Mental Health Promotion

To many health professionals mental health promotion is an emerging field of interest. *Mental Health Promotion* offers a conceptual paradigm approach to analysing and understanding different approaches to mental health and its promotion that will be valuable to students, practitioners and policy-makers alike.

This book traces the history of mental health promotion, defines it, distinguishes it from mental illness and identifies its features within the community setting. The first part of the book reviews the constituent elements: mental health, health promotion and community. Mental health is viewed as a positive concept which is clearly differentiated from mental illness and psychopathology. The second part of the book focuses on the theory and practice of mental health promotion through applications to policy, assessment, consultation, and to education and training in mental health promotion. Drawing on a wealth of international literature **Keith Tudor** offers both theoretical models and practical alternatives and looks to the future for mental health promotion.

Based on the author's own research, *Mental Health Promotion* is suitable for a wide variety of courses at student and professional level in psychiatry, nursing, social work and community work. It is a significant addition to the study of health promotion.

Keith Tudor is a trained social worker, an accredited counsellor (BAC) and a registered psychotherapist (UKCP) in private practice, Sheffield, where he is a director of Temenos. He is also honorary research fellow, King's College, London and a mental health consultant.

This book is a detailed critical analysis of the underlying assumptions, concepts and models of mental health and mental illness and especially of community-based interventions. Tudor helps us understand the confusions, biases, and competing models in the field. He is knowledgeable about the history and trends in community approaches in American and Italian settings and he gives a comprehensive view of (the lack of) mental health policy in Great Britain.

His analysis is scholarly, with hundreds of references that he has woven into a tightly organized volume. It is not an easy read, demanding careful and thoughtful attention from the reader. But anyone making the effort will be rewarded with insights not to be obtained elsewhere. I strongly recommend it to both professionals and politicians.

In addition to detailed and valuable criticism of things as they are, and how they got to be so bad, he provides us with challenging proposals for a new curriculum and even a new discipline in community mental health.

George W. Albee, Professor Emeritus, University of Vermont and Courtesy Professor, Florida Mental Health Institute. Former President of the American Psychological Association.

Mental Health Promotion

Paradigms and practice

Keith Tudor

London and New York

First published 1996
by Routledge
11 New Fetter Lane, London EC4P 4EE

Simultaneously published in the USA and Canada
by Routledge
29 West 35th Street, New York, NY 10001

© 1996 Keith Tudor

Typeset in Times by
J&L Composition Ltd, Filey, North Yorkshire
Printed and bound in Great Britain by

British Library Cataloguing in Publication Data
A catalogue record for this book is available from the British Library

Library of Congress Cataloguing in Publication Data
A catalogue record for this book has been requested

ISBN 0–415–10105–0
      0–415–10106–9 (pbk)

Are you in earnest? seize this very minute –
What you can do, or dream you can, begin it,
Boldness has genius, power and magic in it.
Only engage

(John Anster, 1835)[1]

To Louise and Saul

Contents

Appendices

List of figures

List of tables

List of boxes

Foreword

When, in 1986, Russell Caplan finished his MSc in Health Education at Chelsea (now King's) College, he went into the field and produced creative material on the burgeoning issue of AIDS, later moving to the Health Education Authority (HEA) to develop this work. There he discovered a paucity of work and no priority for projects on *mental* health. With admirable tenacity, and at some personal and professional cost, he argued for attention to be paid to such problems, made ever more urgent by the then impending changes known hopefully as 'care in the community'. After a successful conference in 1989 (HEA, 1990), he persuaded the HEA to fund a one-year, part-time Senior Fellowship in Community Mental Health Promotion at King's College. To my delight we were able to get Keith Tudor to undertake this project. Keith had a background in community politics and mental health social work and as a psychotherapist (then in training), I anticipated that he might overcome the great problem of linking the personal world of mental health and therapy to the social world of 'community' – what we later referred to as 'psyche and society' (R. Holland and Tudor, 1991).

I had long argued for a radically reflexive approach as quite essential in the human sciences (R. Holland, 1977) and was by this time busily expanding and clarifying this approach by means of paradigm analysis, using and extending Burrell and Morgan's (1979) paradigm framework through social work into science education, health education, family therapy and managerial education. The paradigms may be used as a meta-theoretical classification system for theories, but more importantly and more dynamically they provide a way of mapping movement through psychic and social space. In his social work practice Keith had been influenced by this paradigm movement (S. Holland, 1990) later developing it further in his (other part-time) work in social work training and development, using it to design or 'frame' a sixty-day approved social worker post-qualification training course.

Once in post at King's, Keith quickly gathered together therapeutic and educational material into paradigm frameworks and then going beyond them into practical applications in mental health promotion (MHP). We shared ideas, attended conferences and organised an intensive training course in MHP, sustaining each other over a very busy and productive year – and since. The outcome was a manuscript with the exciting title 'Psyche and Society'. This was sent out to readers who came back with many useful suggestions for streamlining the text and clarifying sometimes complex arguments. A revised manuscript was produced and sent to the HEA. We waited for news of the publication date. Time passed with no news of progress. Further enquiries and efforts by Russell Caplan within the HEA failed to remove obstacles to publication. More time passed. We realised that we were in the magical realm of 'Quangoland': that strange territory where supposedly independent authorities speak fine words but are required by government pressure not to rock the boat. Was the manuscript so dangerous? Only if it is dangerous to explore all sides of a question and to follow through the implications of an argument no matter where this leads. In this sense the manuscript was – as the book now is – critical and radical. The next response to further enquiries of the HEA was another reading, this time by a psychiatrist – this itself worthy of paradigm analysis! This reasserted the medical dominance of mental health by suggesting that the manuscript was unbalanced. Eventually (after over two years), the HEA released copyright and thus we were able to find truly independent publication through Routledge. Keith Tudor has since considerably updated and extended his original research (which is reflected in Part II of the book).

When I read the final manuscript, now five years on from its first draft, I was struck by the resilience of the paradigmatic, reflexive approach to human problem intervention and by the fine and continuing labour which has refined the arguments and seen them through into practical application and publication. After many years of trying to fashion a radically reflexive approach to many fields in the human sciences, the most gratifying experience for me is to see some of the basic ideas taken into an area beyond my expertise and elaborated with such passionate commitment that our general understanding is enhanced and our ability to struggle with life's problems is increased. That is exactly what this book now offers.

Ray Holland
Senior Lecturer in Sociopsychology,
King's College Management Centre,
University of London

Acknowledgements

This book has had a long gestation and has been written in two phases. The first, during a year's Senior Research Fellowship in 1990, funded by the Health Education Authority (HEA) and based at the Management Centre at King's College, London. This project was managed by the Mental Health Project Team comprising Russell Caplan, then Education Officer in the Professional and Community Division of the HEA at whose instigation the project was established, Gill Williams, Professional Advisor for the HEA's Professional Development of Teachers Project and former Director of the Health Education Unit at King's College, and Ray Holland, Senior Lecturer in Sociopsychological Studies at King's College, who was also academic supervisor for the original research. I was doubly fortunate in having supportive management for this period as well as stimulating academic supervision, both of which were given willingly and consistently. During this period of the research I met many practitioners, managers and academics as individuals and from organisations in the fields of mental health, mental illness and health promotion who also gave freely of their ideas and support. I wish to acknowledge and thank Kevin Brown, Rob Brown, Peter Campbell of Survivors Speak Out, Louise Capstick, Dr Petrūska Clarkson, Sue Fish, Errol Francis, Derek Gardiner, Maria Gilbert, Graham Holroyd, Yvonne Latawiec of Good Practices in Mental Health, Mike Lawson and Louise Pembroke of Survivors Speak Out, Dr Dennis Trent and the Mid Staffordshire Mental Health Promotion Team, and Colin Whittington for their generosity and contribution to this work. Thanks are also due to Sue Holland, with whom I was privileged to work over a number of years. Both Ray and Sue Holland have contributed to my intellectual development and this book's genesis.

The second phase has been enriched by my move to Sheffield and my contact with a number of professionals who have participated in mental health promotion courses that I have designed and facilitated and without whose critical reflection I would not have continued to develop my ideas. I owe particular thanks to Angus Buck, Gary McCulloch and Sylvia Young from the first course, and also to Rae Magowan, Health of the Nation Co-ordinator at Trent Regional Health Authority (RHA) who, in addition to being a consistent figure supporting initiatives in mental health promotion in Trent Region, has been personally generous with his support, time, ideas and books. I have also had help and support from Richard Goble, Edith Morgan of the World Federation for Mental Health, Guy Robertson, Dr J.G. Sampaio Faria, WHO European Regional Advisor for Mental Health, Ian Stewart, Mathew Thomson of the University of Sheffield, members of the Trent RHA Mental Health Promotion Group, and Peter Williamson of North Derbyshire Health Promotion. I wish to acknowledge the generosity of the Rand Corporation, Santa Monica, California. Stephen Embleton has provided invaluable personal and editorial support and constructive criticism. To all of these, many thanks.

This book could not have been written without access to libraries and, as an independent researcher, I have been fortunate to enjoy the resources of the following local libraries as well as the help and courtesy of their staff: Sheffield Hallam University; Sheffield Health Authority, both the District Health Authority and Health Promotion Libraries; and the University of Sheffield.

I also wish to thank my publisher, Routledge, and in particular Edwina Welham, Alison Poyner and Patricia Stankiewicz for their patience, courtesy and encouragement throughout the stages of this book's development. Thanks to Christine Firth for her precise copy-editing and to Judith Moore for her indexing.

Finally and most fully, I thank my wife, Louise Embleton Tudor, for sharing intellectual as well as personal territory over the years and without whom and whose generous support and encouragement I would not have continued my inquiry into this subject or written this book. My son Saul has been – and continues to be – a source of joy and learning for me as a student of human mental health in general and the development of 'emotional literacy' (Steiner, 1984) in particular. I am only too aware of the stress that a project of this kind has caused my family – and the bitter irony that it is about mental health promotion. To them I dedicate this book with sincere thanks and trust that the end product is worth the cost.

Permissions have been generously given to reproduce the following: Figure 1.2 from Downie, Fyfe and Tannahill (1990) *Health promotion: Models and values* by permission of Oxford University Press; the various figures which draw on Burrell and Morgan's (1979) *Sociological paradigms and organisational analysis* (originally published by Heinemann) by permission of Ashgate Publishing Limited; Figure 1.3 from Barnes (1977) *Transitional Analysis after Eric Berne*, by permission of Harper Collins; Figure 3.3 from Tannahill (1985b) by permission of Margaret Whitehead, Editor, *Health Education Journal*; Figure 8.1 from Hawkins and Shohet (1989)/Hawkins (1993), by permission of Open University Press; extracts from two poems by T.S. Eliot by permission of Faber and Faber Limited; the poem 'Healing' by D.H. Lawrence by permission of Lawrence Pollinger Limited and the estate of Frieda Lawrence Ravagli; the nine Health For All Targets (Appendix 6.1) are reproduced, by permission, from *Health for all targets: The healthy policy for Europe*, Copenhagen, WHO Regional Office for Europe, 1993 (European Health for All series, no. 4).

List of abbreviations

AMA	Association of Metropolitan Authorities
CMH	Community mental health
CMHC	Community Mental Health Centre
CMHP	Community mental health promotion
CSM	Centro per la Salute Mentale (Mental Health Centre)
DHA	District Health Authority
DHSS	Department of Health and Social Security
DoH	Department of Health
GPMH	Good Practices in Mental Health
HA	Health Authority
HEA	Health Education Authority
HoN	*The Health of the Nation*
ICHP	International Conference on Health Promotion
LA	Local authority
MHA	Mental Health Act
MHP	Mental health promotion
NHS	National Health Service
RHA	Regional Health Authority
SSD	Social Services Department
WFMH	World Federation for Mental Health
WFMHERC	World Federation for Mental Health European Regional Council
WHO	World Health Organisation

Introduction

The organisation of mental health promotion (MHP) is one hundred years old, dating back to the foundation of the Finnish Association for Mental Health in 1897. Elements of its history may be traced back to the mental hygiene movement founded in the early years of the twentieth century by the American Clifford Beers. Beers began by exposing abuse in asylums and the mental illness system (Beers, 1908) and advocated a constructive concept of mental health mainly through an emphasis on the development of self-help groups. His ideas spread in the United States through the establishment of the National Committee for Mental Hygiene and were taken up in other countries. In 1922 a National Council for Mental Hygiene was set up in Britain, whose first aim included 'educating the public in all matters which militate for and against good mental health'. By 1930, the first international congress in Washington, attended by over three thousand participants, brought together delegates from twenty-two countries each of which had developed their own national committees. Although in the 1920s the mental hygiene movement was a citizen-based movement supporting the work of professional associations, in the 1930s it focused more on mental illness, institutional care and the emerging professions of psychiatry and psychiatric social work. By 1937, the date of the first European International Congress on Mental Hygiene in Paris, the 'movement' had become more professionalised. Thomson (1995) traces the history of the international mental hygiene movement and the divisions caused initially by the exaggerated influence of Beers himself and the American National Committee on the international movement and, later, by three different strategies which emerged: the propagandist, the research and educational, and the restrictionist.

In 1948 the World Federation for Mental Health (WFMH) was founded, to promote a greater understanding of mental distress and to promote mental health. In its founding document the WFMH defined mental health as involving 'an informed, reflective, responsible allegiance to mankind as a whole' (WFMH, 1948). In 1988 it published a *Declaration 2000 on mental health* (WFMH, 1988) and, in 1989, on its fortieth anniversary, it adopted a *Declaration of human rights and mental health*, Article 1 of which declares that:

> mental health promotion is a responsibility of governmental and non-governmental authorities, as well as the intergovernmental system, especially in times of crisis. In keeping with the WHO [World Health Organisation] definition of health and recognizing the WFMH concern with optimal function, health and mental health programs shall contribute to both the development of the individual and family responsibility for personal and group health and to promoting the highest possible quality of life.
>
> (WFMH, 1989, p. 3)

In 1991, the WFMH's European Regional Council (ERC) produced a manifesto which includes a commitment to user involvment and to viewing mental health in a social context (WFMHERC, 1991). The WFMH, together with the World Health Organisation (WHO), sponsors the annual World Mental Health Day (10 October). The WFMH and its member national associations focus mainly on mental illness and its prevention, and psychiatric patients and advocacy. Some associations have become service organisations, for example the Finnish Association for Mental Health provides services including vocational training; consultation; rehabilitation services, including housing; counselling and information services; crisis intervention; and support persons and groups.

The other international influence in the field of mental health is the WHO. Of the thirty-eight targets of its European regional strategy for *Health for all by the year 2000*, I have identified nine as having implications for MHP. These are developed in Chapter 6 and outlined in Appendix 2.

In Britain the organisation of MHP has fallen to – and between – health promotion, in the form of the Health Education Authority (HEA), and the field of mental health and mental illness, represented by the National Association for Mental Health (NAMH), renamed MIND.

In its original manifesto, the NAMH's first two aims were: '1. To **create concern** for mental health and to challenge apathy and neglect whenever and wherever it is to be found. [and] 2. To **overcome ignorance** of the causes and treatment of mental disorder' (NAMH, 1971, original emphases). Interestingly, the NAMH's journal *Mental Health* was subtitled 'trends in the promotion of mental health', a concern dropped in its successor *OpenMind*. Although MIND is clearly more concerned with mental illness and psychiatry, its uses and abuses, and less with promoting positive mental health, it has at times represented the tradition of MHP, for instance, subscribing to the WFMH's *Charter 2000*. MIND's information line receives numerous telephone calls from people concerned about stress and anxiety and it is equally concerned to respond with initiatives which promote mental health, in addition to its campaigning about mental illness, abuses and prevention. MIND has plans to campaign on MHP and has already produced two leaflets in an ongoing series on MHP: on *How to . . . look after yourself* (MIND, 1994b) and *How to . . . assert yourself* (MIND, 1994a).[1]

The HEA has an ambivalent relationship with the notion and practice of MHP, arguing alternately that it is an integral part of health and therefore an aspect of all its programmes (although this is little in evidence in its *Strategic Plan 1990-95*, HEA, 1989), and then that it needs separate consideration (as reflected in its strategy document: HEA, 1993c). The HEA funded the first National Mental Health Promotion Conference, held in Salford in 1989 and organised by Salford Mental Health Promotion Unit. Two of the recommendations identified by the conference concerned the need for more research into mental health promotion and for further follow-up conferences at regional as well as at a national level (HEA, 1990). Subsequently, in 1990, my research into the field of MHP was funded, although not published, by the HEA. The HEA has acknowledged that it has done 'little work in the specific field of mental health promotion' (HEA, 1993c, p. 9) still arguing, without reference to any literature, that 'the promotion of physical health enhances emotional well-being' (Ibid., p. 9). Despite making mental illness one of its key areas and targets, in response to *The health of the nation*, none of the five areas of the HEA's stated concerns (HEA, 1993c) addresses the mental health and social functioning of mentally ill people. The HEA's latest initative 'Promoting mental ? health' (MacDonald, 1994a) was prepared as a precursor to its commissioning of two pieces of research about indicators for MHP and on the effectiveness of MHP in general. From the limited details available, the research proposals again confuse mental health with mental illness, whilst the research itself appears to consist only of asking practitioners to inform the HEA of any targets and indicators of success in this field (and is behind schedule).

There is widespread and current confusion when anything and everything to do with mental health or mental illness is subsumed under the term 'mental health':

- The *Mental Health Act 1983* (MHA) in fact relates to 'the reception, care and treatment of mentally disordered patients' (MHA 1983, Section 1.(1)).
- Most professionals working with 'mentally disordered patients' are commonly referred to as mental health professionals.
- Community Mental Health Centres (CMHCs) – perhaps more accurately 'hospital outposts dealing with people with mental illness imposed on a particular geographical area' – often represent confused and ultimately dangerous misnaming of terms and services.
- A whole range of institutions and organisations are misnamed and therefore misrepresent their work – from the National Health Service

and the Department of Health to *the Mental Health Foundation* and almost every organisation with 'Mental Health' in its title.

- Job descriptions, titles and the names of units and organisations are changed – in name only. The organisation *Research and Development in Psychiatry*, for instance, changed its name in 1994 to the *Sainsbury Centre for Mental Health*, a change presumably influenced by commerce (and perhaps, as with others, political correctness).
- The new *Journal of Mental Health* is in fact a journal about psychiatry.
- Conferences on mental health and its promotion often focus on mental illness and its prevention as if they are the same concepts (which they are not) and as if they give rise to the same practice (which they do not). Even the annual Promotion of Mental Health Conference has become a forum for eclecticism rather than for MHP with less than 40 per cent of presentations between 1991 and 1993 actually concerned with MHP (see Chapter 6).

Such a widespread misnomer as mental health does no favour either to those with mental disorders or illnesses (however they may be defined) or to those seeking to promote mental health. The usual elision, from mental illness to mental health, serves only to avoid the problems of dealing with mental illness and providing a range of adequate and accessible services and the challenge of promoting genuine mental health.

Despite the lack of organisation and conceptual confusion, MHP is emerging as a new field of theory, policy and practice. It is the concern of a number of professions (discussed in Chapter 9) and has, for instance, been put on the educational agenda in the *National Curriculum* (Department of Education, 1993).[2] It is timely, therefore, to seek some theoretical and conceptual clarity, political direction and practical detail. Theoretically MHP is a largely misunderstood notion, often conflated with mental illness prevention. In addition to theoretical misunderstanding there is conceptual confusion: 'at present . . . we have no concepts for mental health with adequate theoretical substantiation nor well-tested methods for their implementation' (Neumann et al., 1989a, p. 17). This situation is exacerbated by those who are wary of or even hostile to debate about definitions (Childs, 1992) and abstract conceptual frameworks (Trent, 1994), arguing that 'there is a danger that too much emphasis on this can undermine the already limited public (and even professional) comprehension of mental health issues' (Childs, 1992, p. 254). In terms of policy, MHP looks good on paper but few policy-makers, politicians, planners or senior managers have produced specific policies which actually promote mental health. Whilst a number of the World Health Organisation's *Health for all targets* (WHO, 1984/1991a) imply the promotion of mental health, no one has usefully translated these into practical policies. The British Conservative government's major policy on health, *The health of the nation* (Department of Health, 1992), conflates mental illness and mental health and is hesitant about its aims on the promotion of mental health, a hesitancy which has developed into a political abstinence as a result of subsequent policy and circulars (reviewed in Chapter 6). In practice, people are either promoting mental health quietly; struggling with what MHP is; or claiming anything remotely to do with mental health and/or mental illness as MHP which only muddies the debates and diminishes the notion.

These conceptual, theoretical, political and practice issues are of current and urgent importance given the multiplicity of terms, the number of mental health promotion conferences, the expansion of health promotion officers' roles in relation to mental health, and the establishment of mental health promotion posts. In the absence of theoretical coherence, G. Williams (1984) questions the ethics of interventions in relation to the nature of team organisation in this expanding market. Moreover, the potential of MHP remains unfulfilled. Neumann et al. (1989b), in one of the few papers on the subject of 'psychohygiene', suggest that there are four factors for this:

- a lack of public recognition and acceptance
- insufficient material and personal resources
- inadequate knowledge of the system of conditions for mental health
- little cooperation with the institutions, groups or persons participating in the process.

(Neumann et al., 1989b, p. 34)

This book responds to these forces operating against the promotion of mental health and offers a challenge to the lack of public recognition of MHP. It provides material relating to MHP, furthers knowledge about mental *health*, analyses the lack of co-operation between professionals and institutions and offers ways out of such 'paradigm prisons'.

Given that a holistic or integrative view of health includes mental health (as argued in Chapter 1), a fundamental question needs posing: why separate consideration and discussion of *mental* health promotion? Fortunately, the answer is simple: although many theorists pay lip-service to such integration, in practice mental illness, let alone mental *health*, is hardly on the agenda of health promotion professionals. Downie et al. (1990), having made the point that the physical, mental and social *facets* of ill-health and well-being are inextricably interlinked, quote not one example from the field of mental illness/mental health. Killoran (1992), in her discussion about putting health into contracts, cites no example of how to include *mental* health in contracting (thus representing the HEA's 'integrated' approach to MHP). There is a need, then, to put mental health specifically on the health map, and mental health promotion on the agenda of health promotion. This inquiry, responding to this conflation and confusion, develops a clear conceptual framework, reviews debates in several fields, discusses and defines mental health promotion, particularly in the context of community and community care and outlines a number of developments. The field of mental health is defined and developed some-times with reference (although not deference) to the field of mental illness. This is necessary both to clear the ground of mental illness, in order to discuss genuine mental *health*, and because some aspects of mental illness (definitions, concepts, policy, etc.) have an influence on MHP. Before giving an outline of the book, some points are made about its approach and methodology.

SOCIOPSYCHOLOGY

Farr (1984), referring to Wilhelm Wundt (1832-1920), the nineteenth-century philosopher and physiologist, as the 'founding father' of experi-mental psychology, suggests that we can credit Wundt for the 'initial appreciation that *both* a collective *and* an individual psychology were necessary' (p. 126, original emphases). The objects of Wundt's study of collective psychology (*Volkerpsychologie*) included religion, myth, cus-tom, magic, and cognate phenomena. Had Wundt been writing later in the twentieth century, his studies, Farr suggests, would also have included science – and, we might add, language, community and mental health.

However, Wundt argues 'that the mind of the individual could not by itself become conscious of forces of which it was the product, that is the processes of historical change and development' (Ibid., p. 126). Thus Wundt makes a clear distinction between two forms of psychology: his *Volkerpsychologie*, or social psychology, and his experimental laboratory science. The sociologist Emile Durkheim (1858–1917) sharpens this dis-tinction, stressing the differences between 'psychology (focusing almost exclusively on the individual) and sociology (focusing almost exclusively on "society")' (Ibid., p. 127). This has led to over-sharp, exaggerated and often unhelpful divisions between two now separate academic disciplines. Farr traces the lack of dialogue between psychology and sociology to a paucity of creative tension and interchange. Since the early 1980s, how-ever, there has been a developing interest in an integrative approach to the theories, methods and applications of sociology and psychology. In an introduction to a course on sociopsychological studies, R. Holland (1988) makes the point that 'for both disciplines language has taken on great importance. Potentially this provides a meeting point for social and psychological (sociopsychological) study, although conflicts over the own-ership of subject matter cannot be ruled out' (p. 1).

R. Holland (1988) suggests some sample sources from the different disciplines (Figure I.1).

It is from the perspective of this new discipline – or, more accurately, *interdiscipline* – of sociopsychology that this book is written (and reviewed in Chapter 10).

If sociopsychology is the interdiscipline of this inquiry into MHP then reflexivity is its methodology.

Sociology	Psychology
Culture, society, institution,	Culture, personality,
organisation, role, norm,	self, identity,
conformity, deviance,	cognition, behaviour,
social control	experience

Human actions
Human problems
Interventions
Sociopsychological studies

Figure I.1 Sociopsychological studies
Source: R. Holland, 1988, p. 2

REFLEXIVITY

Insofar as he names or defines the term, Reason (1977) proposes an interdisciplinarity which is 'the continual confrontation of the problem of methodology' (p. 206), a meta-perspective of the problems (content) and methodology (process) of our inquiry *as* we inquire: in practice, a critical reflection or reflexivity. *Meta* as a prefix, applied to science, designates 'a higher science of the same nature but dealing with ulterior problems' (Onions, 1933/1973, p. 1313). Thus, meta-theoretical assumptions (to which reference is made throughout this work) are those assumptions which underlie a particular perspective or practice. Critical reflection or reflexivity is the process by which such assumptions are identified and elaborated. Self-reflective, self-critical analysis on the content and process of life is an essential part of being human or 'person' (Harré, 1983) and has been referred to as *reflexivity* by a number of authors from different perspectives and in a number of fields (Bannister and Agnew, 1977; Buss, 1979; Giddens, 1984; R. Holland, 1981, 1987, 1993). Schon (1983) suggests that 'practitioners themselves often reveal a capacity for reflection on their intuitive knowing in the midst of action and sometimes use this capacity to cope with the unique, uncertain, and conflicted situations of practice' (p. viii). R. Holland (1981), writing about and linking reflexivity and sociopsychology, extends the notions of *content* and *process* when referring to a *process* about *process*:

> Discriminating between various transformations and kinds of emphasis is part of the effort to become aware of what we are making of the theory – to become reflexively aware of our activity by means of sociopsychological analysis. And since it is a theoretically guided empirical investigation of theory construction – a theory about theories – it is well described as metatheory.

> (R. Holland, 1981, p. 25)

Thus, the concept and practice of reflexivity links the different levels of content, process and meta-theory which are applied to MHP, and provides both a methodology and a challenge throughout this work; and for all engaged in MHP.

Following one of my presentations on this subject and this approach (Tudor, 1992b), a member of the audience approached me and said that he was disappointed that I had not given him answers. My response was to say that I had provided some relevant questions and a framework within which he could find and define *his* answers. Similarly, this is less a 'This is it, here's how to do it' book than an inquiry (in the philosophical sense and tradition) into MHP which first defines the territory and describes the debates and which then, in proposing a particular paradigm framework for analysis, encourages the reader, practitioner, manager, provider, purchaser, policy-maker, and politician to reflect on their definitions and approaches to MHP. In taking this approach, this book is both conceptual and, as a source and reference drawing on a wide literature as well as examples from the field, is also practical.

THE STRUCTURE OF THE BOOK

The book is divided into three parts. In Part I the elements of the book's concern – mental health, health promotion and the context of community – are defined and explored; first separately and then drawn together in chapters on mental health promotion (Chapter 3) and on community mental health promotion (Chapter 5). The conceptual, paradigm framework (Burrell and Morgan, 1979) of the book is introduced and developed accumulatively through each chapter in Part I. In Chapter 1 mental health (and, to a certain extent, mental illness) is discussed in relation to assumptions about the nature of social science and the nature of society. In Chapter 2, the relevance of health promotion is assessed in terms of Burrell and Morgan's (1979) four paradigm analysis of social theory. In Chapter 3 eight elements of mental health are identified and located within the four paradigm 'map'. In Chapter 4 different concepts of community are discussed, using the four paradigm analysis as a framework for organising different and differing views. Chapter 5, on community mental health promotion, considers possible movements between the paradigms, or 'paradigm shifts' (Kuhn, 1970). The relative length of Chapters 3 and 5 reflect the book's principal concern with the elaboration of MHP.

In Part II four developments of MHP in the community are discussed. Chapter 6 describes the elements of a comprehensive mental health policy. Chapter 7 focuses on mental health assessment, proposing two frameworks for the assessment of individuals, groups and organisations with reference to source material on measurements of mental health. Chapter 8 develops G. Caplan's (1970) notion of mental health consultation, focusing on groups and organisation. Chapter 9 discusses issues of disciplinarity and profession in the development of MHP and outlines my own learning and training in MHP. In Part II the paradigm analysis is used and extended, each chapter being illustrated with examples from practice.

Chapter 10, which forms Part III, moves beyond the field of MHP as it has been defined (in Part I) and developed (in Part II). In the spirit of reflexivity, paradigm analysis is itself subjected to critical reflection and, in a postmodern review of MHP, future directions in the theory and practice of MHP are noted.

Part I
Defining the field

Part 1

Defining the field

INTRODUCTION TO PART I

Part I defines the field of community mental health promotion (CMHP) and introduces its conceptual framework. It discusses the constituent elements of CMHP – mental health (Chapter 1), health promotion (Chapter 2) and community (Chapter 4) – and develops the elements of the four paradigm analysis and framework through the chapters.

Chapter 1 discusses mental health, distinguishing it from mental illness by clearing the ground that is mental illness through discussions of madness, mental illness legislation, the medical response to madness and mental illness, and other, theoretical responses. Definitions of mental health are reviewed and summarised. The conceptual framework is introduced by discussion of its two axes, based on subjectivist–objectivist assumptions about the nature of social science, and about assumptions about the nature of society from social regulation to radical change. These dimensions are elaborated with reference to different notions of mental health.

Chapter 2 discusses the history and definitions of health promotion, health education and illness prevention. The differences and commonalities between different views are understood in terms of the four paradigm analysis of social theory.

Chapter 3 on mental health promotion (MHP) distinguishes between MHP and mental illness prevention. Eight elements of mental health are introduced to provide a comprehensive basis for the promotion of mental health, with a focus on individuals. Through the eight elements, this chapter draws together literature on mental health and other related areas. The chapter considers two areas of MHP – amongst 'the mentally ill' and in the workplace. The conceptual framework is again used as a way of understanding different notions and views.

Chapter 4 on community uses the paradigm framework as an organising framework for discussion of different concepts of community. The eight elements are reviewed, with the focus on the community. The social policy of community care in Britain is compared with 'the Italian experience' of psychiatric reform and community care. The concept of community mental health (CMH) is developed through four discussions about the public's response, the meaning of CMH, community participation and social change.

Chapter 5 on CMHP brings together the chapters and discussions in Part I in a review of CMHP. The literature on Community Mental Health Centres is reviewed as is their practice as regards CMHP. Four discussions – on community psychology, psychotherapy, advocacy and 'the Italian experience' – are developed as making an important impact on CMHP. CMHP is regarded as comprising two elements: challenging myths of mental illness (although not in the usual way in which this is understood) and as promoting mental health. Another aspect of the paradigm framework is introduced, namely, the possible and proposed movement between the paradigms.

1 Mental health

Mental health is predominantly a euphemism for mental illness. This is widespread in legislation, social policy, medicine, psychiatry, sociology and psychology as well as in practice. Such ambiguity has its roots, first, in the fear of the unknown and the irrationality (unreason) of insanity, secondly, in the historical, legislative response to lunacy, thirdly, in the medicalisation of madness, and, finally, in liberal and even radical notions of mental illness. Expanding on these four themes, mental illness is briefly considered in order to clear the ground for discussion of the main concern of this book – mental health and its promotion. A definition of the field of mental health is offered, through discussion of various definitions of mental health. A conceptual framework for understanding the different definitions and their implications is introduced (and further developed in Chapter 2).

MENTAL ILLNESS

The fear of the unknown

The history of madness is the history of people's fear and society's exclusion of the unknown, the 'other'. This operates in a number of ways in relation to gender, race and class.

'Woman', de Beauvoir (1972) argues, represents the 'Other' in a duality based on the male self as subject which is 'as primordial as consciousness' (p.16) and is maintained by dualistic thought and oppression. Chesler (1972) writes about women and 'madness' in mythology and history, the development of female psychology, aspects of the female psychiatric career, as well as aspects of the psychiatric system. Her central theme is the damage to women, perpetuated by psychiatrists and psychiatric institutions: 'women, by definition, are viewed as psychiatrically impaired – whether they accept or reject the female role – simply because they are women' (Chesler, 1972, p.115). Busfield (1988) brings together two arguments about women and mental health: one, that women's mental illness is a product of their oppression; and second, that mental illness is a label used to control and confine women's action, one which involves the exercise of patriarchal power. Thus, in practice, women in Britain are diagnosed and treated differentially.[1]

- Of all people diagnosed by GPs as 'mentally ill', 55% are women and 45% are men and yet men are more likely to be referred for specialist help (D. Thompson and Pudney, 1990).
- Women are twice as likely as men to be diagnosed as suffering from 'clinical depression' (Department of Health and Social Security [DHSS], 1986) and between two and three times more likely to be prescribed minor tranquillisers.
- Women are one and a half times more likely to be admitted to psychiatric hospital than men and admission rates rise steadily for women aged between 35 and 44 (DHSS, 1986).

Drawing on disciplines as diverse as anthropology, history, art and literature, Francis (1991) argues that the very notion of madness suggests the notion of race (and vice versa). The archetypes of unreason all assume the superiority of white Western philosophic thought: from Caliban's lasciviousness and inarticulacy, through the 'discovery' of 'the dark continent' (Africa); through the Darwinian attempts to classify and establish a hierarchy of the species and subsequent racist anthropometry; and the racist connotations of the savage 'animality of madness' (Foucault, 1971); to the psychiatric misdiagnosis of black people (Gabriel, 1987; Fernando, 1988; G. Harrison et al., 1988).[2] Other factors, evidenced by research since the early 1980s, highlight the inequalities of the 'treatment' of black and minority ethnic people within the psychiatric system.

- Black people, in particular young Afro-Caribbean men, are more likely than white people to be removed by the police under Section 136 of the *Mental Health Act 1983* (MHA) (A. Rogers and Faulkner, 1987; Bean et al., 1991).
- Black people are more likely to be retained in hospital under Sections 2, 3 and 4 of the MHA (Department of Health [DoH]/Home Office, 1992).
- There are disproportionate numbers of black people within the psychiatric population (Francis et al., 1989). Afro-Caribbeans are ten times more likely to be diagnosed as white people (G. Harrison et al., 1988).
- Black people receive on average larger doses of medication than white people and have less access to alternative treatment (Littlewood and Cross, 1980; Littlewood and Lipsedge, 1982).
- A disproportionate number of black people have died 'in care'.

Society, in the form of the superior or dominant community, also assumes the moral and practical right to segregate and banish such fearful 'otherness', whether 'hysterical' women, schizophrenic blacks or the feckless (and therefore undeserving) poor: 'this community acquired an ethical power of segregation, which permitted it to eject, as into another world, all forms of social uselessness' (Foucault, 1971, p.58). Foucault argues that the other world is or was defined by labour, that is, one's social usefulness and productivity.[3] This is echoed in class-related aspects of mental illness.

- Hollingshead and Redlich (1958) examined the difference in concepts of mental health and illness, depending on class, showing a correlation between class and *treated* mental illness.
- G.W. Brown and Harris's (1978) study on the *Social origins of depression* found that, amongst those with children at home, working-class women were four times more likely to suffer from depression.
- In a major study on lifestyles, Blaxter (1990) correlated psychosocial illness with class, a situation exacerbated by old age, and commented on the detrimental impact of low income and social isolation.
- People in socially disadvantaged groups have a higher lifetime prevalence of major mental health (illness) problems and poor access to care (WHO, 1991b).
- The impact of poverty, low income and inadequate social security benefits, poor housing, and unemployment, on people with mental health problems is also highlighted by the Association of Metropolitan Authorities ([AMA], 1993).

The legislative response to lunacy

Historically, many of the terms used to describe the unknown distress that people experienced 'in their minds', which are now considered derogatory, then represented both a fear of the unknown and a concern about the social control of vagrancy. Considerations reflected both in early legislation and through the association of 'mental illness' with 'dangerousness'.

Foucault (1971), in his major study of *Madness and civilisation*, traced the history of confinement in Europe, and particularly in France and the legislation supporting this. In Britain, prior to the eighteenth century, common law (and common 'sense') had distinguished between idiots, being 'simple', and lunatics, being less understandably 'mad'. In many ways, although the terms and labels have changed, this distinction has continued to influence both public thinking and governmental legislation and policy: the *Idiots Act 1886*, for instance, provided separately for 'imbeciles' and 'idiots', although the *Lunacy (Consolidation) Act 1890* ignored the distinction between mental illness and mental handicap. The *Vagrancy Act 1714* had associated lunacy with criminal deviance whilst the *Vagrancy Act 1744* defined a 'lunatick or mad person', a definition consolidated one hundred years later in the *Lunatics Act 1845*, which defined lunatics as of 'unsound mind', a redefinition favoured a century later by the *Royal Commission on Lunacy and Mental Disorder*. It was not, however, until early in the twentieth century that the distinctions between and consequences of this terminology were made explicit, both in terms of the responsibility for one's mental state and the provision needed – and this at a time when public and medical opinion favoured the segregation of 'mental defectives'. The *Mental Deficiency Act 1913* distinguished between the *feeble-minded*: those who needed care or control for the protection of themselves or others; *imbeciles*: those who could guard themselves against common physical dangers, such as fire, water and traffic, but who were incapable of managing themselves or their affairs; *idiots*: those unable to guard themselves against common physical dangers; and *moral defectives*: those with vicious or criminal propensities. This history of definitions and names is important in that it lies behind moves in more recent times to rename and reclaim terms in the field of mental illness.

The *Mental Health Act 1959* was the first to be so named, despite its focus on diagnosis, treatment and detention, and was regarded, at least by the Department of Health and Social Security (DHSS), as 'enlightened and forward-looking' (DHSS, 1976, p.1). This Act repealed much of the previous Lunacy, Mental Treatments and Mental Deficiency Acts of the previous seventy years (and repealed or amended twenty-three such Acts, dating back to 1800); defined and distinguished between 'mental illness', 'severe subnormality', 'subnormality' and 'psychopathic disorder'; and introduced and codified the powers and arrangements for various forms of compulsory treatment of patients, the periods of detention, powers of guardianship, and the respective roles of the various people involved in the arrangements for admission and discharge of patients. The *Mental Health Act 1983* (MHA 1983), influenced by professional and civil liberties lobbies and the philosophy of 'the least restrictive alternative' to compulsory treatment, consolidated changes which had occurred since the 1959 Act; updated the 1959 definitions, changing 'subnormality' to 'mental impairment'; and introduced the person and role of the approved social worker. The DoH/Welsh Office's *Code of practice* (1990, 1993) to the MHA 1983 has consolidated much of the 'good practice' implicit in the legislation, and has clarified some of the duties of local and health authorities and other statutory agencies under the MHA 1983.

Other governmental policies which have an impact on the management of mental illness and mental health are reviewed in Chapter 6. An alternative view of the MHA is offered by the Campaign Against Psychiatric Oppression (CAPO) (undated) which demands its withdrawal.

The history of the legislative response to mental illness has been one of definition, categorisation and, commonly, incarceration – what Foucault (1971) refers to historically as 'the great confinement' – of people considered to be socially undesirable or dangerous. The notion of dangerousness in relation to mental illness is an important one as the historical connection remains active in the collective psyche, emerging in often hostile public response to issues of 'mental health', fuelled by tabloid media publicity about 'psycho-killers', and often with a racist twist: 'we would conjecture that the criteria on which bail applications are based [and refused] are related to subjective notions of dangerousness and public menace which bears little relation to objective measures of safety and risk' (Browne et al., 1993, p.108).

The medicalisation of madness

In response to the concern of the social control of madness there was a growth in the establishment of madhouses in the late seventeenth century, given further legitimacy in 1808 by the legalisation of the county lunatic asylum. Porter (1990) argues that, increasingly, medical practitioners took over from the lay 'mental entrepreneurs' who had previously run these institutions for two reasons: the specialisation necessary in a congested occupation (medicine); and the professional and financial benefits to medical career prospects. Foucault (1971) suggests three elements which symbolise society's structures and values and which contribute to the medicalisation of madness:

> Family–Child relations, centred on the theme of paternal authority; Transgression–Punishment relations, centred on the theme of immediate justice; Madness–Disorder relations, centred on the theme of social and moral order. It is from these that the physician derives his power to cure.
>
> (Foucault, 1971, p. 274)

Foucault argues that these relations encapsulate and reify the importance of the doctor/psychiatrist–patient relationship which moves, through the historical development of ideas, from an essentially moral one to one obscured by the 'myths of scientific objectivity' (Ibid., p. 276). Psychiatry also echoes the medical model of the diagnosis-treatment-cure approach: the doctor determines the disease, the diagnosis determines the treatment, and the diagnosis determines the prognosis and/or 'cure' (although in practice this formulation often begins with the prognosis from which follows some experimentation with medication, to which a diagnosis is attached). In the twentieth century, two major events contributed to the establishment of psychiatry as a profession: the formation in 1948 of the National Health Service, and the discovery and development, between 1952 and 1954, of the first major tranquillisers.

The management and treatment of madness has shifted from being viewed as a problem of social control to one of public health, partly through legislation and partly, J. Taylor and D. Taylor (1989) suggest, as a result of the experience of the First World War, the influence of Sigmund Freud on the activities of the 'mental hygiene' lobby in the United States, and in Britain the establishment of the *Royal Commission on Lunacy and Mental Disorder* – a shift which the *Mental Treatment Act 1930* consolidated with the renaming of asylums as hospitals and the first organised development of out-patient services.

Notions of mental illness

Over the last two centuries many people have attempted to draw psychiatry
out of the mists of scientific objectivity and to define and classify mental
illness. There are several ways in which we can consider abnormality or
pathology (and its relation to normality): normatively, statistically, clini-
cally, culturally and subjectively. Due to the influence of positivism on
psychiatry, with its emphasis on scientific objectivity, classifications of
mental illness have become predominantly attempts to construct clinical
models of pathology – and, by implication, of normality. There have
therefore been attempts to codify mental illnesses normatively – the very
act of codifying being to establish norms – and statistically; classically and
currently in the American Psychiatric Association's (1994) *Diagnostic and
statistical manual of mental disorders* (4th edition) (DSM IV) and the
World Health Organisation's (1992) *ICD-10 classification of mental and
behavioural disorders*. Others have attempted to explain mental disorder in
terms of models of mental illness. Siegler and Osmond (1966, 1976),
whose original work came from their experience of working in mental
health centres, construct a typology of madness, in an attempt to elaborate
the implications of different models for treatment strategies in relation to
psychotic illness. Their 'models of madness' are the medical, the psychoanalytic, the social, the moral, the family interaction, the conspiratorial, the
impaired and the psychedelic. Siegler and Osmond (1976) divide their
models into two classes, 'reflecting different ways of viewing human
misfortune': the *discontinuous* – the medical, moral and impaired models
'in the sense that they put forth a partial or restricted rather than a global
view of the problem of madness'; and the *continuous* – the psychoanalytic,
the social, the family interaction, the conspiratorial, and the psychedelic in
that these each offers a global view or explanation of madness. Hill (1988)
considers these models in terms of their implications for mental health
education.

In the 1960s and 1970s, with the popularisation, in sociology, of the
notion of a socially constructed reality (Berger and Luckmann, 1967) and
labelling theory (N. Davis, 1976) and in psychiatry of anti-psychiatry
(Laing and Esterson, 1964; Laing, 1960/1967),[4] there was a movement
away from using terms which, it was argued, stigmatised and reinforced
prejudice. With more questioning of what had passed for objective, clinical, scientific or medical truth and, indeed, a challenging of the very
foundations of 'mental illness' (e.g. Szasz, 1961, 1973) and with the
growth of the users' movement within and outside psychiatric institutions, both professional and lay people shied away from definite and
defining terms such as mental disorder and mental illness, focusing instead
on more subjective, phenomenological perceptions of 'madness'. However,
this shyness, together with the more recent (and false) political correctness,
has given rise to the confused and confusing use of the term 'mental health'

to stand for mental illness. Hendon (1992) argues that the changing language of mental health represents a sincere attempt by those in the vanguard of the community mental health movement, to adopt de-stigmatising language and concepts and to give validity to altered states of consciousness such as hearing voices (e.g. Romme and Escher, 1993), viewing these as health rather than illness. Hendon somewhat undermines his emphasis on the positive point, however, by suggesting that we simply refer to illness as ill-health – an unhelpful conceptual confluence.

MENTAL HEALTH

Such confusion has led to conceptual ignorance and incoherence about mental health. The history of madness and mental illness reveals two common (and flawed) definitions of mental health: one, that it is the absence of mental illness; the other that it is a state of well-being. Both are reductive: to define something by the absence of its opposite is simply a semantic sleight of hand and to define it by substitution is procrastination. Neither option furthers our understanding. The fact that the same term (mental health) is also used to mean or imply its supposed opposite (mental illness) further confuses such conflation.[5]

Definitions of mental health

There are probably as many different definitions of mental health as there are readers of this book (although that very statement implies a personal, subjectivist view of mental health).

> Mental health consists of the ability to live . . . happily; . . . productively; . . . without being a nuisance.
>
> (Preston, 1943, p.112)

> Mental health is a conceptual abstraction. It is a relativistic assessment of man's relations to himself,[6] his society, and his values . . . [mental health] cannot be effectively understood in isolation from the other multifactorial phenomena that constitute the person as he functions in society.
>
> (Eaton, 1951, p.88)

> Mental health is about the way human beings adjust to the world, and are effective, happy, efficient, content, and maintain an even temper, an alert intelligence, socially considerate behaviour and a happy disposition.
>
> (quoted by Wooton, 1959, p. 221)

> [Mental health is] a rubric, a label which covers different perspectives and concerns, such as the absence of incapacitating symptoms, integration of

psychological functioning, effective conduct of personal and social life, feelings of ethical and spiritual well-being and so on.

(Kakar, 1984, p.3)

For a theory of mental health, extra-psychic success is not enough; we must also include intra-psychic health.

(Maslow, 1968, p.180)

Mental health means harmony between values, interests and attitudes with the scope of action of the individuals and, consequently, realistic life planning and purposeful implementation of life concepts.

(Neumann et al., 1989a, p.4)

[Mental health is the] capability of personal growth and development.

(Chwedorowicz, 1992, p.243)

Health of the psyche . . . is a matter of maturity.

(Winnicott, 1988, p.12)

In contrast to the health of the body 'mental health' . . . is not the health of the psyche. It refers to the view, thus to the psychological level of the relations individual–environment. . . . Mental health is only the centre piece of human health insofar as all health-relevant interactions are conveyed (broken, reflected) by the psyche.

(Neumann et al., 1989b, p.28)

[Mental health is] *the capacity to live life to the full in ways that enable us to realize our own natural potentialities, and that unite us with rather than divide us from all the other human beings who make up our world.*

(Guntrip, 1964, p.25, original emphasis)

Mental health is characterized by the ability to love and to create . . . by a sense of identity based on one's experience of self as the subject and agent of one's powers, by the grasp of reality inside and outside of ourselves, that is, by the development of objectivity and reason.

(Fromm, 1956, p.69, original emphasis)

Mental health is thus defined from many different perspectives, and 'every definition of mental health has inherent cultural assumptions' (Chwedorowicz, 1992, p.241). Before introducing a conceptual framework with which such differences may be understood, the relationship between mental health, mental ill-health and mental illness is considered.

MENTAL HEALTH, MENTAL ILL-HEALTH AND MENTAL ILLNESS

It is a commonplace to view the relationship between health and illness – and, therefore, mental health and mental illness – as two ends of the same continuum. Trent (1992a), with reference to Euclidean physics, summarised the problem of placing mental health and mental illness on a single continuum. The importance and relevance of these philosophical arguments is that they underlie the attitudes of many practitioners as well as the policies of national and local health authorities to mental health promotion (MHP) (e.g. Jenkins and Griffiths, 1991). Such policies include, for instance, the notion of promoting positive mental health amongst the mentally ill (DoH, 1992), which is difficult on the basis of a single mental health–mental illness continuum. According to Euclidean physics it is impossible to be in two places at the same time, for example two places on a continuum of mental health–mental illness at once. Equally it is impossible to be moving from two points in two different directions at the same time. It follows that on a single continuum it is impossible to be healthy and ill at the same time or to be mentally healthy with a diagnosed mental illness. The Canadian Minister of National Health and Welfare (MNHW) (1988) suggests defining the relationship between the two by viewing each as on a separate continuum: the one, a mental disorder continuum; the other, a mental health continuum (Figure 1.1).[7]

Trent (1992a) suggests several advantages of this conceptual separation, the most important of which are the separation of health from illness, the consequent focus on mental *health*, and the notion that we can conceptualise and experience being in two places on the two continua at the same time. Thus, respectively, we need to consider notions of health and mental health, distinct from ill-health and disorder, and to develop theory and practice which develop the two continua concept, and thereby promote the mental health or well-being of the mentally ill (discussed further in Chapter 3). Within this concept a person with a diagnosed manic-depressive disorder may also experience good mental health in terms of having a genuine sense of subjective well-being, and be functioning well; equally, someone who is diagnosed as schizophrenic and who is responding well to treatment may be in poor mental health in not feeling good about themselves, in experiencing distress in relation to family, friends, housing and

Range of diagnosis from
severe to mild

Maximal mental_____ Minimal mental
disorder/illness   disorder/illness

Minimal mental_____ Optimum mental
health   health
                                      including, for example
        subjective distress   subjective well-being
        impaired or   optimal development
        underdevelopment of
        abilities

Figure 1.1 The two continua of mental health and mental illness
Source: Based on Minister of National Health and Welfare, 1988

employment and so on. In a similar vein, Downie et al. (1990) link well-being and ill-health and represent their relationship by crossing two axes (Figure 1.2). This perspective has been applied in the field of physical health/illness by Kaplun (1991) and Milz (1991).

Although, obviously, there is a relationship between the two continua, it is more important, both conceptually and in order to promote good practice, to separate them than to merge them. In this sense, it is mistaken to suggest that anyone suffering from a depressive or anxiety state is unlikely to meet the criteria for mental health as, for instance, P. Graham (1986) does, or that there is considerable overlap between mental health and the absence of mental disorder, as Freudenberg (1979) does. Using the two continua concept, a distinction is made between severe to mild mental illness on the one continuum, and minimal to optimal mental health, or mental ill-health to mental health on the other. Thus ill-health is different from and less fixed than ill-ness: it is, to reclaim and reuse the language of medicine, the psychopathology of the average, the ordinary state of dis-ease resulting from unmet needs (Maslow, 1968). This relationship as outlined has two implications: one, that it is possible to have a diagnosed mental illness and to have a good level of mental health and well-being;[8] and, secondly and

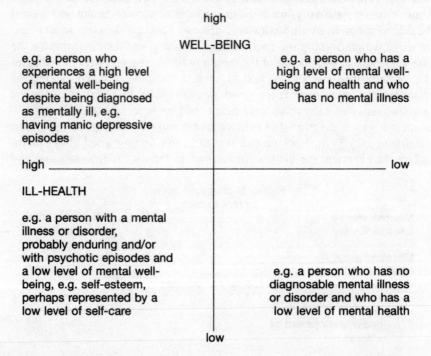

Figure 1.2 The relationship between mental well-being and mental ill-health
Source: Based on Downie et al., 1990

crucially, that it is possible and desirable to promote the mental health and well-being of people with mental illnesses and disorders.

Some notes on language

Having reclaimed the ground which is *mental health* (distinct from that of mental illness), we need to consider the status, meaning and implications of the adjectival noun *mental* when associated and used in conjunction with health. Other terms, such as *emotional*, *psychological* and *spiritual* health, are often used interchangeably with *mental* health and so, again, we need to be clear what we mean. In a paper on the integration of psychotherapies, Groder (1977) extends Erskine's (1975) ABC of effective psychotherapy – affective, behavioural, and cognitive – with the additions of the physiological, social systems, and suprapersonal elements (the latter which he takes to include ethics, philosophy and religious movements and which I interpret as the spiritual and soul aspects of psychotherapy and life (Figure 1.3). These dimensions can be used, on several levels, to describe different aspects of psychotherapy; different approaches to working with individuals (see, for instance, P. Ware's (1983) 'doors to therapy'); the emphases and strengths of different schools of psychotherapy; and, importantly, to define different dimensions of what we might generically consider to be 'mental' health. This describes an *integrative* approach to

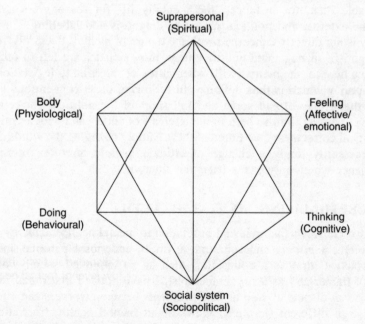

Figure 1.3 Dimensions of mental health
Source: Based on Groder, 1977

mental health, one which might, more accurately (although clumsily), be referred to as affective/behavioural/cognitive/physiological/sociopolitical/ soul/spiritual health. On this basis 'mental' health is used to cover such integration (at least until Chapter 10 when dis-integration is discussed). Evans (1988) combines elements of this integration with Jahoda's (1958) criteria for mental health. This use of mental health means that specific terms – such as 'emotional literacy' (Steiner, 1984), affective well-being (Warr, 1987), the emotional dimension of well-being (Chiu, 1992) and affective education (Sunderland and Clarkson, 1992); cognitive literacy (Afzalnia, 1993); and 'somatic education' (Keleman, 1989) – stand precisely for the specificity of their respective dimensions, whilst mental health remains an integrative, generic term. Groder's octahedron does not have a unifying centre such as 'the self' (and, indeed, in the original Groder did not interconnect all the dimensions). Neumann et al. (1989b), for instance, would argue that the psyche as the agent of all health-relevant interactions is at the centre of all such dimensions of mental health.

Thus, throughout this book, 'mental health' stands for mental health as described; similarly, when 'mental illness/disorder' is used, this refers to mental illness in the sense in which it is introduced. At times mental health (illness) is written to indicate or emphasise the point that, although the subject, policy, etc. referred to is titled mental health, it in fact refers to mental illness. The phrase 'people who are diagnosed or who consider themselves as having a mental illness/disorder' is more accurate and acceptable than, for instance, 'the mentally ill' for reasons concerned with the external and political nature of diagnosis and labelling. As this inquiry is not directly concerned with the nature of mental illness/disorder, its diagnosis, management and treatment, these debates are left to others, referring here to 'the mentally ill' when citing or referring to legislation or social policy which is thus defining. In following these conventions I am aware that I may offend some and fall short of the political correctness referred to earlier. I do so both in the interests of clarity and with a critique of political correctness (see Füredi, 1993). Simply changing the words does not necessarily imply a change of attitude, merely an often resentful compliance which only exacerbates the situation.

CONCEPTUALISING MENTAL HEALTH

Such diverse views (as reviewed in relation to mental health) explicitly or, more often, *implicitly* underpin and, at times, undermine practice. In my own practice, first as a counsellor, then as an approved social worker (ASW), trainer and as a psychotherapist, I have noticed that much inter-professional dispute as well as disagreements between workers and clients was due to different (implicit) views about mental health, frustratingly compounded by apparent or assumed (explicit) agreement. In the field of mental illness, examples include:

- A psychiatrist who admits patients on the basis of their diagnostic category in order to conduct research – a conflict between the needs of patients (for clinical treatment) and the personal gratification of the psychiatrist (for empirical research).
- A psychologist who refuses to speak on the same conference platform as a 'survivor' of the psychiatric system – a conflict between views of mental illness and their legitimacy.
- An ASW who always agrees with 'her doctor' about the efficacy of emergency admission (under the MHA 1983, Section 4) to psychiatric hospital – a collusion about a misinterpretation of the MHA 1983 which was administratively and psychologically convenient.
- A psychiatric nurse who releases the names of patients to the manager of a private nursing home – another collusion, breaching hospital policy, professional codes of ethics and practice over confidentiality, and personal respect.

In the field of mental health examples include:

- Psychotherapists who take different views about human nature, motivation and change.
- Educationalists who propose different pedagogies for learning about the self and its development.
- Trainers who disagree about their respective inputs on an assertiveness course, in terms of how assertively the participants will respond.
- Community workers who work either with community leaders or with disadvantaged members of the community.

In order first to understand differences of definitions of mental health (and mental illness) and in such practices and, secondly, to do something about them, I looked to a conceptual framework:

> a conceptual model can be informed by more than one theory and conceptualized at multilevels (from micro to macro). As importantly in an applied field, it allows the inclusion of processes or characteristics not grounded in formal theory, but that represent empirical findings or the experience of practicing professionals.
>
> (Earp and Ennett, 1991, p.164)

A conceptual framework needs to aid understanding of conflicting views (rather than simply seeing the above examples as idiosyncratic views of malevolent people), to help distinguish between similar views, and to be useful in forming a conceptualisation for use in practice. This is the essential process of conceptualisation to which Craib (1987) refers as the unavoidability of theory: 'we never have a direct access to the world outside ourselves; it is always mediated by our language, which contains implicit and explicit theories of what the world is like and how it works' (p.33). Thus, theory is the best practice.

For the necessary conceptual framework I turned to the work of the organisational sociologists Burrell and Morgan (1979). They argue that 'assumptions about the nature of science can be thought of in terms of what we call the subjective–objective dimension, and assumptions about the nature of society in terms of a regulation–radical change dimension' (p.21).

The subjective–objective dimension

Taking the first dimension, all views about, say, mental health can be placed on a subjective–objective dimension by analysing or reflecting upon the assumptions implicit in a particular view or statement:

> on this horizontal dimension it is evident that scientific knowledge about human affairs in general, and mental health in particular, depends on assumptions about whether we have a subjectivist or objectivist approach to acquiring knowledge, or some combination of the two. How mental health is defined depends very much on what our knowledge base is.
>
> (R. Caplan and R. Holland, 1990, p.11)

Thus, from the quotes about mental health (pp. 21–22), we can identify that, whilst 'feelings of ethical and spiritual well-being and so on' (Kakar, 1984, p.3) and the 'capacity . . . to realize our own natural potentialities' (Guntrip, 1964, p.25) are examples of more personal views of mental health and, therefore, based on subjectivist knowledge, the linking of mental health with socially considerate behaviour (quoted by Wooton, 1959) and productivity (Preston, 1943) and Basaglia's (1981) analysis of (mental) illness as a 'distorted representation' imply certain scientific analyses and, therefore, a more objectivist knowledge-base.

Within their subjective–objective dimension Burrell and Morgan distinguish between four sets of assumptions about the nature of the social world and which I elaborate as they underpin both this dimension and the conceptual framework I develop throughout this book. The first set of assumptions is *ontological* – concerning 'the very essence of the phenomena under investigation' (Burrell and Morgan, 1979, p.1). They argue that:

> social scientists . . . are faced with a basic ontological question: whether the 'reality' to be investigated is external to the individual – imposing itself on individual consciousness from without – or [is] the product of individual consciousness.
>
> (Ibid., p.1)

Thus, the emphasis Maslow (1968) places on 'starting from experiential knowledge rather than from systems of concepts or abstract categories' (p.9) is an example of a subjectivist ontology.

The second set of assumptions, about the grounds of knowledge (*epistemology*), is concerned with how to understand the world and to acquire, or experience and communicate this knowledge. R. Caplan and R. Holland (1990) define the objectivist and subjectivist positions, respectively, in relation to depression:

> if depressive illness is understood and explained in terms of physiological causes, then this mental state would be defined in terms of some genetic make-up . . . on the subjectivist side, it can be argued that depression is defined as a human experience at times experienced in varying degrees of intensity by everyone. The inability to cope with such intense emotional distress by some people has been categorised as an illness by health professionals reflecting their experience of this human condition – depression. . . . Knowledge of mental health here is acquired through engaging with both personal and social meanings.
>
> (Ibid., p. 11)

These two approaches to knowing about (or knowledge of) depression are, in effect, different epistemologies of mental health or of mental illness, depending on which of the two continua (discussed above) depression is placed: 'the norms of mental "health" and "illness" are essentially matters of cultural judgement, although positivism misrepresents them as matters of empirical fact' (Ingleby, 1981, p.43).

The third set of assumptions concerns *human nature* and the relationship between human beings and our environment (the use of 'our' rather than 'their' indicates a certain subjectivism on my part about my inclusiveness with human nature and the environment). The adjectives in the descriptions of mental health collected by Wooton (1959) (quoted above): effective, happy, efficient, content, even (temper), alert (intelligence), socially considerate (behaviour) and happy (disposition) are descriptive of a predetermined view of human nature and its relationship to others and the environment – 'the way human beings adjust to the world'. (Also implicit in this last statement is the desirability of human beings' adjustment to 'the world' which can be located on the second, social regulation–radical change dimension, discussed on pp. 31–33.) A more voluntaristic, as distinct from such a deterministic, view is represented by Fromm (1956): 'the criterion of mental health is not one of individual adjustment to a given social order, but a universal one . . . of giving a satisfactory answer to the problem of human existence' (p.19).

These three sets of assumptions, Burrell and Morgan argue, have implications for the fourth set of assumptions – about the *methodological* nature of the investigation of knowledge. Thus, if our concern is with the objective reality of mental health then our empirical research will be concerned with measuring empirical data and establishing outcome measures. This is the emphasis outlined in *The health of the nation* (DoH, 1992) and its *Key area handbook mental illness* (2nd edition, DoH, 1994c) shared by many health authorities currently concerned with contracting and the measurement of service provision. (A discussion of contracting may be found in

Chapter 6; assessment is discussed in Chapter 7.) Burrell and Morgan (1979) refer to this as nomothetic (or legislative) methodology. If, at the other end of this dimension, our concern is to understand the way in which individuals create, modify and interpret their subjective experience of mental health in relation to their world then such research will be more conceptual and relativistic. Burrell and Morgan (1979) refer to this as ideographic (or symbolic) methodology. In discussing the concept of mental health in the context of health promotion, Neumann et al. (1989a) suggest that 'there is evidence that measurements of subjective perception of the health status [of individuals] allow for more accurate forecasts of health development than many other indicators of health status' (p. 4).

Burrell and Morgan summarise the four sets of assumptions on this subjective–objective dimension of the nature of social science (Table 1.1). In all four sets of assumptions it is useful to distinguish between objectivist and subjectivist approaches to social science. Indeed, the debate between objectivist and subjectivist approaches is a major part of Burrell and Morgan's original work (in relation to organisational theory and analysis) and of this present inquiry into different notions of mental health and of mental health promotion. Table 1.2 shows the application of Burrell and Morgan's (1979) scheme to assumptions about the knowledge-base of mental health.

Of course, many definitions and conceptions of mental health lie somewhere along this subjective–objective dimension. The following quote, for instance, represents an 'interactive' definition of mental health and one which attempts to integrate subjectivist and objectivist positions.[9]

> Mental health is the capacity of the individual, the group and the environment to interact with one another in ways that promote subjective well-being, the optimal development and use of mental abilities (cognitive, affective and relational), the achievement of individual and collective goals consistent with justice and the attainment and preservation of conditions of fundamental equality.
>
> (Minister of National Health and Welfare, 1988, p.4)

Table 1.1 A scheme for analysing assumptions about the nature of social science

The subjective–objective dimension		
The subjectivist approach to social science		The objectivist approach to social science
Nominalism	ontology	Realism
Anti-positivism	epistemology	Positivism
Voluntarism	human nature	Determinism
Ideographic	methodology	Nomothetic

Source: Burrell and Morgan, 1979, p. 3

Table 1.2 A scheme for analysing assumptions about mental health

The subjective–objective dimension		
SUBJECTIVE		OBJECTIVE
The subjectivist approach to mental health		The objectivist approach to mental health
Nominalism	ontology	Realism
Mental health (and illness) are concepts and labels which structure my reality		Mental health is definable and exists independently as a concept and a structure
Anti-positivism	epistemology	Postivism
I am a participant-observer in my own mental health and my study of it		Mental health can be studied objectively through analysis of its constituent elements
Voluntarism	human nature	Determinism
Mental health is representative of human nature which is autonomous and free-willed		People's mental health is determined by situation and environment
Ideographic	methodology	Nomothetic
We can know about mental health only subjectively, personally, through biographies, journalistic accounts and the process of research		Mental health can only be researched through systematic protocol technique, e.g. by testing hypotheses and data analysis

Source: Based on Burrell and Morgan, 1979

The social regulation–radical change dimension

Burrell and Morgan (1979) explain assumptions about the nature of society in terms of a regulation–radical change dimension. In the sociological tradition this is known as the order–conflict debate which Burrell and Morgan (1979), drawing on Dahrendorf's (1959) schema, summarise as order or integrationist views of society which emphasise stability, integration, functional co-ordination and consensus; whilst conflict or coercion views emphasise change, conflict, disintegration and coercion. In order to answer certain ambiguities in this schema, notably the dilution of fundamental differences between the models, Burrell and Morgan (1979) introduce the terms *sociology of regulation* and *sociology of radical change*, defining them separately and respectively as a sociology which is 'primarily concerned to provide explanations of society in terms which emphasise its underlying cohesiveness . . . which is essentially concerned with the need for regulation in human affairs' (p.17); and as one whose

Table 1.3 A scheme for analysing assumptions about the nature of society in relation to mental health

---

RADICAL CHANGE

Radical change
'The destruction of illusions and the analysis of consciousness . . . are the conditions for social change' (Fromm, 1971).

Structural conflict
'Genuine disalienation is . . . impossible without a total restructuring of society' (Bulhan, 1980, p. 260).

Modes of domination
'Clinical judgements about the traits characterizing healthy, mature individuals will differ as a function of the sex of the person judged . . . [and] clinicians' concepts of a healthy, mature woman do differ significantly from their adult health concepts' (Broverman et al., 1981, pp. 87–94).

Contradiction
Developing Erikson's (1968) ideas, Bridges (1980) makes sense of changes and contradictions in life, based on a theory of personality development which views 'transitions as the natural process of disorientation and reorientation that marks the turning points of the path of growth' (p. 5).

Emancipation
Mental health is the possibility and/or achievement of personal and collective autonomy.

Deprivation
The social system prevents fulfilment of mental health needs and, indeed, erodes the possibilities for human fulfilment; the status quo creates and maintains material and psychological deprivation.

Potentiality
Much of the humanistic/existential (psycho)therapeutic traditions represent and reflect mental health as the self-actualising tendency of the human organism.

The status quo
The status quo encourages the achievement and maintenance of individual's mental health.[10]

Social order
'Mental health is about the way human beings adjust to the world' (quoted by Wooton, 1959).

Consensus
Mental health is common sense – the voluntary and spontaneous agreement of opinion.

Social integration and cohesion
'Mental health or illness in this view would have more to do with the individual, or faulty functioning of particular primary institutions in which the individual develops, such as the family. The idea conveyed here is one of regulating individuals or institutions so as to fit them into an otherwise harmonious and integrated social whole' (R. Caplan and R. Holland, 1990, p. 11).

Solidarity
Mental health and well-being is the 'social cement' which holds society together.

Need satisfaction
Mental health comprises the satisfaction of a hierarchy of needs from the physiological to self-actualisation (Maslow, 1954).

Actuality
'[Health] is an appropriate balance of all of what we *are*' (Perls, 1971, p. 6).

SOCIAL REGULATION

Source: Based on Burrell and Morgan, 1979

'basic concern is to find explanations for the radical change, deep-seated structural conflict, modes of domination and structural contradiction which its theorists see as characterising modern society' (Ibid., p.17). Burrell and Morgan's fundamental distinctions between the two views of the nature of society are used to clarify and differentiate between concepts in mental health (Table 1.3). In identifying such concepts and notions mental health is viewed as a legitimate focus of political and personal concern.

Socio(psycho)logical paradigms

Drawing on the notion of paradigm, developed by Kuhn (1970), and putting these two dimensions, the subjective–objective and the regulation–radical change, together as axes, Burrell and Morgan (1979) define four distinct sociological paradigms (Figure 1.4).

Burrell and Morgan make several points about the nature and uses of the four paradigms. First, although each paradigm will contain a variety of viewpoints there will be, nevertheless, a 'commonality of perspectives', an essential unity within the paradigm, defined and described by the differences between the paradigms. Secondly, 'all social theorists can be located within the context of these four paradigms according to the meta-theoretical assumptions reflected in their work' (Burrell and Morgan, 1979, p.24). The paradigms thus provide a useful map with which to explore conflicting theories and practices. Thirdly, the four paradigms are mutually exclusive: 'a synthesis is not possible' (Ibid., p.25).

Having introduced this conceptual, paradigm framework, its development is taken up in subsequent chapters in Part I, through discussions about

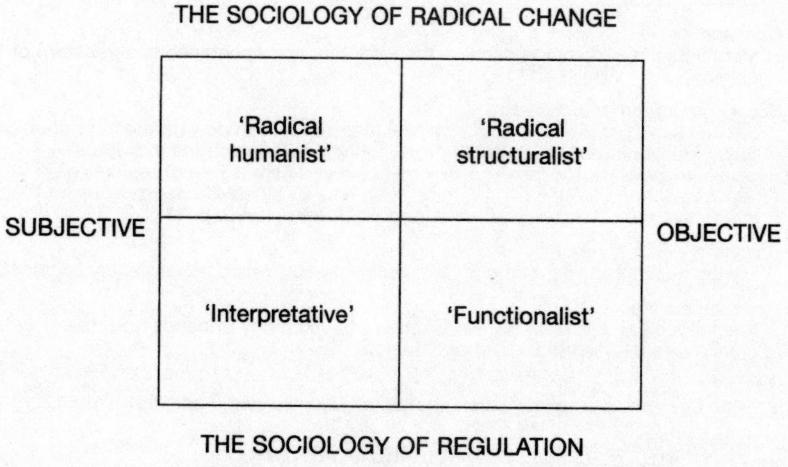

THE SOCIOLOGY OF RADICAL CHANGE

	'Radical humanist'	'Radical structuralist'	
SUBJECTIVE			OBJECTIVE
	'Interpretative'	'Functionalist'	

THE SOCIOLOGY OF REGULATION

Figure 1.4 Four paradigms for the analysis of social theory (Burrell and Morgan, 1979, p. 22)

health promotion (Chapter 2) and notions and aspects of community (Chapter 4) in which different approaches to Burrell and Morgan's point about the meta-theoretical assumptions underlying approaches to health promotion and community are considered, whilst in reviewing the theory and practice of community mental health promotion (Chapter 5), Burrell and Morgan's point about the exclusivity of the paradigms is reconsidered with specific reference to proposed movement between the paradigms.

In this chapter mental health has been separated from the field of mental illness by first discussing aspects of mental illness which militate against consideration of mental health – a theme returned to throughout this inquiry. Different definitions of mental health were reviewed and a conceptual, paradigm framework introduced by which competing definitions and theories may be analysed. The next chapter introduces the other half of the term 'mental health promotion' by discussing health promotion, and furthers our understanding of the paradigm framework.

2 Health promotion

Health promotion has emerged in the 1990s as a unifying concept which has brought together a number of separate, even disparate, fields of study under one umbrella. It has become an essential part of the new public health movement. Less effort has been made, however, in considering the nature of this new form of knowledge and practice, its salient features and the likely constraints on and possibilities for its development.

(Macdonald and Bunton, 1992, p. 6)

This chapter discusses definitions of health promotion and the related concepts of health education and illness prevention as it is the concept of health promotion (and this part of health service provision) which most often forms the context for the development of mental health promotion. This discussion is introduced by a brief history of the evolution of health promotion as a concept through four international conferences and with reference to concepts of health. Developing the paradigm framework (introduced in Chapter 1) as one with which different and competing theories, concepts and models of health promotion can be understood, the territory of health promotion is 'mapped' within the four paradigms. Such paradigm analysis is a more useful way of considering the nature of this form of knowledge and practice than futile health promotion 'versus' health education debates. The chapter concludes by drawing out from the field of health promotion some directions for mental health promotion (further developed in Chapter 3).

A BRIEF HISTORY OF HEALTH PROMOTION

Although health promotion in Britain has its historical roots in the public health legislation of the nineteenth century and public health medicine interventions of the mid-twentieth century (e.g. vaccination and immunisation programmes), the term 'health promotion' first appeared in 1975 in the Lalonde Report (Lalonde, 1975). This report (by the then Canadian Minister of Health and Welfare) introduced into public policy a new perspective on health, namely that all causes of death and disease could be attributed to inadequacies in current health care provision;[1] lifestyle or behavioural factors; environmental pollution; and bio-physical characteristics. The Lalonde Report not only signalled the Canadian government's shift of emphasis in health and public policy, from treatment to illness prevention and health promotion, but also marked the beginning of a world-wide response to the concept and practice of health promotion and a number of World Health Organisation (WHO) initiatives.

In 1977, the World Health Assembly, meeting at Alma Ata in the former Soviet Union, made a declaration committing all member countries to the principles of 'Health For All' and their implementation by the year 2000 – hence 'Health For All 2000' (HFA 2000). Importantly, the Alma Ata declaration (WHO, 1978) incorporated a commitment to community participation, now an essential part of any comprehensive health promotion policy, and practice.

In October 1986 the first International Conference on Health Promotion (ICHP) was held in Ottawa. Jointly organised by the WHO, Health and Welfare Canada, and the Canadian Public Health Association, the conference built both on the Alma Ata declaration and on the WHO's *Targets for health for all* (WHO, 1985). The conference presented a charter for health promotion (known appropriately as the Ottawa Charter) which contained a definitional statement of health promotion:

> health promotion is a process of enabling people to increase control over, and to improve, their health. To reach a state of complete physical, mental and social well-being, an individual or group must be able to identify and to realise aspirations, to satisfy needs, and to change or cope with the environment . . . health promotion is not just the responsibility of the health sector, but goes beyond healthy life-styles to well-being.
>
> (ICHP, 1987, p. iii)

The two subsequent international conferences – in Adelaide, Australia in 1988 and in Sandsvall, Sweden in 1991 – focused, respectively, on healthy public policy and the creation of supportive environments for health, compatible with sustainable development. O'Byrne (1989), in his introduction to a unique WHO workshop on mental health within the health promotion concept, highlights the need for supportive environments such as the home, the school and the workplace in which to promote mental health education and 'intersectoral collaboration' to help provide such health supportive environments.

Whatever the health promotion policy or programme, any concept of health promotion relies on a concept of health.

HEALTH AND HEALTH PROMOTION

Although there are probably as many definitions of health as there are of mental health (discussed in Chapter 1), there is – or, rather, was – a unanimity across cultures and centuries about health and holism. Traditional Chinese medicine links health to energy and disease and illness to interruptions in the natural flow of energy. Ancient Greek physicians viewed health as a condition of perfect body equilibrium with balanced 'humours' supposed to control health and disposition – categorised in European medieval times as blood, phlegm, choler (yellow bile) and melancholy (black bile). The ancient Greek cult of Hygenia viewed health as the foremost good, whilst the Stoics viewed health not as an absolute value but as necessary for the practice of virtue. North and South American Indians see health as a relationship involving humans, nature (including animals and the land), and the supernatural: being healthy is being in harmony with nature.

The unity, universality and integrative quality of such views was broken in Europe in the seventeenth century by René Descartes (1596-1650) who proposed a separation between the mind and the body (Descartes, 1641/1912). This has informed much of the subsequent development of 'Western' medicine with its focus on disease and illness separate from other dimensions of the person. It has taken Western medicine over three centuries to rediscover health.

The English word 'health' has its roots in the Old English 'hælp', 'hæl' (meaning whole) and 'hælen' (heal), and the Old High German *heilida* and *heilen* (meaning whole). Graham (1992) links these origins to the Old English 'halig' and the German *heilig,* which mean holy: 'etymologically speaking, therefore, to be healthy is to be whole or holy, which clearly embraces both spiritual and physical features rather than merely the latter' (p. 53). As Sartorius (1988) points out: 'health is indivisible. It involves and is apparent in mental, physical and social functioning which are interdependent' (p. S3). Money (1993) extends such holistic perspectives on health to the ecosphere, viewing 'human health as ultimately inseparable from the health of the planet' (p. 263).

As regards the relationship between health and mental health, various alternatives are proposed. Winnicott (1949/1975, 1988), in effect takes issue with Cartesian dualism, instead proposing his own, in arguing that the mental and the physical 'are not descriptive of opposed phenomena. It is the soma and the psyche that are opposed. The mind is of an order special to itself, and must be considered as a special case of the functioning of the psyche-soma' (Winnicott, 1988, p. 11). Taking a contrary view, in an article arguing the inseparability of mental and physical health, Sartorius (1988) equates mental with somatic health. In this inquiry, extending Winnicott's view, I argue that 'mental' is a special case within the integrative definition 'mental health' (Chapter 1) and therefore has a

special relationship to each of its constituent dimensions. It follows, therefore, that mental health is *criterial* to health: 'we may proceed from the
assumption that mental health is the centre piece of human health (Neumann et al., 1989a, p. 4).

'Positive health', as Noack (1987) points out, 'is an elusive concept' (p.
6). From a scientific point of view the epidemiology of 'good health' is
difficult to define, let alone measure or study, although Fanshal (1972) and
Galdston (1955) have done. Neumann (1989) suggests that an 'appropriately differentiated symptomatology or syndromatology of health . . .
would be the precondition for a reliable epidemiology of health' (p. 54).
The WHO defines health as 'a state of complete physical, mental and social
well-being and not merely the absence of disease or infirmity' (WHO,
1946, p. 3). 'Health is, therefore, seen as a resource for everyday life,
not the objective of living. Health is a positive concept emphasising social
and personal resources, as well as physical capacities' (ICHP, 1987, p. iii).
Although this sounds positive and is something of an antidote to scientific
definitions of illness and health, criticisms from different perspectives have
been made about the theoretical tautology, vagueness and incoherence of
such positive definitions and restatements of health (G. Williams, 1984;
Tannahill, 1985b; Noack, 1987; Downie et al., 1990). As with the
WHO's definition such definitions actually view health and health promotion as normative and functionalist. Maslow (1968) rejects this
'present easy distinction between sickness and health' (p. 7) implied
by the WHO definition, reflecting in essence much of the complementary medicine tradition which refers to the positive nature and quality of
dis-ease and the 'healing crisis', patient autonomy, responsibility and
choice. Antonovsky (1979, 1987) is concerned with 'the quality of life
in the realm of health' (Antonovsky, 1979, p. 220), a theme and subject
developed in more recent literature (e.g. Baldwin et al., 1990) and in this
inquiry in relation to mental health (in Chapter 3). In his writing
generally Antonovsky focuses on the study of health rather than illness: *salutogenesis* rather than pathogenesis – a concept which Neumann
et al. (1989) take up in proposing that a comprehensive theory of health
should include the equivalence of pathology and *sanology*, pathogenesis
and *sanogenesis*, psychopathology and *psychosanology*.

However, in the same way in which mental health is viewed and
(usually) defined in relation to mental illness, so health is to illness. Health
is – and needs to be – a contested concept (Beattie et al., 1993). Doyal and
Pennell (1979) suggest that in contemporary debates about 'health care'
there are three problematic assumptions: that medicine is a science; that the
determinants of health and illness are predominantly biological; and 'the
belief that scientific medicine provides the only viable means for mediating
between people and disease' (p. 12). Similarly, Shapiro (1983) argues that
the biases in the scientific tradition include 'an effort to reduce all experience to objective laws of "cause and effect" and a reductionist under-

standing of the universe' (p. 26); and that the tradition is itself based on pathology. In an attempt to integrate views of health and illness, Newman (1979) develops an expanded definition of health which views health as a synthesis of disease and non–disease (summarised thus):

1 Health includes conditions described as illness and pathology.
2 Pathologic conditions can be considered a manifestation of the total pattern of the individual.
3 The pattern of the individual that eventually manifests itself as pathology is primary and exists before structural or functional changes.
4 Removal of the pathology only will not change the pattern of the individual.
5 If becoming ill is the only way an individual's pattern can manifest itself, then this illness represents a form of health for that person.
6 Health is an expansion of consciousness.

In a major health and lifestyle survey Blaxter (1990) identifies, from the responses, health: as not ill; as a reserve; as behaviour (i.e. 'the healthy life'); as physical fitness; as energy or vitality; as a social relationship; as functioning; and, as psychological well-being. To summarise, professional and lay concepts, theories and definitions of health describe a number of entities:

- health as a state of being (e.g. WHO, 1985)
- health as a resource (e.g. Ministry of Health [Province of British Columbia], undated)
- health as potential
- health as a relationship or process – with oneself, others, one's environment, and beyond (e.g. Money, 1994)
- health as a value
- health as a belief (M. H. Becker, 1984)
- health as particular behaviours and practices (Tones, 1987)
- health as not ill-health, dis-ease or illness
- health as a status and an indicator (see Box 2.1)

Box 2.1 Health status

Health status refers to the overall health experience of an individual or a population. This is viewed by Neumann et al. (1989a) (alongside health as potential and health as a process) as one approach to the definition of health and, traditionally, as a natural-science definition, as an *objective* status, susceptible to bio-medical verification, although there is no reason why health status cannot equally be defined subjectively.

A *health indicator* is a measure of health status.

A *health index* is a composite of several health indicators.

A *health status index* is a summary measure of health status.

- health as a philosophy of care (e.g. health maintenance)
- health as micro and macro policies (e.g. health priorities, health insurance)
- health as a system of care (health care delivery systems, national health services).

Each of these elements implies certain and different approaches to the promotion of health which, as an organised response to illness and health, needs to respond to these elements and approaches with a comprehensive and coherent health promotion strategy. This in turn defines and describes the relationship between health promotion and, for instance, health status, in a systematic and systemic way. In the development of health promotion as 'a unifying concept', theorists and practitioners have over the years had to define health promotion particularly in relation to health education and to illness prevention.

PROMOTION, EDUCATION AND PREVENTION

Most debates about health promotion include some statements about the relation between promotion and education and promotion and prevention (discussed in relation to mental health promotion and mental illness prevention in Chapter 3). Academics with competing models argue their corner; and Tannahill (1985b) comments that health promotion 'has acquired so many meanings as to become meaningless' (p. 167). Conceptually, Eisenberg (1987) confidently defines health promotion, along with health protection (see Box 2.2), as a part of primary prevention (see Box 2.3). He then subdivides health promotion into those 'measures' which are subject to legislation (e.g. compulsory immunisation, or screening procedures) and those which are more about education and behaviour control. The proselytising perspective on lifestyles (and, therefore, on the quality of life) and behaviour promoted by some health education/promotion programmes has been widely criticised and is now largely discredited. The HEA (1989), for instance, acknowledges that 'people need to be able to understand and accept the need for change before they are willing or able to modify their personal behaviour' (p. 6). Tones (1990), on the other hand, suggests that health promotion is an umbrella which encompasses cure, prevention and policy. Tannahill (1985b) proposes a model of health

---

Box 2.2 Health protection

Health protection, within the tradition of public health, is defined as 'legal or fiscal controls, other regulations or policies, or voluntary codes of practice aimed at the prevention of ill-health or the positive enhancement of well-being' (Tannahill, 1985b, p. 168). Neumann et al. (1989a), from a more psychosocial perspective, suggest a role for mental health as a protective factor for health.[2]

Box 2.3 Illness or disease prevention

Illness or disease prevention generally means *the reduction of risk of disease*. Tannahill (1985a) 'reclassifies' prevention, identifying four foci for preventive action:

- prevention of the first occurrence of a given illness
- prevention of avoidable consequences
- prevention of avoidable complications of an established irreversible disease
- prevention of recurrence of an illness

Whatever the classification, the essential meaning and notion of prevention remains the same: the prevention of something happening predicted to be unwanted or deleterious.

---

promotion 'comprising three overlapping spheres of activity – *health education, prevention*, and *health protection*' (p. 167); for health promotion see Box 2.4 and for health education see Box 2.5. Dekker (1987) differentiates between prevention as programmes aimed at 'risk groups', whilst health promotion is aimed at the general public. Unfortunately, he then detracts from the clarity of this distinction by opting out of discussing promotion and focusing on prevention for the seemingly simplistic reason: 'since it is this concept that has been discussed most' (p. 140). The statement of the then Secretary of State for Health in response to a parliamentary question in the British House of Commons on the balance between treatment and prevention, supports this kind of conceptual confusion and pragmatism: 'it is not possible, or indeed appropriate, to try to quantify the balance between preventive and curative activity' (*Hansard*, 1989, col. 564).

Eisenberg (1981) traces the medical rationale for health promotion to the work of the public health reformer, Theobald Smith (1859-1934), who formulated a 'law of disease' which sets forth the proposition that 'the likelihood of disease is directly proportional to the virulence of the

---

Box 2.4 Health promotion

Health promotion (literally, *a movement towards health*) has almost as many meanings as definitions and covers a range of ideas and paradigms. Downie et al. (1990) propose an all-encompassing definition: '*health promotion comprises efforts to enhance positive health and prevent ill-health, through the overlapping spheres of health education, prevention and health protection*' (p. 2, original emphasis). This is, however, subject to the criticism that it procrastinates definition by substitution. In an article which reflects on different definitions and approaches to health promotion, G. Williams (1984) identifies three categories of health promotion proposals: the all-embracing model, a '*portmanteau . . . into which everything and anything to do with health can be packed*' (p. 192); the selected and separate specialist team; and the 'hard sell', behavioural approach.

Box 2.5 Health education

Health education is the term and concept from (and away from) which health promotion has grown. Traditionally, health education starts with the health and education of the individual and only then refers to groups, community and social context. Its focus is, therefore, primarily on individual and, later, societal behaviour change: '*health education* describes any combination of learning experiences designed to predispose, enable, and reinforce voluntary adaptations of behaviour conducive to well-being' (Green and Lewis, 1986, p. xvii). However, health education may be seen to emphasise a community focus as much as health promotion traditionally does: 'education for health, rather than being restricted to the modification of individual behaviours...is a general reorientation of individuals and the community towards health' (Neumann et al., 1989a, p. 16). Saan (1986) summarises the concepts of health promotion and health education and clarifies the difference of perspectives with reference to the professional and organisational implications, suggesting that 'in shifting from health education to health promotion, organisations have to take into account what shift in effort they envisage. A serious change in organisational policy could imply a reduction of the number of educational professionals and an increase in the number of professionals in environmental sciences, epidemiology and other health information, administration, management and policy development' (p. 254).

provocative agent and inversely proportional to the resistance of the host' (Eisenberg, 1981, p. 5). McPheeters (1976) notes the important elements of an epidemiological model of prevention, based on the notion of 'a) a causative agent, b) a susceptible host, and c) an environment that brings them together' (p. 188). Although medical thinking and practice has moved on from this model, this medical, diagnostic tradition still informs views of and policy on prevention today and nowhere is this more evident than the political policy documents: the British government's *The health of the nation* (Department of Health [DoH], 1991, 1992) and the Labour Party's (1991) response, *The better way to a healthy Britain*. All three refer to and cite 'health promotion' throughout and yet in their strategies and examples both documents confuse promotion with prevention. The government's green paper emphasises health promotion in primary care, extolling the benefits of contracting for general practitioners (GPs) in this respect, and then cites the example that this 'has contributed to the achievement of the national targets for immunisation in only a year' (DoH, 1991, p. 50) – a classic, if controversial,[3] example of illness *prevention*. Of the objectives of fourteen possible 'key areas' of the government's health strategy (DoH, 1991), ten are specifically preventive and only three clearly promotional. The Labour Party (1991), in its thin document, does not elaborate on its understanding of health promotion but comments critically that 'plans to promote better health will not get priority in a health service run as a market for the sale of medical treatment' (p. 1). From the government benches both the prevention of ill-health *and* the promotion of good health are ostensibly considered to be 'major priorities for the Government and the health service' (*Hansard*, 1989, col. 564).

Health promotion is viewed universally as such a 'good thing' that its limitations and dangers are little discussed. These include:

- Viewing individuals as totally responsible for their personal behaviour and consequently blaming them for their choice of behaviour and lifestyle, for example for many psychiatric patients, smoking is much more than simply a behaviour.
- Focusing on individual responsibility at the expense of also accounting for social and environmental aspects of lifestyle, illness and/or ill-health.
- The changing nature of research leading to contradictory advice being given to people.
- The deleterious secondary effects on mental health of some health promotion campaigns, for example obsessive focusing on weight reduction, often particularly aimed at women, may also lead to reduced self-esteem and, again, does not tackle the psychosocial stressors and pressures such as the fashion and advertising industries' promotion of the perfect body or their effect on women's self-image. R. M. Kaplan (1988), reviewing studies on the carcinogenic effects of toxic wastes and food, concludes that 'health promotion efforts designed to motivate avoidance of any carcinogens may result in confusion and anxiety' (p. 230).
- The damaging effect on health and mental health of unrealistic health promotion campaigns such as those promoting healthy eating (which have financial implications) aimed at people with low incomes.
- The partiality of health promotion strategies both in terms of target audience (e.g. healthy workplace policies affect only those at work), and of outcome (e.g. the social class differences in cigarette consumption: Townsend, 1987).

In the face of such confusion, conflation and criticism, it is more important and useful to understand the differences, as well as the commonalities, between particular theories and practices in health promotion. Equally it is more useful to develop and apply a way of thinking – a conceptual framework – with and within which to understand and practice, than to argue for the 'correctness' of a particular definition or position. In the next section, differences and commonalities between concepts of health promotion are identified, following which the paradigm analysis is applied.

Differences and commonalities

Noack (1987) acknowledges that 'concepts of disease and medical care, health and health promotion do not exist in a sociocultural, institutional and political vacuum' (p. 5). He then proceeds to construct what he terms as 'the socioecological paradigm of health', tracing its origins back to both Hippocratic and traditional Chinese approaches to health and medicine. Noack is also refreshingly explicit about his own theoretical framework which is a systems perspective, within the hierarchy of which 'health can be defined as a state of dynamic balance – or more appropriately as a process maintaining such a state – within any given subsystem, such as an organ, an individual, a social group or a community' (p. 14). It is clear that such concepts rest on some 'objective' notions of 'health balance' and 'health potential'; indeed, Noack (1987) discusses these dimensions at the level of both the individual and the community. Green and Lewis (1986) are also explicit about defining their terms: '*health promotion* refers to any combination of health education and related organisational, economic, and environmental supports for behaviour conducive to well-being' (p. xvii, original emphasis). The government's green paper takes this further: 'there is considerable emphasis in this document on the need for people to change their behaviour' (DoH, 1991, p. iv). Green and Lewis (1986) are also open about their interest in 'measurement' and 'the objective quantification of needs, processes, and outcomes' (p. xvii).[4] Such 'objectivity' is also to be found in *The health of the nation*. In the foreword to the green paper the Secretary of State for Health notes his conviction 'that setting objectives and targets for improvements in health is an essential discipline' (DoH, 1991, p. v); and in the introduction to the white paper his successor points out her conviction about 'what individuals and families themselves must contribute if the strategy is to succeed' (DoH, 1992, p. 3). Critics of government health policy – and of the government – see this focus on individual and family responsibility as a strategy which encourages blaming rather than real(istic) responsibility, and a convenient coincidence with the cost-cutting exercise of community care (discussed in relation to mental health in Chapter 4). Similarly, criticisms of the Lalonde Report (1975) have commented on its emphasis on 'healthy' individual lifestyle, individual responsibility and subsequent campaigns to modify individual behaviour in the context of a 'cost-crisis' debate in Canada at the time (Ziglio, 1988).

Raeburn and Rootman (1989) acknowledge the *subjective* dimension of people's experience of health:

> in both a policy and research framework, the usual goal is to obtain hard measures or variables; objectivity is the accepted standard and subjectivity, suspect. In moving away from the old models, however, people must face the importance of subjective aspects of health. Most studies examining the relationships between input (such as living conditions or social support) and health finally arrive at the conclusion that how people appraise or perceive input is more important than the objective nature of the input.
>
> (Raeburn and Rootman, 1989, p. 386)

Aims of health education consistent with this approach are about: improving communication by exploring the meaning of problems and events (e.g. diagnoses), challenging labelling, reconstructing identities by reframing accounts, and representing people (R. Caplan, 1986).

Another difference between theories and practices is the degree to which they are based on notions of change:

at a general level, health promotion has come to represent a unifying concept for those who recognise the need for *change* in the ways *and* conditions of living, in order to promote health. Health promotion represents a mediating strategy between people and their environments, synthesising personal choice and social responsibility in health to create a healthier future.

(WHO, 1986, p. 73; original emphasis)

The WHO working group which produced this document (from its Regional Office for Europe) takes a socioecological approach to health promotion. The difference between this socioecological approach and that of Noack's (1987) is that, whereas Noack's systemic perspective is based upon notions of equilibrium, the WHO's approach – with its references to enabling people to take control over their health, people having access to information, and public participation – emphasises more of a subjective and dynamic approach to knowledge and indicates the need for social change. Stark (1986) suggests that the model of health promotion has developed towards a more ecological approach; 'this was specifically in response to the critique of classical mental health or mental health education methods which turned out to be ineffective and failed to meet the needs of the population' (p. 181), a view echoed and extended by Money (1994). Raeburn and Rootman (1989) argue that the Ottawa Charter (ICHP, 1987) takes a holistic or ecological view and represents a 'major change in emphasis and language in health promotion policies' (p. 386), although L. Mitchell (1989) has struck a warning note about the 'healthism' of some of the WHO's more rhetorical statements on health promotion and the pressure on individual health workers: 'nurses may work or fight for health, but they should beware of posing for it' (p. 49). Consistent with these perspectives, Davidson (1987) describes a ten-week health education programme, the aims of which were 'to increase participants' awareness of the psychological and physical aspects of health, and give them the means to determine their own individual health schedule' (p. 313). The course took place in a variety of settings, such as education and sports centres, workplaces and a psychiatric day centre.

The WHO's principles of health promotion (WHO, 1986) focus on the subjective: emphasising personal choice; people realising aspirations; satisfying needs; etc. However, the subject areas and the dilemmas in health promotion the working group identified, as well as its priorities for the development of policies in health promotion, reflect a concern with social change from an objective stance: 'health promotion best enhances health through integrated action at different levels on factors influencing health, economic, environmental, social and personal' (WHO, 1986, p. 74). The principles of the working group's approach are worth noting:

1 Health promotion involves the population as a whole in the context of their everyday life, rather than focusing on people at risk for specific diseases. . .
2 Health promotion is directed towards action on the determinants or causes of health. . .
3 Health promotion combines diverse, but complementary, methods or approaches. . .
4 Health promotion aims particularly at effective and concrete public participation. . .
5 . . . *health professionals – particularly in primary health care – have an important role in nurturing and enabling health promotion.*

(WHO, 1986, pp. 73-74, original emphasis)

In terms of policy development, 'health promotion stands for the collective effort to attain health' (Ibid., p. 74). The WHO's priorities reflect a social, economic and ecological emphasis on health. The dilemmas identified are political and moral and question the social and structural: 'health promotion *programmes may be inappropriately directed at individuals at the expense of tackling economic and social problems*' (Ibid., p. 75, original emphasis).

PARADIGMS AND HEALTH PROMOTION

Given these commonalities and differences, an analysis of such approaches to health promotion and health education (and to illness prevention) and consequent 'models' of health promotion is vital for planning and practice as it is the often implicit ideology of the model which determines or at least influences strategy (L. Mitchell, 1989) – discussed in relation to mental health policy (in Chapter 6).

Developing the paradigm analysis and framework introduced in Chapter 1, the four paragraphs in the previous section concerning differences and commonalities are viewed as representing concepts of health promotion and education and illness prevention which may be located or 'mapped' within Burrell and Morgan's (1979) four paradigms for the analysis of social theory (Figure 2.1; see also Figure 1.4, p. 34). This mapping is on the basis of the meta-theoretical assumptions underlying the theories or models discussed, that is those assumptions implicit in the theories or models which are made explicit only by critical analysis or reflection. Each subsection is introduced with reference to its paradigm (further details about which are noted).

The functionalist paradigm

The functionalist paradigm 'has developed as a branch of the natural sciences' (Burrell and Morgan, 1979). This paradigm has an extensive history and 'has provided the dominant framework for academic sociology in the twentieth century and accounts for by far the largest proportion of theory and research in the field of organisational studies' (Ibid., p. 48).[5] Thus, concepts of health such as Noack's (1987), which view health as a process maintaining an equilibrium or the status quo, in which the focus is on regulated behaviour – and regulating healthy behaviour – and health promotion strategies which are based on such notions, are, in effect, concepts which have a commonality within the functionalist paradigm.

The interpretative paradigm

The interpretive paradigm embraces a wide range of philosophical and sociological thought which shares the common characteristic of attempting to understand and explain the social world primarily from the point of view of the actors directly involved in the social process.

(Burrell and Morgan, 1979, p. 227)[6]

Thus, concepts and models of health promotion which emphasise people's subjective experience of their own health are representative of and can be located within the interpretative paradigm.

The radical humanist paradigm

The origins of the radical humanist paradigm can be traced back to the same traditions which gave rise to the interpretative paradigm; where they diverge is that, whilst interpretative theorists are content to describe and understand the nature of a *process*, radical humanists offer a critique of such processes: 'reality is socially created *and socially sustained*' (Burrell and Morgan, 1979, p. 306, my emphasis). Thus, the commonality in approaches to health promotion and health education within the radical humanist paradigm emphasises subjectivity and change, with a radical stress on individual experience of health and autonomy in making healthy choices.[7]

The radical structuralist paradigm

'The radical structuralist paradigm is rooted in a materialist view of the natural and social world' (Burrell and Morgan, 1979, p. 326). Its intellectual foundations are based in the works of Marx, although within the paradigm 'Marxism' represents a much broader and differentiated body of social theory than Marx's original thinking, writing and political activity.[8] One radical and structuralist approach to health promotion can be

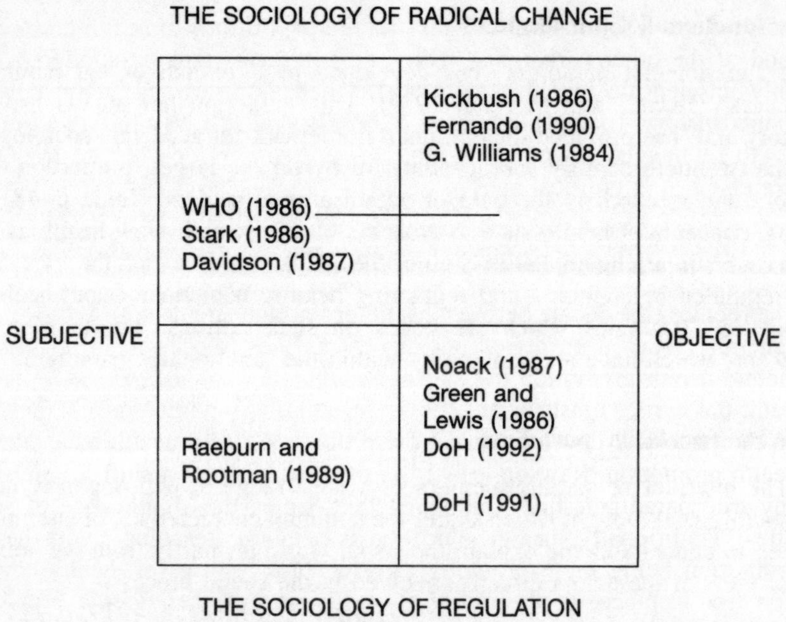

THE SOCIOLOGY OF RADICAL CHANGE

	Kickbush (1986) Fernando (1990) G. Williams (1984)
WHO (1986) ———— Stark (1986) Davidson (1987)	
Raeburn and Rootman (1989)	Noack (1987) Green and Lewis (1986) DoH (1992) DoH (1991)

SUBJECTIVE   OBJECTIVE

THE SOCIOLOGY OF REGULATION

Figure 2.1 Four paradigms for the analysis of social theory (Burrell and Morgan, 1979, p. 22), locating theories of health promotion

summarised by the unequivocal introductory editorial to the journal *Health Promotion*:

> health promotion is positive and dynamic. It opens up the field of health to become an inclusive social, rather than an exclusive professional activity. Its major feature – and here lies its sharp edge – is the challenge to move beyond health services into those areas of both policy and everyday life that regulate access to health.
>
> (Kickbush, 1986, p. 3)

One of the five levels within which a WHO working group has sought to frame integrated action on health promotion was on '*access to health*: to reduce inequalities in health' (WHO, 1986, p. 74) – which implies that the WHO has developed, or is developing, perspectives on inequalities in health, how those inequalities arise and are maintained, and what is necessary to redress them. The fact that this is not explicit bears out Raeburn and Rootman's (1989) argument that one of the criticisms of the Ottawa Charter is that 'in the areas in which the individual has more or less control, the emphasis is on less rather than more' (p. 386). Another subject area was '*the development of an environment conducive to health*' (WHO, 1986, p. 74) – again, this *implies* views within the WHO about present environments being unconducive to health. G. Williams (1984), in her analysis of the three categories of health promotion proposals (see Box

2.5), reflects a serious and radical structuralist critique of health promotion (and of the other paradigms) when she comments that 'promotion is not only unscientific but also mechanistic, behaviourial, and – above all – indoctrinatory' (p. 194). Fernando (1990) has made a plea for practitioners not to get bogged down in definitions: 'health promotion is not an academic exercise – it is political action' (p. 14).[9]

HEALTH PROMOTION AND HEALTH EDUCATION

The focus of the debate between health promotion and health education has generally focused on definitions and disciplines (discussed in relation to mental health promotion in Chapter 9) and which of the two 'schools' or traditions carries most current political credibility (and funding). Reflecting on the historical development in the profession, from health education to health promotion, Rawson (1992) sees this as more of a shift in title than any true paradigm shift – although this denies the significance of such titles. Traditionally, health education is seen as 'teaching', with health promotion being more promotive and enabling. However, health educa-tion, for instance, in the tradition of Freire, who describes a problem-posing education and a pedagogy of the oppressed (Freire, 1972, 1974), is more radical (and humanist) than a 'hard sell' health promotion pro-gramme promoting particular behaviour change. There is no doubt, too, that there is 'an inherent tension' within health promotion, as Thorogood (1992) points out, in commenting on health education and promotion as social regulation:

> to acknowledge the possibility of choice within discourses other than health as equally valid would undermine health promotion's claim to scientific rationality. If health promotion were truly to accept all choices as equally valid, the role of *health* promotion would be reduced to promoting access to and decision making about services, and the dom-inance of the rational, medico-scientific paradigm would be challenged.
>
> (Thorogood, 1992, p. 61, original emphasis)

Rawson (1992) considers the models of health education debate, having earlier identified seventeen published models of health education in Britain alone (Rawson and Grigg, 1988). However, Rawson describes (wrongly) the Burrell and Morgan (1979) scheme variously as an interpretation and, later, as a typology. It is, rather, a model of models or a meta-model which in its four paradigm analysis identifies commonalities of theories or models *within* paradigms as well as the meta-theoretical differences underlying competing theories and models *between* paradigms. This analysis also, ironically, responds to Rawson's (1992) point that 'what is required, however, is debate *between* taxonomies with an attempt to explicate the underlying theoretical principles' (p. 212). What actually matters is the assumptions which underlie the approaches and which therefore influence the direction of particular programmes. This paradigm analysis offers a way out of the futile health promotion *versus* health education debate. The different focus and purpose of health education/promotion within the four paradigms are summarised in Table 2.1.

HEALTH PROMOTION AND MENTAL HEALTH PROMOTION

Mental health promotion, as a new and emerging concept and practice has an inherent, if at times uneasy, relationship to health promotion – and vice versa (as is considered in Chapters 3 and 5). Neumann et al. (1989a) articulate many mental health practitioners' amazement that mental health has been underestimated by health education/promotion and suggest that 'perhaps this neglect has been the real reason for the lack of sustained and reproducible success of many health education programmes' (p. 17). In practice, considerations of mental health, and its promotion, are either marginalised or apparently so integrated that it disappears as an identifiable concept or practice, for example in the HEA's programmes whose strategic plan (HEA, 1989) contains no reference to mental health or its promotion, although this has changed in response to *The health of the nation* (see HEA, 1993b; this is discussed further in Chapter 6).

Equally, however, mental health promotion as a concept and in practice can learn from health promotion policies and practice. The widely-accepted distinction in health promotion that definitions and concepts have *both* individual (e.g. lifestyle) and structural (e.g. economic, environmental) elements is a useful one; although, in a critique of this particular dualism and in offering their own approach, Quirk and Wapner (1991) suggest that it is 'the organismic-development systems approach [which both] elevates the role of the environment and its interdependency with the person' (p. 203).

Despite its inadequacies, the Lalonde Report's (1975) four elements are equally applicable to mental health services:

1 *Inadequacies in current* mental illness/mental *health care provision* and the 'side-effects' of such inadequacies are well-documented (referred to in Chapter 1 and discussed further in Chapters 4 and 6).
2 *Lifestyle or behavioural factors* focus on the individual's contribution to and responsibility for their mental illness and mental health (eight elements of mental health are identified and developed in Chapter 3).
3 *Environmental pollution* also affects mental health, specifically, for example, the association of aluminium and high lead levels in the environment and Alzheimer's disease and, more generally, in terms of the importance of social support systems for mental health (discussed further in Chapters 3 and 5).
4 *Bio-physical characteristics* refer to the organic origins of some mental

Table 2.1 Conceptual approaches to health education/health promotion

	RADICAL HUMANIST HEALTH EDUCATION/ PROMOTION	RADICAL STRUCTURALIST HEALTH EDUCATION/ PROMOTION
Core view of society	Society is oppressive and alienating, characterised by hierarchical and authoritarian institutions of the state, e.g. business, science, work, family, language.	Fundamental conflicts and contradictions arise from economic system giving unequal distribution of wealth, power and opportunity. Society characterised by class, race, gender conflict.
Source of problems	The institutions we inhabit affect human consciousness, relationships and potential, producing alienation. Invalidation of alternatives.	Production: occupational injuries and diseases; distribution: artificial scarcity, inadequate housing; consumption: 'habits' determined by what is produced.
Focus of health education/ promotion	Self-discovery as an individual with *response-ability* (the ability to respond) freedom of choice in health care. Challenging the political aspects of health.	Provide a theoretical analysis of the relationship between health, illness and class structure. Link education/promotion to initiatives which challenge social structures.

	INTERPRETATIVE HEALTH EDUCATION/ PROMOTION	FUNCTIONALIST HEALTH EDUCATION/PROMOTION
Core view of society	Social life proceeds on the basis of the subjective participation of participants. Social structures and institutions are socially created and changed by people's interactions.	An enduring and integrated system based on harmony of interests and common value system. Models and methods of natural science applied to illness/health.
Source of problems	Meanings and definitions that people give to their actions are disrupted by events or reinterpreted/ labelled by others.	Pathological, maladaptive or incorrect (irresponsible) behaviour.
Focus of health education/ promotion	Improve understanding of self and others, reconstruct identities by reframing and 'correcting' stereotypes.	Behaviour and attitude modification based on an ideal/ norm of health.

Source: Based on R. Caplan, 1986

illnesses (see American Psychiatric Association, 1994) and, in relation to mental health, the predisposition to stress.

The Ottawa Charter (ICPH, 1987) and the WHO's (1986) working group's report, the focus on community participation, affirmed at Alma Ata, and the focus of subsequent WHO conferences on healthy public policy and the creation of supportive environments for health, including healthy cities (WHO, 1988), all provide frameworks for equivalent development in the field of mental health promotion (the policy implications of which are discussed in Chapter 6). They include, in addition to the four elements above:

1 *An ecological systems approach* is equally applicable to and inclusive of mental health (as reflected by the integrative approach of this present work and of others, e.g. Bronfenbrenner, 1977, 1979).
2 *Personal control over health*, again equally applicable to mental health (see discussion as regards autonomy in Chapters 3 and 5).
3 *Healthy public policy for urban areas* needs to take account of mental health and, for example, people with mental illnesses, especially in the context of community care.
4 *Environments supportive of health* such as 'cooperative social environments' (Steiner, 1984) are crucial to mental health and its promotion.
5 *Social infrastructure and community action*, again important for the development and maintenance of mentally healthy communities (see Chapter 4).
6 *Developing personal skills*, the practice element of MHP, e.g. the eight elements (see Chapter 3).
7 *Reorienting health and other urban services* which may be undertaken without incurring much expense, discussed as an aspect of mental health policy (see Chapter 6).

Having introduced the fields of mental health and health promotion, Chapter 3 draws these together in discussing mental health promotion.

3 Mental health promotion

Drawing together the chapters on mental health and health promotion this chapter begins to outline the concept and practice of mental health promotion (MHP). It discusses the differences between mental health promotion and mental illness prevention and identifies eight elements of mental health which provide a comprehensive basis for the promotion of mental health. The focus for MHP is on individuals: the implications of the eight elements for groups and communities are discussed in Chapter 5. The chapter concludes with two discussions which take up the challenge of social policy advocated in *The health of the nation*: MHP amongst 'the mentally ill' and MHP at work, in particular staff working in the National Health Service (NHS) and in social services departments (SSDs).

MENTAL ILLNESS PREVENTION AND MENTAL HEALTH PROMOTION

Since the early 1960s there has been much talk in the field of mental health about preventive work – that is, the prevention of mental illness. More recently, the term mental health promotion has been used, often interchangeably with prevention (Eisenberg, 1981; Perlmutter, 1982a; Doxiadis, 1987); and abused, with well-intentioned but naïve connections made with mental illness prevention. Hagard (1988), for instance, reflecting the Health Education Authority's (HEA) approach, links the promotion of mental health amongst the population at large with prevention 'so as to prevent mental illness' (p. 3). An emphasis on preventive services has been given backing by the Council of Europe Committee of Ministers (1976) which recommends that legislation covers factors influencing mental health, such as working conditions, community involvement, and somatic factors; perspectives on primary, secondary and tertiary prevention; and issues about support systems, mental health consultation and education, personnel, research and finance. These recommendations were subsequently taken forward and elaborated by a European *Working Party on the Organisation of Preventive Services in Mental Illness*. I shall look at the often confused and confusing debate between mental illness prevention and mental health promotion by discussing them separately and then the relation between the two.

Mental illness prevention

J. Newton (1988) traces the history of prevention in this country back to the establishment of the *National Council for Mental Hygiene* in 1923 (see Introduction) whose statement of aims, although Newton quotes it as a reference to prevention, is as much about promotion as prevention. Originally, public health practitioners divided preventive activities into primary, secondary and tertiary interventions. These terms were later adopted by mental health practitioners, notably G. Caplan (1961) who distinguishes them as:

> *Primary prevention*: 'the processes involved in reducing the risk that people in the community will fall ill with mental disorders'
> *Secondary prevention*: 'the activities involved in reducing the duration of established cases of mental disorder'
> *Tertiary prevention*: 'the prevention of defect and crippling among the members of a community'.
>
> (G. Caplan, 1961, pp. vii–viii)

J. Newton (1988) criticises this formulation as providing conceptual boundaries which are too wide 'to plan services or research, or educate the public' (p. 9). Nevertheless, most forms of intervention and action can be placed on a continuum, from the educational (primary prevention), the psychotherapeutic (primary and secondary prevention), to the chemical and surgical (tertiary prevention). McPheeters (1976) notes the important elements of an epidemiological model of prevention, based on the notion of 'a) a causative agent, b) a susceptible host, and c) an environment that brings them together' (p. 188) and it is this bio-medical model and tradition which still informs views of prevention today. The primary, secondary and tertiary categorisation of prevention is still current and promoted (e.g. Albee, 1988). Others, for instance Lamb and Zusman (1982), subdivide primary prevention into promotion and prevention, thereby staking a claim for subsuming promotion within prevention, whilst Halm (1989), in a curiously mistitled paper on mental health prevention, argues that prevention 'is part and parcel of the concepts of health education and health promotion' (p. 84). Edwards (1989) comments that 'the term "preventive psychology" is often used to include early *secondary* intervention – such as crisis intervention, mental health consultation, and setting up self-help groups for mental health problems' (p. 62, original emphasis) and suggests that we need to be more precise about our use of terms. Extending this analysis and using G. Caplan's (1961) categorisation (and in an attempt to meet those who emphasise prevention on their own ground), Tudor (1992b) developed this functional division of primary, secondary and tertiary prevention into strategies for mental health promotion and those for mental illness prevention (Table 3.1). Similarly, Trent (1993) uses the categories of prevention in describing primary, secondary and tertiary mental health promotion, defining them as focusing respectively on the removal of illness, the targeting of skills and knowledge deficits, and changing 'the attitudes, opinions and beliefs of the general population concerning mental health and mental illness' (p. 567). The North Derbyshire Mental Health Promotion Group (1991) takes a similar view in its strategy document. The strategies interventions and examples quoted in Table 3.1 are mostly directed to individuals (or groups of individuals), although McPheeters (1976) suggests that in both prevention and promotion there are two strategies: '1) to work with individuals to help them avoid stresses or better cope with them, and 2) to change the resources, policies or agents of the environment so that they no longer put people in stress but rather enhance their functioning' (p. 192). Mental health promotion is discussed in relation to the environment and specifically the community, in Chapter 5.

Vulnerability, targeting and prevention

Theoreticians and practitioners who advocate prevention, and even some who favour promotion, seek evidence of causative factors, are concerned to identify and target 'vulnerable groups', and generally focus their interventions on particular groups or communities. J. Newton (1988), for instance, has been explicit about her focus on the targeting of vulnerable groups, both in her own books (J. Newton, 1988, 1992), at conferences and in interviews: 'the secret is, says Dr Newton, to identify people who are vulnerable to mental illness and refer them to appropriate support systems' (Jervis, 1988, p. 22). This may be 'realistic', given limited resources, and therefore pragmatic. It is also problematic and little to do with promotion.

In the field of mental illness prevention, J. Newton (1988, 1992) has made the most serious attempt, in two coherent and academic books, to draw together research literature on prevention, focusing on depression, schizophrenia and prevention in childhood (J. Newton, 1988). This work is important in view of the fact that many psychiatrists do not accept that preventive action works or even that prevention exists as a scientific truth; at least one psychiatric consultant known to the author has blocked financing of research into MHP because of concern that he will lose psychiatric hospital beds and budgets – and, therefore, power. J. Newton (1988) argues that the question of prevention can be approached from two different perspectives: that of a disease model and that of a health model. She also argues that the two need not necessarily be in conflict, although in the course of her argument she soon drops references to the health model in favour of 'health prediction' and a concentration on predictive factors,

Table 3.1 Mental health promotion subsumed with primary, secondary and tertiary preventive categorisation

Primary prevention	Secondary prevention	Tertiary prevention
Mental health promotion Policy and practice concerned, for instance, with 'improving the ability of people to deal more effectively with everyday life' (McPheeters, 1976, p. 195).	*Mental health promotion* Policy and practice concerned to promote the two continua concept, and public education about mental health and mental illness.	*Mental health promotion* Policies and practice concerned to promote the two continua concept with the specific aim of raising issues of mental *health* within mental *illness* services and settings such as psychiatric hospitals and day centres.
Examples:	Examples:	There are few examples of MHP in tertiary prevention as policy-makers and advisors (e.g. the Health Education Authority), health and social care managers and practitioners are reluctant to enter what is seen as medical/psychiatric territory.
Campaigns, mental health education weeks/roadshows (e.g. Childs, 1992), exhibitions, booklets (e.g. MIND, 1994a, 1994b), seminars, conferences, articles, books, etc.	Northampton Mental Health Project (Gatherer and Reid, 1967). Adult education courses (e.g. Doyle, 1989). Some forms of counselling/psychotherapy with an educative aspect (e.g. Steiner, 1984; Keleman, 1989).	
Mental health education courses (e.g. Spy and Watkins-Baker, 1980; Higgins, 1984).		Examples:
Specific projects (e.g. Milton Keynes MIND's Education Project; the Greater Easterhouse Mental Health Pilot Project's Education Working Group.		Assertiveness courses on psychiatric wards, some forms of group meetings, etc.
Mental illness prevention Concerned with the provision of hospital and community services to ameliorate the effects of mental disorder.	*Mental illness prevention* Policies and practice primarily concerned with the targeting of vulnerable groups.	*Mental illness prevention* Essentially concerned with medical/ psychiatric prevention and treatment of the long-term, chronic 'mentally ill'.

Source: Tudor 1992b

despite her own admission that there is no evidence that such interventions, personal and/or environmental changes 'will affect the chances of those children succumbing to psychiatric disorder in adulthood' (p. 221) – from which it is a short step back to a focus on identifying vulnerable groups. Newton's kind of health model is in fact a functional, medical model of illness.

In debates about prevention and promotion, there is an often serious confusion between theory and pragmatism in relation to 'vulnerable groups'. Following the medical model of *diagnosis–treatment–cure*,[1] preventive approaches take a similar account, in reverse (Figure 3.1).

medical model   treatment   –   diagnosis

preventive model   **intervention–vulnerability–causation–predicted mental illness**

preventive   targeting
interventions   vulnerable groups

Figure 3.1 The preventive approach to mental illness

It follows that those primarily concerned with the prevention of predicted mental illness are interested in causation and causative factors; and, therefore, in identifying people, groups of people or populations who are vulnerable to such factors; and, therefore, in *specifically* targeting *those* people, groups or populations through specific interventions. This is clear and theoretically consistent, although research on stress shows that mental disorders are not caused by assumed risk factors (Scheuch, 1989). In debates and in practice so many people (and particularly groups of people) are loosely identified as being vulnerable that there is an unseemly (and atheoretical) scramble to identify those groups more vulnerable than others. This leads to the second point, often confused with the first: that the targeting of vulnerable groups is seen not so much as an essential element of a preventive approach but more often as a pragmatic exercise in the targeting and allocation of resources: the North Western Regional Mental Health Promotion Group (NWRMHPG) (1994), for instance, links targeting with efficiency – a case of the tail wagging the dog. Such exercises not only undermine any validity in the preventive approach but also lay this approach open to the criticism of creating a class of 'the deserving mentally ill' – deserving, that is, if identified as vulnerable. This leads to a more radical criticism that the identification of people and groups as 'vulnerable' implies a receptiveness and passivity which can foster the passive patient and victim role. Again, research on stress and mental disorder suggests that what is more significant is individual coping styles. A useful and rare insight on vulnerability is provided by Cochran (1988) who, in arguing an ecological perspective on youth and family vulnerability, avoids blaming the individual or groups concerned and identifies specific indicators which focus on social networks, formal institutions and cultural patterns.

Although through informal research in some communities it may be claimed that there has been significant improvement in support and well-being and a decreasing trend in the community's anxiety levels, there is little 'evidence' in terms of 'scientific objectivity' about the future effect of either preventive or promotional activities. Lamb and Zusman (1982) claim that, despite the techniques of primary prevention 'there is no evidence that the incidence of mental illness has decreased' (p. 19); they also suggest, for good measure, that 'there is no evidence that general mental health can be promoted or strengthened' (Ibid., p. 23). This ties in with J. Taylor and D. Taylor's (1989) argument that 'at the organic level there are no major opportunities currently open for the primary prevention of major illness' (p. 27).

Edwards (1989) provides some useful ideas for primary prevention in mental health, based upon three (overlapping) aims: 'to foster the development of a "competent community" via the facilitation of social support systems'; 'to design and implement early intervention for at-risk groups [and] to educate the public about mental health, and maximise the coping skills of the community' (p. 63). These views introduce another perspective on prevention, risk and targeting in which the focus is on the target population, such as individuals, vulnerable groups, the community, and 'the public', rather than on the 'nature' of prevention.

Mental health promotion

Eisenberg (1981) has traced the medical rationale for health promotion to the work of the public health reformer, Theobald Smith (1859-1934), who formulated 'a "law of disease" which set forth the proposition that the likelihood of disease is directly proportional to the virulence of the provocative agent and inversely proportional to the resistance of the host' (Eisenberg, 1981, p. 5). Since then most authors appear to have accepted some notion of promotion being, as its etymology suggests, a 'movement towards' positive mental health. Fernando (1990) acknowledges that, in mental health promotion, 'illness-prevention may be involved but that is not the point of it. Thinking and planning in terms of "illness" merely confuses and often distorts the issues; and in the name of health promotion you end up with an illness-relief service' (p. 14).

Perlmutter (1982a), in a rare book on these subjects *Mental health promotion and primary prevention*, states that 'it is important to note that the terms *primary prevention* and *mental health promotion* are used interchangeably' (p. 1, original emphasis)! A number of reports and reviews on mental health promotion confuse the term with (or subsume it under) mental illness prevention, for example the West Midlands Regional Working Party on the Promotion of Mental Health (undated) and NWRMHPG (1994). Merging promotion with prevention, Perlmutter (1982b) then attempts to draw some distinctions between the two terms and suggests a shift of focus from prevention to promotion and 'competency building'. She argues that mental health promotion is not concerned with the individual, but rather with 'contextual functioning' and therefore that it works with 'institutions in the broader community, not in the mental illness establishment' (Perlmutter, 1982b, p. 11). McPheeters's (1976) strategies for the promotion of positive mental health are (as are his strategies for primary prevention) directed both to individuals and the environment and are again aimed at improving *functioning*. Despite the difference in terms, these approaches to mental health promotion, like mental illness prevention, are in theory and practice still concentrated in the functionalist paradigm. This is why the subsumption of mental health promotion under preventive categorisations and strategies (as represented in Table 3.1) is ultimately doomed as it moves neither debates nor practice forward. It is Albee who, from a background in public health, has done most to move the debates from prevention (Albee, 1979, 1982) to promotion (Albee, 1986, 1990, 1994), with his focus on promoting human potential and social justice. Figure 3.2 represents Albee's formula for prevention; it represents the strategy of reducing 'noxious agents' in the numerator and increasing sources of 'host resistance' in the denominator – the task and strategy of mental health promotion.

In case these differences and discussions are considered academic or irrelevant – as Childs (1992) and Trent (1994) do – the reactions of particular, influential consultants and managers to health authority discussion papers suggesting that the key to mental health promotion rests in the community, are worth considering. Their views, that 'basic services' (i.e. psychiatric beds) are priorities over initiatives in primary care and prevention, have effectively blocked work, research and policy development on mental health promotion – and, for that matter, mental illness prevention – because there is 'no evidence' that promoting mental health 'works'! Albee (1988) counters this kind of criticism by noting that, in the field of public health, diseases have been prevented before knowing their exact causation.

Prevention and promotion

How are the two concepts of mental illness prevention and mental health promotion related, if at all, and, most importantly, what are the implications for practice?

$$\text{Incidence} = \frac{\text{Organic} + \text{Stress} + \text{Exploitation}}{\text{New cases} = \text{Social coping skills} + \text{Self-esteem} + \text{Support systems}}$$

Figure 3.2 Formula for prevention
Source: Summarised in Albee, 1994

Brogen (1985) prefers the idea of a continuum between the two, regarding promoting health and preventing disease as both 'parts of a holistic view of the health concept' (Brogen, 1985, Appendix 1), although he locates promotion within primary and secondary prevention. Promotion, under primary prevention, according to Brogen, takes a health education approach through special programmes in order to promote information and knowledge and to bring about both behaviour conducive to mental health, and increased acceptance of mental disorder on the part of the general population. Under secondary prevention Brogen puts forward the notion of identifying special high-risk groups with regard to their exposure to stress – citing single parents as an example and their risk behaviour, for example people with 'incipient abuse' of alcohol, drugs, and so on. This has echoes of G. Caplan's (1961) work in Israel where he developed the concept of 'key individuals' and those who have 'disordered relationships' and their 'noxious effect' on their community. Significantly, G. Caplan (1961) uses the analogy of the carrier of infectious disease in referring obnoxiously and derogatively in his Jerusalem Study to the identification of 'Typhoid Marys'. Dekker (1987) differentiates between prevention as programmes aimed at such 'risk groups', whilst health promotion is aimed at the general public. Kennedy (1988) describes the difference between primary prevention of mental illness and the promotion of positive mental health:

> the former takes mental illness as its starting point – hence perpetuating the notion that it should remain the preserve of the, misleadingly named 'mental health professionals', whereas the latter takes as its starting point the concept of positive mental health, in which virtually no-one can claim any real expertise.
>
> (Kennedy, 1988, p. 9)

Rakusen (1990) describes the dangers of prevention, suggesting that it 'contributes in no uncertain terms to the maintenance of the taboo surrounding any form of mental dis-ease' (p. 10). Sandford (1972) questions the very notion and validity of prevention, and others, including several users' groups at mental health promotion conferences, have suggested that, as a matter of strategy, prevention should be abandoned in favour of mental health promotion. This is largely because the theories and assumptions which give rise to the notion of prevention and the continuum of preventive interventions can be summarised as having three characteristics. First, they derive from the natural sciences and, in particular, medicine. Secondly and historically, they were located within the institutions of public health/welfare, having a largely functionalist approach, at a particular historical time (post-1945) and place (in the United States) in the development of the welfare state, its theories and practices. Thirdly, they imply a set of assumptions essentially about ideals and norms of mental health. Abandoning mental illness prevention thus represents a paradigm shift away from a medical/functionalist paradigm and towards a salutogenic one.

It appears then that we can merge mental health promotion with mental illness prevention, which more often than not both in theory and practice becomes *submerged* with*in* prevention (Perlmutter, 1982a, 1982b; Brogen, 1985); separate the two concepts (Kennedy, 1988; Rakusen, 1990); or abandon one or other (e.g. Sandford, 1972). The WHO, in its mid-term mental health programme priorities, appears to rank order promotion, prevention and treatment: first, the utilisation of all psychosocial factors for the *promotion* of mental health (e.g. WHO, 1991c); secondly, the *prevention* and control of alcohol and drug use; and thirdly, the prevention and *treatment* of mental disorder. Neumann (1989) sees a greater role for psychiatric research, drawing on both mental and social conditions, in providing more comprehensive foundations for preventive medicine 'as an essential *precondition* for improved strategies of mental health promotion' (p. 54, my emphasis). Verrall (1990) has proposed a framework for mental health promotion using Tannahill's (1985b) framework for health promotion (see Figure 3.3).

Adapting this for mental health promotion Verrall (1990) suggests the following elaborations of the sections:

1 Educational activity aimed at positively enhancing well-being . . . [e.g.] self-empowerment.
2 Preventive procedures . . . [e.g.] counselling services, crisis centres.

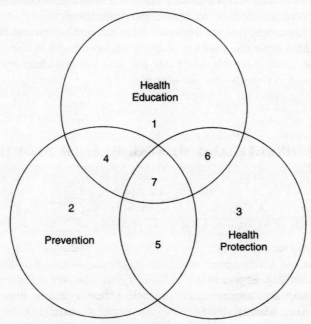

Figure 3.3 A framework for health promotion
Source: Tannahill, 1985b

3 Decisions by local, national or international government or other influential bodies which will positively promote health . . . [e.g.] funding for teachers of relaxation classes.
4 Education for the public or professionals, with a preventive focus . . . [e.g.] education about mental health problems.
5 Decisions by significant bodies which encourage preventive measures . . . [e.g.] funding commitment for a tranquilliser project.
6 Health protective education (i.e. education aimed at decision-makers) with a positive orientation . . . [e.g.] getting positive mental health on the agenda of those with power.
7 Health protective education (i.e. education aimed at decision-makers) with a preventive slant . . . [e.g.] educating managers about the usefulness of providing support for employees with mental health problems.

(Verrall, 1990)

Whilst this framework has echoes of a systemic approach, it is entirely descriptive and static. Individuals can attempt to fit their experience into the various sections; but, because there is no explicit theoretical or conceptual reasoning presented for the framework or its sections, this is a task ultimately without purpose or sense. This framework is not able to account for people's actual experience, which might include, for instance, the experience of de-institutionalisation – a crucial and current issue which any model or conceptual framework of mental health promotion and mental illness prevention needs to recognise and understand.[2]

Having suggested that the mental illness prevention/mental health promotion debate (like the health promotion versus education debate) is, at a definitional level, a largely futile one and that current ideas about mental health promotion are bound and dominated by the functionalism of preventive categorisations, strategies and 'measures', this inquiry develops a dynamic framework which is both conceptually coherent and practical.

MENTAL HEALTH AND MENTAL HEALTH PROMOTION

In Chapter 1 different definitions of mental health were reviewed. However, such statements provide only descriptions; all need to be seen in their cultural context (G. Caplan, 1961; Chwedorowicz, 1992). In a similar way as health was described (in Chapter 2), mental health may be viewed as:

- a state of being
- potential
- a resource (e.g. Epp, 1988)
- a relationship or process – with oneself, others, one's environment, and beyond (e.g. Money, 1994)
- criterial to health (e.g. Money, 1993)
- a value[3]

- a belief
- particular behaviours and practices (elaborated below)
- as not ill-health, mental illness or disorder (on the basis of a concept of one continuum)
- a status and an indicator (see Chapter 7)
- a philosophy and system of care, e.g. community care (see Chapter 4)
- micro and macro policies, e.g. through national mental health (illness) legislation (see Chapter 1) and national and local policies (see Chapter 6).

Depending, in turn, on how these are defined, they may be located within different paradigms with some aspects of mental health, such as potentiality, being more easily located – at the radical change end of Burrell and Morgan's (1979) vertical dimension (see Chapter 1). Trent (1994) describes three criteria for defining mental health: that it is self-contained; explicable, understandable and accessible; and non-biased, non-emotional and non-threatening. Ironically, Trent's third criterion is itself emotional and defensive as well as being atheoretical and unrealistic in arguing for definitions with no bias, that is no underlying meta-theoretical assumptions. In keeping with the reflexive method of this inquiry, it does not offer a definition of mental health or of MHP (at least at a descriptive or content level). This is because numerous definitions already exist, and I have no intention to argue any definition that I may have, as *the* definition above others – MacDonald (1993) also argues against such acts of definition. In any case, the four paradigm analysis suggests that there would be four paradigmatic definitions of mental health and MHP. Furthermore, this inquiry is more concerned to offer a conceptual framework and a reflexive method with which politicians and practitioners may reflect on their own definitions and practice.

ELEMENTS OF MENTAL HEALTH PROMOTION

Having established this conceptual ground, I draw together from the literature and from practice eight elements of mental health for mental health promotion, presented as elements for development amongst individuals:

- coping
- tension and stress management
- self-concept and identity
- self-esteem
- self-development
- autonomy
- change
- social support and movement.

Coping

The notion of 'coping' – and of coping skills – derives from the concept of adaptation, the cornerstone of Darwin's (1859) theory of evolution: as a species humankind is constantly adapting to the environment. Coping refers to efforts to overcome conditions of harm, threat or challenge. Lazarus (1975) identifies two categories of coping: *direct action* behaviours such as fight or flight (or freeze); and *palliative modes* which are those thoughts and actions which relieve the impact of threat or stress. Lazarus (1976) identifies forms of direct action as preparing against harm, aggression, avoidance, and inaction or apathy; and, drawing heavily on Freudian and psychodynamic theories, the various defence mechanisms of identification, displacement, repression, denial, reaction formation, projection and intellectualisation as palliative forms of adjustment. Commonly, coping is viewed as 'putting up with' something, an unwanted circumstance or pressure which has to be endured. In this sense, coping mechanisms and skills are often more about self-regulation and impulse control than, say, about challenging the source of the pressure or the circumstance or our ability to respond. This (functionalist) perspective on adaptation and adjustment is reflected and even encouraged, for example, in psychology ('sane psychology') by McDowall (1943), in personal growth by Worchel and Goethals (1985) and by a 'consumer-friendly' book published by MIND in which in response to the question 'What do you do if you suspect the onset of mental disturbance?' the answer given is: 'The first move must be to go to a doctor' (Melville, 1980, p. 15). More comprehensively, Dalgard et al. (1991) identify three kinds of coping: attempting to change the situation giving rise to the stress; controlling the emotional response; and/or controlling the meaning of the event (e.g. by re-framing).

Coping skills are generally either anticipatory or reactive; the reactive internal defence mechanisms of the latter tend to be experienced as somehow outside of us, not 'me' and/or beyond our control. A positive approach to coping skills takes the view that both direct action behaviours and palliatives modes are necessary skills. If someone or something is threatening someone that person reacts, which reactions are generally referred to (negatively) as 'defence mechanisms'. A positive approach to these defences takes the view that people develop defence mechanisms because they need or needed to defend and/or protect themselves. From a humanistic/existential psychological view these are maladaptations (C.R. Rogers, 1951): 'mal' or bad for our organismic selves but, developmentally, the best we could do in the situation with the information we had at the time. Table 3.2 summarises the traditional defence mechanisms as identified by Freud (1894/1962), M. Klein (1932/1975) and Anna Freud (1936/1966) and supplemented by Lazarus (1976); it sets alongside a humanistic reframing of them as creative adjustment coping mechanisms.

Thus 'defences' may be seen as options for maintaining one's mental health in a variety of circumstances.

Although Darwin (1859) viewed adaptation and adjustment as achievement and others have presented coping as mechanisms, both adjustment and coping can more usefully be considered as a process – or a number of processes – and ones in which people may develop and have a conscious and active ability to respond (*response-ability*). Such conscious reframing is often an important part of reclaiming this ability in the face of disparagement, threat and abuse. Rowan and Eayrs (1982) describe an adult education class on coping with anxiety and suggest that significant reductions in anxiety were achieved by some participants.

Tension and stress management

Stress management (now a multi-million pound industry encompassing psychology, education, management, marketing, publishing and training) and the concept of stress itself is predicated upon the human organism's evolution of homeostasis, together with certain bio-chemical responses to any disruption of this homeostasis. The body undergoes profound neural and hormonal changes in response to stress or, more accurately, tension with the release of adrenaline along with sympathetic changes associated with emotional arousal. Four categories of responses to tension are apparent: physical (e.g. restlessness), mental (e.g. loss of confidence), emotional (e.g. anxiety) and behavioural (e.g. increased or decreased sleep) (Patel, 1989).

Seyle (1956), the early pioneer in laboratory research into stress, formulated a three-stage 'general adaptation syndrome' in response to stress: alarm reaction, an initial phase of lowered resistance; resistance, the stage of maximum adaptation and return to equilibrium; and exhaustion, or the (temporary) collapse of the mechanism of adaptation. Antonovsky (1979), from his salutogenic perspective, distinguishes tension (rather than stress) as the response and a stressor as 'a demand made by the internal or external environment of an organism that upsets its homeostasis, restoration of which depends on a nonautomatic and not readily available energy-expending action' (p. 72), identifying stress as the strain that remains when the tension is not overcome.

Stress management – or 'tension management' (Antonovsky 1979) – comprises seven stages: usual *adjustment* to life; awareness of *vulnerability* to stressors; identification of *stressors*; awareness of *tension* and its negative, neutral or even salutary consequences; *tension management*; *stress*; and *stress management*. These are described briefly:

1 Usual *adjustment* to life (see section on coping). On a conceptual level, Neumann et al. (1989a) view mental health 'as the capacity to cope with unexpected stress or extremely stressful situations . . . [and as] the

Table 3.2 Defence and creative adjustment coping mechanisms

Defences[4]	Creative adjustment coping mechanisms[5]
Having the purpose of 'the protection of the ego against instinctual demands' (Freud, 1894/1962, p. 324).	
Regression	**Conscious regression**
A 'diffusion of instinct' by a regressive form of expression	An ability to 'cathect' a developmentally earlier age or state in order to repair or resolve a particular issue or deficit
Repression	**Conscious repression**
An urge or impulse blocked from expression and thus not expressed consciously	An ability to repress an urge or impulse, e.g. by retroflection, in order to survive a particular danger
Reaction-formation	**Reaction-formation**
When the threatening impulse is reversed to its (usually benign) opposite	As the defence, with an ability to avoid anxiety, for instance, by choosing a less harmful script (Steiner, 1974)
Isolation	**Withdrawal**
The isolation of a traumatic experience, e.g. by an interval of time (amnesia) or disconnection of thought	An ability consciously to withdraw into oneself
Undoing	**Creative de-sensitisation**
The attempt to 'blow away' not only the consequences of the event but also the event itself	An ability to deny certain sensation, e.g. pain, in order to avoid greater pain, e.g. in situations of torture
Projection	**Creative projection**
Dealing with an impulse by attributing it to someone else, rather than accepting it	An ability to attribute to others, e.g. being empathic, and to project oneself, e.g. being artistic
Introjection	**Creative introjection**
Unassimilated accommodation of material (beliefs, values, etc.) from others	Necessary internalisation and socialisation[6]
Displacement/turning against the self	**Creative displacement/retroflection**
Changing the direction of the expression of motivation into different channels, e.g. sublimation, deflection	Holding back certain expression, e.g. altruism
Reversal	**Creative deflection**
Of sequence, of affect, of direction, e.g. displacement of impulse	An ability to turn away a negative stimulus or sensation, e.g. to avoid pain

Projective identification
'Good' and 'bad' parts of the self projected, e.g. to avoid separation

Mechanisms of defence
(A. Freud, 1936/1966)

Sublimation
Directing an obstructed impulse away from its origination to other, usually 'higher' activities

Idealisation
The representation in an ideal form, of an impulse or object

Identification
The unconscious internalisation of characteristics of others, especially parents (not conscious imitation)

Defences
(Lazarus, 1976)

Displacement
Directing the expression of motivational force into different channels, e.g. sublimation, as above

Denial
Directed towards external dangers

Intellectualisation
Emotional detachment from a threatening event

Positive projective identification
An ability to identify: the earliest form of empathy and one which provides the basis of symbol formation

Redirection
An ability to redirect or channel energy into achievable ends

Creative idealisation
An ability to create and hold ideal objects

Imitation
The conscious internalisation/assimilation of the quality of others, e.g. from a positive parental figure

Creative deflection and redirection
(as above)

Discounting
An ability to discount at different levels (Schiff et al., 1975)

Creative egotism
An ability to view oneself with detachment: an important developmental stage

(processual) equilibrium between the individual and the environment (p. 7). Both health and stress, therefore, 'are active and necessary action qualities for the adequate coping with life' (Neumann et al., 1989b, p. 29).

2 Awareness of *vulnerability* to stressors. This varies according to age, stage of life, biological factors, lifestyle, attitudes and beliefs (Patel, 1989).

3 Identification of *stressors,* whether domestic, occupational, social, political and/or economic. The American Psychiatric Association's (1987) multi-axial diagnostic system, for instance, includes two scales of 'psychosocial stressors' – for adults and children.[7] Dalgard et al. (1991) divide psychosocial stressors relevant to mental health into three types: the frustration of needs; 'excess external demands on the internal capacity for change' (p. 427); and stress as an internal event.

4 Awareness of *tension* and its negative, neutral or even salutary consequences. The term 'eustress' describes the agreeable or beneficial reactions to stress: what has come to be seen as positive pressure or optimal stress (e.g. publication deadlines), reflecting the human need for sensory stimulation. Scheuch (1989), however, criticises this category as 'an undifferentiated condition without any conception' (p. 72), preferring to conceptualise and operationalise stress as a dialectical relation between the development of health, performance, personality and disease.

5 *Tension management.* This is the subject of much of what is referred to in the literature as stress management techniques such as breathing exercises, physical relaxation, the development of communication skills, nutrition and healthy lifestyle, physical fitness, etc. (Patel, 1989) – and to which I refer as *first-order management of stressors.*

6 *Stress* is what remains after tension management. It is described variously and measured in various scales, notably in Holmes and Rahe's (1967) social readjustment rating scale.

7 *Stress management*, to which I refer as *second-order management of stressors*, generally comprises more in-depth understanding of stressors and how they affect the individual, and the resolution of stress.

These stages provide an overall scheme for individual mental health development: awareness of individual patterns of adjustment and of vulnerability to stressors; the identification of particular and specific stressors; awareness of tension and how we hold it in our minds, emotions and bodies; the development of (first-order) tension management techniques (as above); awareness of stress and stress factors; and the development of (second-order) stress management techniques.

Traditionally, stress has been viewed as an individual problem; to some extent the seven stages (outlined above) counter this by distinguishing between psycho*social* stressors (the stimulus) and individual tension management (the response). Nevertheless, the social nature of stressors cannot be underestimated: H.B. Kaplan (1983), outlining a complex interaction of mutually influential components,[8] suggests that 'it is precisely the socially influenced nature of distress-inducing psychological processes that delineates the class of determinants encompassed by the term *psychosocial stress*' (p. 196). Following this, the focus for promotional strategies and activities shifts from the individual to the environment (e.g. the community: see Chapter 5).

Details of particular techniques can be found in the literally hundreds (if not thousands) of books and publications on stress management techniques, each with their own categorisation (e.g. Patel, 1989); school of thought and practice, e.g. autogenics and bio-feedback (Mason, 1985); or application, e.g. counselling and stress management (Flanagan, 1990), aromatherapy and stress management (Westwood, 1993). Along with self-esteem (see pp. 71–72), stress management is probably the element of mental health and its promotion (and of mental illness prevention) about which most has been written: in the context of MHP (e.g. M. Harrison, 1993; Sullivan, 1993; H. Graham, 1994), on stress clinics in primary care (P. Gordon, 1992), on occupational stress and stress in the workplace (Jenkins, 1993; Costa, 1994 and see discussion on pp. 85–86); whilst the WHO's European Regional Office is reviewing approaches to stress management by the community (J.G. Sampaio Faria, personal communication, 3 March 1994).

Self-concept and identity

A prerequisite of MHP with individuals (and of the subsequent element of self-esteem) is a concept of the self, although applying this concept beyond the individual becomes more complex. Again, much has been written on this subject from many perspectives and particularly from within philosophy (Glover, 1989), psychology (Gergen, 1971) and sociology (R. Holland, 1977). The 'self' is viewed variously as an innate structure; a structure or process; a behavioural agent ('I'); a conscious behaviour; a unitary concept; a social, an interactive and even a hypothetical construct. Unless we follow Aristotle's – and, later, Descartes's – basic distinction between the physical and nonphysical aspects of human functioning, the self is indivisible: 'my identity is obviously rooted in the continuous experience of my body' (Glover, 1989, p. 87). However, without following the logic of such dualistic divisions, it is nevertheless possible to identify and differentiate different aspects of 'the self' – as the singer/songwriter Joan Armatrading does in her song 'Me, Myself, I'. In this subsection, various theories of the development of self-concept and identity are reviewed briefly, whilst discussion of the evaluation of the self (self-esteem) is considered in the next subsection and exploration of self-development on pp. 72–74.

In terms of the development of the self, the psychoanalytic tradition focuses on psychosexual development (Freud 1905/1977), on a developmental progression (M. Klein, 1932/1975, 1952) and on psycho*social* stages of development (Erikson, 1951/1977) – psychosocial as it is 'a process "located" *in the core of the individual* and yet also *in the core of his communal culture*' (Erikson, 1968, p. 22, original emphasis). Other traditions include educational and developmental philosophy (Montessori, 1936/1966); cognitive-developmental theory (Piaget, 1964; Kohlberg, 1976, 1981); and spiritual development (Alexander et al., 1990). Mahler et al. (1975) suggest a process framework of development and Stern (1985) challenges traditional developmental sequences, focusing rather on the infant's subjective and inter-subjective experiences. Although theories vary, there is some common ground in the description that self-concept and identity are formed through a process of observation and reflection by which the developing individual explores, *knows* – and then evaluates – her/himself. Thus self-awareness is an essential part of this element of mental health and this process: whilst some authors 'use the term "self" as synonymous with "organism" it is here used in a more restrictive sense, namely, the awareness of being, of functioning' (C.R. Rogers, 1951, p. 498). Chiu (1992) links this clearly to mental health: 'a mentally healthy person should be able to consciously be aware of his or her desires, abilities and limitations, responsibilities and rights, acts and their purpose with the minimum of distortions' (p. 33).

Identity is a '*subjective sense* of an *invigorating sameness* and *continuity*' (Erikson, 1968, p. 19, original emphasis). The formative influences of home, school and the immediate and wider environment are also crucial in child and adult development; Nobles (1973), for instance, theorises that there is a 'we' self-concept, an awareness of an historical and cultural reference group. Chiu (1992) suggests that it is only on the basis of a clear (i.e. undistorted) sense of identity that one relates to the world, echoing Stern (1985) who describes the developing sense of the self in domains of relatedness. Gender, race, class and sexuality are also variously described as determinants of or influences on self-concept, identity and development. On gender, the concepts and development of 'masculine' and 'feminine' and the attachment to gender identity have exercised psychoanalysts and others since Freud (1905/1977). On race, Cross (1971) develops a model of 'psychological nigrescence', the process whereby black people who deny their blackness journey towards a confident black identity,[9] which Maximé, in an article reviewing psychological models of black self-concept, illustrates with case examples. On class, Reich (1942/1975) links class identity and the necessity of class consciousness to revolutionary political change, on which Lowe and Tudor (1995) offer a contemporary critique. On gender, through a review of the literature and a self-completion questionnaire, Coyle and Daniels (1993) examine psychological well-being and the formation of gay identity, whilst Hitchings (1994) discusses the psychotherapeutic considerations of Coleman's (1985) model of gay identity development.

Self-esteem

With a conception of self (self-concept) an evaluation of self (self-esteem) is possible: some authors view the relation between the two as developmental, others as an interactive process. Echoing Antonovsky's (1979) notion of mental health being a sense of coherence, Gergen (1971) suggests that with the evaluation of self-concept comes self-integrity, an appreciation of our limitations, and an understanding of the interplay between self and society.

Self-esteem is conceptualised as a psychological response, a personality function, and an attitude (Wells and Maxwell, 1976). Price (1992) offers a view of self-esteem and how to accentuate the positive from evolutionary biology, suggesting that 'the promotion of mental health requires sufficient anathesis (boosting signals) to maintain self-esteem, and the avoidance of excessive amounts of catathesis (putting-down signals)' (p. 89). In his conception of a *locus of evaluation*, Carl Rogers (1951) describes our psychological response being either *external*, based on the judgements and expectations of others and external 'conditions of worth' or value, or *internal*, based on the person's own evaluation of their feelings, actions, thoughts, beliefs, etc. However, if, for a variety of familial, circumstantial, environmental or societal reasons, we introject or perceive values in a distorted fashion which are inconsistent with our self structure we may well (mal)adapt so that such introjected or distorted representations become a function of our personality. This may be apparent only in someone's attitude towards themselves, particularly in discounting (Schiff et al., 1975), putting themselves down, negative self-talk, etc. In a major contribution in the field of MHP, MacDonald (1994b) considers the relationship of self-esteem to mental health and its promotion, commenting on definitions, correlates and antecedents of self-esteem.

Self-esteem skills and the promotion of positive self-valuing may well need to begin with the seen end of this process – of confronting sometimes negative attitudes, of starting where someone *is* emotionally and socially – and then working back to a person's functioning and to how they learned to respond, before working forward to where and how they want to be. Self-esteem skills, then, include the ability to listen to ourselves, self-evaluation (the internal locus of evaluation), and valuing ourselves. In describing the role and skills of the therapist, Fleming (1985) identifies seven levels of listening, at least six of which can equally and usefully be applied to 'self-listening': *passive listening*, a combination of meditation and listening (and elsewhere in the literature, and confusingly, described as 'active listening'); *listening to the content* of what we are saying; *listening to the obvious*; *listening to the message* in the character and quality of our voice (the emotional response of listening); *goodwill* in considering the possibility of making changes (being kind to ourselves); and *listening for the internal logic* of what we are saying.

Self-esteem is another area of growth, both personally and in terms of research. Carl Rogers (1951) describes a change in the valuing process during the course of therapy towards an internal locus of self-evaluation; Eachus (1991) considers the locus of control as a mediating factor in health inequalities. However, Cramer (1994) is critical of the lack of evidence to link the emphasis in certain kinds of therapy of unconditional positive regard or acceptance of the client with mental health in terms of self-esteem. Nevertheless, it is a commonplace to suggest that replacing old, negative (e)valuations with new self-affirming messages is a positive way of promoting our own mental health. Furthermore, Bowling (1991), in reviewing concepts of the quality of life, concludes that

> it encompasses more than adequate physical well-being, it includes perceptions of well-being, a basic level of satisfaction and a general sense of self-worth. It is an abstract and complex concept comprising diverse areas, all of which contribute to the whole, personal satisfaction and self-esteem.
>
> (Bowling, 1991, p. 9)

Self-development

Since the 1960s and 1970s, bookshelves have been bursting with popular psychology books giving advice on everything from abandonment to Zoroastrianism, the term 'self-development' covering a multitude of subjects. However, the literature on self-development has certain common themes: the premise of self-awareness (interestingly, Burnard (1991) links self-awareness to stress reduction by means of particular activities), an emphasis on assessing *existing* strengths, the identification of a 'problem' or something people want to change and the formulation of goals and action plans, usually with some element of time management, the issue of motivation, the identification of obstacles to self-development and how the person will overcome such obstacles, and the maintenance of self-development. Some view such development as self-actualisation, a discovery and reclaiming of our inherent qualities (e.g. Vallet, 1974; Samples and Wohlford, 1975).[10] Given the points made earlier about adaptation, stressors, developmental considerations and psychological responses, I prefer to link self-development as an element of mental health and its promotion to the dimensions of mental health (outlined in Chapter 1). Self-development and optimal functioning (Offer and Sabshin, 1974) may thus be viewed as multi-dimensional. Steiner's (1984) concept of 'emotional literacy' represents one dimension (affective) (although it also has implications for behavioural and cognitive literacy).

Steiner (1984) originally coined the term 'emotional literacy' to describe knowledge of emotions: 'to be emotionally literate we need to know both what it is that we are feeling and what the causes for our feelings are' (p. 165). He proposes, first, the need for 'cooperative social environments' as an ideal ecology for the promotion and development of emotional literacy; and secondly, a series of steps toward emotional literacy:

- asking for permission: to 'check out' feelings
- giving 'strokes' (Steiner, 1974) or recognition to a person
- making feeling/action statements: which are not blaming, e.g. 'When you (action), I feel (emotion)' (rather than 'You *make* me feel . . .')
- receiving such feeling/action statements: by acknowledging them, and, similarly,
- checking out and receiving 'paranoid fantasies', e.g. 'I think you are angry with me'.

Steiner's positive reframing and reclaiming view is that 'paranoia (from the Greek: *para*, to one side; and *nous*, mind) has its origins in heightened awareness. Our intuition is a powerful reality-sensing tool' (Steiner, 1984, p. 170). In order not to escalate our intuitive perceptions into paranoia we need to check out the original intuition.

In her description of psychic hygiene in MHP, Chwedorowicz (1992) argues that 'a high level of energetic emotional involvement is necessary to maintain mental health' (p. 244). Although Steiner used the term '*emotional* literacy', thereby emphasising the affective dimension of his work, it clearly includes behavioural and cognitive dimensions – the ABC of effective psychotherapy (Erskine, 1975) – and has been developed by others.[11] Other examples pertaining to other dimensions include what we might term 'cognitive literacy': Albrecht's (1980) encouragement of brain power through the development of thinking skills; and Afzalnia's (1993) discussion of cognitive literacy through a discussion of the importance of television 'literacy' or 'package of rules' and its impact on children's reading and listening skills. Keleman (1989), a psychobiologist, describes his *somatic*-emotional work and somatic education with its focus on the individual's body and body posture:

> what a person creates and forms remains with him all of his life. If one lives only, if there is nothing he participates in, he becomes passive to his existence. But if he makes the effort to form something for himself, that shape becomes his organisation, body, and life.
>
> (Keleman, 1989, p. 72)

Holden (1993) suggests that laughter works on many levels or dimensions.

Assertiveness may be viewed as an aspect of mental health literacy, also operating on a number of the integrative dimensions, and has an impact on self-esteem (Temple and Robson, 1991). Assertiveness training, another growth area, particularly for and amongst women (e.g. Dickson, 1982), has been applied to the field of sexual health by Painter (1994). It takes many forms, and usually comprises a distinction, a bill of rights, and a number of techniques. In the literature and in practice, assertiveness training distinguishes assertion from aggression (or imposition). It then, commonly, goes on to assert certain rights, for example to be treated as an intelligent, capable and equal human being; to express my feelings, opinions and values; to state needs and priorities; to ask for what I want; to say 'yes' or 'no' (but particularly 'no'); to change my mind; and to make mistakes, etc. It also proposes that everyone has these rights. Epp (1988) proposes a children's Bill of Rights in the context of MHP. In terms of techniques, assertiveness training encourages people to be specific; to make things personal, for example by using 'I', by changing verbs such as 'can't' to 'won't', 'need' to 'want', etc., and by changing questions to statements and the passive voice to the active; and to be able to deal with criticism and conflict. Assertiveness training encourages assertion not only verbally but also through eye contact, voice, posture, relaxation and taking space (often a criticism of men). Assertiveness is the subject of one in a new series of leaflets on MHP produced by MIND (1994a).

Autonomy

Berne, the founder of Transactional Analysis, links psychological health or well-being with autonomy, the attainment of which 'is manifested by the release or recovery of three capacities: awareness, spontaneity and intimacy' (Berne, 1968, p. 158). The concept of autonomy is one which has been developed in both personal (psychological) and political spheres (e.g. Lotringer and Marazzi, 1980). Individual autonomy is traditionally defined as when decisions and actions are a person's own. Dworkin (1988), for instance, conceives of autonomy as

> a second-order capacity of persons to reflect critically upon their first-order preferences, desires, wishes, and so forth and the capacity to accept or attempt to change these in the light of higher-order preferences and values. By exercising such a capacity, persons define their nature, give meaning and coherence to their lives, and take responsibility for the kind of person they are.
>
> (Dworkin, 1988, p. 20)

Autonomy, then, comprises the capacities to be aware, to give meaning, to define, to reflect, to be reflexive, to give coherence to our lives, to take responsibility through a genuine *ability* to *respond* (*response-ability*) and to be spontaneous and intimate. Autonomy may be seen as personal and political freedom *from* . . . as well as freedom *to* . . . This and our ability to express our capacities are, in turn, predicated on being free from psychological and societal restraints and distortions as well as freedom to express ourselves. Erskine and Zalcman (1979) describe and define a 'racket system' as an individual's 'self-reinforcing, distorted system of feelings, thoughts and actions' which is maintained by their decisional life script.[12] The racket system is not only a tool for analysis but also an instrument for change in that any therapeutic intervention which interrupts the system will be an effective step in the individual changing and in becoming autonomous. I. Stewart and Joines (1987) refer to an autonomy system as the positive counterpart of a racket system. A. Lee (personal communication, 29 June 1995) refers to this, more accurately, as the 'alternative system', arguing that as a system it does not represent autonomy: true autonomy integrates both 'systems'. Figure 3.4 shows both systems, with the alternative system shown as a shadow counterpart of an individual's racket system, with examples.

Some Western notions of autonomy and self-actualisation, founded in a tradition of North American 1960s psychology, are open to criticism of monoculturalism and, specifically, individualism (Rigney, 1981; Whitney, 1982; Lukas, 1989). Being a person requires self-consciousness; self-development requires the development of consciousness; and autonomy requires the raising of one's own consciousness in the service of self *and others*. Berne's linking of autonomy with intimacy, both with oneself and others, gives autonomy a connotation of relatedness and interrelatedness (and saves it from self-obsession and self-seeking). Fromm (1956) refers to relatedness as a specifically human need and passion (along with transcendence, rootedness, and the need for a sense of identity). Barrett-Aranui (1989) describes the Māori sense of relatedness: 'whānau means family, whanaunga means a relative, and whanaungatanga means the relatedness of people, one with another' (p. 99). Autonomy, including relatedness, not only provides support in stressful situations, but also as a concept becomes transcultural.

Although consciousness-raising, developed particularly by the women's movement in the 1960s, initially focused on the individual's consciousness about their own lives, it also encouraged a collective view of self in relation, for instance, to issues of gender, sexuality, power and oppression. Taking consciousness-raising further, Freire (1972, 1974), drawing on his experience 'teaching' adult literacy in South America using a problem-posing educational method, describes the egalitarian educative process as 'conscientisation', a kind of two-way, collective consciousness-raising. Freire's critical approach to education is paralleled in the health field by Illich (1975) and Antonovsky (1979), concerned, respectively, with medical damage (iatrogenesis) and 'the quality of life in the realm of health' (Antonovsky, 1979, p. 220).

The movement away from a kind of individualised autonomy to one of relatedness and rootedness is well summarised by two 'prayers' from Gestalt therapy, the original representing the individualistic, rigid 'here and now' focus of some forms of therapy:

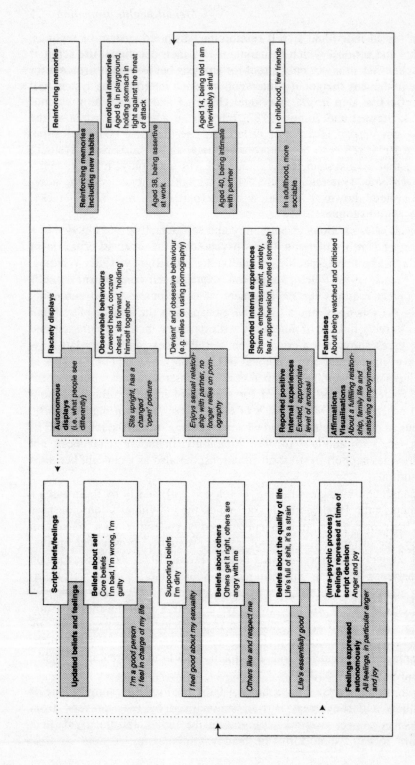

Figure 3.4 An individual's racket and alternative systems
Source: Based on Erskine and Zalcman, 1979; I. Stewart and Joines, 1987

I do my thing, and you do your thing.
I am not in this world to live up to your expectations
And you are not in this world to live up to mine.
You are you and I am I,
And if by chance we find each other, it's beautiful.
If not, it can't be helped.

(Perls, 1971, p. 4)

The second, offers a challenge to this:

You are you and I am I,
And if by chance we find
Our brothers and sisters enslaved
And the world under fascist rule
Because we're doing our thing –
It can't be helped.

(*Rough Times*, 1972, cited in Ivey et al., 1993, p. 329)

Change

Much of what has been summarised about self-awareness, self-esteem and self-development *implies* change: people as individuals changing themselves as individuals. Maccoby (1988), from a social-psychological perspective (and drawing on social marketing), reports on a six-step communication–behaviour–change framework for general health promotion: become aware (gain attention); increase knowledge (provide information); increase motivation (provide incentives); learn skills (provide training); take action (model); and maintain changes (provide support and guidance). Given the elements of self-awareness, self-knowledge *and change*, this might equally be taken as a framework for MHP.

After (self-) awareness and knowledge the elements of change, then, appear to be motivation, which varies from external pressure to internal desire to change; the learning of particular skills (e.g. those implied by discussions in previous subsections); and, crucially, action and maintenance. Watzlawick et al. (1974) suggest that first-order change (the content level of change) is based on 'common sense', whilst second-order change or change at a process level 'is applied to what in the first-order change perspective appears to be a solution, because in the second-order change perspective this "solution" reveals itself as the keystone of the problem whose solution is attempted' (p. 82). So, again, a prerequisite of taking action to change is an ability to reflect beyond the immediate content or common sense of the matter or problem in hand.

Maccoby's (1988) framework suggests that taking action to change requires a *model* of change, a plan, a map – and, perhaps, even a *modelling* of change, someone who has been there before. Both elements provide encouragement, some direction and permission for people to make changes, whether external, in the form of decisions about life circum-stances, such as relationship/s, employment, moving, etc., or internal about, for instance, changing belief systems, a pattern of thinking or behaviour, expressing feelings differently, etc. Maccoby (1988) also sug-gests that in order to maintain changes we need support and guidance. Perhaps the most accessible form of action and maintenance in developing and maintaining personal skills, and in getting support and guidance comes from counselling and psychotherapy. Each 'school' of psychotherapy, of course, has its own views about psychological functioning and malfunc-tioning or maladaptation, about how change is effected and the change skills required.

Maslow (1968) summarises the 'classical approach' to 'undesirable' 'personality problems' such as struggle, conflict, guilt, bad conscience, anxiety, depression, frustration, tension, shame, or self-punishment. Men-tal health problems from this perspective 'cause psychic pain, they disturb efficiency of performance, and they are all uncontrollable. They are there-fore automatically regarded as sick and undesirable and they get "cured" away as soon as possible' (Maslow, 1968, p. 6). Countering this is the originally Eastern view that crisis gives rise and opportunity to change and hence the homeopathic and complementary medicine perspective on dis-ease as a healing crisis. Reflecting this perspective on crisis and change, Bridges (1980) develops Erickson's (1951/1977) ideas in making sense of changes in life, based on a theory of personality development which views 'transitions as the natural process of disorientation and reorientation that marks the turning points of the path of growth' (p. 5).

If this is a macro-level perspective on change, the micro-level is repre-sented by any therapy which carries its own perspective on how individuals change.

Social support and movement

> A substantial convergence is observable in research findings produced in psychiatry, sociology and epidemiology and those from the broader fields of medical ecology and social epidemiology. Collectively, this evidence strongly supports the assumption that the nature of the social environment is significant for health and emotional well-being.
>
> (Turner, 1983, p. 105)

When people change assumptions, attitudes, behaviours, the way they feel and think, a ripple effect can often result which some welcome and others resist. In order to promote and maintain change/s some people come together with others, initially to gain support for their own change as, for instance, Steiner (1984) suggests as the ecology for the promotion of emotional literacy. Others come to exchange views and link up with others in similar positions (women's groups, support groups, etc.); and later to join together and effect changes or movement at wider levels, in their position, situation, environment and society – this movement from individual symptom to collective action is described and considered in Chapter 5. As we are ultimately social beings, any change we make has – and must have – an effect and thus it is important to consider the development of social mental health and social support skills in changing the quality of life.

Social health is viewed variously as a broader concept than health which includes a social dimension; a dimension of individual well-being, distinct from physical and mental health; and a component of health-status outcomes. As far as the social dimension is concerned, there is strong evidence for the significance of the nature of the social environment on health and emotional well-being (Turner, 1983). As social support (such as achievement, family support, friendships, financial security, etc.) is a key concept in the theory and research on social health, it is important to consider the elements of such social support for social mental health. G. Caplan (1974) reviews the taxonomies of social support, all of which acknowledge the relevance of emotional or perceived support and actual aid or availability. Turner (1983) identifies social support as the presence and products of stable human relationships; social bonds, social networks, meaningful social contacts, availability of confidants, human companionship; and developmental contingencies. Parry (1988) reviews the research on social support and social networks, suggesting that mental health(/illness) is related to adequate social support and suggests networking as a way of mobilising social support.

Four reflections on the eight elements of mental health and their promotion

The first reflection on these eight elements is to compare them with other schema or criteria (Table 3.3). Jahoda (1958) identified six criteria for

Table 3.3 Comparative elements of mental health and its promotion

Six criteria (Jahoda, 1958)	Seven indicator groups (Becker, 1984)	The eight elements
Mastery of environment	Capability	Coping Tension and stress management
Adequate perception of reality Integration	Self-centring	Self-concept and identity
Positive regard	Well-being Awareness of own value	Self-esteem
Continued growth to self-actualisation	Expansiveness	Self-development
Autonomy	Autonomy Drive force	Autonomy Change Social support and movement

mental health, whilst Becker (1984) summarised seven indicator groups for mental health: well-being, drive force, expansiveness, capability, self-centring, autonomy; and awareness of own value – with well-being and capability having the greatest importance in characterising healthy people. This reflects Freud's basic requirements for mental health: work and love. However, whilst productivity and intimacy may correspond to central value conceptions of mental health in European culture, this may not be true for other cultures. Maslow's hierarchy of needs is similarly culturally specific with some cultures placing greater emphasis on 'self-actualisation' than others.

The second reflection is to consider the relation of the definitions of mental health (Chapter 1), the categorisation of aspects of mental health (listed on pp. 62–63) and elements of mental health presented here. The Mid Staffordshire Mental Health Promotion Programme Development Group (MSMHPPDG) (1994), in one of the most coherent MHP policy documents around – in part, no doubt influenced by one of its authors (see MacDonald, 1993) – suggests that mental health encompasses three main areas: 'the conditions required for mental health, the skills involved in being mentally healthy, and the feelings and beliefs that this involves' (MSMHPPDG, 1994, p. 5). Using the four paradigm analysis as an organising principle for the definitions of mental health, the following are suggested as unifying paradigmatic principles:

- Mental health as functioning – social functioning (Preston, 1943; Eaton, 1951; Wooton, 1959; Kakar, 1984) and psychological functioning (Kakar, 1984) and development (e.g. Winnicott, 1988).[13]
- Mental health as interpretative and relational (Eaton, 1951; Neumann et al., 1989b; Money, 1994).
- Mental health as ability and capacity (Fromm, 1956; Guntrip, 1964; Minister of National Health and Welfare [MNHW], 1988; Chwedoro-wicz, 1992).
- Mental health as social (Banton et al., 1985; Epp, 1988; MNHW, 1988).

The third reflection is to note that some theoreticians and practitioners adopt a life-cycle approach or framework to health and mental health, its development and promotion (e.g. Pickin and St Leger, 1993; WHO, 1993b; Albee, 1994; Hancock and Hancock, 1993). Although this makes sense, especially in planning interventions in relation to specific target groups by age, the argument of this present work is that the unifying paradigmatic principles (above) will apply in any such targeting and programme. Thus, the development of mental health is functional, relational, to do with ability and capacity, and social.

Such principles are particularly important when authors and organisations propose different and differing definitions or criteria of mental health (e.g. P. Graham, 1986; MNHW, 1988), without also offering any unifying conceptual framework. On this basis, Table 3.4 shows the

Table 3.4 Definitions, aspects, elements and areas of mental health and its promotion

Mental health as functioning	Mental health as interpretative and relational	Mental health as ability and capacity	Mental health as social
Conditions As a state of being	*Conditions* As a relationship	*Conditions* As potential	*Conditions*
As a resource As a status As a philosophy, system and policy	As a philosophy, system and policy	As a philosophy, system and policy	As a resource As a status As a philosophy, system and policy
Beliefs and feelings	*Beliefs and feelings*	*Beliefs and feelings* As potential	*Beliefs and feelings*
As a value As not ill-health, mental illness or disorder	As a value	As a value	As a value
Skills Coping Tension and stress management	*Skills* Self-concept and identity Self-esteem	*Skills* Self-development Autonomy	*Skills* Change Social support and movement

relationship between definitions, aspects, elements and areas of mental health considered.

The fourth reflection is on the location of the eight elements within the four paradigms. Kittleson (1989), in an idiosyncratic article about mental health from a health education perspective (full of assumptions about the nature and content of knowledge and learning), asserts that 'the four major components of mental health fundamental to its development and teaching [are] high self esteem, effective decision making skills, values awareness, and expressive communication skills' (pp. 40-41). The eight elements of mental health outlined in this inquiry incorporate Kittleson's components and have the advantage of representing a comprehensive and coherent approach to the promotion of mental health of individuals:

1 They take account of the integrative perspective on mental health (described in Chapter 1).
2 Each element may be broadly located within the conceptual paradigm framework (see Table 3.5) on the basis of meta-theoretical assumptions about the nature of knowledge and the nature of change of these elements. As such, each element may be analysed from other perspectives and paradigms, thus H.B. Kaplan's (1983) conceptualisation of psycho*social* stress (with its emphasis on the social component) offers a critique of more functionalist approaches to *individual* stress.
3 Each element may be also be viewed as a skill and as such is amenable to development and promotion.
4 Finally, and importantly, these elements may be promoted not only amongst the population at large but also amongst 'the mentally ill', to which we now turn, and in the workplace.[14]

MENTAL HEALTH PROMOTION AMONGST PEOPLE DIAGNOSED AS HAVING A MENTAL ILLNESS

The notion that it is possible to promote the mental health and well-being of people diagnosed as having a mental illness appears a controversial one, both theoretically and in practice. The World Federation for Mental Health (WFMH) sets this out in its *Declaration* (Article 5): 'All mentally ill persons have the right to be treated under the same professional and ethical standards as other ill persons. This must include efforts to promote the greatest degree of self-determination and personal responsibility on their part' (WFMH, 1989, p. 5).

A conceptual prerequisite is an acceptance of the two continua concept (MNHW, 1988; Downie et al., 1990) outlined in Chapter 1. One practical – and political – consequence is a necessary confrontation of existing psychiatric systems and attitudes, one which leads, ultimately, to the acceptance and, indeed, promotion of user-led psychiatric services. Nevertheless, this notion of MHP of the mentally ill was given a considerable boost by the publication of *The health of the nation* (HoN), and the subsequent two HoN *Key area handbooks mental illness* (DoH, 1993b, 1994c). Any optimism about the progressive nature of such social policy has, however, been short-lived in the wake of the paucity of policy on MHP. Despite making mental illness one of its key areas and targets, in response to the HoN, none of the five areas of the HEA's (1993) stated concerns addresses the mental health and functioning of mentally ill people.

One of the often explicit aims in *managing* psychiatric patients both in hospital and particularly in daycare settings, within the community, is 'to keep them occupied' in order that they retain some sense of purpose and usefulness and do not become too inactive (good mental hygiene). Occupational therapies, cutbacks permitting, are seen as an essential part of psychiatric in-patient treatment – and, less honourably, so that 'they' are easier to organise and manage. Another, more often implicit, aim is to promote a safe, low-expressed emotional climate (Leff et al., 1982; Falloon et al., 1985; Tarrier et al., 1988). This is informed by the belief that patients 'suffering' and recovering from mental illness benefit from gentle activity and a calm atmosphere, free of conflict, chaos or ambiguity which enhances the healing process (D.C. Klein, 1968). Such regimes are seen as particularly valuable for patients who have had serious psychotic episodes or who have long-term mental illnesses. Security comes from a regularised (i.e. regulated) environment; one criticism of such environments, however, is that they are unable to offer real patient choice. This may be frustrating for those aware of what they want, especially if it is different from the regime; whilst those unaware of what they want are deprived of the opportunities to discover what they would choose and to exercise more control over their daily lives. In short, such approaches and facilities easily become institutions in which routines often reflect staff convenience rather than patient needs or wishes.

One attempt to avoid the trappings of institutional care, whilst retaining comfortable life-enhancing structures, has been the development practices based on the theory of normalisation (Wolfsenberger, 1972). This theory challenges the necessity and value of broadly-applied guidelines and argues that psychiatric services, as well as those for people with learning difficulties, offer people recreational and occupational opportunities which clients perceive as appropriate to their age, gender and culture, and in the same surroundings as others, for example by using public facilities for activities. Normalisation is an attempt to offer people the ordinary, 'normal' variety and choice in everyday life which most people take for granted. Normalisation, it is argued, encourages clients to improve their daily functioning and challenges society's – and sometimes the clients' own – notions of a person *suffering* from mental ill-health as someone different, that is not normal, strange, and possibly dangerous. However, this very attunement to the generally-held view that different = bad or 'less than' and normal = good are two of the pitfalls of services based purely on the theory of normalisation. People with mental illnesses or disorders *do* have different needs; they may at times be 'less able', for instance, to use public transport confidently and they undoubtedly need special support, help and opportunities. Also, what are 'normal' services are often not necessarily acceptable, useful or good particularly for users with diag-nosed mental illnesses or disorders – a criticism of normalisation shared, amongst others, by Clifford (1986/1991).

Along with these notions goes the widely-held assumption that because someone is 'suffering' from a 'mental illness' they do not have or experi-ence mental health. Two points follow from this line of (un)reasoning. First, given this assumption, there is no point in promoting the mental health of the mentally ill. Secondly, even if the promotion of mental health amongst this population is possible, say, along the lines of the elements of mental health outlined in the previous section or by the use of problem-solving techniques (Loumidis, 1992), it is undesirable as it might be disruptive to the ward, hospital, 'home', mental 'health' centre, or com-munity. Another and most insidious argument is that MHP amongst the mentally ill is dangerous in that it might have a deleterious effect on their recovery from 'mental illness' – this is the high-expressed emotion argu-ment. MHP amongst this population is seen as being disruptive to the regime or to 'normality'. These sorts of arguments, all too often heard in different psychiatric settings are successfully countered (in order):

1 By advocating the dual continuum concept. The concept as outlined has two implications: not only is it possible to have a diagnosed mental illness and to have a good level of mental health, it is possible and desirable to promote the mental health of people with mental illnesses and disorders.
2 Through the promotion of specific elements of mental health promotion.
3 By understanding both the effect of elements of MHP, e.g. the expres-sion and release of emotions on particular patients with specific diag-noses, *and* understanding the effect – and so-called 'side-effects' – of particular medication such as anti-depressants, lithium, Prosac, etc. on the ability of patients to respond to MHP initiatives.

The necessity for sensitivity both ways is particularly important for those wishing to promote mental health entering the psychiatric domain, and for those already there who could – and should – be involved in the promotion of the mental health and well-being of patients. Indeed, from a recognition that physicians are concerned not only with diseases but also with health and that mental health is the centrepiece of health, Neumann et al. (1989a) argue that psychiatrists themselves should be at the forefront of mental health promotion through research, consultancy and the improvement of the patient environment. With the advent of community care, the issue of territoriality in mental health is a crucial one, and one which is discussed in the next chapter on 'community'.

MENTAL HEALTH PROMOTION AT WORK

The notion of mental health at work has a history dating back to the mental hygiene movement of the 1930s and 1940s when a productive workforce was a happy workforce and vice versa (Preston, 1943). Judging by recent government publications, such functionalism, particularly in its aspect of social regulation, is still rampant. The financial costs of mental ill-health (and mental illness) are well-documented; Banham (1993) estimates that 80 million working days are lost to mental health problems each year, costing up to £2 billion per annum.

The health of the nation's strategy on MHP (insofar as it has one), suggests the development of good practice to improve mental health in the NHS and local authority workplace (DoH, 1992, 1993b, 1994c). Subsequent to this, the DoH has produced a series of booklets on *Mental Illness* (*sic*), one of which is *A guide to mental health in the workplace* (DoH, undated), which discusses workplace as well as personal stress. The DoH has also been involved in a major inter-agency initiative, involving the Institute of Personnel and Development, the Health and Safety Executive, the Department of Employment, the Confederation of British Industry, the Trades Union Congress, the Advisory Conciliation and Arbitration Service, the Health Education Authority and the Federation of Small Businesses. This initiative has led to a number of conferences and to the production of a resource pack for employers (DoH, 1994a). The problem with these and many other documents on stress in the workplace is that they tend to concentrate on and ultimately pathologise the individual. At best the aim of such initiatives appears to be to create a more tolerant climate at work towards individuals experiencing difficulties or stress. At worst, the implication is to avoid recruiting people with mental health problems through pre-employment screening. The DoH's bias is revealed in response to this last point: '*unfortunately*, the process [of pre-employment screening] is often discriminatory' (DoH, undated, p. 9, my emphasis). 'Unfortunately' this perspective has given oxygen to those who wish to demote rather than promote mental health issues in the workplace.

Following a landmark legal judgment in favour of John Walker, a former Northumberland social worker, who was awarded £200,000 compensation after suffering two mental breakdowns (reported in *Community Care*, 1994, 24–30 November, p. 1), a Yorkshire law firm, Dibb Lupton Broomhead, advised employers to sack workers suffering from stress (published and reported in the *Independent on Sunday*, 1994, 27 November). In a cynical calculation Dibb Lupton Broomhead advise that, even if the dismissal is subsequently judged to be unfair, the cost of compensation for unfair dismissal is far less than the costs incurred in cases of compensation (sometimes less than 10 per cent). Although Dibb Lupton Broomhead have received much publicity (probably, part of their intention), it is the government, through the DoH, and employers who fuel such attitudes through policies on sickness and sick leave, through implied policy (e.g. DoH, undated), and through the government's lack of explicit policies on mental *health* in the workplace.

Notions of mental health at work generally focus on the individual rather than the organisation. In the DoH's (1994a) resource pack one of the ten fact sheets focus on the mental health components of a health policy and this carries only two references to 'increased stress in the organisation' and 'workplace stressors'. None of the publications cited in the pack represent more dynamic views of workplace stress and anxiety (discussed in Chapter 8). There are inherent dangers in, for instance, the approach of stress management to mental health in the workplace; that the stress is in the individual, rather than the organisation, and that the stress needs to be managed, by the individual rather than the organisation through, for instance, changed work practices. Countering this, Sloboda and Hopkins (1992) and Hopkins (1993) promote a concept of staff care which focuses on relationships at work as promoting mental health.

Rather than simply focusing on individuals *within* an organisation, a comprehensive mental health assessment focuses on *the organisation itself*. In doing so, it highlights workplace stressors, the secondary anxiety (Menzies Lyth, 1959/1988) that workplace practices create, and identifies initiatives and activities designed to promote mental health. In this the organisation could become a context for MHP (discussed in relation to health promotion by Terborg, 1988). The gain to both individuals and the organisation would be reflected in increased mental health and well-being, as well as presence (rather than absenteeism) and productivity: 'helping employees to deal with stress must be secondary to the development of a workplace culture which values and motivates staff' (Trent Regional Health Authority, 1994, p. 5). The recommendations of this focus guide to promoting mental health at work in the NHS back up this statement by first focusing on organisational culture and health promotion and then on issues to do with individuals. In an initiative which goes some way towards a more organisational perspective, the HEA and the NHS Management Executive have launched a long-term initiative (*Health at work in the NHS*: HEA, 1993b) which aims to promote health in the workplace, 'a workplace . . . which reduces the stresses and strains inherent in today's highly competitive economic conditions' (HEA, 1993b, p. 1).

Having established the field of MHP, we now turn to notions of community (Chapter 4) as a prerequisite to consideration of community mental health promotion (in Chapter 5).

4 Community

What life have you if you have not life together?
There is no life that is not in community.
(T.S. Eliot, 1934, 'Choruses from "The Rock"')

In this chapter various aspects of community are discussed with reference to paradigm analysis – this time applied as a way of organising different and differing perspectives on community. The politics, policy and practice of community care in Britain are then compared with the 'Italian experience' of psychiatric reform and community care. Community care as a policy is seen (to use the language of mental illness) as pathological. A distinction is then made between the failure of community care, and positive community mental health (CMH). This is elaborated through four discussions: of the public's response to mental illness, the meaning of CMH, community participation, and social change in 'community'. These discussions serve as an introduction to an elaboration of community mental health promotion in Chapter 5.

COMMUNITY

The functional(ist) community

Whittington and Holland (1985) summarise the functionalist view of community: 'enduring societies, which may be analogous to biological systems, have evolved an integrated equilibrium founded on a broadly common value system, structures that sustain the functioning of the whole, and adaptability to change' (p. 34). This paradigm views community as defined by the functions it both provides and serves. D.C. Klein (1968), in his seminal (yet contradictory) work, *Community dynamics and mental health*, identifies the following basic community functions:

1 Providing and distributing living space and shelter and determining use of space for living purposes;
2 Making available the means for distribution of necessary goods and services;

3 Maintaining safety and order, and facilitating the resolution of conflicts;

4 Educating and acculturing newcomers (e.g. children and immigrants);

5 Transmitting information, ideas and beliefs;

6 Creating and enforcing rules and standards of belief and behaviour;

7 Providing opportunities for interaction between individuals and
groups.

(D.C. Klein, 1968, p. 7)

Klein's work in the field of community dynamics is still valuable in the
mid-1990s, largely because of his detailed analysis of many aspects of
community development and action. However, he unwittingly ranges
across a number of paradigms of community without making his functionalist inclinations explicit (although his chapter headings reveal them: 'The
community as laboratory', 'Epidemiology and community mental health',
etc.). In discussing community mental health, Klein refers to an 'ecologic
perspective' which represents 'the process of adaptation wherein an organism and its significant environment are in a continuously shifting state of
equilibrium and disequilibrium' (D.C. Klein, 1968, p. 58).

One image of a functionalist community is that of a colony of ants:
individuals and groups with defined contributions working to a specific
goal. This kind of community on a human level is one in which systems
fulfil needs (or not). Burrell and Morgan (1979) remind us that 'the
majority of systems models used in the social sciences tend to be based
upon mechanical and biological analogies' (p. 61) and argue that these kind
of models are unable to take environmental analysis into account. Using a
mechanical analogy, a sociopsychology of community – an integration of
sociology of community and community psychology – is interested in the
equilibrium and disequilibrium of the community, and factors influencing
its regulatory balance, whereas those using a biological analogy use the
more organismic concept of homeostasis. Identifying and analysing the
community as a social system is central to the functionalist paradigm, as
such analysis promotes an objectivist view of what constitutes community
(the provision and distribution of services, education, etc. – all of which are
regulated) and is to do with social regulation (maintenance of boundaries
and order, conflict resolution, etc. – which are also based on objectivist
notions). Such an analysis is further developed in relation to organisations
in Chapter 8. D.C. Klein (1968) himself refers to 'the community as a
social system where interaction occurs between people and values; where
needs are met and a vast array of functions performed; where change
occurs while integration is maintained, and where power is distributed,
conflicts managed and decisions made' (p. 183). In a section on 'Change in
the Community' Klein writes on the value of conflict management:
'emotional well-being could hardly be expected to thrive in a conflict-
laden social environment' (p. 154). This is a classic example of a function-

alist approach: there is an implied one 'right' way, 'the mental health approach', an objectivist approach to knowledge; and a statement about conflict *management* which implies a view about social regulation. On the basis of some empirical and comparative studies, Dalgard et al. (1991) link mental health promotion with the incidence and prevalence of mental disorder; arguing that there is a relation between mental disorders and social disintegration in communities, characterised by an absence of local leadership, reduced social interaction, distrust, social fragmentation and anti-social behaviour. Even writers who initially appear more humanistic, such as the American mystic Da Free John, actually propose what might be described as a spiritual functionalism or a functional spirituality: 'communities are rightly established when human beings understand the *functional* design of Man as a totality and as a single or simultaneous whole' (D.F. John, 1980, p. 92, my emphasis).

From this approach, it follows that community organisation and community development work – and within this paradigm it is viewed as such ('organisation', 'development', etc.) – aims at the maintenance of equilibrium and 'integration' or, more accurately, incorporation within the existing body of the community.

The (interpretative) meaning of community

Whittington and Holland (1985) summarise the core views of society implicit within the interpretative paradigm: 'social life is meaningful and proceeds on the basis of the subjective interpretation of participants. Social structures, institutions, roles, identities, and concepts of normality are socially created, sustained and changed by people through their interactions with one another' (p. 34).

Interpretative notions of community focus on what the concept of community *means*. These are many and various: Hillery (1955) identified ninety-four different sociological definitions of community.

A scan through the literature will reveal most psychologists using the term 'community' to mean 'outside a hospital'. This semi-geographical usage ignores the wider possibility of a true community approach. . . . In short, 'community' *may* be defined geographically but can equally be seen as a term referring to any group living together, working together or sharing some other meaningful identity. It is not unknown for the *global* community to be addressed.

(Newnes, 1988, p. 2, original emphasis)

We might add to these references communities defined by ethnicity, gender, class, sexuality or profession. Amongst the multitude of meanings, Bulmer (1987) suggests two elements central to a definition of community in the context of social care: 'the focus upon local social relations within a geographical area and the sense of belonging which is also entailed in the concept' (p. 29).

Views of community within this paradigm are concerned with *interaction* and with *meaning*, raising questions about the role of the community within society as well as those of the inhabitants or members of the community and of (mental health) workers within the community. The community is seen 'as a social system where interaction occurs between people and values; where needs are met and a vast array of functions performed; where change occurs while integration is maintained' (D.C. Klein, 1968, p. 183). Earlier, in a rare reference to an interpretative view, he suggests that 'it is important that the mental health worker raise the question of meaning with himself' (Ibid., p. 25) – the meaning, that is, of community as well as the worker's own sense of community and their own attitudes and responses. Once we discuss the meaning of community, of particular programmes, interventions and professional roles it then becomes possible to talk about processes: that is *how* we do things. Thus, community development work within this paradigm focuses on making meaning and the sense of what constitutes community (e.g. local government policies) and the process of community decision-making (e.g. community dynamics: Randall et al., 1980). D.C. Klein (1968) appears to recognise the importance of this when he refers to what he saw as the goal of a mentally healthy society: 'it is *how* the community goes about meeting problems and making decisions that affects its citizen's social and emotional well-being at least as much as, if not more than, the nature of the solutions or decisions' (p. viii).

Klein acknowledges the influence of interpersonal and interactionist perspectives when he defines community as 'patterned interactions within a domain of individuals seeking to achieve security and physical safety, to derive support at times of stress, and to gain selfhood and significance throughout the life cycle' (D.C. Klein, 1968, p. 11), although he himself admits that this tentative statement, as others, remains essentially functional in orientation. This is not surprising for, as Burrell and Morgan (1979) argue, 'interpretive and functionalist theories reflect a common concern for the sociology of regulation' (p. 254). The difference between interpretative and functionalist theories lies in their approach to the acquisition of knowledge: 'in the context of the interpretive paradigm the central endeavour is to understand the *subjective* world of human experience' (Burrell and Morgan, 1979, p. 253, my emphasis). Thus, Hillman (1993), in a critique of Freud's polarisation of love and work, suggests that one way of recognising community is through the love of work; another is through social justice; and a third is what Adler refers to as *Gemeinschaftsgefühl* – social feeling or community feeling.

Radical humanist community

In the radical humanist tradition (in common with radical structuralism), both community and the wider society are viewed as the locus of change. The difference between the two radical paradigms is based on the degree of subjectivist and objectivist forms of knowledge about the focus and forces for change. Within the radical humanist paradigm, critical theory stands in an idealist tradition which seeks 'to reveal society for what it is, to unmask its essence and mode of operation and to lay the foundations for human emancipation through deep-seated social change' (Burrell and Morgan, 1979, p. 284). In this paradigm the subjectivist aspect of radical change is emphasised; thus, society and community can be changed by the individual's experience of wider social institutions. Radical humanists maintain that 'society is characterised by the political and ideological domination of its members by the *socially legitimate* institutions of the state, business corporations, the professions, science, work and the family' (Whittington and Holland, 1985, p. 34, my emphasis). D.C. Klein (1968), for instance, amongst his references within other paradigms, refers to the community as a *habitat* which 'surrounds the individual and shapes his behaviour with demands and opportunities, with constraints and freedoms, and with rewards and punishments' (p. 22). Another definition is 'a supportive group of like-minded people within any setting over any period of time with a common cause or concern, able to provide an accepting and tolerant culture of genuineness, respect and understanding in and as a result of which personal or organisational change may take place'.[1] This is similar in spirit to M.S. Peck's (1988) characteristics of community: inclusivity, realism, contemplation and a safe place; from which his stages of community-making follow: the pseudocommunity (of conflict avoidance), chaos (including misguided attempts to heal and convert), emptiness and then community. Radical humanist interventions in communities or in helping to create communities are therapeutic (a theme developed in Chapter 5).[2]

Although (as with other paradigms) there are divergent traditions within this paradigm, two theoretical premises maintain the unity of radical humanism: one, about consciousness and the other about change. Radical humanists see 'individual consciousness as a focal point for the understanding of the nature of the social world' (Burrell and Morgan, 1979, p. 281); and, therefore, that 'they seek to change the social world through a change in modes of cognition and consciousness' (Ibid., p. 33). Thus, in terms of community interventions, the radical humanist acts as an 'enabler-catalyst' (Barić, undated).[3]

Radical structuralist community

What differentiates Marxism from idealist philosophy is that it considers that the production of the material conditions of human life ultimately *determines* the social process. This social process, within any particular social formation, comprises a complex and uneven relation of elements within any given mode of production. Under capitalism society is characterised by fundamental conflicts and contradictions which arise from its capitalist economic substructure. This, in turn, gives rise to superstructures such as the institutions of the state (e.g. fiscal and legal systems), the welfare state (e.g. health and social services) and professions (e.g. medicine, social and community work), which distribute wealth, power, services and opportunity disparately to different classes.

Radical structuralist views of society and community provide 'a critique of the *status quo* in social affairs' (Burrell and Morgan, 1979, p. 326) and, in terms of organisation, emphasise the collective groupings of individuals, rather than the individuals themselves, usually defined by structural inequalities in relation to economics, for example class, race and gender. Conflict is viewed as inevitable within capitalism and as the basis of emancipation; thus, a rent strike is seen both as a form of resistance and as a source of individual and collective learning. Any study or conception of the individual or groups within a radical structuralist paradigm must therefore necessarily regard them in the context of their social relations (for further discussion of which, see Chapter 5). Such work must therefore take account of both the personal *and* the political or societal: 'dissatisfaction with the individualistic focus of conventional psychology sets the scene for the development of community psychology' (Bostock, 1991, p. 2) – a psychology concerned with how social environments perpetuate psychological suffering and ill-health (also developed in Chapter 5).

COMMUNITY CARE

Any discussion of community mental health in Britain – and its promotion – needs to consider the politics, policy and practice of community care. Community care is the context in which mental illness and mental health is viewed, particularly by the public; indeed, the fact that community care is concerned with mental illness rather than with mental health inevitably influences the community's ability to care and respond to both mental illness and mental health. Community care is also the context for mental health (illness) policy which has more or, in fact, less impact on the promotion of mental health. Although it is predominantly concerned with the care in the community of elderly people, community care also has a major impact on the care of the mentally ill including the promotion of their mental health and this raises the issue of the extent of community participation in MHP. Finally, consideration of community care policy provides a basis on which to reflect and from which to analyse the implicit principles which lie behind the government's policy of apparent reform of the psychiatric system. These reasons for studying community care as the context for MHP find an echo in the four discussions – on the public's response to mental illness, the meaning of community mental health, community participation, and social change in 'community' – which conclude this chapter.

The political and financial context of community care

Community care is not new. Its origins lie as far back as the thirteenth century in early experiments in a communitarian, mutual aid approach to madness in the Belgian village of Geel (Roosens, 1979; Sedgwick, 1982) (from which twentieth-century community care could learn much and for further discussion of which see Chapter 5). Community care in Britain is governed by thirteen different Acts of Parliament dating from the *Disabled Persons (Employment) Act 1944* to the *NHS and Community Care Act 1990*. The first official use of the term appears to have been as a chapter heading 'The Development of Community Care' in the report of the Royal Commission on Mental Illness and Deficiency which preceded the *Mental Health Act 1959*. In tracing its history, Bulmer (1987) distinguishes four elements or meanings to community care: care outside large institutions, but including small 'institutions' such as some forms of residential care in the community; service delivery; care by the community, that is by voluntary and informal care; and the principle of normalisation. Its recent history may be traced to 1986 when the Audit Commission (1986) reported critically on local government and health authorities and the 'role confusion' between these two agencies in the provision of community care. The government's response to this was to ask Sir Roy Griffiths, then Managing Director of J. Sainsbury, 'to review the way in which public funds are used to support community care policy and to advise . . . on the options for action that would improve the use of these funds as a contribution to more effective community care' (R. Griffiths, 1988, p. iii). Trevillian (1988/9) suggests that Griffiths was able to build on essentially Thatcherite notions of community outlined in the Barclay Report (Barclay, 1982). One of the 'keystones' of the Griffiths Report was a re-orientation of the role of social services so as to ensure that individual needs are identified, 'care packages' drawn up, 'care managers' assigned, and co-ordinated services

> provided within the appropriate budgets by the public or private sector according to where they can be provided most economically and efficiently. The onus in all cases should be on the social services authorities to show that the private sector is being fully stimulated and encouraged and that competitive tenders or other means of testing the market, are being taken.
>
> (R. Griffiths, 1988, p. vii)

One reading and reaction to Griffiths was that, in its recommendation (1.5.1) on the transfer of resources from central to local government, it was somehow challenging government attacks on the power of local authorities. That this is a superficial reading of Griffiths, we can see both from Griffiths itself and in the government's subsequent white papers and legislation. Central government's notions of community and community care belie an essentially fiscal policy of monetary control of the social security expenditure on residential care for the elderly, whereby local authorities are used as the means of controlling expenditure and therefore of regulating the community.

As far as 'services for people with a mental illness' are concerned, in *Caring for people* (DoH, 1989a) the government set out three key initiatives (summarised in Box 4.1).

Box 4.1 Caring for people (Department of Health, 1989a)

Three key initiatives:

Continuing health care This was concerned with collaborative arrangements between health authorities and social services on a patient's discharge plans. This extended the principle and practice of cooperation between District Health Authorities (DHAs), local authorities social services departments (SSDs) and relevant voluntary agencies to provide after-care services for patients detained under certain sections of the *Mental Health Act 1983*, outlined in Section 117 of the Act.

Capital for building new facilities This provided a way of generating capital for new projects by selling off existing health authority assets.

Provision of social care This proposed a 'specific grant' to SSDs, payable through Regional Health Authorities (RHAs) 'on the basis of plans for the development of social care agreed between social services authorities and the matching district health authorities' (DoH, 1989a, p. 57).

As far as acquiring capital for building new facilities is concerned, this kind of asset stripping backfired in some areas because of the slump in the property market; due, at least in part, to the high interest rates determined by the government's economic policies. Some RHAs committed themselves to spending on new facilities on the basis that they would generate a certain income from land and hospital sales. The subsequent depreciation in property prices jeopardised some of the projected new facilities in the community (see British Medical Association, 1992). Money also leaked away due to lack of government concern, with the consequent failure on the part of government to provide adequate community facilities (Association of Metropolitan Authorities [AMA], 1993; Utting et al., 1994). The provision of a social care 'specific grant' (the *Mental Illness Specific Grant* [MISG]), went some way towards answering the criticisms of Griffiths, levelled by the Royal College of Psychiatrists, which, under the guise of care and concern for the funding and organisational difficulties of social services attempted to gain control over community care for the medical establishment, through fiscal control and statutory power:

> the mentally ill of all ages require a great deal of continued input from the psychiatric services whether at home or in some sort of sheltered accommodation. The Health Service contains by far the largest fund of expertise in the assessment and care of the mentally ill and evaluation of services. In our view, Social Services Departments are not the appropriate organisations to provide or to bear the responsibility of developing community care for the mentally ill. This responsibility must be invested mandatorily in the Health Authorities.
>
> (Royal College of Psychiatrists' Council, 1988, pp.386-7)

The predominance of the medical model in this statement and in the recommendations of the Royal College – which, for instance, reduced the role of social workers to that of assistants – is clear. As Nocon (1990) points out, the white paper arrangement whereby health authorities (HAs) hold the purse-strings (for the MISG) 'may allow health authorities to determine priorities in social care for people with mental health problems. It would thus undermine the ability of local authorities to plan services in an area in which they have both experience and expertise' (p. 27).

The broader economic policies on which *Caring for people* was based are 'managerialism and the denial of inequality' (Trevillian, 1988/9, p. 67), and the regulation of the community. In terms of inequality, it is generally women who are expected to be the 'care(rs) in the community'. Four out of every five of an estimated 5.5 million people caring for elderly or disabled relatives at home are women (Finch, 1986). H. Smith and Brown (1989) ask the question: 'how can any movement advocate "care" in the community without acknowledging how and why women hold together other people's fragmented lives' (p. 234). The answer they suggest is a strategy of using equal opportunities policies and structures in order to rectify the situation as regards women's role in community care. At the same time women express the fragmentation of their own lives: to which the statistics on mental illness and mental health (see Chapter 1) bear witness. Women as carers impact on the community. As Rose and Hanmer (1975) put it: 'to study community is to study women' (p. 29).

Financially, the government has been concerned about the escalating costs of care provision in the community, for example social security costs of income support claims towards accommodation and care costs in private care and nursing homes. In the field of private residential care for the elderly and disabled people, for instance, costs increased from £10 million to £878 million between 1978 and 1988 (Viney, 1990). With an increase in the proportion of elderly people in the population these costs were predicted to rise further. Under the white paper proposals the government transferred those monies they predicted it would have spent (had the old system remained in place) in the form of social security payments to local authorities through the revenue support grant. Such grants are cash limited (and do not exceed current social security payments), thereby in effect transferring the responsibility to local authorities to limit care according to finance, rather than providing care according to need. Specifically, local authorities have become responsible for the shortfall known, incidentally and incorrectly, as the 'care element', one element of which is the shortfall between the housing benefit and income support a resident receives and the rent they must pay. This additional cost to local authorities will inevitably be reflected by the placement of fewer people in residential accommodation: thus 'care in the community'!

In contrast to the lengthy gestation of the concept of 'community care', the development of the policy of care in the community – from the Audit Commission's Report (1986) through the Griffiths Report (1988) to its enactment in the *NHS and Community Care Act 1990* (the key elements

---

Box 4.2 NHS and Community Care Act 1990

Key elements

For the NHS

- The separation of the responsibility of commissioning services (the purchaser) from the responsibility of providing services (the provider).
- The creation of 'internal markets' whereby providers (e.g. an NHS Trust or part thereof) compete to sell services to purchasers.
- The reorganisation of the financing and management of primary health care services (e.g. Family Health Service Authorities (FHSAs) replacing Family Practitioner Committees, and GPs having the option to hold budgets for the purchase of a variety of services for their clients).
- The requirement on DHAs (with the co-operation of SSDs) to implement the 'care programme approach' by formulating individual care plans, based on a multi-disciplinary assessment, for those to be discharged from psychiatric care (in conjunction with the requirements of the *Mental Health Act 1983*, Section 117).

For Local Authorities (LAs)

- The annual preparation and publication by each LA of a plan for the provision of community care services in their area (S.46 (1)(a), such plans to be prepared in consultation with appropriate DHAs, FHSAs, housing departments and 'such voluntary organisations as appear to the local authority to represent the interests of persons who are or are likely to use any community care services' (S.46 (2)(d)).
- The responsibility and duty to take over financial responsibility (e.g. for residential care); to develop care management systems, including the development of care managers; and to provide assessment services.

of which are summarised in Box 4.2) – has been a hasty and interrupted induction. When challenged in the House of Commons on the government's delay in implementing its programme, the then Deputy Prime Minister Sir Geoffrey Howe said that the implementation date and the pace of the reforms 'must depend on the scale of the resources available' (quoted by Travis and Brindle, 1990, p. 20). This postponement was in order to stem the rise in the following year's poll tax bills:

> it would cost £830 million to introduce the programme next April. Some £370 million would be transferred from the social security budget to local authorities, but an extra £460 million would be needed from the Treasury. Postponement could save nearly £15 a head on poll tax bills.
> (Travis and Brindle, 1990, p. 20)

The government's cynical delay of the community care reforms caused confusion, disappointment and anger from virtually all sectors of care, levels of management and shades of political opinion (Cervi, 1990). The reforms were subsequently phased in over a three-year period beginning on 1 April 1991 (see Box 4.3).

Box 4.3 Community care reforms 1991–4

Phase one (from April 1991) included:

- The introduction of the centrally funded MISG (of £21 million for three years) 'for a planned improvement in the quality of provision' (DoH, 1990b).
- The introduction of a specific training grant for training social services staff.
- The continuing development work (already started) on planning arrangements, assessment and case management procedures, purchasing and related budgetary and information systems, all of which were to be implemented within existing resources.

In *phase two* (April 1991–March 1992) local authorities were

- to publish their first care plans (on 1 April 1992)
- to continue their development work
- to 'top up' the government's care grant with £9 million.[4]

In *phase three* (from April 1993 onwards):

- Resources were to be transferred, whereby local authorities took on full responsibility for funding care services.

The requirement on local authorities to publish community care plans is particularly significant as regards MHP as it provided an opportunity for the voluntary/independent sector to influence local government policy. The then parliamentary Under-Secretary for State for the Department of Social

Security added: 'we shall also require local authorities in drawing up their care plans to consult local statutory, voluntary and other agencies to ensure that the approach to community care becomes much more user driven than fitting clients into existing services' (*Hansard*, vol. 518, cols 1477–8). Some initial plans reflected these political perspectives in containing commitments to MHP alongside and, in some cases, even ahead of policies focusing on responses to mental illness. This onus on the local authority to include the voluntary/independent sector and user voices in the drawing up of community care plans was somewhat reversed in a subsequent governmental direction which stated that each local authority shall consult 'where that organisation notifies the local authority in writing of their wish to be consulted in respect of the authority's community care plans' (*Community Care Plans (Consultation) Directions 1993*, released 1 May 1993 with DoH circular no. LAC(93)4 and applying only to England). Despite this discouraging change of emphasis, one practical piece of MHP at an organisational level is that organisations may notify the local authority of their wish to be consulted. Furthermore,

> by making community care functions social services functions these too are brought within the scope of the general powers of direction and inquiries, of the complaints procedures and of the default action set out in addition to the 1970 [Local Authority Social Services] Act effected by s.50 of this [NHS and Community Care] Act.
>
> (R.M. Jones, 1993, p. D1/383)

This little known passage is crucial. If notifications are ignored, consultation (timetables and methods) unreasonable, views not considered, parties not properly informed of meetings, etc., then LA complaints procedures may be invoked.

In the two-year lead up to April 1993, plans were further delayed, criticisms of the concept and practice of community care were levelled (e.g. Tudor, 1990/91; Pelikan, 1991); and the original spirit of community care was soured by bureaucratic and political manoeuvrings over implementation, for instance, noting 'unmet choice' rather than 'unmet need' in care assessments in order to avoid possible legal action by dissatisfied clients.

The government's care in the community policies have escalated the previous decline in hospital/residential psychiatric beds in a dramatic programme of closure of psychiatric hospitals and hospital-based services (see Davidge et al., 1993). However, despite assurances to the contrary, the government has failed to provide sufficient financing, through health and local authorities, for a consequent development of services in the community to meet the mental health (illness) needs both of those discharged from hospitals and of the general population. This is well-illustrated in the following figures, taken from a Mental Health Foundation (MHF, 1990) report. In 1989 it was estimated that there were about 6 million people, in

Britain, with an identified mental illness, of which 60,000 (1 per cent) were NHS psychiatric in-patients, maintained in hospital at a cost of £26,250 per person per year. By contrast, the 99 per cent – people with an identified mental illness, living in the community – had only £107 per person per year spent on their care and support. According to the MHF (1990): 'there are at least 3 million people with a serious mental illness living in the community who receive minimal professional treatment and care' (unpaginated). It is clear that care in the community in respect of people with mental illness frequently means that people are discharged from (or not admitted to) psychiatric hospitals with little, inappropriate, or even no support in the community. This lack of community care has its roots in policies which are led by budgets rather than principles, unlike its Italian counterpart.

THE 'ITALIAN EXPERIENCE' OF PSYCHIATRIC REFORM AND COMMUNITY CARE

Heginbotham (1990) suggests that the *NHS and Community Care Act* is 'pre-eminently a piece of strategic law rather than one of detailed provision' (p. 25). This is in marked contrast to Italian Law 180/1978, a piece of enabling legislation which precisely *enabled* local Health and Social Service Authorities politically, strategically and financially to develop community mental health care facilities and support networks. It is worth looking briefly at the provisions of Law 180/1978 as they reflect the philosophy of de-institutionalisation and community care of the original reformers and as such it provides a useful yardstick against which to measure both the *Mental Health Act 1983* (England and Wales) and the *NHS and Community Care Act 1990*.

Law 180/1978

There are three important principles underlying Law 180. The first is that the Law, whose first Article is entitled 'Voluntary and compulsory health treatment', is concerned not with definitions or classifications of disease but with the forms of and reasons for treatment.

Secondly, Law 180 emphasises patients' rights, already guaranteed under Italy's written constitution (Articles 13 and 32), but specifically as regards personal freedom and the right to treatment (Law 180/1978, Art. 1). In the context of compulsory health treatment for *general* illness (confirmed by Law 833/1978 on the organisation of health and social services, Articles 33 and 34) Law 180 clarified the conditions under which compulsory treatment could be applied to those with a 'mental illness' and this is the only category to which compulsory treatment is applicable (Law 180/ 1978, Art. 2.1). The emphasis on treatment gives rise here to an important distinction: that between compulsory *treatment* in Italy and compulsory *hospitalisation* in England and Wales (the *Mental Health Act 1983*, Ss

2.(2)(a) and 3.(2)(a)). In Italy the moral and legal emphasis is on treatment in the community, under the auspices of the local Community Mental Health Centre (CSM).

The third important principle of Law 180 was its shift of emphasis from the behaviour of the 'mad' person to the importance of the provision of appropriate services. The previous 1904 Law had legalised compulsory admission to the asylum of individuals due to their dangerousness as certified by a doctor or a legal ordinance. Law 180 dropped this notion of social dangerousness.

The reactions to Law 180 were many and varied. One, as Dell'Acqua et al. (1986) point out, was a certain polarisation:

> it seems to us that in Italy such application [of the law] has given attention exclusively and in an absolutely *ambiguous* and perverse way, on the one hand to the guarantee of personal freedom (non intervention) and, at the other extreme, to compulsory treatment.
>
> (Dell'Acqua et al., 1986, p. 5, my emphasis)

This led, on the one hand, to a scarce realisation of integrated, local resources, and, 'at the other extreme', to a proliferation of 'diagnosis and cure' emergency services (SPDC) within general hospitals. Crepet and De Plato (1983) suggest that 'these two negative aspects of the reform – compulsory treatment and psychiatric service in the general hospital were intended by this law to constitute exceptional and short-term instruments. Instead, they have become almost the norm' (p. 127). However, between the passing of Law 180/1978 and 1986 there were, in Trieste, only thirty-one orders for compulsory treatment – an average of under four per year – of which 70 per cent were managed directly by the local CSM and 30 per cent were admitted to the Trieste SPDC (quoted in Dell'Acqua and Mezzina, undated, p. 6n).[5]

De-institutionalisation and de-hospitalisation

The importance and significance of these phases was that de-institutionalisation *preceded* the process of de-hospitalisation and that there was a developmental relationship between these two processes. As Franco Basaglia, the 'founding father' of the reforms puts it: 'the humanization of asylum life was not seen as an end in itself, but only as a first step: the ultimate goal was the abolition of the asylum itself. Thus the project was not seeking simply to make the asylum "work better", but to lay the groundwork for its total destruction' (Basaglia, 1981, p. 184). In this Basaglia rejects the essentially reformist approach of the therapeutic community movement as propounded by Maxwell Jones, with whom he had worked in Britain. Whilst the therapeutic community broke down an unconscious complicity between the professional medical staff and 'the sick', the institutional barrier remained and Basaglia maintained was made more elastic and therefore subtly reinforced by the fact that the patients/ residents appeared to play a more active role. Basaglia developed his politics of abolition as he viewed the central contradiction of psychiatry as a social institution as being that between treatment/cure and custody/ control. He saw a dialectical relationship between his two conclusions – of abolition of the institution and reintegration into the community of the individual – and, although in practice this was a gradual process, Basaglia's theory and language was at times as violent as the institution he wanted to destroy. On this relationship, he is reported to have said at a dinner for professionals and politicians held soon after his arrival in Trieste that 'with the very presence of "mad" people on the streets of Trieste, my aim is to put the psychiatric institutions themselves in crisis'. That this process – from de-institutionalisation to de-hospitalisation – was not a hierarchical or bureaucratic one is important to note:

> administration and regulation at Trieste always followed real changes, and the closure of the hospital was not a bureaucratic operation but the collective effort of patients, psychiatrists, nurses, and the public, all of whom worked together in a project of emancipation and the social reproduction of those with little or low contractual powers. It is in this that the difference lies between the de-institutionalisation of Reaganomics and the practice and projects of de-institutionalisation which reach out to liberate resources, power, subjectivity and autonomy.
>
> (Del Giudice et al., undated, p. 9)

POLICY AS PATHOLOGY

This project of abolishing the institution of psychiatry and psychiatric hospitals as we know them in order to achieve genuine care in the community is some way from the Royal College of Psychiatrists' Council's notion of the medical responsibility for community care (noted above). The original meaning of asylum (from the Latin asylum and the Greek αδυλον) is 'refuge' – reflected and retained in the modern usage of political asylum. However, historically, asylum became a place of exclusion rather than refuge, of segregation rather than integration, in practice the removal of 'mad' people from their community. What follows is that 'madness' too is removed from the community: it is not seen, we do not see it, therefore we do not have to think about, feel or act in relation to it, our reaction or indeed, our own distress. Banton et al. (1985) make the point that distress 'is not a private matter at all, but is generated in and through the social domain' (p. 188). Furthermore, because we have only one phrase (mental health) for both mental health and mental illness we do not have a sense of our mental health: dis-ease becomes illness and disease.

The policy of community care, of placing people in the community – and not always their own – without de-institutionalisation, without addressing notions of 'madness', 'mental illness' or mental health, let alone the financial, political and organisational issues which need to be addressed, may in itself be considered madness. It is simply an inversion of the exclusion, through sectioning, of 'the insane'/'the mentally ill'; such an inversion may itself be diagnosed as pathological. As such community care as a policy can be seen as an example of distorted thinking, disturbed perception, and irresponsible and unpredictable behaviour – all 'symptoms' of schizophrenic psychoses, according to the World Health Organisation's (1992) ICD-10. Many individuals showing signs of such symptoms would, of course, be assessed under the *Mental Health Act 1983* (MHA); similarly organisations or policies showing signs of such symptoms could be assessed under the MHA (a parallel process explored further in Chapter 7). Such policy inversion does not challenge notions of mental illness and health, rather it perpetuates them. Thus, community care as proposed in Britain becomes an extension of the psychiatric hospital as the quote from the Royal College of Psychiatrists' Council (p. 95) virtually acknowledges. Worse, such inversion disrupts and indeed can provoke often adverse reaction from the community.

Such policy inversion is retroflective and blaming rather than reflexive and illuminating. Neither does it address the more obvious and well-documented failings of community care such as:

- The lack of enabling resources, in particular the level of the MISG (House of Commons Social Services Select Committee, 1991; AMA, 1991).
- The problem of the required contribution to the MISG of 30 per cent from local authorities (Social Services Inspectorate, 1993).
- Organisational problems and lack of co-ordination between NHS and SSDs e.g. over procedures for the care programme approach, care management and after-care (Utting et al., 1994).
- Lack of coherent central government strategy (Utting et al., 1994).

'The counterpart of the myth of deinstitutionalization was the myth of collective care' (Castel et al., 1982, p. 124). Although 'community' has many meanings and is a concept subject to much discussion, the concept of care is ill-considered. Both its meanings are relevant to this work: first, mental suffering; a burdened state of mind, and secondly, charge; oversight with a view to protection, preservation or guidance (summarised from Onions, 1933/1973). In elaborating the concept of care, Bulmer (1987) identifies three components: physical tending, material and psychological support, and more generalised concern about the welfare of others. Such distinctions raise the questions of who does what for whom and where? Generalised concern does not cost much economically or emotionally, and may be expressed through donations to deserving (but distant) groups. It is only when we and others near or dear to us need material and psychological support and especially when more intimate physical care is required that care (oversight) often becomes care (a burden), in response to which the community (individuals, families, neighbours, friends, etc.) may well want, in this free market economy, to contract it out. The appropriateness of the care required and the suitability of the carer are other important considerations.

Collective care is a myth. Given the fear of mental illness and the ignorance and confusion about mental health, when the concept and practice of community care is applied to those with 'mental health' problems, it is not surprising that the public reacts unfavourably, influenced as it is by its response to mental illness. Thus, community mental health (CMH) also needs reclaiming.

COMMUNITY MENTAL HEALTH

The fact that we need to examine the impact of community care and its pathology before we consider positive CMH is a parallel to clearing the conceptual ground of mental illness before considering mental health, and is a reflection of how practice in this field is so often driven by pragmatism rather than principle – a theme considered in developing mental health policy (Chapter 6). Linking community with mental health, D.C. Klein (1968) suggests that: 'community represents the single most important social matrix which man has invented and that it is upon this matrix that the concept of mental health can be developed most fruitfully' (pp. 4-5). Castel et al. (1982) summarise the original goals of the CMH movement, one of which is 'to inform psychiatrists and their coworkers of the desires, needs, and priorities of people in the community' (p. 143). Dalgard et al. (1991) see CMH as 'at the crossroads between social, cultural and political processes at the community level, and family and small group processes at the individual level' (p. 422). By way of introducing community mental health promotion four aspects of these processes are discussed: the public response to mental health, the meaning of CMH, the relevance of community participation, and social change in the community.

The public response to mental illness

The public, in the form of local communities, has not always responded or reacted positively to unplanned and under-resourced decanting of psychiatric patients into the community. In their review of three years' worth of American literature on social and community interventions Iscoe and Harris (1984) conclude that 'discharge from the institution, in many cases, has resulted in increased exposure to a hostile environment, lack of health care, and deterioration of living conditions' (p. 348). One geographical survey of attitudes found that mental health facilities came lower than sewage facilities in preference about proximity to the community (C.J. Smith and Hanham, 1981). Rabkin et al. (1984), in their survey of public attitudes, however, suggest that 'in general, respondents' geographic proximity to psychiatric facilities was not related to attitudes about community services for the mentally ill' (p. 311). One or two British studies appear more optimistic about the public's response. A street interview survey, for instance, concludes that 'the public appears to be not against the idea of treating clients in the community, and recognises the advantages, as well as the disadvantages, of people continuing their normal lives while receiving treatment' (Barnett, 1987, p. 32). A DoH survey also provides an optimistic picture of public attitudes towards mental health, showing that more than three in four people support the policy of care in the community (cited in DoH, 1994c). In a survey of people's attitudes towards the mentally ill, Hall et al. (1993) report predominantly positive attitudes (only 2 per cent had negative scores on an Opinions about Mental Illness Scale); and, amongst most (85 per cent), an absence of fear of the mentally ill. Not surprisingly, relation to or acquaintance with a person with mental illness are significant determinants of benevolence, absence of fear and rejection of authoritarian attitudes, although in another study on views and attitudes, the responses of relatives 'were less critical of institutional care and more cautious about the ability of ex-patients to lead normal lives' (Manktelow, 1993, p. 399).

These different conclusions are not as incompatible as they initially appear in that the public may well take the view that if patients are going to live in the community then they should receive *treatment* in the community. This view is supported by the Royal College of Psychiatrists in its advocacy of community treatment orders by which a doctor could require a patient to receive treatment with the threat of a return to hospital if they do not comply. Such orders, however, beg a number of questions about who should be treated, the means of treatment, and the degree of choice about treatment (Scott-Moncrieff, 1988). More recently, the government has introduced the power of supervised discharge (DoH, 1993a; NHS Management Executive, 1994a).

One of the key issues in the public's antipathy to mental health facilities appears to be the lack of public consultation, for example, about the siting of half-way homes (e.g. Tissier, 1993). However, if 'Not in our back yard' is the answer/solution, the real question is not 'Where do we site this mental health facility?' but rather 'What is the problem people are expressing through their negative reaction to "mental health"?' Rather than having, and often being given, only a limited choice (e.g. which 'back yard'), another more radical solution is for the community to determine the principles of community care and of CMH.

The meaning of community mental health

Community mental health is an ambiguous phrase, particularly as the context in which it is used is often one of illness and disease and a medical/psychiatric model of emotional and mental distress. In view of the pragmatism of government policy, the fear of the unknown that is mental illness, and the lack of genuine public consultation, it is not surprising that 'the community', however defined, shows little understanding of CMH and little care. This is functional in that the community is defining mental health (illness) as objectivist, as outside the community. On further investigation, however, such definition may be seen as a defence, a denial both of the impact of mental illness and of addressing mental health in the community. There is, according to Barić (undated), 'a general shift in responsibilities from the health care system onto the people themselves. Although this shift concerning the doctor–patient relationship is widely recognised, there is no shift in the health care–community relationships' (p. 211).

From the 'Italian experience' it is clear that in order for 'the community' to develop awareness and positive responses to mental illness and to mental health, it first needs to challenge and change the theoretical foundations and practices of the asylum, and to take itself into those challenges and debates directly. A rare example of this in embryonic practice in Britain is reported by R. Doyle (1989), describing an adult education course as a part of which the public spent structured time on the wards of a psychiatric hospital with discussion and support groups facilitated by medical and nursing staff. One result was that 'two members have expressed an interest in setting up a day care facility in their town with the support of a community psychiatric nurse' (p. 1407). Only through this kind of process can patients move out of the hospital into the(ir) communities – which will be ready to receive rather than reject them.

Community participation

In an attempt to 'work with the community' by establishing contacts within a particular community, some professionals identify community 'leaders' and work with them, thus developing a kind of lay professional and, ultimately, a professionalised leadership of the community and its institutions and organisations who become 'opinion leaders'. Other identified community figures or roles in the change process are the practitioner, the adopter (client), and the change agent (promoter) and change agency (Artemis Trust, undated). Although the Artemis Trust's work in identifying and developing how the field of 'personal growth' is promoted through community networks, it represents a professionalised 'top-down' approach to community and change.

Miller and Rein (1975) trace the emergence of genuine community participation to 'sources of discontent in the urban scene' (p. 3). Rose and Hanmer (1975) review theories of scientific sociology, in particular cybernetics, as central to an understanding of community mobilisation or participation whereby 'relationships hitherto characterised by domination move towards reciprocity' (p. 37). There has been a further shift since the mid-1980s in participation through community organisation and community development approaches (as promoted by the Artemis Trust) to those which encourage genuine community participation: that is, participation by members of the community in decision-making. In a debate about the public health origins and model of prevention, counterposed to the medical model, it is arguable that it is a public health perspective which is more focused on the community: initiating consultation, diagnosing problems within the community, and even defending the community. Reviewing US and Italian 'experiences' of mental health reform, Mosher and Burti (1989) suggest that four elements are necessary in order to achieve programmatic success in CMH: strong leadership, professional support groups, a consensus that change is needed, and a stable and predictable source of financial support. Applying principles for effective partnerships for citizen participation in the field of community health, Bracht (1991) suggests that any community health project typically entails a six-stage process: community analysis; design and initiation; programme implementation, consolidation and maturation; maintenance and incorporation; and dissemination and reassessment (Appendix 1 gives more detailed notes on the stages of community organising). Arnstein (1969) identifies eight rungs on a ladder of citizen participation ranging (from the bottom) from the non-participation of *manipulation* and *therapy*, through degrees of tokenism in participation of *informing*, *consultation* and *placation* (although placation should be placed earlier in the sequence), to degrees of citizen power of *partnership*, *delegated power* and *citizen control*. However, both these models imply a certain professionalisation of the community and its concerns. Concerns quickly become issues, issues problems, and the community pathologised. It is only citizen control which expresses independent power, derived from the citizenship, as distinct from that expressed by the professional for and on behalf of the citizen, and which leads to social change.

Community groups and voluntary organisations are particularly relevant and interesting as settings for health promotion (Trojan et al., 1991) for two reasons: one, they may themselves have health-damaging effects (e.g. meetings in smoke-filled rooms) but, equally, they are the source of untapped resources. Trojan et al.'s research in Hamburg showed that, of 309 health-related community organisations, 42 per cent claimed 'psychosocial' as an area of activity they covered. In Britain, however, in one survey of 4,264 voluntary organisations in Birmingham, only 1 per cent were classified as being relevant to health (K. Newton, 1975).

Social change in the community

Communities often become the site of a struggle between two groups with unequal power: professionals and residents/tenants/consumers. The professionals work there and are visitors; the inhabitants live there. Professionals have a greater say in the provision, allocation and delivery of services: they are often the gatekeepers to resources; the consumers are too often supplicants at the gate. Barić (undated) goes on to comment that 'the roles of initiation, enabling, advocacy and action are still firmly in the hands of the external agents who are members of the health care delivery system and often health education specialists' (p. 211). Examples of communities taking control over resources and decisions are, therefore, noticeable by their rarity. Castel et al. (1982) report that one black neighbourhood in Harlem, New York, refused to allow a mental health centre to open as it was seen as another way of controlling the black population – that it was to be run by blacks was seen to be the most insidious part of the project. Bracht and Kingsbury (1990) suggests that 'community activation requires not only the creation or presence of an issue, but also the identification and activation of community groups and individuals to deal with the issue' (p. 71).

As society changes so communities change. The economy determines international and *intra*national migration. Patterns of employment and unemployment affect communities. The housing market dictates access to employment opportunity. All these changes affect mobility and family life. New roads cut communities in two. Car ownership rises, bringing with it increased mobility. There is a 'decline of community' in cities (Wirth, 1938) and in the countryside, where dormitory villages with a predominance of commuters affect life in rural communities and drive house prices up: so societies and communities change. Alongside the benefits of change, there is an ambivalence about such changes. In 'community care' policies there is an implicit appeal to 'community' which finds at once a resonance in romantic and idealised notions of a 'golden age' of idyllic urban and rural communities as well as a dissonance in this age of individualism.

CONCLUSION

The hospitalisation of the community is already in progress and exists in the form of many so-called Community Mental Health Centres, a critique elaborated in the next chapter. Learning from the Italian experience that de-institutionalisation must precede de-hospitalisation, it is crucial that psychiatric hospitals and the people involved in and with them – psychiatrists, managers, patients, families, SSDs and the voluntary/independent sector – critically challenge the ideology of current psychiatric health care and social work practices. As a practical strategy we can use the paradigm map in this task. First, the origins of 'community care' initiatives and the predominant location of the psychiatric and public response are analysed – within a functionalist paradigm which is concerned with social regulation and 'objective', scientific reality. Secondly, critiques of such 'objectivity' and social regulation may be made from a number of perspectives. From an interpretative perspective the meaning of certain policies, actions and reactions needs to be examined; from a radical humanist perspective it is important to account for people's subjective desire for and experience of change and for participation in structures which affect their lives; from a radical structuralist perspective inequalities within the psychiatric system have been referred to as well as the impetus for social change. Thirdly and urgently, more critical practice in mental health (from perspectives other than a functionalist one) needs to be elaborated – a challenge taken up in Chapter 5. Fourthly, conceptual and practical movement around the paradigm map from individual symptom to collective, social action must be described (see Chapter 5). Such movement can and should involve everyone concerned with mental health and mental illness, with the community and with the closure of psychiatric hospitals and in every forum: committee and policy meetings, local authority/health services joint planning meetings, staff groups, ward rounds/case conferences, community forums and other local meetings.

In the field of mental illness, de-hospitalisation without de-institutionalisation changes nothing. In 1990 community care was predicted – by the editor of the magazine of the same name – to be 'a policy set to advance from anarchy to chaos without the redeeming interregnum of rational thought' (Philpot, 1990, p. 13). Despite optimistic readings (such as E. Murphy, 1991) community care has unfortunately fulfilled such predictions and warnings (e.g. Tudor, 1990/91) and indeed has provoked 'the abandonment to objective, regulatory models of disease and mental illness of both individuals and of notions of positive mental health care within the community' (Tudor, 1990/91, p. 21). Chapter 5 seeks to redress this balance in the field of community mental health promotion.

5 Community mental health promotion

Community mental health promotion (CMHP) not only comprises an integration of its constituent elements – community, mental health, health promotion, mental health promotion – but is developed here as a concept and practice in its own right. As a contribution to this development, this chapter offers a critique of examples of CMHP theory and practice. The implications of various definitions of mental health (Chapter 1) and the elements of mental health (Chapter 3) for CMHP are reviewed. A critique of Community Mental Health Centres (CMHCs), as potential bases for the promotion of community mental health, is offered. The role and impact of community psychology, psychotherapy, the advocacy movement, and 'the Italian experience' of mental health reform on CMHP are considered as background to a discussion of CMHP which comprises two elements: *challenging myths of mental illness* and *promoting mental health*, elements which are elaborated and examined. In this chapter the paradigm analysis is again used as an organising framework and developed as a tool for understanding and facilitating the process of reflection and change.

COMMUNITY MENTAL HEALTH PROMOTION PRACTICE AND THEORY

In 1963, one of the earliest initiatives in mental health (illness) education in recent times was introduced by the Northampton Mental Health Project. It aimed:

1 to make the public aware of mental disorder as a social problem;
2 to spread some knowledge of the aetiology (in general terms) of mental disorder;
3 to indicate the advances made in the treatment and care of the mentally disordered;
4 to explain what community care means, how lay people can themselves play a part and why it is, from the medical point of view, important that they should do so.

(Gatherer and Reid, 1967, p. 6)

The functionalist frame of reference, explicit in the language ('aetiology', 'treatment'), the medical legitimation of the importance of this work and the public's role was in line with the government's thinking (then and now) about community care: 'the aim of enabling the mentally disordered to take their part in the life of the community cannot be realised without the co-operation of the public' (Ministry of Health, 1963). The relationship between early discharge of patients and the high rate of readmission – the so-called 'revolving door' policy – and public reaction, and therefore the need for some kind of 'education', was identified by the Northampton Project:

> there is a suspicion that patients may be discharged with inadequate consideration of the after-care which they will require and of the burden which will result on the family and on the community. Many of these challenges can only be met by mental health education of everyone in the community.
>
> (Gatherer and Reid, 1967, p. 2)

Such challenges of course need to be met by 'the community' which, as we have seen in the previous chapter, has not always responded or reacted positively to unplanned and under-resourced decanting of psychiatric patients into the community.

There are principally two foci with which CMHP must concern itself. First, that which requires a focus on the community itself: mental health *of* the community. This may take the form of a developmental, educational, organisational or locational function – for which C.J. Smith's (1976, 1984) geographical paradigms, analysis and research are useful. Secondly, mental health promotion (MHP) *in* the community has the community as its context but focuses on the individual, whether promoting mental health in the individual or promoting the individual (e.g. the former psychiatric patient) within the community. Several projects have drawn on community mental health promotion in one of these two ways. An example of a project with the focus on community is the Greater Easterhouse Mental Health Pilot Project (cited by Kennedy, 1988), whose Education Working Group proposed a piece of research and evaluation around the impact of a play and follow-up tutorials. Its functionalist perspective is made clear in the Working Group's main aim: 'to promote a greater understanding of issues surrounding mental health and mental illness and thus attempt *to correct erroneous ideas and attitudes previously held*' (Kennedy, 1988, Appendix E, my emphasis). Hollander et al. (1989) describe a training course in mental health development studies for psychiatrists, introducing a primary health care approach to their work. An educational example in which the focus is predominantly on the individual, both the school child and the diagnosed patient, is provided by the West Lambeth Health Authority Mental Health Unit Mental Health Education Group's (1989) booklet on *Mental health problems* in which facts about and definitions of mental health and mental health problems are presented, along with case histories, in accessible language. In a book reviewing the Torbay experience of mental health (illness), one page is devoted to community mental health education. Its limited programme is conceptually mixed with clearly promotional aims such as 'to create a caring and informed community . . . and to help people live happier lives' (Beardshaw and Morgan, 1990, p. 73) included alongside principles of de-stigmatisation and normalisation. These initiatives are given legitimacy by the Council of Europe Committee of Ministers in its statement on the aims of a mental health education programme: 'being [the] modification of attitudes, [and] the body of knowledge of social pathology pertaining to change of attitudes should be utilised when planning such a programme' (Council of Europe Committee of Ministers, 1976, p. 44).

These approaches to mental health promotion of the community are generally based on certain objectivist notions of mental health and of community (and therefore lie nearer to the objective boundary of the functionalist paradigm). Insofar as such functionalist perspectives are also concerned with the regulation of mental illness and health, particularly in behavioural terms, they are conceptually closer to the social regulation boundary of this paradigm.

These distinctions of focus and statements are also useful in reviewing what little has been written from a theoretical or conceptual perspective on community mental health promotion. Brogen (1985) in a rare title *Promotion of mental health* takes a largely functionalist approach in locating and subsuming promotion within primary and secondary prevention (see Chapter 1). Promotion, under primary prevention, should (according to Brogen) take a health education approach through special programmes, in order to promote information and knowledge and to bring about both behaviour conducive to mental health and increased acceptance of mental disorder, on the part of the general population. Under secondary prevention Brogen puts forward the notion of identifying special high-risk groups with regard to their exposure to stress, citing single parents as an example and their risk behaviours, for example people with 'incipient abuse' of alcohol, drugs, and so on. This carries echoes of G. Caplan's (1961) work as regards the concept of 'key individuals' and those who have 'disordered relationships' and their 'noxious effect' on their community.

Verrall's (1990) elaboration of Tannahill's framework has been discussed (in Chapter 3) and criticised for its rigidity and lack of sociopsychological analysis. Similarly, given Brogen's concern with *measuring* the 'problems' of mental health, significantly in terms of an epidemiological approach and of financial costs, he makes only a passing reference to sociological stressors such as unemployment. He makes no reference to the impact of poverty or homelessness or any sociopsychological stressors such as racial oppression (e.g. Guernina, 1994).

At best such functionalists only confuse the debate. At worst they promote deterministic and static notions of 'good mental health'; they tend to blame individuals not subscribing or conforming to such notions; and they 'foster people's use, and the functioning of existing systems; promote reintegration and adaptive change of people and systems' (Whittington and Holland, 1985, p. 34).

COMMUNITY MENTAL HEALTH: DEFINITIONS AND MEANINGS

Concern about differing views about mental health, for instance on the basis of different personal and sociocultural backgrounds, is not only of conceptual interest, but also intensely practical. As has been suggested the underlying (meta-theoretical) assumptions of different perspectives influence practice. Thus, someone interested in correcting 'erroneous ideas and attitudes' will be less interested in the *self*-development of people holding those views. Equally people taking different sides on the mental illness prevention/mental health promotion debate will have different perspectives. Thus, someone concerned with prevention may be interested in which elements of mental health should be promoted so that people are less susceptible to certain identified or predicted risks. Someone more concerned with promotion may be interested in the promotion of autonomy and interrelatedness for their own sake. The developmental therapeutic, curative, promotional and/or social intentions connected with different concepts of mental health are equally important. Thus, with regard to community, the definitions of mental health (from Chapter 1) – i.e. mental health as functioning, as relational, as ability or capacity, and as social – all these are mediated between the individual and their environment. To paraphrase Maslow (1968) 'for a theory of mental health, intra-psychic health is not enough; we must also include extra-psychic success'. Thus (in terms of capacity), an individual's desire for personal autonomy and its achievement will, at some point, come up against someone else's view of, say, 'socially considerate behaviour' (social functioning) – in which case there may be some recourse to the negotiation of their respective mental health needs (relational). To complicate matters further in this particular example, as has been suggested, the very notion of personal autonomy is only one view of mental health – and a culturally specific one at that.

The implications for CMHP follow, being: the promotion of social and psychological functioning and development; the promotion of relations and relationships including, for instance, their contradictions; the promotion of the abilities and capacities of individuals, groups and communities; and the promotion of social change in support of mental health. Thus, for instance, mental health education may comprise information about *not* using local mental health (illness) services, unlike the educative aspect of the Torbay experience (see Beardshaw and Morgan, 1990).

Elements of mental health

Mental life is described as 'inner experience linked to interpersonal group experience' (World Health Organisation, 1981b, p. 5). The challenge as regards the eight elements of mental health (Chapter 3) is to apply them not only to individuals but to link them to groups and to the wider community (see Veit and Ware, 1983). Such application is in the tradition of viewing the community as a focus for health promotion (e.g. Maccoby, 1988).

Coping

The CMHP approach to this considers how different groups and communities respond to tension and stress. The notion of group or community coping mechanisms relies on a psychology of group, community or nation and coherent analytic tools such as the Jungian concept of the 'collective unconscious'. Thus, Margaret Thatcher's infamous reference to being 'swamped by an alien culture' may be seen as a fearful, collective defence – and one which leads to fight (more often than flight) responses.[1] However, Jung's work on collective and, in particular, 'national psychology' is the subject of serious criticism (e.g. Dalal, 1988). For Samuels (1993) it marks 'an unwarranted expansion of his psychology . . . into complicated fields where psychology on its own is an inadequate explanatory tool' (pp. 307-308). A *socio*psychology of community and coping is needed in order to move beyond the assumption of innate differences between communities and nations, to integrate economic, historical, social and political factors.

Having established this, and with due analysis of the *social* conditions in a given community or setting then the defences and creative adjustment coping mechanisms identified in Chapter 3 (Table 3.2) may be usefully applied to groups, institutions, communities and even nations. This carries resource implications: 'enhancing people's capacity to cope both individually and collectively means committing a greater share of resources to community development and community-based programs and services' (Minister of National Health and Welfare, 1988, p. 10).

Tension and stress management

As Bostock (1993) suggests: 'although contemporary psychological models of stress purport to represent a transactional relationship between individuals and their environments . . . in actuality the main thrust of empirical and practical work is with individuals' (p. 144). The WHO (1993a) goes some way to redressing this imbalance in a report on approaches to stress management *in the community setting* in which stress prevention and management in the community is defined as a set of co-ordinated activities with the purpose of:

(a) preventing potentially noxious stressful life situations;
(b) reducing stress-related health problems in the workplace and other settings; and
(c) assisting individuals and groups exposed to particularly stressful situations to reduce the risk of negative health outcomes.

(WHO, 1993a, p. 4)

It is a short step from this to consider this element of *community* mental health promotion as concerned with psychosocial stressors – or 'socio-psychological pain' (Guernina, 1994) – such as hunger, homelessness, poverty and oppression and, equally, with the promotion of minimum standards of poverty levels, wages, housing rights, etc. and of anti-discriminatory practices.

Self-concept and identity and self-esteem

As discussed in Chapter 3, self-esteem requires a concept of self and self-identity – and thus these two elements of mental health are linked.

Here we need to consider not so much the social creation of self but rather the self-identity of the social, that is the community. Again, we face the problem discussed above: that of applying concepts from individual psychology (such as self-concept and identity) to the wider social context. Groups may have a 'sense' of identity (e.g. gay identity) and/or identifying as a community, etc. which is gained by expanding the 'we' self-concept (Nobles, 1973). This is especially true at particular moments in time such as on a demonstration or in campaigning for or against something. Significantly, the concept of group or community identity is strongest in opposition, even though the differences between individuals within such a group or community may, outside that particular time or place, be as great as those between the identified oppositional group and the wider society.

Group- or community-esteem arises from a sense of self-concept and identity. Again, the issue of identity through opposition is an important one. If a group or community has a sense of its value only through and in opposition its self-esteem is fragile (the British Labour Party might be considered a case in point). Here, psychological models of the development – and interruption – of self-esteem in individuals (e.g. C.R. Rogers, 1951) are easily applicable to groups, organisations and communities.

Linking self-esteem to mental health promotion, Milton Keynes MIND's Education Project runs workshops in schools and produces a bi-monthly magazine as well as an education pack *Feeling good about ourselves and others*, its title reflecting the belief that 'development of a positive view of ourselves will also provide fertile ground for the preservation and promotion of mental health and the breaking down of the myths and prejudices surrounding mental illness' (Milton Keynes MIND, undated, unpaginated).

McIlmoyl (1994) describes a group approach to enhancing self-esteem in older women.

In a comment on self-esteem as an element of MHP which impacts on policy and the prevention–promotion debate, J.K. Davies and Kelly (1993) postulate:

> if early childhood development programmes enhance children's self-esteem, producing higher literacy levels and better job prospects resulting in an improved work record, less work strain and less heart disease, *then clearly early childhood development could be viewed as (and perhaps funded as) a heart-disease-prevention procedure.*
>
> (J.K. Davies and Kelly, 1993, p. 18, my emphasis)

Self-development

In applying this element of mental health to community the issue is whether community building and community development is an aggregation of individual self-development or whether aspects of self-development may be applied to the community *per se*. The two examples of emotional literacy and assertiveness are reviewed.

Emotional literacy or 'integrative mental health literacy' may be applied to a group (e.g. a psychotherapy group) or a community (e.g. a school). A Transactional Analysis psychotherapy group, for instance, may be introduced to Steiner's (1984) concepts of emotional literacy as a result of which such concepts may be integrated into the culture of the group, expressed in their language and through the transactions of group members – and, if not explicitly, thereby implicitly passed on to new members. In some tribes, every fifth day is an opportunity to 'clear the air' between members; this may take the form of literally yelling at each other. A school or a workplace may have a policy as regards bullying (on which there is an emerging interest in and literature on the issue in both settings). The government's recent initiative focuses on bullying as a (bad) behaviour to be eradicated whereas more considered responses conceptualise and design responsive interventions to bullying as roles people play and between which they switch. In either case a school or workplace may develop a collective policy on and response to this (and other) issues which constitute a development of that community.

Classically, assertiveness is developed in groups, for example of women. It is therefore not difficult to imagine the transition from a group of (individually) assertive women to an assertive group of women. In discussing assertive behaviour and assertiveness training (AT) in its societal context, Rakos (1991) offers a number of critiques of AT: its rationalist philosophical underpinnings; its cultural determinism, suggesting that: 'the social and political activism that provided the initial impetus to the AT movement has given way to various forms of individual activism' (p. 4); its rejection of absolute standards of morality and its pragmatism.

The focus of this element of mental health is also on the autonomy and relatedness of groups and communities, for instance, as described by Barrett-Aranui (1989). As such it must be considered closely with the self-identity of groups (discussed on pp. 114–115), their autonomy and *interrelation* to other groups and communities.

Change and social support and movement

In order to think about and promote the social support of groups and communities and the consolidation of change, the interface between community and environment needs consideration: 'the very quality of mental health as a centrepiece of human health is decisively determined through man's relationships with the environment and the latter's actual state as well as its susceptibility to human influence' (Neumann, 1989, p. 54). This is a two-way process: 'there is a good deal of evidence that whilst social isolation and the lack of confiding intimacy do affect mental health, so do mental health and personality affect the amount and quality of social support received' (Parry, 1988, p. 88). Neighbours and social networks are important for the mental health of individuals and the community, as are families and tribes (Money, 1994). This, combined with Parry's point, takes CMHP into the dynamic realm of the individual/group/community's relationship with wider, ecological approaches (e.g. Bostock, 1993).

On this, in developing a socioeconomic model of health, J.K. Davies and Kelly (1993) pose a radical question about priorities: given the absence in many situations in the world of basic salutogens such as food, shelter, clean water, safe environments and peace, how important are social networks and self-esteem – and, for that matter, any of the identified elements of mental health?

It could – and indeed should – be argued that the growth of Community Mental Health Centres (CMHCs) in Britain from the 1970s has led to a respective increase in awareness and understanding within the community at large, not only of mental illness but also of mental health, its elements and their promotion. That this is patently not the case is worth some consideration in this inquiry.

Community mental health centres

Perlmutter (1982b), commenting on mental health promotion in the United States, takes this further, affirming that 'the responsibility for primary prevention was conceptually and programmatically viewed as the responsibility of the mental health system (primarily of the community mental health centres)' (p. 12). Criticism has also been levelled at the role of CMHCs – and at the community mental health teams (CMHTs) which operate within them – in particular on the low priority they have placed on working with people with severe and long-term mental health (illness) problems (Sayce et al., 1991; Patmore and Weaver, 1991). Falling between the two – neither promoting mental health nor supporting the acute or chronic mentally ill – CMHCs are currently in crisis.

In order to ascertain the role of CMHCs, it is useful to trace the historical development of CMHCs on both sides of the Atlantic – from 1961, when, in Britain, the move from psychiatric hospital to the community was given its first ministerial direction and, in the United States, the Joint Commission on Mental Health first reported. This transatlantic perspective is important as developments in practice in North America have often preceded events in Britain and the theoretical implications of such developments have usually been clearer. Whilst there are still some parallels, more recent US and British history, policies and practice in CMH, diverge.

In the United States President Kennedy presented a Bill to Congress in February 1963 following which, in October 1963, legislation (PL 88-164) authorising a federally funded system of CMHCs was passed. This was followed in 1965 by the *Community Mental Health Centres Act 1965* which mandated centres to deliver services and to establish governing boards of citizens. However, the federal funding was not forthcoming and, by 1984, only 760 CMHCs out of the 2,000 proposed were operational. The *Mental Health Systems Act 1980* reaffirmed the emphasis on prevention and would have improved scope and quality of CMHCs, but again the Act was not funded. Nevertheless, despite the lack of financial backing, CMHCs in the United States have a richer and, in many ways, more radical tradition than in Britain.

In Britain CMHCs were first established in the 1970s, under the administrative auspices of the National Health Service (NHS), social services departments (SSDs) or under some kind of joint management arrangement between the two. By 1985 *Good Practices in Mental Health* (*GPMH*) had identified twenty-two CMHCs in Britain. Sayce (1989), reporting on her survey of CMHCs and commenting on the difficulty of defining CMHCs, suggests further increases in the number of CMHCs established during the mid-1980s and again in the late 1980s and early 1990s. Sayce (1989) also reviews the policies in Britain which have given rise to community care with specific reference to CMHCs, suggesting that 'the CMHC is . . . one model that is being adopted with some enthusiasm' (p. 161). However, in considering the conceptual and political background to the development of CMHCs, the management of CMHCs and of the community, and the political implications of the present state of CMHCs, Sayce's enthusiasm and optimism is questionable.

Conceptual, theoretical and political background

E. Peck and Joyce (1985) make the point that the very term community mental health centre (or team) implies a lack of homogeneity. Arguably the most ambiguous and rhetorical word is 'community', a word (as discussed in Chapter 4) encompassing a diversity of interests. C.J. Smith (1984), in his original work in the United States developing 'a geography of mental health', presents a number of alternative conceptual models of community and their implications for CMHC services.

The context of the development of CMHCs, both in the United States and in Britain, is one of de-hospitalisation (rather than de-institutionalisation): 'the now well established model of the CMHC forms the stepping stone onto which psychiatry has made its territorial move out of the hospital into the community' (S. Holland, 1988, p. 127).[2] However, the problem with CMHCs is that 'psychiatry, by bringing its "eclectic" baggage of psycho-social language and pharmacological treatments with it into the commu-nity, has contributed, not to the communalisation of the patient, but to the hospitalisation of the community' (Ibid., p. 128). This is in sharp contrast to the radically different history and perspective of 'the Italian experience' of community mental health. Mosher and Burti (1989) comment on the reputation of CMH in the United States:

> it suffers from attributions of having overpromised and not delivered, of being unscientific, of being dominated by non physicians, of being a major accomplice in the 'failure' of deinstitutionalisation, and most of all, of being ineffective in dealing with the most severely disturbed patients, except insofar as it fosters medication compliance.
>
> (Mosher and Burti, 1989, p. 1)

The management of CMHCs and of the community

Mosher and Burti (1989) explain their reference to 'non-physicians' by observing that it is non-physicians who largely took over the management of the CMHCs in the United States by default, when psychiatrists left partly for more lucrative and prestigious hospital-based jobs and partly because the psychiatrists no longer enjoyed the power they were used to in the domain of the hospital.

In Britain the early CMHCs were dominated by medical interests, although the trend, particularly since the Griffiths Report (Griffiths, 1988), has been towards joint funded projects. In a survey 59.3 per cent of CMHTs surveyed are funded jointly by health and social services (Onyett et al., 1994).[3] However, despite joint funding, 'physicians' are mainly still in charge of CMHCs with many largely funded (35.8 per cent) and managed (47 per cent) by health authorities/trusts alone and the co-ordinator/manager role often taken by the senior health authority/trust professional (i.e. the psychiatrist or the psychologist). Not one of the 302

CMHCs surveyed was managed by a social services employee let alone someone from the voluntary/independent sector (and only one CMHC is known by the author to be managed by a social worker). The establishment of such centres is often marked by long and protracted negotiations between the NHS and SSDs over capital and revenue financing, management and professional accountability. Neither has joint funding eased 'difficulties in multi-professional teams in terms of locating power and responsibility' (Sayce, 1989, p. 169) about, for instance, the weight given to medical/psychiatric opinion, the issue of clinical responsibility as well as that of management and leadership, case allocation, etc.[4]

The predominant medical management of CMHCs themselves is paralleled by the CMHCs' own medical model management of the community. Like the patients they aim to serve, CMHCs in Britain are too often imposed on communities with little or no consultation or sensitivity, and propagate a medical model of mental illness and disease. In one case the author knows of, the launch of a local CMHC was sponsored by a drug company. When this was questioned the psychiatrist involved remained (or chose to remain) blissfully ignorant of the implication or meaning such sponsorship conveyed to the community, other professionals and potential users. This represents the Janus face of the functionalist medical response: a hospital outreach mental illness service, often thinly-disguised as a community-based mental health service. At worst, this hospitalisation of the community perpetuates an ideology of mental illness:

> this transfer of hegemony and legitimation 'depoliticised' the issues and continued the focus of concern on patterns of service delivery rather than on redefining an entire new set of needs that former patients incur as a result of being either de- or reinstitutionalised into community settings.
>
> (Rose and Black, 1985, p. 4)

The political implications of CMHCs

CMHCs may, wittingly or unwittingly, also set themselves up in a 'leading' role in the community they are serving, with problematic implications for notions of both community (leadership, advocacy, empowerment, etc.) and of community mental health. D.C. Klein (1968) expresses creative doubts about 'the notion that the way to mentally healthy communities is to be found in the institutional hallways of comprehensive mental health centres' (p. viii). CMHCs rarely engage in substantial community development activity, such as developing self-help or engaging with community action groups and are rarely accountable to local people through management groups or other structures. This is despite the fact that two of the original goals of the community mental health movement were 'to inform district residents of what services were available in the centers . . . and to involve clients in organizing and running the facility' (Castel et al., 1982, p. 143). Onyett et al. (1994) found that not one CMHC is funded or managed by voluntary, private or non-profit organisations only; only 17.8 per cent of CMHCs involve community members in management/steering group meetings with any decision-making role, a statistic which drops to 8.3 per cent when applied to users of the services. Remarkably 72.2 per cent of CMHCs surveyed state that they do not plan to involve users in decision-making. In the light of such criticisms, ambiguities and statistics it is therefore naïve, dangerous and disempowering to argue, particularly post-Griffiths, that: 'CMHCs could and should take on the coordinator role in mental health care' (Sayce and Charman, 1988, p. 17).

Sayce (1989) suggests that 'the promotion of positive examples of community provision . . . was a key part of the rationale for setting up a study of community mental health centres' (p. 160). However, the conflict within and without CMHCs between their role in treatment and social reform (as Sayce suggests it is) is a false dichotomy. The conflict is rather between a medical/psychiatric model and view – of mental illness and health and of community – and other 'models'. Theories and practice which emphasise people's own experience of mental illness and mental health, challenge the predominant medical model from a subjectivist (interpretative) point of view, notions of societal change (radical structuralist) challenge the social regulation of the medical/psychiatric establishment, whilst notions of empowerment and personal change (radical humanist) challenge both realism and regulation. CMHCs can – and should – take a role in promoting such paradigm shifts. Both Iscoe and Harris (1984) and Sayce (1989) report estimates that only about 5 per cent of CMHC workers' time is spent on consultation and education (or 'C&E' as it is referred to in the United States), staff being almost totally dedicated to treatment services. J. Newton (1988) makes the point that prevention falls within the C&E category and McPheeters (1976) comments generally on the low priority of preventive work in CMHCs. Goodbody (1992), in her survey of CMHCs in the South Devon Healthcare Trust area, suggests that a wide range of preventive work is being done, although only a small proportion of the working week is spent on prevention. Rose and Black (1985) make the point that whilst CMHCs 'were mandated to provide "five essential services", all clinical in approach . . . "C&E" . . . was often little more than a marketing mechanism for psychiatric intervention' (p. 3). Of the twenty-one DoH-funded projects for people with long-term mental health (illness) needs, reviewed by GPMH, only four describe amongst their principal service components 'health education and promotion', 'public education' or 'community information and education' (GPMH, undated). In the survey of services offered, less than half of CMHCs surveyed offer public education – defined as preventing mental health problems – an activity which is significantly associated with community psychiatric nurses.

D.C. Klein (1968) argues that: 'rehabilitation of former mental patients will be successful in the final analysis when there is a community that accepts the person as a valued, if not fully functioning, member or citizen' (p. 6). This must be the aim of every genuinely community-based and community-focused CMHP programme and practice. In order to do this, however, CMHCs need to shift their 'thought structure' and practice away from the medical/psychiatric model:

> the pattern of psychiatric control continuing into community-based programs meant that the shift from hospital-based care to community-based care was in reality only a shift in locus (as opposed to the focus) of the mental health service delivery system without a concomitant shift in approach to the redefining of, and therefore intervening into, problem situations.
>
> (Rose and Black, 1985, p. 3)

The actual *meaning* most CMHCs carry into the community and promote is essentially a medical model of illness, of community and of individuals. 'Mental patients', still seen as passive recipients of treatment and/or 'care', are maintained largely by Depo injection in this hospital in the community. Little CMHP work is directed at the community itself and individuals remain largely isolated from the community: within and yet without.[5]

CMHCs have their origins in policy which, as S. Holland (1988) observes: 'has elements of both progressive reform and reactionary opportunism' (p. 127). There are, of course, many examples of good practice within CMHCs, providing positive examples of strategies for access, co-ordination and user responsiveness. Examples of good policy and practice with clients, however, does not negate the economic and political context in which CMHCs have been established, their predominantly medical funding and management (at least in Britain), their lack of theoretical or conceptual coherence, and the difficulty experienced by many multi-disciplinary teams in establishing agreed and precise objectives. All these points indicate the urgent need for reform. Progressive reform, however, is dependent on a commitment on the part of CMHC staff both to a critical view of mental illness and to a positive view of mental health. Whilst there is some evidence that there is a shift in CMHCs towards a greater prioritisation of working with people with severe and long-term mental illness problems, there is no evidence that CMHCs or CMHTs have a critical view of mental illness or have a concept of positive mental *health* and promote it.

Realising that neither CMHCs or CMHTs are in the business of community mental health promotion, we turn to considering the contribution of other disciplines and experiences.

CONTRIBUTIONS TO COMMUNITY MENTAL HEALTH PROMOTION

In this section contributions from four sources are considered as crucial to our understanding of CMHP: community psychology (which, in the spirit of our inquiry, should more accurately referred to as community socio-psychology); social aspects of psychotherapy; the user/advocacy movement and empowerment; and 'the Italian experience' of mental health reform.

Community (socio)psychology

Sociology, as the science or study of human society, makes a major contribution to the study of 'community', and within it people's primary groupings, family and kinship networks, social relationships, personal and informal ties, and so on. Bulmer (1987) suggests that a shift in emphasis from the study of 'community' to that of the primary group is that it gets away from what he refers to as 'the metaphysical problem of community' (p. 39): the study of neighbours and neighbourhoods, for instance, 'does not involve the reification of a geographical or structural entity which has proved so problematical in the case of "community"' (Ibid., p. 39). A sociology of community is concerned with issues such as social class, age, race, gender, etc. as well as patterns of contact, involvement and the impact of these variables on the life of the community. Social change (and social regulation) is also of interest to the sociologist of community. Psychology, as the science of the nature and phenomena of the human mind or soul, has traditionally focused on the individual – the live*s in* the community – being concerned with their environment only so far as it impacts on the individual. Even Wundt's collective psychology (*Volkerpsychologie*) was concerned with the influence of religion, myth, etc. *on the individual.* More recently, community psychology, in response and in reaction to prevailing paradigms in psychology, has refocused the attention of psychology on social environments such as communities; thus 'community psychology is concerned with how social environments perpetuate psychological suffering' (Bostock, 1991, p. 2). With its concern about structural inequalities such as poverty and racism, community psychology is seen – at least in psychological terms – as radical. Similarly, in discussing social psychiatry, Neumann (1989) argues that 'more than any other medical speciality, psychiatry is concerned with **human personality** and man's **informational, i.e. communicative, interaction** with the environment' (p. 54, original emphases). In a model of primary illness prevention which includes mental health promotion, Castel et al. (1982) acknowledge their ambition for primary prevention: 'it aims at nothing less than a metamorphosis of psychiatry into a new form of social and political action' (p. 126).

There is often an unnecessary and unhelpful division, however, between the disciplines of sociology and psychology. The *interdiscipline* of *socio-psychology* acknowledges the value of both sociological and psychological analysis, the influence of both disciplines on each other, and the roles of both sociologists and psychologists in community mental health and in community care. In a seminal article, Bostock (1991) outlines some characteristics of community psychology. Elaborating some of her points, the characteristics of community *sociopsychology* are outlined:

- A rejection of models of mental health based on illness and pathology in favour of salutogenic ones.
- An emphasis, therefore, on the strengths of individuals, groups and communities rather than on their perceived weaknesses or vulnerabilities (see Rappaport, 1977).
- A focus on groups and communities rather than on individuals.
- An emphasis at least on the practice of prevention (e.g. Albèe, 1979, 1982; Bostock, 1991; S. Holland, 1988, 1990) and, increasingly, on the practice of promotion.
- The application of a wide range of interventions and activities such as policy formation, mutual assessment, consultation and training (see Part II).

> These characteristics . . . go beyond the idea of mental health services locating themselves in the community. They represent a more pervasive paradigm-shift in the way we understand and respond to human distress.
>
> (Bostock, 1991, p. 3)

Castel et al. (1982) apply the semantic point about the ambiguity of 'community' to community psychiatry: 'the truth is that much of what is ambiguous about community psychiatry results from the multiple meanings of the word *community*, which readily lends itself to ideological distortions' (p. 142). S. Holland makes the more radical point that despite the fact that psychiatry

> has had to adopt the language of social causal models such as 'psycho-social transitions' or 'life events' . . . none of the issues concerning the effects on mental health of the environment, work, housing, poverty, racism, sexism, ageism [are] considered to be appropriate subjects for preventive action.
>
> (S. Holland, 1988, p. 127)

Social aspects of psychotherapy: psyche and society

Psychotherapy is, at best, about understanding the past in the present in order to assure the future. If psychotherapy carries implications of radical change on a personal level, its historical development, and particularly that of psychoanalysis, is rooted in objectivist analysis, 'scientificity' and social regulation. Auerswald (1987), in discussing some controversial assumptions on which family therapy is based, suggests that: 'the study and treatment of families is at least partly rooted in science' (p. 321) and that the evolution of this field of study cannot be separated from that of the physical and biological science.

Within psychotherapy, as with other fields encompassed by this inquiry, there are different traditions,[6] 'schools',[7] and theories which inform practice. Edwards offers a critique of psychological and psychotherapeutic models as they impact on mental health:

> within mental health, our therapeutic models tend to perpetuate victim-blaming. The biomedical model enquires into genetic or biochemical abnormalities to explain people's distress; behavioural approaches imply that victims have faulty learning histories, which can be corrected by more appropriate reinforcement schedules; cognitive models suggest that the victim is simply thinking in the 'wrong' way; while psychodynamic theory and systems models . . . also tend to 'pathologise' the individual and the family respectively.
>
> (Edwards, 1989, p. 62)

Set against this criticism, however, are other approaches to health psychology, mental health and psychotherapy. C.R. Rogers (1951, 1961), the proponent of 'person-centred therapy',[8] for instance, emphasises the human self-actualising tendency as the motivating force for change in therapy. Berne refers to *physis*, the force of nature (Berne, 1961/1981, 1963, 1972/1975); Clarkson (1992) traces the origins of *physis* or *phusis* back to Heraclitus and Aristotle. Humanistic/existential approaches to health and mental health generally emphasise attitudes towards one's self, perceptions of reality, self-actualisation, autonomy, control of one's environment, and an integration of personality (Jahoda, 1958). There are, of course, in turn, radical critiques of these humanistic approaches (e.g. Jacoby, 1977).

Whatever the orientation, in practice psychotherapy predominantly focuses, at least initially, on impaired functioning. Mental health promotion, or what Neumann et al. (1989a) refer to as 'psychoprophylaxis', 'is aimed at preserving and stabilizing unimpaired, normal mental function and developing new, additional possibilities of active coping' (p. 12). However, this distinction between psychotherapy and MHP is not as stark as it might initially appear. By implication, if not explicitly, psychotherapy has always had an educative element. This dates back to the early 1930s when Wilhelm Reich established sexual hygiene clinics for workers and employees in Germany which included sex-affirmative education.[9] Other examples have been discussed in Chapter 3 and, again, they may be subject to paradigm analysis. Jaspers (1913/1964), for instance, summarises his own (highly functionalist) approach to psychotherapy and its educative nature:

the more the patient turns to the doctor to accept his authority and be guided, the more the relationship may assume the character of re-education. The patient is taken out of his usual environment into a hospital, a spa or sanatorium. Within the authoritative atmosphere of an ordered existence, he then becomes re-educated.

(Jaspers, 1913/1964, p. 3)

In order to redress this historical (im)balance, radical approaches to psychotherapy are considered.

Individual and society

The central thesis of radical structuralist approaches to the individual is that of alienation: the notion that as individuals within a conflictual society operating and maintaining oppressive power relations by class, race, gender, and so on we are alienated from nature, from ourselves, from our 'species-being', our 'human-ness' or 'person-ness', and from other people. Therefore, in order to understand and develop an accurate and complete understanding of the individual they must be understood within their social and political context (R. Holland, 1977). In his work exploring a Marxist theory of personality K. Brown (1979) points out 'the false divorce between the personal and the political . . . [and the need for] an analysis of the individual, a science of biography' (p. 6). Radical structuralism criticises traditional psychological theories for isolating the individual, refusing to see them as a social entity. Equally, materialist accounts need to be subjected to the same rigorous analysis with regard to their traditional lack of insight into individual psychology. From these different starting points Leonard (1984) suggests two alternative ways forward. One is to attempt to transform psychological theory, and specifically psychoanalysis, from a materialist standpoint. This way is represented by the work, amongst many others, of Reich (1942/1975), Marcuse (1968, 1969) and J. Mitchell (1975). Jacoby (1977) criticises this project: 'a harmonious synthesis of Marxism and psychoanalysis presupposes that society is without the antagonisms that are its essence' (p. 73). Embleton Tudor and Tudor (1994), drawing on Burrell and Morgan's (1979) subjectivist–objectivist analysis of assumptions about the nature of social science, counter this with an integrative conceptual approach to issues of power, authority and influence in psychotherapy. The other way forward for Leonard (1984) is 'beginning to build, on the basis of the principal concepts of historical materialism, an entirely new psychology of the individual' (p. 39). This possibility is reflected in the work of Séve (1975, 1978) and applied to a materialist and psychological account of class consciousness by Lowe and Tudor (1995). A third way forward is the development of a theory of the social individual within sociopsychology and is represented by the approach reflected in this present work. Sociopsychology provides an interdisciplinary or, even, transdisciplinary framework (for discussion of which see Chapter 9). This framework does not ignore antagonisms or differences but seeks to understand them and to develop and integrate theory and practice on a number of levels – of content, process and meta-theoretical analysis. Beyond this integration is a fourth approach, represented in the field of depth psychology by the work of Samuels (1993) in which he engages with political issues (such as the market economy, environmentalism and nationalism) using depth psychology and *at the same time* explores and expresses personal experience (as regards fathers and the male body) in a public and political way. Such postmodernist dis-integration and deconstruction of disciplines and ways of thinking and writing is the result of reflexive analysis *beyond integration* and is the subject of further reflection in Chapter 10.

Social action psychotherapy

> Dealing with human relations in the here and now demands a multi-dimensional approach that is at once psychological, social and political.
>
> (Castel et al., 1982, p. 160)

S. Holland, whose background is within the psychoanalytic tradition of object-relations, has described her work on a multi-racial housing estate in West London with 'depressed women' and suggests a therapeutic and social movement, using the paradigm map, from individual symptom to collective social action, 'using psychodynamic counselling as a tool for action, rather than as an end in itself' (S. Holland, 1990, p. 256).

> Women originally presented themselves at the GP's using the functionalist language which they had learned was the correct way to describe their discomfort . . . the programmes of therapy offered in the project aim to move her through into the interpretive mode or paradigm: 'What does your depression mean and where does it come from?' Then, by way of group work into the radical humanist mode: 'What do you want of yourself and others?' Finally, and this is the most difficult, into the radical structuralist mode: 'What is to be done?' 'How can we change the bit of the world we inhabit?'
>
> (S. Holland, 1988, pp. 132–133)

The development of a subject's thinking over time is analogous to movement between paradigms, a movement as it were from psyche to society.

Holland's work in the well-established White City Mental Health Project offers a critical example of MHP and CMHP. The project helps depressed women to move from passive individual and individualised recipients (functionalist/ symptom); through an understanding of their personal pain (interpretative/meaning); through desire for personal change (radical humanist/desire); to action (radical structuralist/action) (see Figure 5.1).

THE SOCIOLOGY OF RADICAL CHANGE

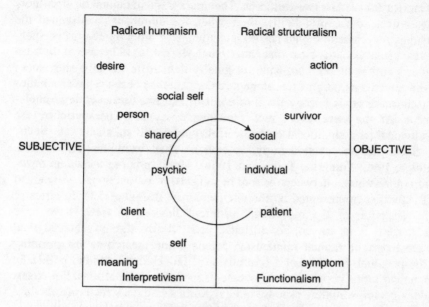

THE SOCIOLOGY OF REGULATION

Figure 5.1 Social action psychotherapy
Source: Based on Burrell and Morgan, 1979, p. 22; S. Holland, 1990, p. 258, and 1993

This is 'social action psychotherapy' (S. Holland, 1985, 1988, 1990). Social action on the part of ex-clients has led to the establishment of an independent sister organisation, Women's Action on Mental Health (WAMH) – a title and organisation which the women who run it promote vigorously.[10]

Kuhn (1970), in a seminal work on *The structure of scientific revolutions*, discusses periods of of revolution in which the principal features of the dominant paradigm change. He suggests three basic stages of scientific development: a pre-paradigm stage in which different theories compete for dominance; a period of 'normal science' when a single paradigm (such as the functionalist paradigm) dominates; and a crisis stage when one paradigm is replaced by another. Thus, development in natural science is not so much evolutionary as revolutionary. This may be applied in a historical analysis to the field of mental health. The history of the early legislative responses to lunacy may be seen as a period of struggle for 'the mind' between the acceptance of difference on the one hand and the interests of social control allied with those of medicine on the other. As a result, the dominant approach to lunacy/madness/mental illness was one which drew on notions of objectivist science as well as social regulation – a functionalist paradigm which has dominated thinking and action, becoming the 'normal science' in the field of mental health/illness in Europe and North America for the last two centuries. The crisis stage in mental health/illness dates back to the mid-1970s, since when the dominant paradigm of the medical/psychiatric model has been challenged from a number of perspectives. From this, it is clear that Burrell and Morgan's (1979) use of the term 'paradigm' is looser than Kuhn originally defined it. Equally, movement between two paradigms (let alone three or four) is not the same as a major disciplinary crisis in the natural sciences: it is, rather, an *analogous* movement. At the same time, such movement may be experienced by the individual as a significant and powerful (paradigm) 'shift'.

Social action psychotherapy, as well as other examples (R. Holland, 1990a, 1992; Embleton Tudor and Tudor, 1995), propose a specific direction of movement between the four paradigms, from functionalist to radical structuralist (represented by the circular arrow in Figure 5.1). In terms of the direction of the movement, different theoretical views have been advanced. It is argued, for instance, that 'desire (the psychoanalytical counterpart of radical humanism) comes before searching for meaning (the personal correlate of interpretivism)' (R. Holland, 1990c, p. 43). In practical terms people make movements in different directions. For example, a person who may espouse radical politics (radical structuralist/action) may decide to explore what they want (radical humanist/desire) personally (subjectivist) rather than collectively before understanding the meaning (interpretative/meaning) of their actions: 'posited directions for "progressive" movement depend on interpretation of the defined spaces' (Ibid., p. 43).

Social action psychotherapy focuses on the social context in which both practitioner and client are located, often a common and very immediate one. As such it requires self-critical reflection and personal involvement. It is not insignificant that, until the early 1990s, Holland lived in the same area in which she worked:

> this kind of therapeutic method demands not only that therapists be well versed in the use of sophisticated techniques but also that they be immersed in the same milieu as their clients. If therapists and clients truly form an endogamous community, then the boundaries between personal problems and social problems vanish; the personal and social become merely polar points on a spectrum, and therapy can deal with the whole spectrum by working to transform the individual and his surroundings at the same time.
>
> (Castel et al., 1982, pp. 160-161)

These authors see this approach as 'a concrete realization of G. Caplan's vision, combining crisis intervention with preventive action in the community' (Ibid., p. 160).

Having focused on one professional approach to and view of CMHP, it is timely to consider the view of the client or user.

The user/advocacy movement and empowerment

In widening the concern of MHP to that of the population at large the users of such services may be defined as the general public; this makes the identification of potential service users an all-inclusive task. From the social action perspective and in describing her work in developing psychotherapeutic interventions and social action, S. Holland (1985) makes the point that mental health workers seeking to promote positive community mental health and social action should identify and promote the *least* powerful members of the community (e.g. depressed women). This is a reversal of the approach of much community development work which has traditionally identified community 'leaders' rather than those marginalised by the community. Within the broad picture of CMHP and given an important focus of MHP on 'the mentally ill', it is important to consider the user/advocacy movement within this field in order that CMHP is sensitive to the needs and priorities of this particular population. With this in mind, Bassett et al. (undated) offer a rare and positive discussion about involving service users in CMH services.

The plethora of terms to describe people with mental health problems – from patient to survivor – not only reflects great debates within the field of mental health/illness, but also illustrates the issues and 'positions' which give rise to such terminology. The terms used and their implications are reviewed and located within the paradigm map (Figure 5.2). Definitions of advocacy and the advocacy movement are examined, as are the implications of such terms and definitions for theoretical and practical developments in the context of the government's policies on *Caring for people* (Department of Health [DoH], 1989a) and *Working for patients* (DoH, 1989b) as enacted in the *NHS and Community Care Act 1990*.

A cursory brainstorm throws up some of the terms or 'buzz-words' (Tyson, 1987) used to describe or label people: patient, client, sufferer, victim, survivor, user, recipient, consumer, customer, member, resident, trainee. All of these carry their own implications. 'Patient' implies a diagnosis and a medical view of 'the problem'. 'Client' is perhaps a more liberal version and one more familiar to social work, but nevertheless implies an unequal professional–client relationship. 'Victim' can be seen as individualising and pacifying; it is both worse and, some would argue, more accurate. 'Survivor' has taken on a particular and now more political connotation with the founding in 1986 of the organisation Survivors Speak Out, which represents all survivors of the mental health (illness) system. 'User' is a more popular and in some senses a relatively value-free term and, interestingly, the one adopted by users (*utenti*) in Italy; it has, however, an unfortunate connotation with drug and substance use and abuse. 'Recipient' is another passive term, although again some would see it as accurately reflecting that people *receive* (as opposed to choose) treatment. Similarly, 'consumer' can imply receipt, although it carries a sense of choice which is generally not true – Rose and Black (1985) offer a critique of consumerism, set against participation. Even less true is 'customer' which, in the present economic context of internal markets and increasing privatisation of service provision and poverty amongst the mentally ill, is bitterly ironic and patronising. 'Member', often used liberally and usually associated with day centres and mental health projects, is at best ambiguous and at worst dishonest. Such facilities are in the main not open to 'membership' with the kind of democratic control and participation this implies. 'Resident' and 'trainee' usually describe people in particular settings. Finally, in increasingly popular usage, is the phrase 'people with . . . ', for example, people with mental health difficulties. This sounds nice but has been criticised for its libertarian value, disguising the very real differences between people.[11] These terms strongly imply a view of the individual, of mental illness and of mental health. Unfortunately, many people, usually professionals (e.g. Renshaw, 1987; Tyson, 1987), use them interchangeably and sloppily.

Sang (1989) reviews the state of the concepts and role of advocacy by identifying and defining four forms of advocacy: *self-advocacy* and *citizen advocacy*; and *professional advocacy* and *patients' advocacy*.[12] The difference between these two sets of terms is, as becomes self-apparent, a difference between forms of advocacy (self- and citizen-advocacy) which emerged 'as a response to two fundamental characteristics of traditional services and their various institutions . . . "labelling" . . . and [lack of] choice' (Sang, 1989, pp. 192-193), that is a grass-roots approach to the need for change; and forms of advocacy 'generally stimulated and organised by professionals' (Ibid., p. 203) in a kind of 'top-down' approach (professional and patients' advocacy). Sang warns, as others before and since (e.g. MIND, 1992), against the take-over of the former forms of advocacy by professionals. Sedgwick (1982) reviews mental health movements in the United States and in Europe and notes the difficult task of integrating the diverse demands of mental health workers, patients and the public. Even self-advocacy and citizen advocacy, however, is subject to professional influence; hence the more recent use of 'independent advocacy'.

In addition to these terms there is the relatively new concept of legal advocacy which can take the form of professional advocacy or citizen advocacy of legal issues. This continuum is represented in practice by the unique Springfield Advice and Law Centre (SALC), an independent law centre operating within a large psychiatric hospital (SALC, 1990), and, at the other end, the role of the patients' advocate within Dutch psychiatric hospitals. R. Brown, in some innovative research, has developed ideas about the extension of the meaning and purpose of guardianship under the *Mental Health Act 1983*, arguing that there is no reason why the role and powers of the guardian could not be extended to a nearest relative or friend and away from the approved social worker (R. Brown, personal communication, 18 June 1990). Indeed there is a precedent for this under the *Disabled Persons (Services, Consultation and Representation) Act 1986*, Sections 1 and 2 of which define the appointment and rights of authorised representatives of disabled persons. These enabling sections are largely not currently implemented.

At a strategic level, the DoH's Mental Health Task Force (MHTF) has promoted consumer involvement in mental health (illness) services through a series of regional conferences, the whole project being steered by user groups (NHS Executive, 1994a, 1994b, 1994c).

Focusing on self-advocacy, Campbell (1989b) identifies three main types of groups involved: the national campaign groups, campaigning on major issues regarding the psychiatric system; locality-based groups of which Survivors Speak Out (1989) identified over thirty; and groups 'connected to existing service provision or which are themselves supplying significant services' (Campbell, 1989b, p. 211).

The various terms and themes discussed may now be located and placed within the paradigm map (Figure 5.2). Whilst their general positioning is accurate and significant there may be examples which may be located within another paradigm. Thus, whilst self-advocacy groups are placed broadly within the radical humanist paradigm some of their work, such as that of the Camden Mental Health Consortium's (1988) *Treated well? A*

Figure 5.2 Forms of advocacy
Source: Based on Burrell and Morgan, 1979, p. 22; S. Holland, 1990, p. 258

code of practice for psychiatric hospitals, contains elements of a radical structuralist analysis. There is a growing number of advocacy groups and citizen advocacy groups and organisations, many of whom were represented at MIND's Annual Conference 1990 on Speaking Up: Advocating for a Different Future. In locating the various forms or elements of the mental health/illness user/advocacy movement, there is no purpose (or presumption) to assess the worth or practice of individual groups or organisations. Neither is it for MIND to present them as examples of 'exemplary services', defined simply (and simplistically) as those services 'which meet the real needs of the people whom they exist to serve' (MIND, 1990). Rather, the location of such organisations on the paradigm map depends on the explicit and implicit assumptions on which they operate and on an analysis of an organisation's aims, structure, policies and practice. The Insane Liberation Front (ILF), for instance, given its views on the 'capitalistic system' and the need for 'a socialist society based on cooperation' (ILF, 1971, p. 109) would be located within the radical structuralist paradigm. Similarly, the Mental Patients' Union (MPU) makes the link between the position of women, medication and psychiatric admission, and between unemployment and mental illness (MPU, 1973, reported by Durkin and Douieb, 1975). It is not insignificant that the ILF, the MPU, as well the more recent Campaign Against Psychiatric Oppression (CAPO) all identify themselves as offering a radical structuralist critique of present medical/psychiatric and social services systems.

Many of the applications of the paradigm approach imply an historical development – from functionalism, through the interpretative paradigm to radical humanism and radical structuralism (e.g. S. Holland, 1988; R. Holland, 1990c). In tracing the historical development of advocacy we can locate and describe slightly different developments and reactions. In the social work profession, for example, there has traditionally been an advocacy (professional advocacy/interpretative) role. From Octavia Hill and the Victorian social reformers on, many well-meaning social workers had (and still have) the role or 'sense' of being an advocate *for* and *on behalf of* their clients in relation to, for example, social security and housing departments, literally interpreting and representing their clients' needs. Fewer professionals have a practice of encouraging or enabling their clients themselves to take an active part in accessing resources and services: 'the vocational assumptions, which underpin the various professions and their approved training schemes, ignore the unresolvable conflicts of interests and values that exist between service users and service providers' (Sang, 1989, p. 203). A publication from MIND gives guidelines on advocacy for mental health workers (Read and Wallcraft, 1994). Campbell (1989a) notes the hostility of workers to the idea of user involvement in mental health services. It was largely in response to this kind of professional hostility or take-over, and often reinterpretation or mistranslation of the 'problem' or issue, that many individuals in hospitals, residential institutions and 'homes' took up the struggle to represent themselves (e.g. the Union of the Physically Impaired Against Segregation, 1981). That this was a struggle reflects an essentially radical view of society, its institutions and the process of change. The paradigm distinction between self- and citizen advocacy (above) depends on the objective–subjective dimension of the particular conditions and nature of that struggle and the forms of knowledge and organisation which inform these. Historically then the development of advocacy may be viewed in terms of a movement from professional advocacy (interpretative) to self- and citizen advocacy (radical humanist and radical structuralist, respectively). A worrying aspect of this historical development worth noting is the subtle take-over, freezing out, or incorporation of self-advocacy. The groups identified in Figure 5.2 are threatened by these three dangers. The national campaign groups are always in danger of being taken over by well-meaning professionals (e.g. the 'professionalisation' of National MIND in the 1980s). The locality-based campaign groups either suffer from a lack of funds and if given funds, are then in danger of becoming professionalised or incorporated.[13] Finally, groups in the voluntary/independent sector providing services in the form of drop-in centres, telephone advice lines, emergency accommodation, etc. are, through community care legislation, in danger of becoming dependent on local government finance, control and regulation.

In the current context of community care, with its interest in consumer involvement, there is an increasing interest amongst professionals in the notion of empowerment. Empowerment is seen by some as the same as advocacy: 'being able to assert our views and make choices is a form of *power*' (MIND, 1990). Rose and Black (1985), in a seminal book on the subject, usefully distinguish the two terms: defining advocacy as 'issue-oriented, focused on objective conditions' (p. 16) and empowerment as characterising 'an ongoing process of direct interaction covering all contacts with all clients' (Ibid., p. 15). There is both a conceptual and a practical problem with the notion of empowerment: that of the necessity for professionals to 'give up' or 'give away' their power.[14] The consequent democratisation of services is also, therefore, limited. Renshaw (1987) acknowledges that for professionals this is 'not an easy move or gesture to be made lightly. It could mean taking some risks and stepping into hitherto unknown territory' (p. 10). Commenting on the extent of professional influence, Durkin and Douieb (1975) remain critical of professionals whilst Campbell (1989a) refreshingly suggests that 'many mental health workers are comparatively powerless within their own systems' (p. 23). From the point of view of the disempowered, Tyson (1987) comments on initial 'consumer' resistance from 'institutionalised, routinised people' (p. 12) to the opening up of meetings and decision-making.

While professional allies may open up some services and resources to a limited extent in seeking to empower clients they are doing no more than perpetuating a system in which professionals can choose what to dispense, including power. In reality this is the acceptable face of patients' advocacy:

> from beginning to end patients' advocacy is run to suit the interests of institutions which are being forced to change in the face of new policies. The fact that it appears progressive is a reflection of the power of the controlling forces which exist within psychiatric services and which come openly into play as soon as 'clinical judgement' and other professional rights are challenged.
>
> (Sang, 1989, p. 204)

Ultimately it is the patients/clients/users/survivors who take and will continue to take power for themselves in the form, for instance, of independent groups such as Insight in Brighton (Beeforth, 1991). The difficulty of *em*powerment is thus resolved when seen from the users' perspective – of seizing power – rather than from the perspective of the professional giving it up: self-advocacy is thus about people regaining power over their own lives. 'Mental patients' taking power does not mean that professionals do nothing. From a radical humanist perspective the professional's task is to be aware of their own role and power and to develop, for instance, congruent, respectful and empathic relationships with their clients (C.R. Rogers, 1951, 1961). Radical structuralists suggest a more radical shift of perspective, one which Rose and Black (1985) have described, asserting 'the primacy of reconnection to objective circumstances as the central problem to be addressed' (p. 36). They develop a 'practice theory', applying it to case management, day programmes, legal advocacy, programme evaluation and community organisation, which 'validates the person, reconnects her/him to the *objective context* in which she/he lives, legitimates the impact of psychiatric history or self-expression, and engages the person in a process of transformation' (Ibid., p. 40, original emphasis).[15] Those who promote this notion of empowerment see the person as an active – or, at least, a potentially active – agent in their own process of health and change. Beresford (1994) discusses empowerment in the context of MHP, identifying three reasons as to why empowerment is important:

> first to ensure that people have more control over what happens to them in the service system; second, to challenge the broader discrimination, oppression and disadvantage they experience; and third, to offer a way of addressing any link there may be between their disempowerment and distress.
>
> (Beresford, 1994, p. 33)[16]

'The Italian experience'

'The Italian experience' of psychiatric and mental reform has been discussed in the context of community care. Here it is presented as having a radical impact on the community and the public's attitude to mental illness and mental health, in its theory, its practice and its organisation.

Although the first phase of reform, that of de-institutionalisation (1971–4), was centred on the hospital, the movement was strongly from the hospital into the community with the re-establishment of daily contact with patients' families, outings, and, where possible, reintegration at home and in the workplace. The city, too, had contact with the hospital through festivals, concerts and other cultural initiatives. This was a period of effervescence, of anti-psychiatry, of 'everything is possible'. Perhaps the most famous and public metaphor of this period was that of Marco the Horse, built inside the psychiatric hospital in Trieste and then paraded, like its Greek/Trojan forerunner, around the streets of the city, symbolising the theoretical view of Franco Basaglia that illness was located (and hidden) in the external world:

> the conflicts which had previously been regarded as internal to the patient, or at least to the asylum, are thrown back on the wider society from whence they came – for the illness is seen essentially as a distorted representation of specific contradictions of the subject in his social relations.
>
> (Basaglia, 1981, p. 190)

As more people, including other professionals, became drawn to this practice, so the need to organise the emerging movement became more pressing. In 1967 *Psichiatria Democratica* (PD: Democratic Psychiatry) held its first conference and in 1976 it was formally founded. It comprised professionals involved in the psychiatric system, as well as patients and relatives.[17] In line with its critique and perspectives, PD quickly became a political and social movement and a reference point for political parties, trade unions and activists. Its initial aims are worth noting:

> to fight against any form of segregation and institutional repression, in favour of improving on the present special legislation concerning mental diseases; to fight against noxiousness in factories and in the district; to fight against selection and isolation as practised by educational and assistance authorities; to fight for the democratic cooperation of social assistance services, no longer mystified by the corporative, speculative, and bureaucratic logic typical of the current health system; and the need to establish in practice a new work method in the field of health, which will give priority to prevention, in cooperation with worker organisations.
>
> (Minguzzi, 1974, quoted by Crepet and De Plato, 1983, p. 123)

PD contains diverse views. In the early years there were those who favoured an autonomous, anti-institutional approach, and those who believed in the need for an alliance with the institutions and parties of the Left. It was the latter grouping that sought legislative change in order to promote the practices of alternative psychiatry in Italy as a whole.

The crisis of the psychiatric institution – and the institution of psychiatry – cannot be viewed outside the context of Italian politics at the time. In the 1970s there was a mass movement to the Left which in its parliamentary expression gave the Italian Communist Party (PCI) a majority and a governmental role for the first time since the Second World War in the famous 'Historic Compromise' with the Christian Democrats (DC): at this time 'anti-institutional experience became an organic part of the actual change process' (Crepet and De Plato, 1983, p. 122).[18] It has been particularly since this period, that the question of constitutional and institutional reform, what has been referred to as the 'crisis of the institutions', has been on the parliamentary political agenda – with little or no resolution and, indeed, further recent regional fragmentation and polarisation with the rise of the Right.

COMMUNITY MENTAL HEALTH PROMOTION

CMHP is viewed as comprising two elements: challenging myths of mental health (illness), and promoting mental health.

Challenging myths of mental illness

In the context of CMHP, this refers not so much to de-stigmatising mental illness but, more specifically, to separating mental illness from mental health.

If the community is to develop an awareness of more positive responses to mental illness as well as to mental health, the theoretical foundations and practices of the asylum need to be shaken: by reform of the hospital, supported, for instance, through the WHO's project on health promoting hospitals (WHO, 1991a; NHS Executive, 1994d) and by public access to psychiatric hospitals and other facilities. Secondly, the conceptual complacency of the community needs to be challenged: by 'madness' entering the community (e.g. Marco the Horse); and by users, carers and professionals bringing home to the community debates about mental illness and health, resources, care in the community and other policies, the siting of residential and daycare facilities, etc. At a conceptual level as well as a matter of strategy the dual continuum concept (Minister of National Health and Welfare, 1988) is useful in this process. CMHCs and CMHTs could and should take a central role in this process, although (as discussed above) they appear currently incapable of this. Whilst there are some examples of this kind of challenging and promotional work, it is significant, although not surprising, that none of the initiatives or examples reviewed originated from CMHCs or CMHTs.

One positive example of this approach to CMHP is the adult education course reported by Doyle (1989) (referred to in Chapter 4). Also, in 1980 Tooting Bec's hospital Voluntary Services Department set up a mental health education group to provide education about mental illness and mental health for teachers and pupils in the form of a four-week package for schools and as a way for involving volunteers, school and hospital (Spy and Watkins-Baker, 1980). Higgins (1984) describes a mental health education project run as part of a (then) CSE social biology syllabus with the three objectives of: education/information, self-awareness and counselling. The Hastings Health Authority/East Sussex County Council SSD's (1989) joint statement of intent includes references to the education of people in health matters, including school and college programmes; promoting health in local communities; and encouraging sensitivity in the community to the needs of those who are vulnerable. It is an example of a coherent LA approach to CMHP and to joint planning. The Harpurhey Resettlement Team in Manchester describes its work in secondary schools: 'to help young people to challenge the general assumptions that ex-psychiatric patients are "other people" who are not like us, and at the same time foster a tolerance of and sympathy for people whose problems lead them to behave differently' (Harpurhey Resettlement Team, 1990). The national curriculum for schools now contains guidance on psychological aspects of health education focusing on, in various key stages: self-value, human emotions, co-operation; differences and consequences; labelling and self-confidence; and self-assessment (Department of Education, 1993). There are an increasing number of information, educative and teaching packs about mental health, notably ones produced by the Northern Ireland Association for Mental Health (now curiously unavailable) and the more recent teachers' resource pack produced by the Northern Ireland Centre for Learning Resources (1993) and the Westminster Association for Mental Health (Wood, 1986). The Workers' Education Association (WEA), for instance in its North Yorkshire District, has taken up courses on adult education and mental health.

The common feature of many of these initiatives is their involvement of the public with the psychiatric institution and/or with psychiatric patients. This may initially be on a personal level, via an individual or small group and then developing from that contact to operating in larger groups and at a wider community level with further ideas and interventions. Some of these ideas and involvements – such as expressing an interest in establishing a daycare facility (Doyle, 1989) – have radical and structural implications.

Promoting mental health

Making a conceptual separation between mental illness and mental health has the consequence of making space for the promotion of mental health whether at an individual level or with groups, organisations or communities.

Working with individuals and groups many Transactional Analysis psychotherapists use and actively promote with their clients Steiner's (1984) concept of emotional literacy, for example in working with groups of children (Tudor, 1991). Rakusen (1990) also describes examples of what she refers to (and without reference to Steiner) as 'emotional education'. Coyle and Daniels (1993) discuss strategies for promoting mental health among gay men by means of discussion groups and group exercises as well as improving clinical services for gay men. A rare example of a consciousness/awareness raising programme is presented by Mubbashar (1989) who describes a community-based rural mental health care programme, involving schools in particular, in Gujar Khan, a sub-district of Rawalpindi in Pakistan. The programme included providing counselling to children, changing attitudes towards healthy living, training teachers in the recognition of mental ill-health. The results are impressive in terms of increased educational achievement; a reduction at school in absenteeism, the use of corporal punishment, and, amongst teachers, a reduction in smoking; and a greater knowledge and sense of mental illness and health amongst the community. Another positive example is the promotion of children's mental health in Czechoslovakia, organised through the Czechoslovakian Psychological Society's working group, reported by Krejčiřova (1989). The programme works first through the support of individual health and positive development amongst a *healthy* population; and, secondly, through preventive work in which the focus is on *situations* in risk groups (rather than on the vulnerable person/s themselves.

CONCLUSION

The examples referred to here are neither comprehensive nor exhaustive. The important issue is to analyse the various and increasing number of initiatives in MHP and CMHP so that the underlying assumptions which inform their practice may be understood. This is partly so that we may understand differences and commonalities and partly so that the examples may be transferred. It is important that the theories – of society and of knowledge – and assumptions on which policies and programmes are based are made explicit. This has a direct bearing on developing good policy and good practice. Also, it is only when we put other people's positions in context that we begin to make realistic decisions about working together, on what basis and with what purpose.

  Having defined the field and process of CMHP over these five chapters, we now turn our attention in Part II to developing this field through a number of discussions: on mental health policy, assessment, consultation and learning through education and training.

Part II
Developing the field

INTRODUCTION TO PART II

In Part I the components of community mental health promotion were assembled along with a conceptual framework which was developed through the chapters. The four paradigm analysis is seen to operate on a number of levels: of comparing and contrasting the *content* of theory and practice; of analysing the *meta-theoretical* assumptions underlying such content; and of *process* (between these levels) or movement (between paradigms).

In Part II, developing the field of mental health promotion (MHP), four key areas of concern to any inquiry into mental health and its promotion are examined. In each case I am concerned to develop the field by first wresting it from the context of mental illness. Following this, each subject is discussed and developed with reference to the relevant literature; Chapters 6 and 7, in particular, are intended for use by politicians and practitioners at all levels in conveying the theory and practice of MHP through macro and micro policies.

In Chapter 6 the social policy context to MHP is discussed and developed. Mental illness policies are given critical attention and a *politica* of mental health policy is proposed. A schema is developed which integrates the many elements of a coherent and comprehensive mental health policy. One element – mental health assessment – is considered separately (in Chapter 7). Together, they provide a unique translation and elaboration of existing policies such as the World Health Organisation's (1984/1991a) *Health for all targets* into practical policies.

Chapter 8 develops the notion of mental health consultation, a notion and practice described by G. Caplan (1961, 1970), although since fallen somewhat into disuse. Mental health consultation is distinguished from psychotherapy and supervision, elaborated with reference to the analytic literature, and given direction by means of the four paradigm analysis. MHP is linked particularly with secondary prevention and four case studies offer a range of how mental health consultation may be used to promote the mental health of individuals, groups and organisations.

Part II concludes with reference to the implications of these discussions (and those in Part I) for learning. My own training/education courses in MHP are subject to reflective analysis as is the notion of a 'discipline' of mental health or a (separate) profession concerned with its promotion.

6 Mental health policy

Social policy on mental health has been concerned more with mental illness, its management, amelioration and prevention than with mental health. Mental *health* policy is new and relatively uncharted territory. Developing the ground defined in Part I, this chapter brings together disparate elements of policies and strategies in mental health promotion (MHP), describes them with reference to examples of good practice, and suggests a progressive and reflexive interrelationship between them. In doing so, it inevitably draws on policies and strategies concerned with mental illness and with secondary and tertiary prevention. My own strategy in drawing on such sources is to locate MHP within existing international, national and local governmental legislation, circulars, guidelines, policies, etc. in order to claim some ground for MHP whilst offering a critique of the limitiations of existing mental illness policy. It is for this reason that the chapter is titled mental health *policy*, in the Italian sense in which *la politica* means politics, policy and political action. Thus, *mental health policy* includes macro politics, their implementation (through policy), as well as the (political) action necessary to implement policy.

The social and political context of mental health is that of social control, medicine and, more recently, social and community care services. Historically, national health policy in Britain has been administered through health authorities (HAs) – from Regional Health Authorities (RHAs) to District Health Authorities (DHAs) – and social policy through local authority social services departments (SSDs). The *NHS and Community Care Act 1990* has led to an integration of health and social services with the intention that these services are influenced by and accountable to people at a local level, involving user groups as well as an expanding independent sector, in the provision of services to purchasers. However, with devolution has come complexity. International law is often taken as advisory rather than mandatory. Other legislation defines relationships, for example between national and local government. Partnerships, such as those between health and local authorities and the independent sector, are affected by competing ideas, for instance about mental health and mental illness, and are determined by (so-called) 'free' market forces, that is the economics of purchasing. Contracts often operate one-way or from the top down. Indicators, targets and measures frequently derive from medicine and epidemiology and are not always sensitive to nominalistic, anti-positivist, voluntaristic and ideographic notions of mental *health*, community and quality of life. The implementation of policy and the delivery of services are too often based on pragmatism; whilst the idea of critical self-reflection on any of this is seen as indulgent.

Figure 6.1 illustrates a structure which describes all the elements relevant to the development and implementation of MHP policy, and the relation between the elements. The structure of this chapter reflects the interrelationship between all these elements: from principles to reflection on the implications of mental health services which, in turn, provides a review of objectives, and so on; (mental health assessment is considered in Chapter 7). In practice, some elements are passed over or not considered. For instance, the tripartite relationship between principles, objectives and policy is more usually driven by policy rather than by principles or objectives. Reflecting this, the chapter begins with consideration of mental health (illness) policy. The numbered elements of Figure 6.1 refer to the following sections in this chapter which elaborate the relevant discussions and practices pertaining to each element. Policy (3), objectives (2) and principles (1) are discussed – in the order of their usual consideration (but numbered according to a more coherent conceptual sequence) – before progressing on to consider how policies are applied in practice through strategy (4), etc. The chapter concludes with an example of genuine mental health policy elaborated according to this scheme.

POLICY (3)

The journey commences with consideration of mental health policies (rather than objectives or principles) as this is whence most politicians, policy-makers and managers begin. All the major and influential policies make the usual elision from mental health to mental illness: the *Mental Health Act 1983*, *The health of the nation* (Department of Health [DoH], 1992), *The health of the nation key area handbook mental illness* (DoH, 1993b, 1994c). To date, there is no *la politica*, there are no specific *policies* on mental health promotion. There are objectives for the promotion of mental health which are not elucidated as policy, and there are strategies which draw on implied policies. Thus for genuine policies on mental *health* promotion we need to consider the existing fields of mental health (illness) policies and health promotion policies, to redefine them, and if necessary to break out of them.

In the field of mental health (illness) policy it is impossible to ignore the impact of community care (see Chapter 4). Whilst community care in this field focuses on the needs, assessment and management of the mentally ill,

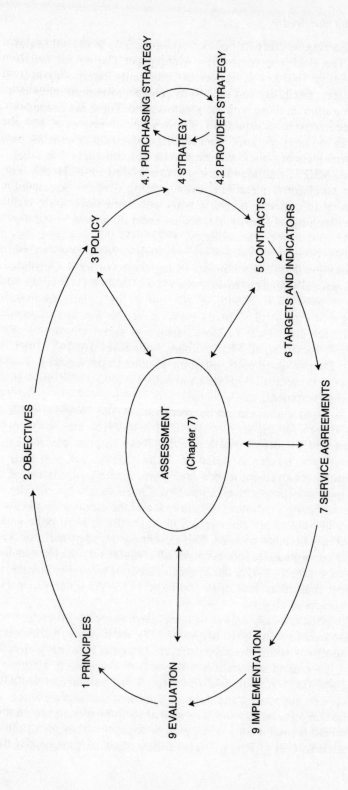

Figure 6.1 A macro scheme for the development and implementation of mental health policy

it is worth considering whether its policies are applicable to mental health
and ill-health. The British government's white paper *Caring for people*
(DoH, 1989a) set out four key principles of community care policy in its
delivery of services: flexibility and sensitivity, choice, minimum intervention, and concentration on those with the greatest need. These are examples
of what may be referred to as *principles of policy* (the objectives of which
are considered in the next section). One important question to consider is
whether such principles of policy may be transferred and applied to other
policy as regards MHP. Brian Mawhinney, the then Minister of Health, in
speaking about purchasing, identified seven guiding (policy) principles,
including listening to patients; knowing what you want to achieve; and
establishing challenging efficiency targets in order to create space for
improving health and quality (Mawhinney, 1993b). In this inquiry a distinction is made between *principles of policy* (such as Mawhinney's) and
the *policy in practice*, that is, those pieces of legislation or local decisions
commonly and generally referred to as 'policy' (see Table 6.1). It is worth
noting that as a policy *The Health of the nation* itself fails to meet
Mawhinney's guiding principles. In its revision of the *Key area handbook*, the DoH does not appear to have listened or taken any notice of
criticisms (e.g. Association of Metropolitan Authorities [AMA], 1993;
MIND, 1993c). Despite its rhetoric of joint planning and services, *The
health of the nation* is medically oriented and does not focus sufficiently on
the role of local government.

In the health promotion field some elements of the World Health
Organisation's *Health for all targets* (WHO, 1984/1991b) can be interpreted and promoted as mental health policies (both in principle and in
practice), although the targets as stated are in fact objectives, and their
elaboration through achievement targets and aims, appear as a mixture of
policies (principles and practice) and strategy. Those targets specifically
relevant to mental health promotion, their aims, and the strategic implications for their achievement are summarised in Appendix 2. Most policies,
in turn, imply or rely on other policies. This is acknowledged by the way in
which the WHO conceptualises its *Health for all targets* as those concerned
directly with goals (targets 1–12), those which elaborate strategies (targets
13–31), and those defined as developmental targets (32–38) which support
the previous two sets of targets.

Mental health policy, as any aspect of more general social policy, is of
course subject to paradigm analysis. Mishra (1977), for instance, examines
five major perspectives which describe different relations between society
and social policy: social administration or the empirical approach, citizenship, industrialism, functionalism, and Marxism. Thus, any mental health
policy or strategy, its supporting and defining contracts and service agreements, indicators, targets and measures, as well as its implementation, each
phase of any overall mental health policy may be located within any of the
four paradigms elaborated in Part I. It also follows that an ill-considered

general policy with (theoretically) conflicting elements will ultimately fail. On the other hand, one which is coherent in terms of the underlying cohesion of all its elements (and one which preferably starts from well-conceived and conceptualised objectives) is more likely to succeed. Significantly, Utting et al. (1994), in an inquiry into community care, considers that 'policies for mental health appear to have become detached from the principles and practice of community care' (p. 36).

For better or worse, policies are in practice the usual starting point. In the next sections I reflect on the objectives which, explicitly or implicitly, influence such policies and the principles which underlie those objectives.

OBJECTIVES (2)

The objectives of *la politica* of mental health promotion are – or should represent – the translation of principles into practice. Thus, the policies described in *Caring for people* follow from identified objectives:

to enable people to live as normal a life as possible in their own homes or in a homely environment in the local community;
to provide the right amount of care and support to help people achieve maximum possible independence and, by acquiring or reacquiring basic living skills, help them to achieve their full potential; and
to give people a greater individual say in how they live their lives and the services they need to help them to do so,

(DoH, 1989a)

However, on closer examination, such 'objectives' comprise in essence one objective ('to enable people' . . . etc.), together with a *principle of policy* (i.e. the provision of 'the right amount of care and support' etc.) and a *policy in practice*, in this case the acquisition of basic living skills (see Table 6.1).

Such objectives are, of course, driven by principles and, specifically, political principles and, again, warrant analysis. The principle of 'normalisation', for instance, is one way to view care. The provision of normal, 'homely' environments in the local community may be a worthy objective; it is certainly seen as a controversial one when, say, applied to the mentally ill whose local communities may well be at best ambivalent and at worst hostile about them living 'next door'.

PRINCIPLES (1)

The provisions of the *Mental Health Act 1983* are concerned with 'the reception, care and treatment of mentally disordered patients, the management of their property and other related matters' (S.1.(1)), elaborated in 149 sections, in addition to delegated legislation, circulars, the subsequent *Codes of practice* (DoH/Welsh Office, 1990, 1993), etc. Although often

Table 6.1 The relationship between principles, objectives and policy in mental health policy*

Principles	Objectives	Principles	Policy	Practice
Normalisation	To enable people to live as normal a life as possible (CfP)	The provision of the right amount of care and support to help people achieve maximum possible independence . . .		Community care
Independence				. . . by acquiring or reacquiring basic living skills (CfP)
Individuality		Giving people a greater individual say (CfP)		
Choice Independence		Services which respond flexibly and sensitively, allow a range of options, foster independence, concentrate on those with the greatest need (CfP)		
Self-actualisation (Hfat)	To enable people to lead socially, economically and mentally fulfilling lives (Hfat)	Comprehensive, co-ordinated and accessible services		Promotion of mental health skills in a variety of settings (e.g. schools, workplaces)
Opportunity	To develop health potential and quality of life (Hfat)			
Self-development	To achieve the comprehensive support of children and their families (Hfat)			
	To improve public and professional competence . . .	. . . through education and training (Hfat)		Emphasis on lifestyle issues e.g. self-esteem, support and coping skills (Hfat)

		The development of comprehensive community-based services (Hfat) Community participation (Hfat)	The treatment and management, the alleviation, and prevention of mental illness/disorder
	To improve the quality of life of people with mental disorders (Hfat)		
Citizenship Freedom	To improve significantly the health and social functioning of mentally ill people (HoN)	The least restrictive alternative Continuity of care[1]	Consultation with existing user groups, open access to information
Autonomy	To enable people to access information as a result of which they are able to make informed choices	Users to have informed choice	

Note: [1]italicised type represents existing principles, objectives, and policies, while normal type represents the author's elaboration of these.

quoted in its progress through parliament, the guiding principle of the Act – the concept of the 'least restrictive alternative' – nowhere appears in the Act. Similarly, the principles behind mental *health* objectives, policies, etc. are seldom stated. Of many regional, district and local 'policy' documents reviewed in the course of this inquiry, Trent RHA's (1992) document is one of the few which makes explicit the *principles* of a required joint mental health service in which 'individuals have a right to be involved in decisions which affect their lives' (p. 4b). The Northern Region Minds Matters Group (1993) draws on the WHO's principles of equity, participation and collaboration in its policy framework for promoting mental health.

This apart, within the limited literature on mental health policy (even including mental illness policy), it is apparent that principles are seldom directly applied to objectives or policy; objectives are confused with policy (e.g. Trent RHA, 1992) and targets with objectives (e.g. DoH, 1992); no distinction is drawn between principles of policy and the practice of policy (e.g. Mawhinney, 1993b); and there are gaps in a necessary coherent relationship between principles, objectives and policy. Drawing on *Caring for people* (*CfP*) (DoH, 1989a), *Health for all targets* (*Hfat*) (WHO, 1984/ 1991b), *The health of the nation* (*HoN*) (DoH, 1992), Table 6.1 summarises and organises these points and completes a policy framework for mental health promotion by filling the identified gaps.

As with the structure of this chapter, in drawing up Table 6.1 I started with objectives and the principles of policy, working back to principles and forwards to policies in practice. What is noticeable – although unsurprising – is that very different philosophical principles inform the various objectives laid out or implied in the various policy documents. *Caring for people* and *The health of the nation*, for instance, are both informed by free market economics and Thatcherite notions of 'independence'. Nowhere is the notion of *inter*dependence – perhaps politically less correct (at least from the Right), but psychologically a more mature development than an insistent independence. In contrast, the WHO's (1984/1991b) *Health for all targets* appear, like other of its policies, more humanistic and even radical.

Local mental health promotion policies reflect these elements – to a greater or lesser extent. Trent RHA (1992), for instance, sets out the principles of its strategy. Within Trent RHA, the North Derbyshire Mental Health Promotion Group (NDMHPG) identifies important elements of mental health promotion strategy or principles of policy such as the active involvement of service users, carers and relatives in all stages of service planning and delivery (NDMHPG, 1991). This is in line with the DoH's policy, implemented principally through the Mental Health Task Force (MHTF) of encouraging a wide range of activities aimed at empowering users and voluntary groups. The Mid Staffordshire Mental Health Promotion Programme Development Group (MSMHPPDG, 1994) outlines the ethos which informs its strategy and which includes notions that mental health promotion should be an empowering process; one which aims to reduce the stigmatisation of individuals or groups, and one which is respectful of the developmental needs as well as current needs and aspirations of people.

STRATEGY (4)

Noticeable by its absence from Table 6.1 is the *The health of the nation: Key area handbook mental illness* (DoH, 1993b, 1994c). This is because neither version elaborates MHP principles or policies. However, unlike *The health of the nation*, the *Key area handbooks* do refer to mental health promotion – the first devoting 4 of its 163 pages to the subject, the second edition, 6 out of its 179 pages. The material as regards MHP is insubstantial and the tone of both handbooks is hesitant, outlining *predicted* outcomes through developing strategy rather than clarifying *The health of the nation*'s objectives or even setting their own objectives.

If these criticisms seem severe, what is even more remarkable is the revision of the first handbook in the second edition. The first handbook suggests, for instance, that increasing awareness (about mental illness), changing public attitudes and developing strategies to prevent illness will:

• improve coping abilities in stressful situations
• *'create a more positive social climate in which it becomes more accep-table to talk about feelings*, emotions and problems and to seek help without fear of labelling or feeling a failure' (DoH, 1993b, p. 27, my emphasis)
• improve the quality of life of people with mental health problems
• maintain and improve social functioning.

In the second edition the second point is changed to 'to help people to talk about feelings' etc. (DoH, 1994c, p. 27). There is then an *explicit deletion* of concern about the creation of positive social climate, or a 'cooperative social environment' (Steiner, 1984), in which it becomes more acceptable *for all* to be, for instance, emotionally literate. The second edition of the *Key area handbook* clearly places the emphasis on the individual (rather than the community) – and the 'mentally ill' individual at that.

Although none of the major pieces of social legislation cited provides either *plans* (C. Newton, 1992) or a strategy for mental health policy and even the *Key area handbooks* set out these areas in a somewhat roundabout way, they nevertheless reflect government thinking and as such act as a reference point, particularly for NHS and (to a certain extent) SSD managers and others to develop strategy for the purchase and provision of mental health services. In this sense, the *Key area handbooks* represent the meaning of the word *strategy*, defined as the art – and perhaps science – of projecting and directing movement. At best, strategy is *how* policy is translated and how its subsequent implementation is framed, targeted and measured.

The health of the nation's reference to MHP is to the significant improvement in the health and social functioning of *mentally ill people*. The *Key area handbook* (DoH, 1993b) appears to extend this to the population as a whole in suggesting that 'a major area of direct health promotion work is the detection of at risk groups *and the provision of advice and counselling*' (p. 28, my emphasis). This appeared to open the way to a wide interpretation of and focus for MHP. Presumably influenced by J. Newton (1988, 1992) (whom it cites under references to MHP), the *Key area handbook* frames mental health promotion in terms of primary, secondary and tertiary prevention. Under primary prevention the areas it identifies include:

- disemployment – redundancy and retirement
- family circumstance (e.g. bereavement, single parenting)
- social isolation – from friends, family and other support structures
- living conditions – homelessness or inadequate housing
- sensory or physical impairment – to reduce the additional risk of disabling depression
- child abuse – the early detection and management of emotional and physical abuse
- awareness of mental health – increasing people's ability to recognise their own stress and look after themselves.

Under secondary prevention, measures include:

- the early detection and effective management of depression in primary care
- developing personal coping strategies to minimise the effects of certain conditions (e.g. hearing voices).

Under tertiary prevention it includes measures such as:

- countering discrimination in health provision to people with a history of mental illness
- developing coping strategies with carers and people with long-term physical or mental illness
- providing support for carers

(DoH, 1993b, p. 29).

Thus, apart from the specific targeting of mentally ill people (in *The health of the nation*) and on the development of good practice to improve mental health in the NHS and local authority workplace (in the *Key area handbook*, DoH, 1993b), *The health of the nation* as a strategy might have been read as providing a wider brief for developing mental health promotion strategies. However, the second edition of the *Key area handbook* again edits out important points. Under primary prevention, significantly the area of social isolation, and the one reference to awareness of mental health are both excised.

In the light of the Clunis inquiry and report (DoH, 1994d), the government has produced a stream of coercive policies and guidance such as the 'Ten Point Plan' to reinforce community care (DoH, 1993a); the introduction of supervision registers (National Health Service Management Executive [NHSME], 1994b); the guidance on the supervised discharge of mentally disordered people and their continuing care in the community (NHSME, 1994a); and the draft guidance on inter-agency working (DoH, 1994b). The second edition of *The health of the nation: Key area handbook mental illness* is but a logical extension of these policies, focusing on the care, control and management of the mentally ill; MHP is off the agenda.

Local strategies reflect these different emphases. The North Western Mental Health Promotion Group (1994) in its response to *The health of the nation* targets for mental illness identifies the contribution of preventive approaches and in doing so places – and justifies – all its examples of mental health promotion (e.g. approaches to stress management) within a preventive model. In contrast, the MSMHPPDG (1994) argues that mental health – and, therefore, that its promotion – is worthwhile in its own right:

> the merits of promoting mental health do not rely on the idea that doing so will result in the prevention of mental and physical ill health. This argument suggests that it is a worthwhile and basic human responsibility to help others improve their mental as well as their physical well-being.
> (MSMHPPDG, 1994, p. 5)

As if highlighting this difference, the Wolverhampton Health Authority (undated) distinguishes between preventive, pro-active counselling (within primary care settings) and remedial or reactive counselling (from psychiatrists).[2]

In terms of improving mental health in the NHS and in local authorities, many local strategies reflect this. South Birmingham Community Health Trust has a separate policy on mental well-being at work, concerned with stress (Phillips et al., 1992); and Trent RHA has produced a focus guide on promoting mental health at work in the NHS (Trent RHA, 1994).

Where *The health of the nation* refers to the need for DHAs, Family Health Services Authorities (FHSAs), LAs and relevant voluntary bodies to establish joint mechanisms for purchasing, with the RHAs identified as taking the lead for promoting the development of a strategic framework, the *Key area handbook* has a more specific action summaries, including:

- For all NHS and SSD managers to

    build alliances for health promotion outside the NHS and local authority social services.

develop alliances with a wide range of other local and national organisations to develop mental health initiatives.

(DoH, 1994c, p. 27)

• For DHAs (with GP fund-holders), FHSAs, SSDs and service providers to seek local views from interested parties and, in doing so, maximising user involvement.

(DoH, 1994c, p. 59)

Mawhinney (1993a) reinforces this inter-agency emphasis with a seven stage approach to purchasing and contracting which requires identification and joint ownership of needs; shared vision and value system; shared service objectives; definition of service objectives and identification of key elements/indicators; shared construction of health gain investment programme including identification of indicators, measures, data sources and targets; joint management and information systems; and shared monitoring and feedback.

Such inter-agency agreement is crucial, especially between purchasers and providers of mental health services. The purchaser/provider split is not yet entirely clear. In general, elements within the NHS have made more progress in defining themselves according to this, whilst local authorities, in particular SSDs, have taken more time since the *NHS and Community Care Act 1990* to implement an internal market. Purchasers of mental health services include HAs, GP fund-holders as well as SSDs, whilst providers comprise elements within the NHS, SSDs and the voluntary/ independent and private sector (see G. Robertson and Tudor, 1993). Nowhere is this split more acute as regards mental health promotion than within Health Promotion Units, many of which fulfil the functions of both purchaser and provider.

A critique of the rigid purchaser/provider split is offered by the Association of Metropolitan Authorities (AMA, 1990, 1991), making the points that local authorities need to invest in 'the infrastructure of the voluntary sector' (e.g. training and other professional services) and that local authority grant aid should continue to have a significant role in funding projects. From the perspective of the voluntary/independent sector, many small organisations are wary of the professionalisation of their often unique services and burdened by the paperwork of the contract culture but, as C. Thompson (1989) points out, tempted by the chance of funding even if it diverts a group from its primary purpose.

Given *la politica*, the political and policy context of the distinction between the purchase and the provision of mental health services, it is important to consider the elements of purchasing strategy (4.1) as well as that for providing (4.2), and how they are brought together through contracting (5).

PURCHASING STRATEGY (4.1)

Mawhinney (1993c) sets out the British Conservative government's vision of purchasing for health in general; there are seven stepping stones which need to be present and by which it assesses and ensures effective purchasing through: strategy, effective contracts, knowledge-base, responsiveness to local people, mature relationship with providers, local alliances, and organisational capacity. (Unfortunately Mawhinney does not elaborate his metaphor by identifying the running waters over which his government is stepping.) The Royal College of Physicians' Committee on Health Promotion (RCP), in conjunction with the Society of Health Education and Health Promotion Specialists, propose various practical guidelines designed to promote health through the contracting process between purchasers and providers (RCP, 1992). Following *The health of the nation* and the *Key area handbooks*, these include the notion that purchasers themselves need to consider their own role as health promoting organisations as well as building that into contracts with providers (see pp. 156–159). In addition to those action summaries concerning purchasers seeking local views and developing local alliances, the *Key area handbooks* also contain specific guidance for purchasers on identifying and assessing available interventions; identifying research and development needs (dropped in the second edition); and importantly, agreeing strategies (albeit for service development in mental *illness*). South Thames RHA has drawn up a useful checklist for promoting mental health through purchasing with a view to purchasers developing a specification for mental health promotion 'based on understanding and quality communication' (South Thames RHA, 1994, p. 1). In developing local mental health strategies, purchasers also need to take account of the specific needs of particular groups, such as women (J. Williams et al., 1993).

In terms of resource allocation and investment, purchasers often identify particular groups on which to focus mental health promotion services. Whilst 'targeting' is pragmatic it is also problematic. One outcome of this approach to purchasing has been a focus on the mental health of mental health professionals. In ensuring that health promotion takes place through the mechanisms of contracts for services, the RCP (1992) identifies three groups as the focus of such contracting, prioritising the *employees of the providers*, over patients/clients of the providers, and the population at large. Whilst it is undoubtedly important that the NHS and local authorities promote the health of their employees, such prioritisation may be viewed cynically by under-resourced bodies outside these authorities (not to mention the staff within them). Surprisingly, the most promotional point of prioritising employees with the NHS and SSDs appears lost in the literature: that of these staff passing on good and positive (mental) health practice to the people with whom they work. In effect, this may be seen as MHP by example (some might say by stealth) and is the sort of mental health consultation advocated by Caplan (1970) (see Chapter 8).

In response to the requirements of the *NHS and Community Care Act*, *The health of the nation* and the *Key area handbooks*, different local models of purchasing have arisen, involving: locality managers (e.g. in Stockport HA); joint boards with the local Family Health Services Authority (e.g. Cambridge DHA), and/or involving 'reference groups' of key agencies (e.g. Sheffield DHA); and multi-agency health committees (e.g. Winchester DHA).

PROVIDER STRATEGY (4.2)

Very little literature exists on mental health strategy from the perspective of the providers. This is not surprising given the fact that strategies are driven by the necessity of economic management by purchasers, and given the weight of responsibility for activity placed on NHS and SSD managers particularly by the *NHS and Community Care Act 1990* and *The health of the nation: Key area handbooks*. Even the notion that provider units should include health promotion in all their contracts and their strategies for training and professional development comes within and is ensured by the role of the purchasers (RCP, 1992). Also, 'it could be incompatible for a voluntary organisation to be both a major service provider and act as a critic of current service provison' (C. Thompson, 1989, p. 2).

In a response partly to this lack of strategy, the Trent RHA's Mental Health Promotion Group conducted an exercise in 1993 which was subsequently developed by the author on a mental health promotion course. The exercise, involving providers, identified those providers across a range of services; identified the need for mental health promotion in the general population, of those in 'vulnerable groups', and those within mental illness/ psychiatric services; and then cross-referenced these with examples of mental health promotion (Table 6.2). Only one or two examples are given under each heading. Table 6.2 is intended for use as a framework for others to develop local strategy, sensitive to the ideas and practice of providers as well as the needs of specific local populations.

CONTRACTS (5)

The relationship between purchasers and providers is – or should be – expressed through contracts. The purchaser negotiates the contract; the provider defines their operational strategy in order to deliver the contract. In the context of the market economy, internal contracts, and the 'contract culture', the concept of contracts and contracting is worth considering.

Drawing on the parallel with legal contracts, Steiner (1971) outlines four basic requirements for contracts: *mutual consent*; *valid consideration*;

Table 6.2 Purchasing mental health promotion services – a provider's perspective

Provider	Promoting mental health amongst the general population	Promoting mental health of those in 'vulnerable' groups	Promoting mental health of those within mental illness psychiatric services
Healthy alliances	Through joint finance policy, information re. services on database with joint access	Through local needs assessment	Through promoting mental health status, Patients Charter, etc.
Health services GP services	Primary health care staff training in counselling skills, cultural awareness, etc.	Primary health care staff training in identification of predictive factors in suicide prevention	GP training re. prescribing practices sensitive to mental health status
Community services	Outreach work promoting 'emotional education'	Training CMH workers in tension and stress management	Provision of 'safe' havens (asylum in community)
Mental health services	Interventions designed to de-stigmatise mental health and illness	Counselling and psychotherapy services	Assisted and supervised living projects
Acute services	Mental health liaison nurses at hospitals	Identification of links between alcohol and mental health/illness	Access to psychiatric units for users, advocates and carers
SSDs	Comprehensive advocacy schemes	Fulfilment of all aspects of relevant legislation and policy on after-care	Comprehensive and rapid response to people in crisis
Voluntary/independent sector	Grants to support self-help groups	Secure funding for organisations such as Samaritans	Funding for specialist workers (e.g. for black clients)
Education departments	Curriculum development (Department of Education, 1993)	Counselling and psychotherapy services for children	Adult education within psychiatric hospitals
Housing departments	Staff training in mental health/illness	Emergency accommodation for people in crisis	Support for people in group homes
Trade unions	Raising awareness of mental health component of occupational health	Negotiation re. rapid access to appropriate counselling and support services	Negotiation re. 'sick leave'

competency; and *lawful object*. In the field of psychotherapy mutual consent involves a request for treatment, an offer of treatment and the acceptance of treatment. Valid consideration refers to the (mutual) benefits of the treatment (e.g. cure for money) or, in the case of mental health policy, the provision of services in exchange for a grant. Competency covers both parties' suitability, applicability and capability to deliver what is agreed. That contracts should have 'lawful object' reminds the parties that they are operating within the laws of the land, although the contracts may not be legally binding – as in the case of NHS contracts. Berne (1966) identifies three levels of contract for the psychotherapist in private/independent practice to have with their patients: *administrative*, to do with the practical demands of the therapeutic situation; *professional*, the potentialities and limitations of the treatment; and the *psychological*, involving those aspects 'which become part of the therapeutic struggle' (p. 20). Both Steiner's four requirements and Berne's three levels are usefully applied to contracts between purchasers and providers. The concept of competitive tendering for services has the elements of mutual consent: from the notice inviting tenders, through the submission of a proposal to its acceptance. Valid consideration of the mutual benefit is defined in the negotiated and agreed contract (administrative level). Prior to signing the contract the purchaser must satisfy themselves as to the competency of the provider/s (professional level), whilst the whole process is framed by legislation and policy. The parallel in the field of mental health policy and strategy of Berne's 'therapeutic struggle' is often expressed in practice by a breakdown in services or funding and is usually a result of a lack of clarity in the contracting process. Given that according to Berne (1966) 'the behavioral outcome of an ulterior transaction is determined at the psychological level and not at the social level' (p. 227), this is unsurprising. In order to make the process of contracting as explicit as possible, again we draw on the psychotherapeutic literature on this.

James (1981) formulates six questions as foundations for effective contracting:

> What do I *want* that would enhance my life?
> What do I *need* to do to get what I want?
> What am I *willing* to do?
> How would I measure my success?
> How might I sabotage myself?
> If I do, what positive steps can I then take?
>
> (James, 1981, p. 174, my emphases)

The changes of verb in the first three questions are significant: from wanting something (desire) to the identification of a need to fulfil that want (thought) to a willingness to do something (action). The measurement of success in achievement is important in terms not only of intra-psychic change but also of the external, social change observers see and measure. In working with individuals in psychotherapy these questions have the advantage of informing the therapist and the client – and in group psychotherapy each member – of their contract as well as its behavioural manifestation and possible sabotages at the psychological level. This approach to and process of contracting applies equally to individuals, groups (Berne, 1966) and organisations (Berne, 1963).

In mental health policy, contracts not only lie at the centre of the whole process of mental health policy, but also define the relationship between purchasers and providers. Although along with the finance the purchaser has the purchasing power, it is the provider who has the knowledge of their field and is often in the position to write their own service specification. Contracts vary and various government policy documents give direction on different aspects of contracting. The policy guidance on *Caring for people* (DoH, 1990a) makes the point that contracts reflect the relationship between purchaser and provider:

> those contracts which are based on partnership arrangements are likely to be strong on intended outputs and outcomes for clients, and to be flexible – those contracts covering highly standardised activities and negotiated following a highly competitive process, are likely to contain more detailed specifications in terms of inputs and process and to leave less scope for flexibility.
>
> (DoH, 1990a, p. 42)

Mawhinney (1993a) focuses on the principles underlying contracting, suggesting seven imperatives for making the mechanisms of purchasing and contracting happen: better working between purchasers and providers; the involvement of both doctors and nurses (i.e. the providers of services); realism about activity and the impact of change; appropriate contracts; robust information on prices and activities; and effective monitoring. From a provider's perspective, Lishman (1989) suggests some key points for contracting including good standards of quality; overall service design; relevant structure; proper budgeting; consideration of the implications of any reorganisation for employment and property including the transfer of both; and monitoring.

Contracts bring together many of the elements of mental health policy, translating objectives, via strategy, through indicators and specific service agreements into practice.

TARGETS AND INDICATORS (6)

That services need to be evaluated is a fact of life. The fact of evaluation, as with other 'facts', can be approached from different methodological perspectives – from the objective (nomothetic) to the subjective (ideographic). In *la politica* of MHP, the polarities of this horizontal axis are represented by various terms and debates about measurement and methodology.

First the terms. A target is something to aim at (perhaps on the basis that if you aim at nothing you will hit it!). It has a specific end point, usually measured in time, quantity, etc. Internationally, the WHO's (1984/1991b) *Health for all targets* are an influential example of targets and, nationally, *The health of the nation* (DoH, 1992) provides one target which can be taken as a target for MHP: that of improving the health and social functioning of mentally ill people. Similarly, an indicator provides a point against which to measure achievement (or failure). Although they are often used interchangeably, the difference between the two terms is that whereas the implication of establishing or agreeing a target is that someone or the provision of some services will hit it, an indicator is more something which measures the progress towards the target. A measure is an instrument by which we can ascertain the quantity or quality of an input, process or outcome, by comparison with a fixed unit or starting point. Whilst targets are predictions (one senior health service manager was quoted as saying that *The health of the nation* targets are acts of faith), services are evaluated retrospectively. Thus, for example, the WHO's target 2 – Health and quality of life: 'by the year 2000, all people should have the opportunity to develop and use their own health potential in order to lead socially, economically and mentally fulfilling lives' (WHO, 1984/1991b, p. 23) is a *target*, something at which, in this case member states, agree to aim. The *indicators* by which the WHO assesses this target to be achieved include a greater emphasis on the quality of life in the provison of care, amongst others (for details of which see Appendix 2).[3] The *measures* by which this particular target could be assessed include those discussed and produced by McDowell and Newell (1987), Fallowfield (1990) and Bowling (1991) (see also Baldwin et al., 1990).

This apparently straightforward example and scheme, however, has many complex implications. Targets need to be agreed and to be compatible at all levels – international, national, regional and local. This alone requires political understanding and economic resources, both of which are sadly lacking in the field of MHP. Thus, the WHO's target 2 is much broader, both in vision and application, than *The health of the nation* which applies the 'target' of health and social functioning only to mentally ill people. Worse, the British government has set *no specific targets* for improving health and social functioning, even in its limited application to mentally ill people – which, given its prioritising of this group in the population, reveals the paucity of its policy on MHP. Two sets of conferences on, respectively, the measurement and common profile of 'mental health', organised jointly by the Faculty of Public Health Medicine, the Royal College of Psychiatrists and the DoH (Jenkins and Griffiths, 1991; S. Griffiths et al., 1992) are further examples of lost opportunities – at least, as far as mental health is concerned. Similarly, the Health Education Authority (HEA) in its most recent five year strategy has 'to be determined' as its health education targets for improving the health and social functioning of mentally ill people (HEA, 1993b). Measures require a fixed starting point which, in turn, requires a level of assessment to ascertain, for instance, people's existing quality of life, from which improvement and the achievement of targets (or not) may be measured. (The issues involved with assessment across a range of mental health needs and of populations are considered in Chapter 7.) Where people start, as well as what people want to achieve are also subject to differences, economically, politically, socially, geographically, etc. Even agreeing the starting point and the end point of a particular strategy, the measures used in assessment are subject to methodological differences, such as the quantitative/qualitative debate in research circles. The RCP (1992) acknowledges these differences in relation to health promotion in distinguishing between *measures of process* (e.g. the percentage of a staff group involved in health promotion activities); *measures of impact* (e.g. the percentage of the public attending a particular event); and *measures of outcome* (e.g. changes in health-related knowledge of a target group), all of which are indicators. These indicators are applied by MacDonald (1994a) in his report for the HEA on evaluation methods used in MHP. Finally, the magnitude of the problem of applying measures to targets is represented by the fact for *one* target (the WHO's target 2), *six* broad indicators are noted, for *each one of which* there are any number of measurement scales, questionnaires, grids, etc. – and an equal number of concomitant controversies.

In response to the government's restricted thinking in its green paper on *The health of the nation* (DoH, 1991), MIND (1993c) put forward a number of alternative 'key targets':

- to realign resources currently spent on specialist psychiatric services into local community based services
- to create access through every GP surgery to a range of options for people in mental distress (including counselling and information on self-help groups)
- to ensure that affordable housing, with support where necessary, is available to people with mental health problems by the year 2000
- to reduce levels of unemployment amongst people who have/have had a psychiatric diagnosis
- to provide all children with education geared to helping them look after their mental health, by making this part of the national curriculum.

Although monitoring is, properly, one aspect of evaluation (see pp. 166–167), the prerequisites for monitoring, such as quality standards, volume specification, cost per volume (Christmas and Ewles, 1992), as well as monitoring methods such as quality tools, spot checks, reports, review meetings, peer review/audit, special research/evaluation projects (Christmas and Ewles, 1992) are worth noting. The criteria by which MHP is measured need to be consistent with and relate to the principles and objectives of the policy. On the quantitative end of measurement scale, increase in investment and/or activity may be targeted for future evaluation. One example of this is the joint strategy agreed between the Sheffield Health Authority and two departments within Sheffield City Council, namely Family and Community Services and the Housing Department. In the section on mental health, action for 1994/95, the planned investment and activity increases (totalling £244,000) are noted alongside the summary of strategy. Each element of the joint mental health strategy is therefore costed and serves for subsequent evaluation. On the qualitative end, there is a parallel between the debates about the quality of life, its definition, targeting and measurement and those about the quality in and of service provision (e.g. Clifford et al., 1991; H. Smith, 1992; Audit Commission, 1993; C. Murray et al., 1993).[4] The AMA identifies two key components to quality: the *fitness of purpose* or appropriateness of a service (including its 'fit' or consistency with its policy objectives); and the *standards* of a service which, in turn, comprise both values/policy objectives (e.g. choice, responsiveness) and practice requirements (e.g. consistency, courtesy) (AMA, 1991).

The North Western Mental Health Promotion Group (1994) argues that there is a need for local approaches to target setting, identifying a number of considerations, including the following three.

First, the *extent of local control* over factors affecting target achievement, such as the extent of 'isolation and disaffection within our society which local policies will have only limited power to change' (p. 47). Regional and local variations in unemployment and homelessness will also affect the impact of local policies and need to be taken into account when setting targets.

Secondly, *other important local objectives for mental health*. This raises the issue of the allocation of limited resources. Should aiming to meet *The health of the nation* targets divert resources from financing other mental health services (such as secure units for mentally ill offenders)? The answer to this dilemma lies in the separation of mental health promotion from mental illness prevention and the provision of mental illness services. Each needs to be resourced. Ultimately it is for national and local politicians to allocate resources for each, without setting one against the others or subsuming one within the others.

Thirdly, *reducing local inequalities*. Local strategies need to balance the need between reducing inequalities between district and region, between region and the rest of the country, and between different and particular groups.

SERVICE AGREEMENTS (7)

Service agreements or service specifications describe the elements of services required such as those promoting mental health promotion, and usually include details about quantity and quality and how these are to be monitored. Service agreements, therefore, are in effect a subset of contracts. They are drawn up usually as a result of consultation between purchaser and provider and define the services to be provided and purchased in a particular geographical area, such as a DHA or local authority for a particular period, usually a financial year.

Service agreements should include a statement of purpose which again should be consistent with overall principles, objectives and policy, and should include targets, indicators and outcomes by which the service will be evaluated. It should include the terms and conditions by which the service is provided and its cost. The more specific the service agreement the more likely it is to be implemented. Detailed service agreements may include principles of policy such as accessibility as well as principles of practice such as the provision of advocacy services; details about the provision of assessment procedures, information and research; requirements for training, etc. Birmingham City Council SDD provides a comprehensive example of a service level agreement (reproduced in AMA, 1991).

IMPLEMENTATION (8)

In terms of the macro scheme (Figure 6.1) this element is the least written about and yet the most important as it is the delivery of *la politica* in practice. That implementation or delivery is the most important element of a mental health policy is not a statement which prioritises pragmatism over principle. On the contrary, it is an assertion which acknowledges the fundamental purpose of any mental health policy: that of increasing the mental health of the population. That it is implementation about which least is written is unsurprising given that to date mental health promotion as a concept has been open to wide interpretation: equally, claims as to its practice have been varied and various. Table 6.3 shows my analysis of the presentations at three years of the annual Promotion of Mental Health Conference. Presentations subsequently published (see sources in Table

Table 6.3 Analysis of presentations at the annual Promotion of Mental Health Conferences 1991–3

Source	Mental health promotion		Mental illness prevention/ mental health promotion		Mental illness prevention		Not relevant to either	
	no.	%	no.	%	no.	%	no.	%
Trent (1992b)	18	53	7	21	4	11	5	14
Trent and Reed (1993)	17	30	18	32	8	14	13	23
Trent and Reed (1994)	10	28	16	46	2	6	7	20

Table 6.4 The elements of mental health policies

Principle	Objective	Policy		Strategy
		Principles	Practice	
Coping: To maximise people's individual coping mechanisms	To educate people about the effects of tension and stress	Co-ordinated services	Promotion of coping and stress management	To provide services (e.g. stress management courses)
Self esteem: To maximise individual's self-esteem	To increase awareness of the factors which contribute to the development of self-esteem	Co-ordinated services	Promotion of self-esteem in a variety of settings	To encourage participation in activities which develop individual's self-esteem
Self-development: To maximise people's mental health and well-being	To increase awareness of the factors which affect emotional well-being	Comprehensive and co-ordinated services	Promotion of mental health in a variety of settings	To encourage participation in activities which develop people's mental health and well-being
Social change: To maximise the abilities of individuals and communities to participate in assessment and planning	To effect social change	Comprehensive, co-ordinated and accessible services	Promotion of social change	To encourage participation and empowerment

Indicator/s	Targets	Service agreements	Implementation	Evaluation
Percentage of the population who have developed their coping skills (WHO, 1984/1991b, Targets 2, 16 and 25)	To have stress management courses in all workplaces (WHO, 1984/1991b, Target 14)	To be agreed between local businesses (purchasers) and various providers	Design, negotiation and delivery	Through monitoring of physical activity, social interaction, coping mechanisms and stress scales
Percentage of the population who have positive self-esteem (see Chapter 7, Table 7.2; MacDonald, 1994b)	To have facilitated staff support groups in the NHS (see WHO, 1984/1991b, Target 36)	To be agreed between the local HA (purchaser) and the provider/s e.g. Health Promotion Unit/independent consultants	Design, negotiation and delivery	Through quantitative measure, e.g. volume of input, numbers involved and qualitative measures (see Table 7.2)
Percentage of the population who have a concept of well-being (WHO, 1984/1991b, Target 2)	To have 'emotional literacy' (Steiner, 1984) as an integral part of the school curriculum	To be agreed between the local HA (purchaser) and the provider/s	Design, negotiation and delivery	Through quantitative measures, e.g. numbers of staff and pupils involved, and qualitative measures, e.g. focus groups, and regional HA lifestyle surveys
Percentage of the population involved in organisations and/or movements for social change (see WHO, 1984/1991b, Targets 1, 2 and 24)	To adopt community planning approaches to all MHP initiatives (see WHO, 1984/1991b, Target 24)	To be agreed and implemented by the local HA in respect of all providers	Design, negotiation and delivery	Through quantitative and qualitative measures of process

6.3) are allocated according to their own references to mental health and/or mental illness or neither.

As may be seen from Table 6.3 the number of presentations and the percentage of the total presentations specifically and directly concerned with MHP has fallen over the three years of the conferences, with a total of only 37 per cent of presentations concerned with MHP. In the first volume (Trent, 1992b), in which contributions were subdivided between theoretical issues, research and programmes, of eleven contributions classified as programmes only two are unambiguously about mental health promotion (Chwedorowicz, 1992; Sloboda and Hopkins, 1992) whilst three focus exclusively on preventive programmes and five on a mixture of promotion and prevention (the other contribution being about local policy rather than a specific programme).

EVALUATION (9)

As has been indicated, a comprehensive evaluation of any particular mental health policy needs to consider the complete policy from principles onward and, in particular, needs to be based on identified targets and indicators. On the second, general point, the AMA (1991) similarly regard quality as a cycle: from quality policy through quality assurance and quality service to *quality audit* which in turn influences quality policy. Evaluation is generally about measuring outcome against the target at which the policy was aimed or against the indicator indicated, although Day and Klein (1984) argue that there is a crucial distinction between 'input' and 'outputs'. Thus, standards may be as equally measured in terms of appropriate staffing levels and suitable physical environments as the production of adequate levels of care or service provision. Using paradigm analysis, evaluation also involves a critical self-reflection: a reflexivity which evaluates each element of mental health policy.

This kind of reflexivity is in stark contrast to *The health of the nation* in which the DoH somewhat apologetically proposes an unquantified target for improving health and social functioning. It then rather unfortunately draws attention to this by two statements remarkable only for their ignorance of conceptual and practical realities. The first attempts an unsubstantiated connection between services: 'the professional and service developments which will be necessary to progress towards the suicide targets will also have a broad beneficial effect on health and social functioning' (DoH, 1992, p. 84). This implies that services designed to intervene in and to prevent suicides will have an effect on services designed to promote the health and social functioning of mentally ill people – which, by and large, do not exist. The DoH goes on to claim that: 'success in meeting targets for improving the health and social functioning of mentally ill people will mostly be achieved by continuing developments in the services provided by the NHS, social services and others' (Ibid., p. 85). This is startling; in its complacency that such existing services will have this effect, in its arrogance in that success is defined and described by service development rather than an individual's development, and in its paucity in that in its inability to identify any specific targets for health and social functioning let alone MHP, the DoH reveals its intellectual bankruptcy. Instead of promoting health and mental health, *The health of the nation* 'perpetuates a medical view of mental illness and adopts a rather crude and unhelpful fixation on suicide rates as a proxy for mental health' (AMA, 1993, p. 35).[5]

CONCLUSION

The British government has no mental *health* policy. Its mental illness policies, and in particular community care, have been sacrificed on the ideological altar of the free market economy. The word 'sacrifice' is not used lightly. That community care is failing is principally due to lack of economic resources, with dire and sometimes mortal consequences for individuals with mental illnesses, their carers and, in some instances, the general public. The answer to the problems of community care is not, as the government appears to react, met by ever more coercive measures which only pander to the worst myths about mental illness. Genuine MHP policy would begin by responding along the lines suggested throughout this present inquiry, for instance, as regards the priority of de-institutionalisation over de-hospitalisation.

Critical, reflexive analysis – in this case on existing mental health policy – is needed not only in order to distinguish the elements of social policy on which it is possible to draw but also in order to clear the ground for mental health policy which genuinely promotes mental health. Table 6.4 outlines four examples of mental health policy (representing the four paradigms), with reference to the elements outlined in this chapter.

Having discussed all but one of the elements of mental health policy, mental health assessment is now considered (Chapter 7).

7 Mental health assessment

In Chapter 6 the various elements of positive mental health policy were outlined and connections made between them. Mental health assessment forms another link in this schema and, indeed, needs to be seen in the context of a coherent and comprehensive mental health policy (see Figure 6.1). The criteria for assessment need, for instance, to be written into contracts and service agreements. They influence indicators and targets. However, the concept and practice of mental *health* assessment has a particular association with mental illness and its assessment. Thus, as with discussion of other developments in the field of mental health promotion (MHP), this chapter wrests mental health assessment from the context of mental illness by, first, acknowledging the mental illness context of mental health assessment. Following this, and an introductory discussion of needs assessment, new directions for the assessment of mental health which draw on and develop notions defined in Part I (in particular Chapters 3 and 5) are proposed as reference points for the many existing measures of mental health. Mental health assessment is considered in terms of individuals, groups and communities.

MENTAL HEALTH (ILLNESS) ASSESSMENT

In general usage, mental health assessment is, in fact, an assessment of a person's mental illness or mental illness status. Under the *Mental Health Act 1983* (the MHA), for instance, one of the duties of the approved social worker (ASW) is to co-ordinate the process of a *mental health* assessment. This mental health assessment involves (or should involve) the ASW and one or two doctors (depending on the situation), the patient's nearest relative, other relevant parties and, of course, the individual patient. The objective of this assessment is to consider all the relevant factors of the subject's situation into account; to 'consider and where possible implement appropriate alternatives to compulsory admission' (DoH/Welsh Office, 1993, p. 4) and to do so in compliance with the MHA.[1] Similarly, at the other end of the process, when a patient is due to be discharged from psychiatric hospital, a multi-disciplinary care-planning meeting should be held to decide the after-care plans with and for the patient (MHA, S.117; DoH/Welsh Office, 1993). Importantly, the relevant health and social services authorities should agree procedures for after-care and have joint plans for after-care which implies a level of joint organisation, maintenance and review of 'needs assessment' of psychiatric patients. Developments since the MHA have consolidated this (see Chapter 6). The assessment of mental health (illness) needs now takes place in context of the *NHS and Community Care Act 1990* which provides a structure within which the health needs of defined individuals and populations have to be assessed and packages of services planned, purchased and provided (see Chapters 4 and 6). That this system is breaking down is the subject of widespread criticism (e.g. Association of Metropolitan Authorities, 1993; Utting et al., 1994).[2]

There is no reason (other than a lack of political and financial commitment) why the care planning and case management model of managing mental illness services may not be transferred to mental health, its assessment and promotion. Assessments of individuals – and, indeed, of groups and communities – could be made, according to the principles, objectives, policies and strategies of the particular service; needs identified; contracts negotiated; targets and indicators set. Service agreements could also be agreed, including the provision of resources, that is the allocation of funds and an appropriate nominated person such as a clinical co-ordinator or consultant to manage or supervise the process. Each element of a mental health policy could thus be implemented through to evaluation.

The two assessments – of mental health and mental illness – could, of course, go hand in hand if clinicians and managers grasp the concept of the two continua (Minister of National Health and Welfare, 1988). Macias (1994), for instance, reports an evaluation of a case management model in the United States which was implemented *in conjunction with* psychosocial rehabilitation. After a year, consumers were found to be functioning at a higher level of competency and experiencing lower levels of psychiatric symptoms. Psychosocial health is an integral part of mental health and is affected by psychological stressors and social conditions. Commenting on a lifestyle survey, Blaxter (1990) links psychosocial health with class, concluding that 'over 60, and especially over 70, class differences in the more subjective dimensions of health – illness and psychosocial health – continued to be great, and indeed it was amongst the most elderly people that psycho-social health differed most' (p. 66).

MENTAL HEALTH NEEDS ASSESSMENT

In a guide for people wanting to promote healthy communities the Ministry of Health (in the Canadian Province of British Columbia) (undated) defines a need as 'a problem or barrier that makes people or communities less healthy than they could be [and/or] a situation that causes pressure, or interferes with optimum health' (p. 11). Bradshaw (1972) identifies four dimensions or types of need, each identified by different methods:

- *normative need* identified and defined by 'the powers that be' who establish the norms
- *felt need* what the individual or community states (usually in the form of solutions rather than needs)
- *expressed need* inferred by observation (e.g. of attendance rates)
- *comparative need* identified by examining and comparing different services.

Needs are, of course, potentially limitless and thus there is a relationship and often a tension particularly between expressed need and felt need identified by clients and normative need and comparative need as identified by 'experts'. In the original article, Bradshaw develops a taxonomy of social need which represents the interrelation between the four definitions of needs and whereby 'real need' may be identified. H. Graham (1992), however, highlights the dangers of framing professional judgements – and, for that matter, decisions and resources – in terms of needs. Accepting them 'on face value as authoritative statements of fact' (p. 58) neither addresses the value position from which needs are made or what may be in the best interests of all concerned. Pickin and St Leger (1993) suggest one way out of this dilemma: 'essentially, health needs assessment is the process of exploring the relationship between health problems in a community and the resources available to address those problems in order to achieve a desired outcome' (p. 6). They go on to suggest there are three elements of health need assessment: health status measurement; ways of maximising health gain (e.g. through health promotion); and the measurement of health resources (e.g. through existing health services, local authority and voluntary/independent sector provision). In all of these both quantitative and qualitative research needs to be used: 'quantitative research will tell you how many people in a locality "need" different kinds of services; a qualitative approach will give you a sense of the range of health needs in a locality and the strength of feeling about different issues' (Ibid., p. 37). Applying this to mental health, there is a need:

- to develop mental health status measurements in terms of perceived mental health status and positive mental health indicators (rather than focusing on the incidence of mental illness)
- to find ways of maximising mental health gain (e.g. through health promotion initiatives in MHP)
- To measure mental *health* resources in public, voluntary/independent and private sector provision.

These three elements are expanded.

Mental health status

Mental health status is predominantly linked to mental illness and its incidence, the classic example of this being in *The health of the nation* (Department of Health [DoH], 1991) and even in economic approaches to health promotion (e.g. Godfrey et al., 1989).

Mental *health* status refers to the overall mental health experience of a population ascertained through formal and informal research. Such research is based on conceptualising and measuring mental health in terms of psychological manifestations such as the quality of life rather than physiological states. Most indices of mental health or psychological well-being are incorporated into studies of general, health-related quality of life – a perspective which may be conceptually coherent but, again, one which is often to the detriment of clarity and specificity about *mental* health status. The McMaster Health Index Questionnaire (Chambers et al., 1976), which measures physical, social and emotional functioning, for instance, has twenty-five emotional function items including self-esteem, feelings towards personal relationships, etc. Perhaps the most widely-applied measure of psychological disturbance (and health) in Britain is the General Health Questionnaire (Goldberg, 1978; Goldberg and Williams, 1988), used in relation to measuring psychological well-being in the context of MHP by Moore and McAdoo (1992) and Daniels and Coyle (1993). Although it limits respondents to assessing the effects of *illness* on behaviour, the Nottingham Health Profile (NHP) (Hunt et al., 1986) is a widely accepted questionnaire designed to measure the health status of a population. The second part of the NHP asks about seven areas of performance in life affected by health: employment, looking after the home, social life, home life, sex life, hobbies and holidays – thereby ascertaining some information about mental health. In a paper reviewing their work, the authors of the NHP suggest that it contributes, amongst other things, to:

> the identification of individuals and groups who may be in need of care . . .; the development of social policy . . .; mass aspects of the evaluation of health and social services; [and] the identification of consumer concerns.
>
> (McEwan et al., 1987, p. 601)

The most comprehensive and specific study in this field is the Rand Health Insurance Study (HIS), an eight volume series which covers all aspects of health: physical, physiological, mental and social health as well as perceptions of health. The volume on mental health (J.E. Ware et al., 1979/1987) includes literature reviews on mental health and on measurement and an HIS Mental Health Battery (MHB) comprising forty-six questions designed to ascertain subjective general well-being. The HIS MHB is designed:

- to elicit specific constructs such as positive well-being and self-control
- to measure positive and negative definitions of mental health (i.e. ill-health)
- to be valid in association with anxiety and depression scales – which has the advantage of being sensitive to the distinction between mental health and mental illness. Thus the levels of well-being and functioning of depressed patients, for example, has been researched by A.L. Stewart, et al. (1993).

More work in terms of research design is needed in order to prioritise mental health status – either within overall health status or separately – and in linking mental health status with socioeconomic factors. An unemployed miner may not see the immediate relevance of an assertiveness course for men; he may be more focused on his changed social status and relationships; further he may be exhibiting signs and (psychiatric) symptoms of concern to health professionals. K. John et al. (1987) suggest that the psychosocial status of the general population may be assessed by using three types of measurement: measures of subjective well-being; social adjustment scales, 'measured in terms of either the ideal or actual norms of his or her referent group' (p. 133); and psychiatric screening instruments. A combination of schedules, questionnaires, etc. from the three approaches will provide a comprehensive assessment of the psychosocial/mental health status of a population.

Mental health gain

Based on a base assessment of mental health status, mental health gain measures the mental health gain in individuals, groups and communities of policies and practice interventions. Thus, many of the scales, schedules and questionnaires referred to in this chapter operate on a 'before and after' basis, being administered before the implementation of a policy or intervention and then again after – and the gain measured. There is also a need for disadvantaged groups to 'gain' equity and, therefore, a need to monitor health potential and quality of life targets (McDowell and Newell, 1987; Fallowfield, 1990; WHO, 1984/1991b).

Mental health status and mental health gain has, thus far, been considered predominantly in relation to individuals. To some extent the situation as regards groups and communities may be totalised and generalised from research on numbers of individuals. Nevertheless, such wider groupings have their own systems which warrant further analysis (considered in more detail in Chapter 8). Mental health gain in the workplace, for instance, arises from addressing organisational issues as a priority, as distinct from individual issues (see Chapter 3).

In terms of the community focus of health promotion, the Province of British Columbia Ministry of Health suggests that any health promoting group will be working simultaneously on two tasks: 'to gather many perceptions of health needs – facts, opinions, and resources; [and] to gain public acceptance that health needs are *real* and that they *matter* [in order] to determine community priorities and gain commitment' (undated, p. 11, original emphases). Such gathering of community opinions commonly takes place through surveys of individuals, the organisation of focus groups, the identification of key members of the community whether leaders, initiators, influencers, etc. or the most disadvantaged. The community as the context for health promotion is described by Maccoby (1988) and the process of facilitating community participation in MHP has been discussed (in Chapter 4).

Mental health resources

An increasingly popular method of determining mental health (illness) needs is the use of registers of patients; their use in health services planning and research has been identified (Wing, 1989). Focusing on individual needs, again there is no reason (apart from the lack of commitment noted above) why a similar register may not be kept of resource needs for MHP, whether normative, comparative, felt or expressed, whether identified by request from clients or by professionals, such as coping skills, stress management and self-development groups, input to develop social support in a local community, etc.

There now exist a number of mental health resource directories which provide information, linking individuals to resources. The problem with many of these (unsurprisingly) is that they often list more resources for mental illness and its prevention than for the promotion of mental health and that they lack conceptual clarity in their layout. The implication of this current work is that such information and resources are more clearly and thoroughly edited and organised to focus attention on MHP resources. They would therefore exclude (or place under a suitable and separate entry), for instance, Community Mental Health Centres unless they offered some form of mental health education/promotion or consultation to the community (see Chapter 8). They would include, for instance, contacts for user groups promoting the mental health of the mentally ill; local counsellors/psychotherapists who, as part of their work, offered, self-development groups promoting emotional literacy or somatic education, etc. Such information would also include resources which promote mental health in the workplace as well as initiatives, such as employee counselling programmes or arrangements, outside the workplace.

Having established the background of mental health needs, the scene is set for elaboration of genuine mental health assessment.

MENTAL HEALTH ASSESSMENT

Drawing on frameworks and discussions developed in Part I, two approaches to mental health assessment are proposed: an integrative approach (from Chapter 1) and one based on the eight elements of mental health (Chapter 3). Of course, these approaches and the scales, schedules and questionnaires referred to each carry their own meta-theoretical assumptions particularly as regards the essence of phenomena under investigation (ontological) (mental health) and the method(ological) nature of the measure (assessment). Statements such as 'Only I know what I need. Only I know what comprises my mental health. Only I know if I feel better' represent the subjectivist end of the dimension, whereas 'Mental health is definable and can be researched only empirically through data analysis' represents objectivist assumptions. Whilst both frameworks are integrating ones, they represent different points on this subjective–objective dimension, with the dimensions of integrative mental health more a framework for personal reflection, self-assessment and development (see Table 7.1), whereas the eight elements reflect a comprehensive and paradigmatic approach to mental health and its promotion, one which is more amenable to validated measurements. H. Graham's (1992, 1994) writing on the imaginative assessment of needs in mental health represents a middle point, using creative methods to ascertain subjective truths.

The dimensions of integrative mental health

The dimensions of integrative mental health – affective, behavioural, cognitive, physical, social, and suprapersonal (Groder, 1977) – may be used as an integrative framework for the mental health (self-) assessment of individuals, groups and communities.

G. Caplan (1961) views assessment in terms of the quality of ego structure and the stage of its development or maturity. Similarly, Winnicott (1988) suggests that the health of the psyche 'is to be assessed in terms of emotional growth' (p. 12). Thus, appreciation of child and adult development is central to any mental health assessment as are the cultural values of the assessor (G. Caplan, 1961). The need for this kind of assessment is noted by the Trent RHA Psychology Advisory Committee (1990) although, as with the majority of health authority documents regarding psychological and/or psychotherapeutic input which refer only to psychodynamic (or cognitive-behavioural) approaches, it discusses only psychodynamic assessment of people with long-term mental health (illness) problems. Table 7.1 represents a schema for self-development, based on the dimensions of integrative mental health, with reference to development, together with awareness and communication (or congruence, see Tudor and Worrall, 1994). Development refers to developmentally appropriate growth in each dimension; awareness to self-awareness of fulfilment or lack in each

Table 7.1 Schema for assessment of integrative mental health

	Developmental	Awareness	Communication	Measures
Affective				The happiness question (Gurin et al., 1960)[3]; Bradburn's Affect-Balance Scale (Bradburn, 1969)[4]
Behavioural				The Sickness Impact Profile (Bergner et al., 1981) measures health (and sickness) in relation to its impact on behaviour
Cognitive				Intelligence Quotient (IQ) tests[5]
Physical/ physiological				Many standard measurements of physical health, particularly in relation to functional ability[6]
Social				Quality of life measures (referred to above)
Suprapersonal[7] spiritual				

dimension; and communication to the ability to communicate (i.e. express) needs in each dimension. Whilst this may be completed on a purely personal (subjectivist basis), Table 7.1 also makes reference to various (objectivist) measures and scales, linking them to the integrative dimensions.

Several measures span two or more or a combination of dimensions. Andrews and Withey's (1976) seven point satisfaction scale is designed to combine a cognitive evaluation ('positive'/'negative') of feelings. The Sickness Impact Profile (Bergner et al., 1981) also incorporates questions on emotional well-being and functioning. The McMaster Health Index Questionnaire (Chambers et al., 1976) measures physical, social and emotional functioning. The Rand Health Insurance Study Batteries cover physical, physiological, mental and social health as well as perceptions of health. The General Health Questionnaire (Goldberg, 1978; Goldberg and Williams, 1988) is the most widely-applied measure of psychological disturbance and health in Britain – and, as has been noted, has been used in relation to measuring psychological well-being in the context of MHP.

The elements of mental health

The elements of mental health already identified (in Chapter 3) and developed (in Chapter 5) may also be used as a focus for mental health assessments. Each element is reviewed along with a number of relevant scales, questionnaires and schedules, thereby offering a comprehensive mental health assessment (summarised in Table 7.2).

Assessment of coping

There are a number of scales developed to measure functional ability, many of which focus on the elderly, disabled and ill (see Bowling, 1991). Amongst others, the Quality of Well-Being Scale (QWBS) (R.M. Kaplan et al., 1976) is designed to translate 'wellness' into an operationalised scale in which respondents are asked to indicate how they have coped with different symptoms/problems in the preceding six days. In the American Psychiatric Association's (APA, 1994) *Diagnostic and statistical manual of mental disorders* (DSM-IV), Axis V in its multi-axial diagnostic system is a Global Assessment of Functioning (GAF). This is used by the clinician to assess the patient's psychological, social and occupational functioning both currently and at the highest level of functioning in the past year. Although the GAF is a clinical assessment, it may also be – and is – used by many clinicians in conjunction with clients. In the field of mental illness, Clifford (1987) has developed a Problems Questionnaire (PQ), designed to enable an assessment of the problems of people suffering from long-term psychiatric disabilities; and, along similar lines, Clifford

Table 7.2 Summary of measures for mental health assessments

Coping	Quality of Well-Being Scale (R.M. Kaplan et al., 1976); Problems Questionnaire (Clifford, 1987); Social Functioning Questionnaire (Clifford and Morris, undated)
Tension and stress management	Social Readjustment Rating Scale (Holmes and Rahe, 1967); Severity of Psychosocial Stressors (APA, 1987)
Self-concept and identity	The Tennessee Self-Concept Scale (Fitts, 1965)
Self-esteem	Self-Esteem Scale (Rosenberg, 1965); Self-Esteem Inventory (Coopersmith, 1967); Culture Free Self-Esteem Inventory (Pro-Ed, 1981)
Self-development	Happiness Question (Gurin et al., 1960)
Autonomy	Ladder of Life (Cantril, 1965); Autonomy system (I. Stewart and Joines, 1987)
Change	Racket system (Erskine and Zalcman, 1979; Script system (Erskine and Moursund, 1988) and the alternative system (as above)
Social support and movement	Inventory of Socially Supportive Behaviours (Barrera, 1981); Interview Schedule for Social Interaction (Henderson et al., 1980); Global Assessment of Functioning (APA, 1994); Perceived Social Support from Family and Friends (Procidano and Heller, 1983); Perceived Social Support Network Inventory (Orritt et al., 1985)

and Morris (undated) have developed a Social Functioning Questionnaire (SFQ) to enable a detailed assessment of an individual's social functioning particularly for rehabilitation purposes, focusing on self-care skills, domestic skills, community skills, social skills and responsibility.[8]

Assessment of tension and stress management

The assessment of an individual's ability to manage tension and stress may be ascertained by using the seven stages (as outlined in Chapter 3). This will include (at stage 3) the identification of stressors through, for instance, the Social Readjustment Rating Scale (Holmes and Rahe, 1967) (commonly referred to as the stress rating scale) or the DSM-III (APA, 1987) Axis IV Severity of Psychosocial Stressors (for Adults and for Children and Adolescents). Whilst this is, again, intended to be rated by a clinician assessing the effect of the psychosocial stressors on the patient in comparison with an 'average' person, it may, like the Holmes and Rahe scale, be scored by the individual concerned. Holmes and Rahe note their concern that such a predictive measure could become a self-fulfilling prophecy and remind us of the preventive purpose of the scale.

Assessment of self-concept and identity

Based on Maslow's theory that individuals who are more self-actualising will develop their potential and function more creatively and effectively, Fitts (1965) developed and revised the Tennessee Self-Concept Scale, consisting of 100 self-descriptive items. Given that self-concept and its development is central to many psychological theories of development, adjustment and growth, each theorist and clinician will have an understanding of self-concept and an assessment of the process of its change. C.R. Rogers (1951), for instance defines the self as 'the awareness of being, of functioning' (p. 498) and develops a theory of how the structure of the self is formed and organised – and disorganised. He also reports extensive research on how the process of therapy affects self-concept (C.R. Rogers, 1951).

Assessment of self-esteem

Carl Rogers (1951) cites studies by which he confirms his thesis that clients perceive and evaluate themselves more positively as a result of therapy (e.g. Raimy, 1948; Seeman, 1949; Sheerer, 1949). Following Rogers and on the basis of describing self-esteem as self-acceptance (or positive self-regard), Rosenberg (1965) developed a ten item Self-Esteem Scale. In the same vein, Coopersmith (1967) has designed a Self-Esteem Inventory which measures attitudes towards the self, and Pro-Ed (1981) has developed a Culture Free Self-Esteem Inventory.

Assessment of self-development

The subjectivity which marks quantitative or qualitative considerations of self-esteem is also necessarily a feature of any (subjective) assessment of an individual's interest in and view of their self-development (see previous section). This may be initially in terms of pathology, for example Clarkson and Gilbert's (1990) confusion, conflict and deficit model, or sanology, for example Gurin et al.'s (1960) happiness question.

Asessment of autonomy

Cantril (1965) has developed a scale on which respondents range their actual conditions and their ideal situation in terms of satisfaction with life. Maslow's (1968) hierarchy of needs may be used similarly as an identification and assessment of need – from physiological needs to self-actualisation. As has been discussed (in Chapter 3), individual self-actualisation as a concept is culturally determined and needs to be mediated by relatedness or whanaungatanga (Barrett-Aranui, 1989). The autonomy system (I.

Stewart and Joines, 1987) or alternative system (also elaborated in Chapter 3) is one way of describing autonomy.

Assessment of change

Each school of psychotherapy has its theory of change. Used in relation to the racket or script system, the autonomy or alternative system is one way of describing individual change. Maccoby's (1988) model of change may be used as an assessment for change on an individual and a community level.

Assessment of social support and movement

Concern to assess levels of social support is expressed by G. Caplan (1974): 'the extent to which an individual perceives that his/her needs for support, information, and feedback are fulfilled by friends . . . and by family'. The Perceived Social Support from Family and Friends measure, devised by Procidano and Heller (1983) to assess the functions of social networks is a specific response to Caplan's concern. It has been updated by Orritt et al. (1985). Bowling (1991) reviews social-network analysis and the number of other measures measuring social support including the Inventory of Socially Supportive Behaviours (Barrera, 1981; Barrera and Ainley, 1983); and the Interview Schedule for Social Interaction (Henderson et al., 1980).

MENTAL HEALTH ASSESSMENT IN PRACTICE

In terms of practice, mental health assessment – of individuals, groups and communities by those involved as well as by a mental health consultant – may be summarised as a process comprising:

1 An identification of needs (felt or expressed).
2 An assessment of the meaning of these needs both in terms of the subject/client and in terms of the assessor/consultant. This, in turn, should include
  2.1 an acknowledgement of any sociocultural differences between the parties undertaking the assessment
  2.2 any differences between the parties involved in the assessment (e.g. between expressed and normative needs)
  2.3 any influences on the assessment (e.g. between expressed and comparative needs, including financial constraints).[9]
3 An assessment of the subject's mental health status.
4 A prediction of mental health gain. (In psychotherapeutic terms, this may be linked to the process of contracting – see Chapter 6.)

5 An assessment of the subject's resources, including those in and of the local community.
6 An assessment of the different dimensions of mental health and mental ill-health (as discussed on pp. 174–176, see Table 7.1).
7 An assessment of the different elements of mental health (as discussed on pp. 176–179 and, for the measures of which, see Table 7.2).
8 A conclusion which forms the basis for an overall mental health care plan and the response to which could form a mental health care package, the subject of mental health 'case' management/community development, etc.

8 Mental health consultation

Mental health consultation, as one of the essential ingredients of an organized program of community mental health, must articulate in a planned way with its other elements in forming a body of methods and techniques that are designed to fulfil the overall mission of promoting the mental health of the population and reducing community rates of mental disorder.

(G. Caplan, 1970, p. 35)

Following Caplan's influential work on mental health consultation, this chapter develops the notion and practice of mental health consultation as an essential ingredient of community mental health promotion. The chapter begins with a discussion of Caplan's definition of consultation, and of its methods and techniques. Its 'articulation' with other elements is explored through first, distinguishing between consultation, supervision and psychotherapy. The articulation of mental health consultation with other elements of mental health promotion (MHP) and the 'overall mission' of consultation are considered by means of a discussion which draws on the psychoanalytic tradition of organisational analysis and consultation, with specific reference to Menzies Lyth's (1959/1988) work on the dynamics of social and organisational structure. In concluding this chapter the paradigm framework offers a development of this analytic approach with case study examples of consultation designed to promote mental health, and to reduce mental disorder.

DEFINITIONS OF CONSULTATION

For G. Caplan (1970), consultation denotes:

a process of interaction between two professional persons – the consultant, who is a specialist, and the consultee, who invokes the consultant's help in regard to a current work problem with which he is having some difficulty and which he has decided is within the other's area of specialized competence.

(G. Caplan. 1970, p. 19)

Caplan's subsequent definitional elaboration of consultation can be summarised:

- Consultation aims not only to help the consultee but also to add to their knowledge.
- 'Mental health consultation is a method for use between two professionals in respect to a . . . client or a program for . . . clients' (Ibid., p. 28).
- The relationship between the two professionals involved is 'coordinate', that is non-hierarchical in terms of management authority.

In addition:

- The consultant is a specialist: 'the consultant must have expert knowledge' (G. Caplan, 1970, p. 28).
- The consultant has no administrative or coercive responsibility as regards the client.
- The consultant has no liability for outcome.[1]

G. Caplan (1970) also defines the remit of mental health consultation from the client/consultee's point of view:

the consultee's work problem must be defined by him as being in the mental health area – relating to (a) mental health disorder or personality idiosyncrasies of the client, (b) promotion of mental health in the client, (c) interpersonal aspects of the work situation.

(Ibid., p. 28)

It is the 'help *and knowledge*' aspect of Caplan's view of consultation that marks its importance for mental health promotion as, for Caplan, it is the educational aspect of consultation that makes it a community method, since 'its goal is to spread the application of the specialist's knowledge through the future operations of those who have consulted him' (Ibid., p. 20). It is this same view which attracts criticisms of elitism, for example from A. Brown (1984), who prefers a more (arguably, all-) inclusive definition that consultancy is 'any help which one person offers to another who has sought their help and advice, that is, has *consulted* them, *in a professional context*' (p. 3, original emphases). If Caplan's view is hierarchical, and Brown's egalitarian, it is Schein (1969) who emphasises the knowledge-in-the-client and the interaction or *process* between the consultant and the client. *Process consultation* 'is a set of activities on the part of the consultant which help the client to perceive, understand, and act upon process events which occur in the client's environment' (Schein, 1969, p. 9). These three definitions lead to different methods of consultation.

Method, techniques and skills

In elaborating these views of consultation, a distinction may be made between *method* as relating to methodology, the broad approach to any scientific investigation such as consultation; and, following from this, the *methods*, that is the techniques and skills employed to further the method.[2] Both method and methods of consultation, as in any other sphere of activity, follow explicitly or implicitly from its theory or conceptualisation. Thus, if consultation is about knowledge and expertise then the method will be concerned with passing on that knowledge or expertise from the expert whilst the methods employed will focus on the skills of teaching and communication. If consultation is about offering 'any help' then both the method and the methods required will be many and various. If consultation is about the development of a process then the method will focus on establishing, maintaining and reflecting on that, whilst the methods required will include diagnostic, communication and facilitative techniques and skills. As I have indicated, G. Caplan (1970), A. Brown (1984) and Schein (1969) represent, respectively, hierarchical, egalitarian and facilitative approaches to consultation.

Caplan's mental health consultation, whereby a relatively small number of consultants work with a large group or network of consultees is a method which has some merit in a community programme in terms of both influence and economy. One methodological implication of this view is that 'the amount of time devoted by a consultant to helping a consultee deal with the mental health problems of a current case must be relatively short, and there must be a maximum educational carryover to the consultee's work with other cases' (G. Caplan, 1970, p. 21). This, in turn, has implications for the supervision (as distinct from consultation) of the same mental health practitioner's clinical work. Caplan views mental health consultation as a method of communication. However, he is less clear about the particular techniques and skills required by the consultant in developing such communication for instance about their expertise, or in increasing the consultee's knowledge or skills, or in offering support or reassurance.

In contrast, A. Brown (1984) proposes no *method* (in our terms),[3] but many methods in consultation such as the use of counselling skills (problem-solving facilitation skills, confrontation, feedback, etc.) and other techniques such as role-play, sculpting, use of video and brainstorming. Kadushin (1977) produces evidence from American research studies which report that consultees tend to emphasise the importance of problem-solving. Brown's is an eclectic, supermarket approach to consultation and does not add to our understanding of mental health consultation; nevertheless, his particular and useful contribution is to emphasise the value of consultation in groups.

Following on from his definition of process consultation, Schein (1965, 1969) acknowledges his historical roots, elaborates his method as *process* and, in doing so, indicates his methods. He identifies the field of group dynamics, the study of group process, the development of group dynamics

Table 8.1 Distinctions between consultation, supervision and psychotherapy

	Consultation	Supervision	Psychotherapy
Primary goal	Increased effectiveness in the work setting	Increased effectiveness in the work setting	Cure or amelioration (variously defined)
Focus	On job performance (and not on sense of well-being: G. Caplan, 1970)[4]	On workload; on supervision and work matrixes (Hawkins and Shohet, 1989)	On past; on intrapsychic processes; on behaviour, etc.
Function	Facilitative; educational (G. Caplan, 1970); 'any help' (A. Brown, 1984)	Administrative, educative, supportive; encouraging objectivity (Westheimer, 1977)	Facilitative – on analysis, behavioural change, growth etc.
Selection	By consultee, on the basis of having relevant knowledge and competence	Allocated by role in organisation	By client, on the basis of knowledge and interview
Profession of consultant and supervisor	From same, related, or different profession	Same profession	Usually same profession and initially same 'school'
Entered into	Voluntarily	Compulsorily, usually as a requirement of role	Voluntarily
Payment	Fee charged, usually to organisation	No direct fee in public sector	Fee charged
Time commitment	Time-limited, by negotiation	Continuous activity	By negotiation
Agenda	Initiated by consultee	By negotiation, although supervisor may initiate 'overview'	By negotiation

Process	Help and knowledge (G. Caplan, 1970); facilitation to encourage the client's insight (Schein, 1969)	Learning within a 'therapeutic triad' (Hawkins and Shohet, 1989)	'Treatment' facilitating change; support
Responsibility for subsequent decision-making	Rests with the consultee	Is shared, according to role, and policy	Rests with the client
Responsibility to consultee, supervisee, client	Professional, subject to negotiation and contract	Administrative/managerial	Professional/ethical, subject to codes of practice
Accountability for work to others	None, unless negotiated	In turn to supervisor/line manager	No direct accountability, although usually to supervisor and to professional organisation

training, and the study of group and intergroup relations as direct influences on the study of organisational *and human* processes, arguing that:

> as long as organizations are networks of people, there will be processes occurring between them . . . the better understood and better diagnosed these processes are, the greater will be the chances of finding solutions to technical problems which will be accepted and used by the members of the organization.
>
> (Schein, 1969, p. 9)

The method is the process: 'the process consultant seeks to give the client "insight" into what is going on around him, within him, and between him and other people' (Ibid., p. 9). The methods (techniques and skills) required to facilitate such process consultation, focusing as it does on human actions, interactions, meetings and encounters at work, follow: communication skills, the analysis of roles and functions in groups, group problem-solving and decision-making skills and awareness of group processes. Schein develops each of these and describes particular process consultation interventions which he categorises (in order of preference) as agenda-setting, feedback, coaching or counselling, and structural (Schein, 1965, 1969).

Historically prior to Caplan and Brown – although apparently not influential on them: no references to Schein's work appear in either Caplan (1970) or Brown (1984) – it is Schein who synthesises the historical roots of the study of organisation. In doing so, he marks the conceptual link between organisational and human processes in the context of organisational development (OD) work, specifically through consultation. Before considering whether this can be considered as MHP, as a way of looking at the 'articulation' of consultation with other elements of MHP, consultation, supervision and psychotherapy are distinguished.

CONSULTATION, SUPERVISION AND PSYCHOTHERAPY

In defining mental health consultation, G. Caplan (1970) distinguishes it from supervision and psychotherapy.[5] Undoubtedly, there are aspects of supervision and psychotherapy which could be classified – and which would certainly be experienced – as promoting mental health such as the educative elements of Transactional Analysis. This and any of the eight elements of mental health identified in this work may be developed through psychotherapy, supervision or consultation or, indeed, other means. Nevertheless, as a method, each of these has different goals, focus, function, etc. (summarised in Table 8.1). It is only when the differences between them are identified that their interrelation and 'articulation' with each other may properly be seen.

The primary goal of psychotherapy, as Table 8.1 suggests, is cure or the amelioration of symptoms or, more vaguely, 'growth'. As has been indicated earlier (in Chapters 3 and 5), psychotherapy has elements of MHP and particular forms or 'schools' of psychotherapy focus on the promoting of mental health. Insofar as supervision is about coping with clients,

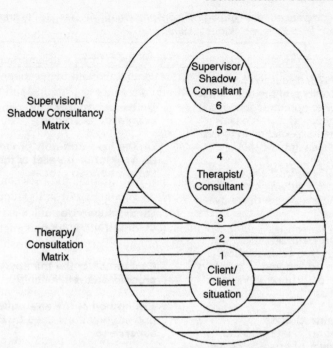

Figure 8.1 The double matrix process model of supervision and shadow consultancy
Source: Hawkins and Shohet, 1989; Hawkins, 1993

professional and self-identity and development, it is certainly a form of MHP and, although it is not usually viewed in this way, good supervision is often experienced as such. There is a developing literature on supervision to which Hawkins and Shohet's (1989) double matrix model has made a significant meta-theoretical contribution (see Figure 8.1 and Box 8.1). Of the three, and depending on the context, contract and circumstances, consultation is the most directly concerned with promoting mental health – of individuals, groups, organisations and communities. Hawkins (1993) has applied the double matrix model (Hawkins and Shohet, 1989) to supervision of the consultation or 'shadow consultancy'. The double matrix model is applied to both supervision and consultation (Figure 8.1).

This inquiry has stressed the methodology of reflexivity. Supervision is essential in facilitating this process. Good supervision is crucial to the development of a reflexive process in mental health promotion. Another reason for focusing on supervision is the element of mental health consultation and 'shadow consultancy'/supervision required in the role of the person promoting mental health (G. Caplan, 1970). Thus, people involved in MHP may be called upon to act as a consultant to a community group; a local religious leader may ask for advice about how to approach a particular mental health problem; a mental health social worker might ask for non-managerial supervision of their work.

Table 8.2 A comparison of a typology of consultation (G. Caplan, 1970) and foci for supervision (Hawkins and Shohet, 1989)

Typology of consultation	Foci for supervision
G. Caplan (1970) discusses the possible distortions of the consultant who 'may suffer from preconceptions and culturally based distortions of perception and expectation in regard to the consultees' (pp. 59–60)	**On the supervisor's countertransference** **On the here-and-now process as a mirror or parallel of the there-and-then process**
• **Consultee-centred case consultation**, in which the focus is on the consultee's difficulty with cases	**On the supervisee's countertransference**
• **Consultee-centred administrative consultation**, analogous to the above but with the focus on programming and organisation	**Exploration of the therapy/work process and relationship**
• **Client-centred case consultation**, relating to the management of specific cases	**Exploration of the strategies and interventions used by the supervisee**
• **Programme-centred administrative consultation**, focusing on the planning, management and development of specific programmes	**Reflection on the content of the therapy session/work**

G. Caplan (1970) identifies a fourfold classification of consultation which is summarised and compared with Hawkins and Shohet's (1989) foci for supervision (Table 8.2).

Box 8.1 The six modes of supervision/shadow consultancy in relation to mental health consultation

II   Focus on the supervisee/consultee's work as it is reflected in the super-vision/consultancy process

6 – Focus on the supervisor/consultant's (counter-transferential) feelings.

Here the supervisor/consultant reflects on their own feelings evoked by the supervisee/consultee's work 'to provide reflective illumination for the therapist' (Hawkins and Shohet, 1989, p. 58).

For example, a consultant reacts to a mental health worker's pressure of work and their busy response by deliberately drawing a deep breath.[6]

5 – Focus on the 'here-and-now' process in the supervision/consultation session as a mirror or parallel of the 'there-and-then' process.

For example, an officer working in a Health Authority is a consultant to a social worker having a similar brief in a social services department. Through acknowledging and reflecting on the competitiveness in their own relationship they identify areas of competition and conflict between the two organisations in which they work.

4 – Focus on the supervisee/consultee's (counter-transferential) feelings.

Here the supervisor/consultant attends to the conscious and unconscious in the work presented.

For example, by focusing on the language and metaphors used in supervision ('us', 'entrenched', 'them', 'the chronically mentally ill'), a member of a community mental health team highlights their own ambivalence about the work and ethos of the team.

I   The work presented by the supervisee/consultee is reported and reflected upon in supervision/consultancy

3   Exploration of the supervisee/consultee's own work – in terms of process and relationships.

Here, the focus is on the process (both conscious and unconscious), of the supervisee/consultee's work and the systems the supervisee creates with the client/s with the purpose of enabling the supervisee to develop greater understanding of the dynamics of the work.

For example, a mental health (illness) social worker realises in supervision that she has not been clear in establishing boundaries in developing a consultancy relationship with colleagues.

2 – Exploration of strategies and interventions used by the supervisee/consultee.

Here the focus is on the choices of intervention used by the supervisee/consultee.

For example, a mental health worker discusses options (a focus group, attending community meetings, meeting with user organisations, setting up a group, etc.) in promoting user involvement in planning mental health services.

1 – Reflection on the content of what the client/s presents.

The focus here is to enable the supervisee/consultee to become more aware of what actually takes place in their session/s with their client/s.

For example, a supervisee/consultee describes his client and tells the client's story.

MENTAL HEALTH CONSULTATION AS MENTAL HEALTH PROMOTION

Taking up the challenge of what Caplan views as 'the overall mission' – of promoting mental health and reducing mental disorder, this section first draws on Menzies Lyth's (1959/1988) work in developing analytic perspectives on the relation between the individual and the organisation within which they work and, secondly, develops her analysis, using the paradigm framework, presenting specific examples of mental health consultation aimed at promoting mental health and reducing mental disorder.

Anxiety and objectivity

Menzies Lyth's research, and in particular her classic paper on 'The functioning of social systems as a defence against anxiety: A report on a study of the nursing service of a general hospital' (Menzies Lyth, 1959/ 1988), develops Jaques's (1953) work on the dynamics of social structure by linking the objective situation of work with 'the phantasy situations that exist in every individual in the deepest and most primitive levels of the mind' (Menzies Lyth, 1959/1988, p. 46).

Menzies Lyth argues that 'the intensity and complexity of the nurses' anxieties are to be attributed primarily to the peculiar capacity of the objective features of her work situation to stimulate afresh . . . early situations and their accompanying emotions' (Menzies Lyth, 1988, p. 47). The intensity of the link between the objective and phantasy situations of nursing is due to the intimate nature of the work itself. Menzies Lyth's analysis is equally applicable to the functioning of social systems such as the organisation of community mental health (CMH) services, in which objective and phantasy issues all too often remain unaddressed such as mental health workers' acknowledgement of their own mental health, distress and dis-ease. In developing and applying her analysis to CMH, then, both the 'objective features' of the institutions and organisations of mental health as well as their capacity to evoke emotional responses in their staff need to be considered.[7]

The objective features of community mental health services

CMH has two primary tasks. The first is the promotion of mental health and the reduction of mental disorder or illness, as expressed through social welfare legislation and policies. The second is to offer a variety of personal, health/social care services to people of all ages, abilities and states of health who are in particular need or in special circumstances. The philosophy and principles of services are, however, as has been discussed, often at odds with increasing financial and ideological constraints. Thus, the first task is devalued and, in the process of carrying out the second task, social/health care managers and other staff may frequently be obliged to act against the express wishes of one person in the 'best interests' of another. This has led to other critiques of the nature and task of social and health services from predominantly two perspectives. The radical tradition conceptualises and contextualises the oppressive nature of social services (e.g. Corrigan and Leonard, 1978; Simpkin, 1979; Hoggett, 1990) and health services in relation to clients and workers. The (psycho)analytic tradition analyses the unconscious forces and motivations of health workers (Menzies Lyth, 1959/1988) and of social work and social workers (e.g. Guggenbühl-Craig, 1971/1978; Roberts, 1984; Lousada, 1993).[8]

The stimulation of early situations in community mental health

A crucial aspect of Menzies Lyth's analysis is that such intense anxiety can provoke regression to more primitive methods of defence, which are 'projected and given objective existence in the social structure and culture of the nursing service, with the result that anxiety is to some extent contained, but that true mastery of anxiety by deep working through and modification is seriously inhibited' (Menzies Lyth, 1959/1988, p. 64). Hoggett (1990), writing about public hostility to public service workers, suggests that the business of the welfare state is 'to satisfy need, develop human potential and alleviate distress whilst simultaneously managing our neediness, restricting our potential and concealing our distress' (p. 212). Another view is that institutions of social/health care have to evolve mechanisms with which to deal with *some* anxiety of staff at a certain level (e.g. through supervision), as the distress of a person with mental illness is, at least at some level, obvious. These same institutions however ultimately deny the *extent* and *intensity* of the anxiety because of the greater anxiety/fear: of individual psychological breakdown and/or the potential of individual reaction and collective action. Thus, whilst restricting the promotional aspect of the work or the opening times to the public may protect CMH workers from overload and some immediate anxiety, the greater anxiety of a (f)ailing system is still carried by individuals and may not be addressed at an organisational level.

Menzies Lyth (1959/1988) describes the principal mechanism by which the nurse/worker links and re-enforces her objective and phantasy situations:

the nurse projects infantile phantasy situations into current work situations and experiences the objective situations as a mixture of objective reality and phantasy. She then re-experiences painfully and vividly, in relation to current objective reality, many of the feelings appropriate to the phantasies. In thus projecting her phantasy situations into objective reality, the nurse is using an important and universal technique for mastering anxiety and modifying the phantasy situations. Through projection, the individual sees elements of the phantasy situations in the objective situations that come to symbolise the phantasy situations.

(Menzies Lyth, 1959/1988, p. 49)

Examples of this in CMH operate in two directions. People working in CMH may well project their own issues of, say, dependency on to their clients, thus rendering clients in some way more dependent. The rescuer role on Karpman's (1968) drama triangle appears to be an occupational hazard or even a professional proclivity, although as Menzies Lyth stresses, these projections and other defence or coping mechanisms described operate largely at an unconscious level. As the drama triangle suggests, the rescuer role can belie a more persecutory position, what Guggenbühl-Craig (1971/1978) refers to as the 'power-shadow': 'whenever something must be imposed by force the conscious and unconscious motives of those involved are many-faceted. An uncanny lust for power lurks in the background; dreams and fantasies show motives which consciousness prefers to ignore' (p. 8).

The other direction of projection is that by CMH workers on to their managers of, for instance, their own anxiety about competency. Thus social/health care workers may project their own feelings of incompetency and inadequacy on to their managers. Whilst we can view this as a projection of the worker's own defensive coldness in the face of pain and deprivation, it also protects the worker from the anxiety that their other projections – of incompetency, etc. – will destroy or provoke their managers.[9]

Organisation and institution

Having described mechanisms at work in the individual, Menzies Lyth moves from the individual to the organisation. She describes three factors important in the development of a social organisation:

its primary task, including such environmental relationships and pressures as that involves; the technologies available for performing that task; and the needs of the members of the organisation for social and psychological satisfaction and, above all, for support in the task of dealing with anxiety.

(Menzies Lyth, 1959/1988, p. 50)

Menzies Lyth, however, underplays the interrelation between these three factors of primary task, technologies, and needs and the extent to which the accomplishment of the organisation's tasks is limited in an era of legislation, increasing need and decreasing resources. These three factors are briefly considered in the context of CMH services.

As has been suggested, one of the primary tasks of CMH is to deliver the services which are set out in social welfare legislation. However, unlike in some other countries, British law in general and social welfare legislation in particular is not 'enabling' in that it does not enable, identify or release monies with which to implement the legislation. This contradiction has been openly acknowledged, for instance, in the *Code of practice* to the *Mental Health Act 1983*: 'this Act does not impose a duty to comply with the Code but failure to follow the Code could be referred to in evidence in legal proceedings' (DoH/Welsh Office, 1990, p. 1). At the same time: 'where adopting the recommendations of the Code would have significant resource implications, it is recognised that this can only be done *as resources permit*' (Ibid., p. v, my emphasis).[10] The contradiction between needs and resources has also been acknowledged in the changes made between the two editions of *The health of the nation: Key area handbook mental illness* (DoH, 1993b, 1994c). It is often the front-line workers who carry and 'contain' the anxiety of these contradictions.

As far as the 'technologies' in community mental health are concerned, Menzies Lyth generally discusses the social system as part of the technology, equating this with what is delivered, whether this is specific resources, the care management of individuals, or a particular therapeutic model. Roberts (1984), also drawing on Menzies Lyth, points out how individual social workers' response to institutional instability may take the form of obsession with technology and task: 'a slavish adherence to rules and regulations for safety's sake' (p. 45). On an organisational level, Critchley and Casey (1989) describe ways in which organisations get stuck in focusing exclusively on the task, becoming 'the task organisation'.

Social defences

Socially structured defence mechanisms are

> an attempt by individuals to externalise and give substance in objective reality to their characteristic psychic defence mechanisms. A social defence system develops over time as the result of collusive interaction and agreement, often unconscious, between members of the organisation as to what form it shall take. The socially structured defence mechanisms then tend to become an aspect of external reality with which old and new members of the institution must come to terms.
>
> (Menzies Lyth, 1959/1988, p. 51)

The socially structured defence mechanism or 'pathology' of the organisation is then the pathology of the sum of its individual members: in a sense defences and coping mechanisms are operated only by individuals. However, 'membership [of an institution] necessitates an adequate degree of matching between individual and social defence systems' (Ibid., p. 73). This then implies an existing social defence system, a collection of the sum and history of individuals' defence systems. The mechanism by which this is constructed and maintained is one of complex inter- and intra-psychic processes within the individual and between the individual and the institution which 'depend heavily on repeated projection of the psychic defence system into the social defence system and repeated introjection of the social defence system into the psychic defence system' (Ibid., p. 73). The institution seen, for instance, at interview is, including its social defence systems, part of the 'objective situation' for the candidate. The institution and its defence system is thus confirmed, re-enforced and introjected as such by the new employee: 'in the process of matching between the psychic and social defence systems, the emphasis is heavily on the modification of the individual's psychic defences' (Ibid., p. 74), rather than on organisational change.

Menzies Lyth distinguishes between defensive techniques through which the social defence system fails to alleviate (and indeed denies) what she refers to as 'primary anxiety' within the individual, and ways in which 'the social defence system itself arouses a good deal of secondary anxiety' (Menzies Lyth, 1959/1988, p. 65). Following Menzies Lyth, examples of social defences against *primary anxiety* are distinguished from the *secondary anxiety* evoked by the social defence itself. Thus, the social system of CMH functions in such a way as to deprive workers of necessary reassurance and satisfactions (primary anxiety). Roberts (1984), for instance, makes the point that social work organisations, as other institutions, are no longer felt as dependable – either by their clients or by their workers. Secondly, the social defence system itself through, for example, rivalries between a District Health Authority and an SSD over the management of a Community Mental Health Centre (CMHC), arouses a deal of (secondary) anxiety (see *Case example 4* below). Of the nine separate, although interacting, defensive techniques against primary anxiety and the four defences against secondary anxiety in the nursing service identified by Menzies Lyth it is possible to cite parallel examples in other settings, such as from SSDs (Embleton Tudor and Tudor, 1995).

Menzies Lyth's (1959/1988) analysis leads her to put forward the proposition: 'that the success and viability of a social institution are intimately connected with the techniques it uses to contain anxiety' (p. 78). Applying this to the 'social institution' of CMH, the relation between the promotion of mental health and the reduction or amelioration of mental disorder and primary and secondary anxiety, may be expressed in terms of primary and secondary prevention thus:

Primary prevention/	Secondary prevention/
Mental health promotion	Reduction of mental disorder
encompasses the	encompasses the
alleviation of	alleviation of
Secondary anxiety	Primary anxiety

Edwards (1989) views mental health consultancy as an example of preventive psychology – secondary prevention.

It is, according to Menzies Lyth, the intense anxiety evoked by the nursing/social/health care task which precipitates individual regression to primitive types of defence (see Chapter 3). It is the fact that Menzies Lyth writes in terms of 'intense anxiety' and 'primitive types of defence', that places this primary anxiety more within the range of secondary prevention (although some types or forms of defence may be viewed and 'prevented' within the scope of primary prevention – indicated in parenthesis in Table 8.3). These individual defences are then projected and given objective existence in the social structure and culture of the particular service under analysis. The socially structured defence system fails to support the individual thereby arousing secondary anxiety as well as failing to alleviate primary anxiety. The focus here is on the institution/organisation. The fact that its social defences evoke secondary anxiety is fundamentally an organisational issue (most of Menzies Lyth's examples of secondary anxiety are organisational) with personal implications for those affected. As such it is subject to diagnosis, analysis, intervention and change: organisational mental health promotion (primary prevention). The fact of the system failing to alleviate individuals' primary anxiety is also an organisational issue but one which has an exacerbating impact on

Table 8.3 Application of primary and secondary anxiety to primary and secondary prevention

Primary prevention/Mental health promotion	Secondary prevention/Reduction of mental disorder
(Individual and group primary anxiety)	Individual and group primary anxiety
	Case example 1: Peace-making in a conflictual relationship
(Individual and group secondary anxiety)	Individual and group secondary anxiety
	Case example 2: The 'anxious team'
Organisational social defences/ secondary anxiety	(Organisational social defences/ secondary anxiety)
Case example 3: The approved social worker, the 'mad' hospital and the mental health assessment	
	Organisational non alleviation of primary anxiety
	Case example 4: The Community Mental Health Centre

individuals and is therefore placed within the secondary prevention. Taking into account the different foci on the individual (or group) and the organisation, this application produces the matrix (Table 8.3) in which reference is made to the case examples of mental health consultation described on pp. 198–205.

By way of introducing the case examples of mental health consultation as interventions aimed at alleviating primary and secondary anxiety in the context of MHP, some limitations of Menzies Lyth's work are reviewed.

PSYCHE AND SOCIETY

Menzies Lyth (1959/1988) presents her conclusions in terms of the importance of analysis, insight and an understanding of anxiety as a defence in the functioning of a social institution as 'an important diagnostic and therapeutic tool in facilitating social change' (p. 78), but gives no details of how this insight is applied as a therapeutic tool. Reference is also made to the restructuring of social defences, although again no detail is given. Earlier she comments that due to the structure and culture of the (nursing) service 'true mastery of anxiety by deep working through and modification is seriously inhibited' (Ibid., p. 64). Whilst it may be that this is desirable, if indeed acknowledged and requested by nurses, health and social care workers, etc., Menzies Lyth's focus on the individual (nurse), precisely and ironically re-enforces the individual and individualising approach which her work on social defences appears to confront. The social defence is an extension of the individual defence. Such analysis locates the problem and the pathology in the defence and, ultimately, in the individual. It is an approach which epitomises Menzies Lyth's analytic inheritance and its fundamental pessimism is summarised in her concluding paragraph: 'it is unfortunately true of the paranoid-schizoid defence systems that they prevent true insight into the nature of problems and realistic appreciation of their seriousness' (Ibid., p. 81).[11] Developing this, Hoggett (1990) suggests that public service workers need to retain the Kleinian 'depressive position' in order to maintain 'a commitment to the object in spite of its damaged state' (p. 216), the 'object' in this case being the damaged institutional 'bodies' of a benign welfare state. If welfare workers are unable to maintain such a commitment and remain unsupported they may well turn on the damaged bodies of their clients. In the context of the destructuring of the welfare state through successive rounds of financial cutbacks, the increasing distance between central and local government, and the damage to workers within institutions and organisations such as health authorities and SSDs, we should perhaps not be surprised at the public rejection of the mentally ill or their physical abuse by carers. Indeed, as Hoggett (1990) implies by linking these points, such reactions may exemplify the true primary task of social services: to oppress through amelioration. Workers 'constitute an institutionalized buffer between the blandness and complacency of public life and the intensity of private and privatized need and distress. . . . For many workers, lacking adequate resources or institutional support, this pain must be quite unbearable' (Hoggett, 1990, p. 212).

For a more explicit statement about effecting change we must turn to Menzies Lyth's own source. Jaques's (1955) statement that 'effective social change is likely to require analysis of the common anxieties and unconscious collusions underlying the social defences determining phantasy social relationships' (p. 24) provides a clear direction for the consultant and an echo of the analogous paradigm movement from functional analysis to social change. Indeed Jaques makes a useful distinction between manifest change (in the organisation's structure, culture, etc.) and change at the phantasy level, arguing that both are essential. Whilst individuals may master their anxiety through deep individual work, through supervision, support groups and even counselling, analysis or psychotherapy, the concern here is to focus on the more systemic response of process consultation within an organisation. Brearley (1985), also drawing on Menzies Lyth in describing her own experiences of consultancy, suggests that 'we need a psychological model of the individual and an organisational model of the institution which are mutually consistent'. Menzies Lyth's work, in itself, is ultimately lacking in providing an adequate conceptual *and practical* framework for individual and organisational change. Others from different theoretical backgrounds offer analysis of and practice for change in organisations (e.g. Merry and Brown, 1987; Stein and Hollwitz, 1992) and consultation (e.g. Colman, 1992; Alevras and Wepman, 1994).

As with the other developments of MHP in this enquiry, the work of Burrell and Morgan (1979) is used. It is particularly pertinent in this context as their work is on organisational analysis. The four sociological paradigms are taken as a metaphor and a 'map' to describe the movement of individuals, groups and organisations from individualising symptom (anxiety) to collective, organisational action. An individual's development and/or change over time is analogous to movement between paradigms: a movement, as it were, from psyche to society. In organisational analysis and mental health consultation a similar movement is proposed: from Menzies Lyth's *analysis* of symptoms (the defence system of the organisation); through an understanding of the *meaning* that organisation holds for individuals working within it, as well as for the organisation itself; through a sense of individual *desire* (what do the elements of the organisation want of themselves, others and the organisation?); to collective *social action* (how can we/do we change the organisation?). Whilst it is unrealistic to claim paradigmatic change in all cases (let alone change through three or four paradigms), the paradigm map can be used as one in which psychological models of individual and organisation are identified as consistent (or inconsistent), and as vehicles for effective personal and social change.

Case example 1: peace-making in a conflictual relationship[12]

The situation

The manager (X) of an organisation in the voluntary/independent sector (dealing with aid to developing countries) was experiencing difficulty with a particular member of staff (Y). The manager described Y as unmanageable, as Y disagreed with everything he said and would not take his directives. X recognised that Y was a good worker, being competent at her job, but was getting increasingly angry and despairing about her resistance to and rejection of his proper authority as her manager and as director of the organisation. X called the consultant as 'a mediator', and Y had agreed to this process.

The consultation

The consultant met X and Y for three sessions. She commented on the fact that they had both acknowledged that there was a problem and agreed to some 'mediation'. X and Y then proceeded to air their grievances which, initially, took the form of complaining about each other to the consultant and referring to a number of incidents in the past about which one or other had felt resentful (and had not said anything). They each blamed the other and each said they felt in 'a double-bind' with no way out. Each acknowledged that this situation was affecting not only their work but also their lives outside work; towards the end of the first session Y commented that 'this seems bigger than both of us'. They each went away from the first consultation session feeling quite pessimistic about whether they could ever resolve their differences. It was clear to the consultant that each party was extremely distressed by this conflict and that the situation was evoking intense anxiety which was affecting their social and personal functioning.

At the beginning of the second consultation, the consultant commented on the nature of their work, co-ordinating aid to developing countries. X and Y both responded by saying how difficult the work was at present, given the political situation in many of the countries with which they were involved. They both felt angry about situations such as war and conflicts which were beyond their control and acknowledged their feelings of impotence and impotent rage. The consultant then commented on how they appeared: as 'they', as 'both', as united in the face of a common enemy (war, poverty, famine, etc.) and as having much more energy than in the previous session. Both X and Y then talked much more about their personal anxieties in response to the work they did. In doing so, and supported by the consultant, they acknowledged the political realities with which they were dealing *as well as* their own reactions and personal sociopsychological histories in response to these realities. In effect, they each acknowledged how much they projected their individual reactions and defences (for X isolation and introjection and for Y identification and displacement) on to not only the social and political world but also on to and into their working relationship, thus giving their defences 'objective existence' in their relationship. From being angry at the world to feeling personally and professionally stuck, both X and Y realised how much energy they had invested in their own conflict.

Although in the first two sessions X and Y had done most of the analysis of their problem and had given meaning to their conflict; they agreed to come to the third session as negotiated. This focused on what they each and both wanted and what they were prepared to do (thus completing their journey through the paradigms). In this third session they also looked at their differences, including that of gender, both as representative of and as a parallel to the conflicts in the world with(in) which they worked.[13] This led them to make certain agreements: the manager agreed to trust Y with work he delegated to her and Y agreed to report in more detail, including about any area of difficulty she experienced. They also reflected on the parallel between conflicts in the world and inner conflicts and the impact this had on the social structure and culture of the organisation and agreed to review this on a regular basis. They each reported generally feeling better, being able to detach themselves from work and having more fun in their social lives.

Reflection

The consultant had realised the significance of the theme of conflict from the initial referral when the manager talked about 'mediation' and from the context of the work. This also came at a time of various high-profile peace negotiations about conflicts in the world. The content of the first session paralleled the lack of understanding, history, mistrust, blaming and intran-sigence common in such situations. This consultation is identified as concerned with secondary prevention partly due to the timing of the work: the consultant was not initially contacted to promote the mental health of the relationship or of the organisation; and partly due to the degree of dysfunction engendered by the situation. It is identified as an example of consultation focusing on primary anxiety as the anxieties were clearly within the individuals concerned and which had not been identified or alleviated by the organisation. The fact that, as a result of this consulta-tion, the role and defences of the organisation would be reviewed on a regular basis was an important conclusion to the work.

Case example 2: the 'anxious team'

Situation, consultation and reflection[14]

The staff of a hostel for single people recovering from mental illness was in conflict with their senior management, based elsewhere, about the fact that the manager and her team had not responded to repeated requests from the senior manager that they submit detailed proposals for developing the service offered to the clients to include some off-site support and co-operation with staff from other teams and agencies. *The staff team was the identified client and 'problem', being seen as rather anxious and precious about their independence. The warden was seen by senior management as ineffectual, i.e. not 'managing' the ('objective') situation. The senior management wanted a particular and defined outcome which was essentially about regulating the staff and the warden. The problem presented was thus firmly within the functionalist paradigm.* When the consultant met the team of eight for the first time they appeared anxious and defensive and were reluctant to focus on the identified issue and gave routine answers to his questions. The warden without prompting informed the consultant several times that it was 'an excellent team', that they 'pulled together' and that there was a low rate of staff sickness. The warden was described by the staff as 'wonderful' and as 'having a tough job on her hands' (i.e. dealing with the managers). The staff team identified the problem as lack of support from senior management and the lack of co-operation and interest of staff in other teams. *The staff team and the warden too, were operating from within the functionalist paradigm, describing the problem, and labelling themselves and blaming the behaviour of others. Their primary defence lay in idealising the warden, minimising doubt and conflict, maintaining their feelings and position of powerlessness ('They tell us which clients we have to accept into the hostel'), and focusing on the 'objective', social regulatory task of running and overseeing the hostel.*

The consultant asked the team to focus on two pieces of joint work between hostel staff and field social workers: one in which their experience had been negative (deskilling and disabling) and one positive (promoting skills and enabling). Much time was spent listening to each individual describing their interactions with their colleagues and what this meant for them. *Here the consultant was facilitating the staff as individuals and as a group to shift their position from a purely descriptive and blaming mode to one which acknowledges interaction and meaning. The consultant's listening encouraged them to share and acknowledge their subjective experience (rather than claiming it as 'objective' reality – an analogous movement to an interpretative paradigmatic position.* The consultant also worked explicitly on the team's subjective image of the senior management (Berne, 1963, 1966).

After further work the consultant, through a series of short, focused exercises, encouraged the staff team to draw up a list of developments and changes they would make 'if we could'. *Here, the staff team, by focusing on 'what they want' was operating in a way which is analogous to the radical humanist paradigm.* This was picked up by the team which began to make requests of the consultant (e.g. to help them with their negotiation with senior management). At this point the consultant also offered to work individually with the warden, acknowledging her desire for change as well as her different subjective experience from that of the team.

The team then initiated changes by selecting two particular areas for potential development, planning the action in terms of content and process, anticipating problems and arranging dates. For his part, the consultant also agreed to take up with senior management appropriate organisational issues such as support and lack of key policies *The effectiveness of this approach can be seen in this final analogous movement into the radical structuralist paradigm of social action and objective change.*

Throughout this piece of work the consultant used the paradigm map within which to use a variety of theories and hypotheses as well as his overall experience of the team. Boundary issues (both in form and content), and anxiety about the clients' and individual team members' mental health were acknowledged, interpreted and explored in the changes the staff team made. They began by being seen and seeing others as individual (and individualising) 'symptoms' or 'problems'; they then explored what this really meant to and for them; after formulating their desires, they finally identified and took appropriate action as a team and were able to respond with some thought, enthusiasm and creativity to requests made of them by their manager and to initiatives from other teams. That this is an example of secondary anxiety is evidenced by the fact that the social defence system of the organisation, through lack of management, support and clear policies and, indeed, by labelling the team as 'anxious', had itself evoked a deal of ' secondary' anxiety in individuals.

Case example 3: the approved social worker, the 'mad' hospital and the mental health assessment[15]

An extremely distressed and angry patient/client, in need of a mental health assessment involving a psychiatrist, was held – by security guards and the illegal use of drugs, in the casualty department of a general hospital. Some of the hospital staff and the hospital authorities wanted to move the patient against his will (and, therefore, illegally) to a psychiatric hospital for assessment.

The approved social worker (ASW) on duty confronted these and other proposed illegal actions.

As a result of these confrontations it transpired that the hospital had no available psychiatric cover. The hospital authorities, unable to provide a psychiatrist of their own, initially refused and eventually agreed to ask a psychiatrist from another hospital (and Health Authority) to attend to make an assessment.

The ASW and others then spent time organising the people necessary to make a mental health assessment under the *Mental Health Act 1983* (MHA), including contacting a psychiatrist from another hospital.

As this agreement was reached it transpired that the second hospital (and Health Authority) had refused to provide psychiatric cover for the first hospital due to administrative and political disagreements. The hospital authorities at the first hospital then came up with various 'solutions' to the developing crisis (including that they should discharge the patient and then call the police to remove him from the hospital premises). These solutions attempted to 'solve the problem' by shifting the psychiatric responsibility to other hospitals and authorities. The patient had by then been held in the casualty department for eight hours.

The ASW who, in addition to his clinical responsibilities, was now acting as a consultant to this process, confronted these attempted 'solutions' by questioning how this situation – of lack of psychiatric cover and of ignorance of the law amongst key hospital staff - had arisen in the first place.

As a result of this questioning the first hospital's senior administrators and medical management were involved and eventually resolved the crisis by formally requesting a psychiatrist from the second hospital to participate in the assessment.

After the incident (the patient was admitted to a psychiatric hospital under S.2 of the MHA), the ASW and others concerned took up this and other related issues at a senior management level within the social services and the health authorities in order to effect changes of policies so that there would be no repeat of the situation. This is a classic example of an organisation's social defences in action (and reaction to) a crisis. It is a case of unnecessary secondary anxiety (i.e. lack of policies, planning, training, etc.) which exacerbate the situation for the patient and all concerned. It is classified as MHP/primary prevention specifically in relation to the institution and the organisation of its services. The ASW's role as consultant focused in the short term on confronting the institution's social defences ('mad', crazy-making ones at that) and, in the longer term, on institutional/organisational responses which were legal and appropriate and promoting of mental health.

Case example 4: the Community Mental Health Centre

The situation

A CMHC was planned which would principally accommodate a social services mental health team together with a health services team of community psychiatric nurses (CPNs) as well as some other health service staff. These two groups had been working in the same community over a number of years. There had always been some mutual suspicion (projection) and rivalry (splitting) between the two, which the design, planning and consultation process in relation to the CMHC did nothing to alleviate. The whole process described may be set against the background of the wider funding, management and administrative issues as regards CMHCs (discussed in Chapter 4).

The capital expenditure on this CMHC was almost exclusively funded by the local District Health Authority (DHA); the SSD contribution was promised but withdrawn, a state of affairs seized upon by some of the health authority staff as (further) evidence of a lack of commitment by the SSD and its staff and, indeed, resented by the DHA which picked up the extra expenditure. The design and planning stage had gone badly. Neither the community nor the staff had been consulted either about the location of the CMHC or its design. The result was a certain amount of hostility on the part of the local community, and anger from users about its inaccessibility. This was exacerbated by some glaring design faults, such as a lift far away from the entrance, thus creating further problems of access for some clients. The establishment of the CMHC coincided with cutbacks in both authorities. Thus, what had been some (covert) anxiety about possible conflict, for instance, about roles, management, organisation, accountability, referrals, systems, etc. escalated into overt competition for jobs. In an attempt to involve people involved more widely, DHA and SSD management (which was also in some conflict about a number of other issues in the field of mental health) then threw open the consultation process. The result was that bitter disagreements erupted between the two teams about the style of chairs and the colour of carpets (symbolically reminiscent of Gilbert and Sullivan's famous carpet quarrel which, in effect, ended their collaboration). This was the point at which joint training for the two teams had been organised.

The initial consultation

The consultation began when the joint training, perhaps not surprisingly, had broken down as a result of poor attendance on the part of the CPNs which was traced back to their manager's resentment, repressed and 'acted out' in not informing staff about training dates.

The trainer, now consultant, set up a series of meetings with the various parties involved, including user groups (who had been denied office space in the CMHC). He quickly established that there were several defences in operation. There was a widespread denial of differences ('We've all got the same goal in sight', 'We all want what's in the best interest of the clients') alongside a lot of splitting along professional lines, for instance about counselling (not quite but almost as crude as 'Social workers do counselling, CPNs don't': the fact that neither profession is trained as counsellors *per se* seems to have escaped their attention). There was a general repression of feelings, as well as a number of projections of fantasies about others and introjections of doubts about self and 'our side'.

Reflection

The consultant considered that many of the problems identified predated the planned CMHC. They were, in effect, primary anxieties carried by individuals concerned with their work and future: job security, changing and future roles, professional identity, management, etc. These anxieties had been manifested by the staff involved through discontent, posturing and positioning, in increased sick leave, and by numbers applying for jobs elsewhere. Their primary anxieties had not been alleviated by their organisations.

The consultation (continued)

As a result of this analysis, the consultant decided to encourage those involved (the social services mental health team, the CPNs, other health services staff, DHA and SSD management and users) to take a step back by initially working with them separately. In doing so, he asked them to focus on their current difficulties and dissatisfactions. Some of these were with 'the others' but there were a number of other unresolved issues within the respective authorities. He then reintroduced the joint training in stages and over specific issues. These were, by and large, well attended. From these, a small representative group were nominated to co-ordinate the remaining planning issues and decisions about the CMHC.[16]

SUMMARY

Mental health consultation varies in terms of how it is conceptualised (including its methodology) and introduced into a situation, and as far as the methods used and its focus are concerned. This chapter has drawn on the historical roots of mental health consultation and has developed its conceptualisation in terms of the four paradigm analysis.

The introduction of consultation varies; in the first two case examples the consultant was called in explicitly as such; in the second two the person who acted as consultant began in a different role and, in each case, had at some point to renegotiate their role, task and focus. In these particular cases (3 and 4), the consultant was internal, that is an employee of the authority concerned; otherwise there might also have been a financial implication and a renegotiation.

In terms of methods, the examples cited reflect more of a 'process consultation' (Schein, 1969) than, say, A. Brown's (1984) skills-based approach. The focus also varied: in the first, with two individuals, the consultation focused initially on their relationship; in the second, with a team, on their relationship with others; the third on a process and the institution involved; the fourth with an issue between two teams representing two authorities being refocused on existing issues.

Having developed the field of MHP attention so far in Part II, attention now focuses on the individuals doing this work, the disciplines upon which they draw, their professional allegiance/s and their training and learning.

9 Mental health education and training

The final development in the emerging field of mental health promotion upon which this work reflects is that of learning and training. This chapter begins by considering the implications of what has been described, throughout the book, as community mental health promotion work, with a discussion of the role of those involved in community mental health promotion (CMHP) in a variety of applications and settings. The characteristics of CMHP are defined as are the different levels of MHP. Special consideration is given to radical perspectives on CMHP. Following this, in the spirit of reflexivity, I reflect on the mental health promotion (MHP) courses I have designed and led. The chapter concludes with consideration of the issue of the disciplines involved in promoting mental health and discusses whether mental health promotion should be seen as and become a separate discipline and profession, or whether it is a concept and practice which integrates various disciplines through specific processes, policies and programmes.

COMMUNITY MENTAL HEALTH PROMOTION: PRACTICE AND PARADIGMS

It has been argued throughout this book that there are many different and differing approaches to CMHP – which may be located within Burrell and Morgan's (1979) four paradigms for the analysis of social theory. The four paradigmatic views on CMHP are briefly summarised as are their implications for the person promoting community mental health (CMH).

In his work on community dynamics and mental health D. C. Klein (1968) identifies various functions of the community, including the facilitation of the resolution of conflicts, the education and acculturation of newcomers, and the provision of opportunities for interaction between individuals and groups. It follows that someone fulfilling these functions would need facilitative and teaching skills with a view to maintaining the boundaries of the community and its functions; and educating and instructing individuals and groups in how to maintain their own and the community's mental health, through, for instance, tension and stress management skills and coping skills. The focus for MHP would be on behaviour and attitude modification, based on a norm or ideal of mental health.

Elsewhere Klein suggests that 'it is important that the mental health worker raise the question of meaning with himself' (1968, p. 25) – the meaning, that is, of community, their own sense of community, their attitudes and responses. This raises important issues of what sense the person promoting mental health makes of the community, how they communicate that, and to whom (discussed in Chapters 4 and 8). Within approaches which take more account of meaning and interaction there is often a shift away from a narrow 'medical' view, a shift represented by Ashton and Seymour (1988), who, working within a 'Health for All' framework, advocate an expansion into the five areas of self-care; integration of medical care with other related activities; integration of the promotion of health with preventive medicine, treatment and rehabilitation; meeting the needs of 'under-served' groups; and community participation. The skills required to do this work are generally more therapeutic, reflective and interactive (than didactic) and include an ability to help individuals and groups to identify and value themselves. Here the mental health worker is interested in promoting people's (subjective) understanding of themselves and others and, therefore, in self-concept, self-identity and self-esteem.

A third paradigmatic approach to CMHP emphasises a participative and collaborative relationship with individuals, groups and communities. Here the CMH works *with*, rather than *for* or *on behalf of* individuals and the community. Promotion and 'education' (literally, a 'leading out') take on a more radical libertarian, problem-solving perspective. The mental health worker takes account of people's subjective experience of themselves, others and the environment as well as their views about what it is that they want to change. Whilst the therapist focuses on individual change, the radical CMH worker is concerned to generalise and to 'collectivise' individuals' experiences and, in terms of McPheeters' (1976) strategies, is generally more concerned with the environment and its relation to mental illness and mental health. Much of the CMHP work undertaken in Salford through the appointment of the first Health Promotion Officer (Mental Health) has been based on fostering the notion of the competent individual acting and active within a competent community (Holroyd, 1991). The skill-base of the person working within this approach to CMHP needs to include therapeutic skills and competence in areas of self-development such as emotional literacy and assertiveness, as well as in promoting autonomy and interrelatedness.

The fourth approach is one in which CMH workers understand the relationship between mental health and mental illness, dis-ease and distress in terms of oppression and exploitation arising from structural differences and conflicts within society on the basis, for instance, of class, race and gender. Approaches to this work are influenced by the notion of empowerment, developed by users and survivors of the psychiatric and mental health system (see Chapter 5). CMH workers develop new services and promote awareness and initiatives, which make existing services more accessible, and which empower users; often by forming alliances of users which challenge health care and local authorities as well as social structures. This approach lies at the heart of mental health promotion work in Salford where there has been an emphasis on the involvement of users of services and other members of the community. To enable effective communication and consultation a self-help network has been established:

> minimised dependence on statutory care and maximising self-coping mechanisms will diminish the likelihood of future need . . . one of the most effective ways of doing this has proved to be through a series of self-help groups co-ordinated by a central body, the Salford Forum for Mental Well-being.
>
> (Holroyd, 1990)

Holroyd also suggests that the strengthening of community action aids effective mental health promotion precisely through the participation and involvement of the community, taking control and power over its activities and initiatives. As people experience these activities and struggles they themselves gain experience of change and social support and movement. A framework for describing the interface between various elements of radical practice forms Appendix 3.

By now the reader will recognise the broad outline of these different approaches. The usefulness of the paradigm framework is apparent. The reality is that people involved in CMHP do have conflicting approaches. Rather than arguing one approach over another ('My approach is better than yours'), it is more conceptually coherent and more useful in practice to be aware of differences, not least so as to be able to develop practice and theory. For CMHP to have any form and meaning, let alone become a discipline, or an interdiscipline, it must comprise more than ill-informed or atheoretical eclecticism:

> *it is very important to recognise that choice of a particular theoretical stance is not merely a technical decision: in the human sciences it implies moral commitment to a certain interpretation of what is to be human and to be involved in various kinds of social structure.*
>
> (R. Holland, 1991, p. 3, original emphasis)

Drawing these considerations together with the characteristics for community sociopsychology (Chapter 5), the requirements or specification, then, for anyone seriously involved in or wanting to promote coherent initiatives and interventions in CMHP include

- knowledge and awareness of salutogenic models of mental health
- ability to work with individuals, groups and organisations

- abilities to apply and promote a wide range of interventions and activities (e.g. formulating policy, and in assessment, consultation and training/education)
- abilities to promote a range of positive mental health skills
- ability to be self-reflective at a level of practice, process and meta-theory.

The first four points have been discussed in this inquiry. The last point deserves some elaboration.

The paradigm analysis and framework presented in this work may be viewed as operating on the three levels of content, process and meta-theory. This is conceptually coherent as well as highly practical. In terms of content, the four paradigm analysis provides a framework within which to describe different theories, elements and practices of MHP and CMHP. This is linked to the meta-theoretical level, as it is the analysis of the meta-theoretical assumptions implicit in definitions and descriptions, by which these are located within the four paradigms. The third level – of process – describes the level of interventions made in order to promote the mental health of individuals, groups, organisations, communities, etc.; this level includes the analogous movement through the paradigms described by the Hollands (S. Holland, 1985, 1988, 1990; R. Holland, 1990c, 1992) and others. Of course, there is also a meta-theoretical level at which the assumptions underlying *processes* may be analysed. Meta-theory, then, is that theory which distinguishes various orders or forms of content and process/es in order to understand their relation to each other, whether complementary or conflictual. The dynamic relationship between these levels may be represented as shown in Figure 9.1.

From this it follows that there are three definitions of MHP. As argued earlier (in Chapter 3), this inquiry does not seek to define the content level of MHP (beyond an obviously reductive definition such as initiatives designed to promote the positive mental health and well-being of individuals, groups and communities). However, two other definitions are

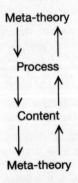

Figure 9.1 The relationship between content, process and meta-theory

offered. A *meta-definition* defines MHP as a transdisciplinary epistemological framework within which to analyse and locate the assumptions implicit in different and differing theories, models, practices and processes of mental health and its promotion, in all its elements. Thirdly, a *process-level* definition defines MHP as interventions made in order to promote the mental health of individuals, groups, organisations, communities, etc. including those which encourage movement analogous to paradigm shifts and which, thereby, increase their mental health and further its promotion. From these definitions there are three implications or commitments and three levels of intervention for people involved in MHP and CMHP who take a reflexive stance on the subject.

The first implication, at the level of content, is the commitment to questioning practice. This means challenging content, such as of a particular policy or lack of policy, or about what a colleague or client may or may not be doing, thinking, feeling, etc. The act of questioning often makes explicit people's practice and (implicit) thinking. Secondly and following from this, is the commitment to making explicit what is implicit, a movement from content to identifying the meta-theoretical assumptions which belie that content.[1] Thirdly, is the commitment and intervention to encourage movement and change at a personal, social, collective and organisational level (e.g. through paradigm shifts). These interventions are summarised in Table 9.1.

Finally, a job description for a person involved in CMHP is outlined (Appendix 3).

Radical practice

Before considering the implications of the different approaches to CMHP for training and learning, in order to redress the balance in the literature

Table 9.1 Levels of interventions in MHP

Level	Level of intervention	Examples of interventions
Meta-theory	Meta-intervention	Further reflexivity, reflecting on the process of process Asking questions ('Which theory . . .?')
Process	Process interventions	Reflexivity Making explicit what is implicit Advocating movement and change Asking questions ('How . . .?')
Content	Content interventions	Promoting alternatives Asking questions ('What . . .?')
Meta-theory	Meta-theorectical understanding	Reflexivity Understanding underlying meta-theoretical assumptions

some priority is given to the development of the radical tradition within CMHP. There is a rich tradition of radical practice, particularly from political thinkers contesting a number of fields relevant to CMHP:

- In social policy, the London Edinburgh Weekend Return Group (1980), the *Bulletin on Social Policy*, the journal *Critical Social Policy*.
- In social work, the radical magazine *Case Con*, Bailey and Brake (1975, 1980), the discussion group *Socialists in Welfare*.
- In health, the Politics of Health Group (1980, 1982), groups of radical GPs, midwives, etc.
- In health promotion, the magazine *Radical Health Promotion*, Rodmell and Watt (1986).
- In psychology, S. Holland (1979), Bostock (1991), Samuels (1993).
- In mental health, the group *Black Workers in Mental Health*, Banton et al. (1985).
- In therapy, the group *The Radical Therapist Collective*, Agel (1971), the *Humpty Dumpty Radical Psychology Magazine*, J. Mitchell (1975), Séve (1975, 1978), S. Holland (1990), Samuels (1993), etc.

Radical practice is a form of opposition. Banton et al. (1985) distinguish between radical *therapy* and radical *mental health practice*: 'the latter includes the former but is not co-extensive with it' (p. 164). If we add to these consideration of health promotion practice we then have three

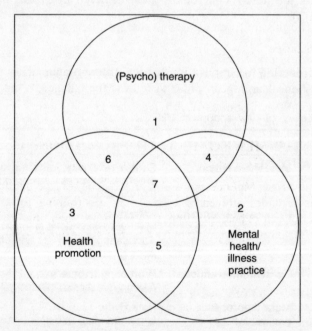

Figure 9.2 The interrelationship between radical therapy, mental health/illness practice and health promotion

spheres of work and influence which overlap each other (Figure 9.2). Figure 9.2, however, marks an important difference from Tannahill (1985b) and Verrall (1990) in that the spheres themselves as well as the interrelated spaces between them are all located within, in this case, a radical paradigm.

That any of this practice is radical is by virtue of the analysis which informs it (not by the mere prefix of an adjective). The interrelated spaces between therapy, mental health/illness practice and health promotion are thus summarised:

1 Radical (psycho)therapy focuses on the individual with the aim of 'subjectification'.
2 Radical mental health/illness practice 'involves grasping hold of [politics], of taking power and the discourses that surround it and regenerating our perceptions' (Banton et al., 1985).
3 Radical health promotion combines radical perspectives on (in this context) mental health, together with radical political action, probably with an emphasis on MHP in and of the community.
4 Psychopolitics/radical (psycho)therapy (the interface between 1 and 2) is 'a form of psychopolitical enlightenment' (R. Holland, 1992, p. 143).
5 Radical community work (the interface between 2 and 3) aims to develop community strategies for mental health and its promotion, taking an oppositional view of mental illness.
6 Radical MHP (the interface between 1 and 3), promotes radical forms of (psycho)therapy, and develops therapeutic perspectives of health education/promotion.
7 Social action psychotherapy (the interface between and combination of 1, 2 and 3) aims to combine all aspects of these areas or spaces in promoting personal psychological and social awareness and change and action in the community.

COMMUNITY MENTAL HEALTH PROMOTION: TRAINING AND LEARNING

In the mid-1970s McPheeters noted that 'none of the mental health professions provides any amount of systematic training for prevention and promotion' (McPheeters, 1976, p. 197). Since then, this has changed to a degree. The rules governing nurse training, for instance, require branch programmes to achieve certain outcomes, including:

the recognition of common factors which contribute to, and those which adversely affect, physical, mental and social well-being of patients and clients and take appropriate action [and] the identification of physical, psychological, social and spiritual needs of the patient or client.
(*Nurses, Midwives and Health Visitors' Rules Approval Order 1983*, Section 18. See also *Approval Order 1989*, Rule 18A.)

This and other bodies, to some degree or other and with varying degrees of political analysis, commitment and monitoring, make reference to the need for an appreciation of social, political and cultural factors affecting service users. Notwithstanding these references, it is unclear that any of these professions have a claim on or an interest in CMHP.

R. Holland (1990c) reflects on this problem as regards health education/ promotion:

> ˙since professions are defined partly by their possession of a body of knowledge, health educators need to assemble a credible, saleable corpus of knowledge capable of legitimizing their practice. To their embarrassment, nearly everything they need already belongs to other professions. Epidemiology belongs to the public health areas of the medical profession, although some part of it can be gained from demographers. Personal intervention theories belong to clinical psychologists and social workers, family intervention theories belong to family therapists, and mental health knowledge belongs to psychiatrists and clinical psychologists. The only bodies of knowledge without strong commitment to professional sectors of activity are the academic disciplines of education, psychology, and sociology, and the two latter disciplines are notoriously unpractical in their academic form. How can the group aspire to professional status on a knowledge base which is fragmented, incoherent, and in many aspects already spoken for?
>
> (R. Holland, 1990c, p. 30)

Mental health educators too, faced with the stark reality of a market economy of health and social care, may feel embarrassed by what some see as the fig leaf of interdisciplinarity. Currently no one profession – health promotion, psychology, medicine, nursing, social work or education – has the monopoly on this new field of mental health promotion. Neumann et al. (1989a) suggest 'that the promotion of mental health requires the framework of a coordinated concept of education' (p. 5).

In response to this, and based on my initial research, I designed a training course, offering professionals in various disciplines an overview of the constituent elements of CMHP and, on a practical level, introducing them to – or consolidating and developing their existing – counselling, supervisory and consultative skills. Influenced by such educationalists as C. R. Rogers (1951, 1977/1990), Freire (1972, 1974) and Illich (1973), I am interested in a reflexive approach at all levels, thus each training course and each day is influenced by, and changes as a result of, my own reflection and that of others, as well as the interaction between participants and new ideas and practice. As a part of this critical self-reflection, 'training' has been changed to training/learning on the basis that 'no man can reveal to you aught but that which already lies half asleep in the dawning of your knowledge' (Gibran, 1926, p. 67). The 'trainer'/teacher thus becomes a facilitator, someone who genuinely educates or 'leads out' (*e ducare*). The current aims of the course reflect this:

- To review and extend existing notions of mental health, health and health promotion, and community, by introducing participants to a sociopsychological conceptual framework.
- To help participants distinguish between mental health promotion and mental illness prevention and to draw out the implications of this for their practice.
- To introduce participants to a number of identified mental health skills.
- To introduce participants to practice skills relevant to mental health promotion such as: reflexivity (self-critical reflection on practice), mental health consultation skills, and an appreciation of the elements of mental health policy (principles, strategies, targets, measures, etc.).
- To suggest different foci for promoting mental health: with individuals, groups and organisations and communities.
- To integrate anti-discriminatory theory and practice throughout the course.

An outline of the course forms Appendix 4. Of course, in facilitating such a course it is important that the method is congruent with the content and process, taking account, for instance, of the emotional state of the learner – a contribution of education to health promotion (Weare, 1992).

H. A. Becker (1981), looking at personal construct psychology from a 'dynamics of science' perspective, identifies four structural obligations, or demons, chasing social scientists: the first clamouring for the enhancement of scientific knowledge, while its paired second clamours for practicality and for 'helping people'; the third clamouring for scientific proof, prediction and control, and the fourth for insight and understanding – existential truth. Becker warns of the dangers, or 'pathology' of listening to any one demon, becoming, respectively: an academic in an ivory tower; a social mechanic; a positivist; or an 'autistic phantast' (egotist). In designing, facilitating and reflecting on the CMHP course, I recognise the obligations or my impetus, and the danger or my tendency, at any one time. Becker's response to what he describes as the lonely task of fighting the demons is to find and maintain an uneasy balance in the middle. In the field of CMHP, another and important option is to link up and network with others and to exchange ideas on a regular basis, thereby maintaining a more social and easy balance between these demons.

DISCIPLINARITY

'Progress in the promotion of mental health and the prevention and treatment of mental disorders depends on increasing, integrating and sharing relevant knowledge from many fields' (Minister of National Health and Welfare, 1988, p. 14). In the proposal for the original research from which this book has developed, R. Caplan (1989) conceives 'the interface between psychoanalytic/psychodynamic theory of individual and group psychic processes and the social theory of social processes' (p. 2) as the ground of any conceptual 'model' of mental health promotion. Both this and the introductory discussion of the interface between psychology and sociology – and its interdiscipline, sociopsychology – imply the need to consider the various disciplines relevant to the field of community mental health promotion (CMHP) or whether it constitutes a discipline in its own right.

On the question of interdisciplinarity, Reason (1977) suggests, paradoxically, that it can be approached only in terms of disciplines: 'the labour of academic division produces nothing but the recombination of names: multi-, pluri-, inter-, cross-, and trans-disciplinary set a royal fashion, but it is noteworthy that a- and anti- are never nominated' (p. 204). Different solutions to this paradox are offered. Brown and Tudor (1981) assert that one should 'not talk about *inter-disciplinary* but *integrated* approaches as once the barriers between disciplines have been discarded the disciplines as such no longer exist' (p. 103). More recently it has become fashionable to talk about *transdisciplinary* theories and ways of working which, R. Caplan (1989) suggests, 'start from the premise of the holistic nature of knowledge which cannot be mechanically separated into different disciplines' (p. 3). H. B. M. Murphy (1986), in tracing the historical development of transcultural psychiatry, acknowledges the different connotations of the term:

> the 'trans' part of the term even caused some unease, since it appeared to imply that the field would be concerned only with features that transcended cultural boundaries, not those that remained within them; but on the other hand it could be taken as implying intercultural comparison.
>
> (H. B. M. Murphy, 1986, p. 13)

Reason (1977) proposes 'a positive, concrete conception of knowledge, understanding and enquiry which would be interdisciplinary in all but name' (p. 206) for, he argues, once interdisciplinarity is named it becomes in essence another 'discipline'. Insofar as he does not name or define the term, Reason proposes a (kind of) interdisciplinarity which is a methodology of 'the continual confrontation of the problem of methodology' (p. 206). Thus, the *way* we do things (process) becomes as much a part of our study or inquiry as *what* we do (content) through a process of critical reflection or reflexivity which is essential to our method and inquiry. This concords with Money's (1993) (interpretative) argument, in discussing the origin of disenchantment (of which depression is a symptom), that:

> the problem, the origin of disenchantment, is the loss of meaning and of purpose. We have disciplines such as theology, psychology, gerontology and so on. But the missing -ology is teleology – the perception of

purpose and meaning in the universe and thence in the life of the individual.

(Money, 1993, p. 455)

The problem with interdisciplinarity or transdisciplinarity, however, is that in order to integrate something or 'transdiscipline' we again need a method and a concept. Again, we may draw upon the notion and reality of paradigms – it is significant that, since his original work, Kuhn came to regard a paradigm as a disciplinary matrix (Kuhn, 1976). In the field of psychotherapy, for instance, it is becoming increasingly fashionable to call oneself an integrative psychotherapist. Too often this is eclecticism in all but name: the method of integration is doing 'what *feels* right at the time'. A more serious view of integration is one which requires training and experience in at least two approaches or disciplines (in psychotherapy, preferably ones which represent the different schools or traditions) *and* a method and a concept which integrate the approaches or disciplines in a way which deals with theoretical similarity and difference, thus providing direction for making choices between approaches at the interface of theory and practice. On the basis of this definition, one *method* of integration is reflexivity, this time a reflection on *process* which enables us to understand the meta-theoretical assumptions at work in any method, theory or model, policy or practice. The coherent organisation of this material then provides us with a conceptual approach to integration, in this case the paradigm analysis (of meta-theoretical assumptions) and framework.[2]

This concern for reflexivity at all levels is reflected in the job description for CMHP (Appendix 3).

COMMUNITY MENTAL HEALTH PROMOTION: PROFESSION OR PROFESSIONS?

Having discussed the role of the person involved in CMHP, the training/ learning required and the problem of disciplinarity, it is pertinent to discuss whether mental health promotion should become a separate discipline and profession or whether it is – and should be – 'Mental health for all', by all.

The hitherto lack of conceptual clarity and consequent pragmatic practice is reflected in the current confusion of terminology and role. People are appointed – at present, mainly within the health care professions and Health Authorities/Trusts – as Health Promotion Officers (sometimes with Mental Health in parentheses), or with a special interest or specific brief in mental health. In addition to 'Officers' there are 'Workers', 'Specialists', 'Advisors', 'Consultants', 'Facilitators' who, in the current contract culture, may be purchasers and/or providers. These terms are important: they often carry an organisational and theoretical significance beyond their title. Whilst 'Officer' has a professional ring to it, the term 'Worker' implies an active activist, especially when linked to 'community', the focus for much mental health promotion work. 'Specialists' are special and their expertise is often seen as exclusive (e.g. G. Caplan, 1970), whilst the advice of 'Advisors' can be taken or not, and a 'Promoter' sounds pugilistic. The terms 'Consultants', 'Facilitators' and 'Supervisors' all describe different aspects of a person's role. All these terms are significant in terms of their *meaning* and have implications for a person's role. In a booklet on approaches to stress management in the community setting, the World Health Organisation (1993a) advocates advocacy for action, implying that the health promotion worker needs to be an active advocate in and for the community.

The lack of a theoretical, professional or training base for people in CMHP has been noted. Despite this, the establishment of mental health promotion posts or officers for whom a part of their job is mental health promotion, is increasing. Against a background of confusion in theory and practice, a burgeoning interest and investment (despite competing priorities and governmental directives), and the breadth of mental health as a field of inquiry and promotion, relevant to the general population as well as specific groups such as the mentally ill, the organisation of CMHP, in Britain, is at a crisis point.

It therefore faces both opportunity and change. In response to this there are essentially two principal strategies: that of separation and separatism or of integration and entryism.

The first strategy is to argue that mental health, including community mental health, and its promotion is a separate discipline. Given the influence of the medical/illness model of 'health', mental health needs separation from medicine and psychiatry in order to develop a distinct, separate and saleable body of knowledge. Taking up R. Holland's (1990c) challenge, this would include the epidemiology of health (Galdston, 1955) including mental health; a sociopsychology of mental health, individuals, their social context and of interventions which could draw on other disciplines such as the performing arts (Kane, 1994); and an integrative methodology and conceptual framework. From this a coherent training and professional base could be developed – and one no more fragmented, incoherent or borrowed than, say, that of social work. In many ways, and especially in the short term, this is an attractive proposition, as it separates and highlights mental health and its promotion which is so often subsumed (and ignored) by health and health promotion. To the extent that present work is a separate volume, it represents this strategic approach. The danger of this approach lies in becoming fixed; there is often a rigidity of thought created in the definition of a new discipline or profession, particularly at the edges where it meets other disciplines and professions, arising from the need to identify itself as different.

The second strategy is to insist that just as mental health is an integral part of life, so its promotion must be integrated into every discipline, profession, policy and practice. Thus the health visitor checking the child's health needs to inquire and take account of their mental health (stress, coping, self-concept and self-esteem, etc.), appropriate to their age and development. In advocating the interdisciplinarity implicit in mental health promotion, Sartorius (1992) argues that the promotion of mental health:

> is not restricted to mental health workers. In fact, the more different people participating in the effort the better: changes of values of a society must include many professionals and people from all walks of life, speaking a variety of professional jargons and class or group idioms.
>
> (Sartorius, 1992, p. 21)

Conceptually, this is a more coherent and integrated (and long-term) strategy for CMHP. In practice, however, it requires practitioners to act as entryist/advocates for mental health wherever they practise. This has enormous implications for policy and practice. It would mean, for instance, that, instead of writing a separate book, I would need to find a means of influencing every contribution to, for example, the volume on *Health Promotion* (Bunton and Macdonald, 1992) to make explicit and to integrate mental health in their understanding of health. The danger of this approach is of vagueness and, literally, a lack of discipline; mental health and its promotion may be seen as too nebulous and intangible and the intellectual and practical tasks as too enormous to tackle.

A third strategy which emerges from consideration of the previous two, is one of combining both: of arguing, at least in the short term, for a separation and distinction of terms, definitions, concepts, policies, practices, etc. in order to establish some defining ground. This may involve training and learning but need not – and, I would argue, needs to not – involve the establishment and consolidation of a separate profession. It does, however, require the identification of specific people within a range of professions and at all levels who have the task of promoting the promotion of mental health. Once established, theorists and practitioners, reflecting a truly reflexive methodology, would then seek to de-construct such separation, promoting an integrative definition and concept of mental health in all disciplines and professions, and training and learning, as a longer-term strategy for CMHP.

It is this third approach which has been developed in this book, first by defining the field of MHP and CMHP and secondly, by developing it in a way which is both conceptually coherent and fundamentally practical. Now, following the methodology of reflexivity, and before the definitions and developments of this inquiry become too fixed and rigid, Part III deconstructs MHP.

Part III
Breaking out of the field

INTRODUCTION TO PART III

In Part I the field of mental health promotion (MHP) was defined through an exploration of its component parts and of how they fitted together – or not. The conceptual framework and methodology of the inquiry was also introduced and developed accumulatively. In Part II, four key areas for the development of MHP were discussed in the course of which the four paradigm analysis and framework was used as a way of describing the material (the content); as a way of understanding it, through understanding its meta-theoretical assumptions (meta-theory); and as a way of organising the material and moving from one approach to another (the process). These points, along with some further discussion about paradigms, paradigm shifts and how the framework could be used as a practical tool for effecting change in a number of areas, were also developed in this part.

It was also indicated that the logic of the methodology used throughout this inquiry – of reflexivity – was to continue to reflect critically. In this part (Chapter 10), I seek to break out of the field as defined and developed, initially, by reflecting on the method itself.

10 Beyond mental health promotion

Throughout this book Burrell and Morgan's (1979) four paradigm analysis and framework has been used as a meta-theoretical map and therefore, in effect, as a conceptual framework for integration of different and differing approaches to mental health promotion (MHP). In the spirit of critical reflection and in response to the postmodernist movement, this paradigm analysis is itself subjected to reflexive scrutiny. Dis-integrative and deconstructionist views of mental health are offered and some future directions for community mental health promotion (CMHP) are noted.

BEYOND THE PARADIGMS

Various critiques of Burrell and Morgan's (1979) original work have been offered including whether their frameworks are indeed paradigms, and on the issue of their incommensurability (D. Cox, 1979; Harvey, 1982). Three related critiques of Burrell and Morgan's paradigm analysis are examined here, each of which take us in some way beyond the paradigms: the choice of dimensions, the applicability of the analysis to other fields, and the problem of knowledge.

Other dimensions

One critique of the paradigm analysis centres on the two dimensions chosen by Burrell and Morgan (1979). Social science (subjective–objective, horizontal dimension) and society (regulation–radical change, vertical dimension) may not be *the* two dimensions which frame all theories of (social) organisation. Hofstede (1980), in a major piece of international research (in twenty languages) investigating the main areas of differences between cultures, identified four major criteria/dimensions of cultural difference (Figure 10.1). (Hofstede defines culture as the collective mental programming of a people in an environment.)

Hofstede's dimensions may be equally, if not more, applicable to theories of societies – and, if plotted as axes with Burrell and Morgan's (1979) sets of assumptions about the nature of social science (about ontology,

Power	Uncertainty	Individualism	Masculinity
Distance	Avoidance	Collectivism	Femininity

Figure 10.1 Dimensions of culture/society
Source: Based on Hofstede, 1980

epistemology, human nature and methodology), may provide a more sophisticated and cross-cultural framework for the analysis of science and society (Figure 10.2).

Applicability

Burrell and Morgan's search for a framework took place in the context of their study of theories of organisation. Whilst it may be the case that the paradigm analysis is applicable to theories of individuals, mental health, community, etc. this should not be assumed. To some extent this critique is

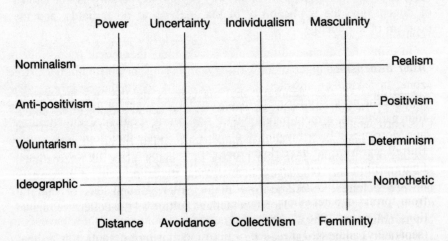

Figure 10.2 Dimensions of science and culture/society
Source: Developed from Burrell and Morgan, 1979; Hofstede, 1980

met by moving from the single discipline of sociology (Burrell and Morgan's background and interest) to the dynamic interdiscipline of socio-psychology with a focus on individuals, groups and community – concerns explicit throughout this inquiry. Nevertheless, the transferability of theory and especially of meta-theory, like that of skills, needs to be taken and questioned seriously.

If we take paradigm analysis as the analysis of the paradigms within a particular field of study, then we need to look within a particular field, for the dimensions by which we can develop an analysis particular to that field. Although developed in the context of the four paradigm analysis, either the eight elements of mental health (Chapter 3) or the summary of the common elements of mental health (Chapter 5) – as functioning, as relational, as ability/capacity, and as social – may themselves be taken as frameworks by which to analyse and influence policy and practice in mental health promotion.

The problem of knowledge

It has been suggested that the four paradigms for the analysis of social theory – or, rather, sociopsychological theory – may be viewed and used as an integrative framework. In Chapter 9 certain requirements for integration were defined, including the necessity of a meta-theoretical framework – which the four paradigm analysis fulfils. However, the possibility of paradigm unification is itself a (functionalist) assumption; separateness and incommensurability is safer! Equally, whilst this inquiry has been careful not to overstate the notion of paradigm shifts, particularly in describing movement between the paradigms (see Chapter 5), arguing that the development of a subject's thinking is *analogous* to movement between paradigms, this does not tackle the epistemological issue of what constitutes knowledge at the level of 'integration'.

In using the four paradigm analysis as a meta-theoretical framework *in itself* there is a danger of unwittingly proposing an epistemological-free zone, in a kind of abstract space somewhere above the paradigms. The logic of the necessity for meta-theory is that for coherent integration of the four paradigms, a meta-paradigmatic position is required. Neither Burrell nor Morgan resolves this philosophical issue. Since their joint publication, Burrell and Morgan have developed different interests. Burrell, a leading figure within critical management theory in Britain still advocates the incommensurability of the paradigms, whilst Morgan has moved away from formal debates about knowledge to work on metaphors in organisations (Morgan, 1986).[1] Nevertheless and significantly, they have both (separately) addressed the issue of postmodernism in organisational theory (Burrell, 1988; Morgan, 1986, 1993) and it is to postmodernism that we turn in order to take these critiques further.

POSTMODERNISM

Postmodernism is important not only as offering a critique of modernism but also as a movement which is having a significant influence on many spheres such as art, architecture, literature and literary criticism, the media, music, organisation, philosophy, politics, psychology, etc. At its extreme, in representing the 'death of reason' (Power, 1990), it also has a relevance for mental illness and for mental health.

Postmodernism, however, is also seen as abstract, elitist, reflexive to the point of obscurity and absurdity, and irrelevant. Whilst the writings of some of the leading writers on postmodernism such as Derrida (1978, 1981, 1982), Lyotard (1984) and Baudrillard (1988) are difficult in parts, there are a number of works which elaborate postmodernist ideas in accessible language (e.g. Ahmed, 1992; Hassard and Parker, 1993).

Perhaps the most famous author on postmodernism is Derrida. His postmodernism is founded on deconstruction (as opposed to construction); irrationality (as opposed to rationality); logical undecidability (as opposed to predictability); and separation and difference (as opposed to unity and identity). Derrida's critical deconstruction comprises two movements: 'overturning' and 'metaphorisation'. Derrida (1981) suggests that to deconstruct the opposition we need initially to 'overturn the hierarchy at a given moment' (p. 41). However, Derrida also warns against deconstruction becoming the new construction or hierarchy. In order to avoid this he activates 'metaphorisation' whereby metaphors are used to emphasise mutation, uncertainty and ambiguity. Metaphors have been applied to images of organisations (Morgan, 1986) and to psychotherapy (M. Cox and Theilgaard, 1987). Derrida's view of a double-dynamic within the opposition or deconstruction distinguishes him – and it – from the Hegelian and later, Marxist triadic and linear formulation 'thesis – antithesis – synthesis'. A postmodern version is represented in Figure 10.3.

Writing about postmodern organisational analysis, Hassard (1993) identifies five key concepts: 'representation', 'reflexivity', 'writing', '*differance*' and 'de-centring the subject'. These concepts are briefly defined, compared with Burrell and Morgan's (1979) assumptions about the nature of social science (see Chapter 1), and discussed in relation to mental health.

thesis -

- antithesis -

- asynthesis –   synthesis -

- anti-synthesis -

Figure 10.3 A postmodern thesis

'Representation' acknowledges the notion that we cannot know things directly, but only through a representation of them. This pushes the subjectivity of ideographic methodology further than Burrell and Morgan's (1979) description. As far as mental health is concerned, the concept of representation reminds us that descriptions of mental health through language, for instance, are framed by existing scientific (i.e. medical and psychiatric) discourses: 'findings produced through empirical science reflect pre-existing intellectual categories' (Hassard, 1993, p. 12). A postmodern representational discourse on mental health, therefore, deconstructs existing, empirical scientific notions of mental illness and mental health and recognises that any representation of mental health through, for instance, a metaphor such as 'I'm as happy as a sandboy' in turn needs deconstructing – including, in this case, the racist representation/association of mental health with happiness with carefree, naïve, black innocence.

'Reflexivity' needs little introduction in this inquiry and, indeed, follows from the above reflection on representation: 'propositions which remove representations from the grasp of the factual are themselves representations' (Ibid., p. 12). There is a deconstruction of knowledge itself implicit in postmodern reflexivity. Derrida's unique interpretation of ambivalence transcends the sociology or psychology or even the sociopsychology of the individual, locating itself in the 'text' which is the interplay of discourses whether sociopsychological, political, philosophical, medical, linguistic or whatever. Our epistemology is thus challenged and widened. Such deconstruction takes place by means of 'serious play' through which ideas are taken seriously and not seriously at the same time. In the field of mental health this irreverence is represented by metaphors and language which encourage reflexivity such as Marco the Horse of 'the Italian experience' in Trieste; by the poetry of Survivors Speak Out (1992); by a client who made and wore a T-shirt showing the results of his MMPI test,[2] thereby encouraging others to reflect upon his and their mental health/illness.

> Where is the Life we have lost in living?
> Where is the wisdom we have lost in knowledge?
> Where is the knowledge we have lost in information?
>
> (Eliot, 1934, p. 161)

'Writing', in postmodernist terms, is about the structure rather than the written word or even the meaning of such representations. Writing – and reading – is linear, at least formally. Even though I may have written this chapter before writing others, by virtue of its position in the ordering of the text it is presented as my last word: it is fixed in time, space and its (modernist) significance. Despite formal conventions (such as reading from beginning to end), readers, at least, have some flexibility about how they relate to the text, whether through the back cover, the index, by reading the last chapter first, etc. Whilst it is easy to imagine a buffet presented as a smörgåsbord comprising sweets, starters, decorations and savouries, it is more difficult to present non-fictional 'writing' as other than linear. The deconstruction of the form of writing involves challenging linguistic forms and structures in writing as Daly (1978) and Spender (1980) have, as well as finding other forms of expression such as art, music, performance, video, and the latest computer internetwork. As far as mental health is concerned, the former is represented by critiques of 'mentalist' and stigmatising language (Hendon and Lawson, 1990), the latter by creative and non-written or non-literal forms of MHP (e.g. Sunderland and Clarkson, 1992; Kane, 1994).

In inventing the term *'differance'*, Derrida (1982) incorporates two meanings of the French verb *différer* – to differ (in space) and to defer (put off) (in time), arguing in effect against ontological realism in favour of phenomena being both present and absent; 'our traditional understanding of the sign [or representation] is that which we substitute for the absent thing we wish to be present. The sign represents the presence in its absence – it is deferred presence' (Hassard, 1993, p. 14). There is no fully present reality; all is relative and continually deferred. The concept of *differance* provides us with an insight on the usual conflation of mental health with mental illness.

Neither mental illness nor mental health have a present reality. They exist as concepts which structure my reality (nominalism) and have a relationship to each other of *differance*.	By substituting mental health (present) for mental illness (absent) we defer the *differance* and 'realities' of mental illness, thereby exiling madness.	By conflating mental illness (present) with mental health (absent) we do not realise our mental health needs or that the two concepts may exist independently and differently.

So far, in terms of Burrell and Morgan's (1979) analysis of assumptions about the nature of social science on the subjective–objective dimension, postmodernism looks like a radical subjectivity. 'De-centring the subject' challenges the tidiness of this conceptual congruence. As 'consciousness is never a direct and unmediated experience . . . [so, human] agency is an artefact and subjectivity is a process of locating identity in the language of the "other" ' (Hassard, 1993, p. 15). Thus, the subject is no longer self-directing; it becomes instead 'a convenient location for the throughput of discourses' (Ibid., p. 15). This is the sense in which the subject becomes de-centred. Instead, subjectivity, including our mental health, becomes a fragment of who we are. The focus of analysis and discourse shifts to 'agency' – action personified – as a system of relations. Thus agency rather than psyche stands at the centre of the dimensions of mental health (Chapter 1). Another implication of this is that mental health and its promotion is seen as relational: a process view of MHP and CMHP (for a definition of which, see Chapter 9).

NOTES ON THE FUTURE FOR MENTAL HEALTH PROMOTION

Having subjected the conceptual framework used in this work to some reflexive analysis and outlined concepts from postmodernism relevant to mental health, I end this present inquiry (the use of 'inquiry' throughout this work indicates a certain continuity) with some notes on the future of and for mental health promotion.

Mental health and chaos

> To approach an understanding of the postmodern age is to presuppose . . . a spirit of pluralism; a heightened scepticism of traditional orthodoxies; and finally a rejection of the view of the world as a universal totality, of the expectation of final solutions and complete answers.
>
> (Ahmed, 1993, p. 10)

Mental health is plural: it is, as we have seen, multifaceted both within and between individuals, groups and communities and over time. It is diverse. It is disputed. It changes. It is unstable. It should, on reflection, perhaps more accurately be referred to as 'mental health*s*'. Salutogenic concepts of mental health imply at the very least a scepticism of medical/psychiatric orthodoxies, whilst postmodern approaches to positive mental healths reject any universal notion of an objective, defined, regulated – or even, *a* subjective, phenomenological, liberated – view of mental health.

Chaos challenges our traditional notions of order. Mental illness is viewed as chaotic and whilst this may be experienced from the inside or the outside as distressing, there is also a significant tradition in mythology and history of 'divine madness' which carries truth from the Gods. Thus, hearing voices may be thought of or experienced as mad (Department of Health, 1994c) or as a form of insight or spirituality (see Romme and Escher, 1993). The psyche – and psychotherapy – is no stranger to chaos. Chaos theory provides a view of 'organic order' (Weiss, 1973), examined in relation to society and psychotherapy (Wieland-Burston, 1992). From this perspective psychotherapy may be seen as 'serious play' in which clients find their organic order – for Gestalt therapists in the 'fertile void' – rather than achieving a particular (functional) solution or (re)solution. Lax (1992) considers how, in therapy, the way in which people describe their lives is limiting in terms of developing new ideas of structures.

Healing

I am not a mechanism, an assembly of various sections.
And it is not because the mechanism is working wrongly that
    I am ill.
I am ill because of a wound to the soul, to the deep emotional self
and the wounds to the soul take a long, long time,
    only time can help

and patience, and a certain difficult repentance,
long, difficult repentance, realisation of life's mistake, and the freeing oneself
from the endless repetition of the mistake
which mankind at large has chosen to sanctify.

(D.H. Lawrence, 1964, p. 620)

The media

MHP in the postmodern world must address discourse itself and the 'language' or medium of that discourse.

Increasing attention is paid to 'the media' as a medium for promoting mental health (e.g. White, 1992); many mental health initiatives such as roadshows now use the media to counter the stigma of mental illness and to promote positive mental health. Maccoby (1988) has examined the effect of the application of a sophisticated and integrated mass media campaign in health promotion. This needs to be taken further, particularly in analysing the promotion of mental ill-health, for instance, the emotional illiteracy contained in everyday media messages (R. Shohet, personal communication, 1 October 1994).

A poem is a medium as is the choosing, the reading (or writing) and the placing of it here, now. In developing the practice of mental health we need to be prepared to focus on discourse, on the layout, on the process of our words and world/s. For instance, I am aware that a lot of the time I find it easier to read – and write – in the style and manner of the other (left-hand) column. I find it more comfortable to be literal, rather than metaphorical. Sometimes this is different and I want to be told or to tell a story or to read about a myth rather than to learn or re-count a 'fact' or to construct an argument.

These two traditions – the literal and the metaphoric/poetic or reflective – often come together when people talk about their mental health, their 'nerves', feelings, emotions, and so on. It's as if, when we come down to it, we have few words for this aspect of our lives. Furthermore, much of our learning, whether through families, schools, or other cultural influences, such as the media, discourages such literacy and imagery.

Mental health and social change

The social world has always been changing; during the twentieth century the pace of change has gathered pace and change is now exponentially fast. As we near the end of this millennium, we are faced with change in two directions. Societies in the form of countries appear to be splitting into ever smaller communities along ethnic, religious and 'nationalist' divides, often with dramatic and tragic consequences. At the same time many national governments, sometimes of those same states in internal conflict, are moving towards ever larger federations and international 'communities'. At a psychological level, such apparently contradictory social and political movement perhaps represents both an impetus for separation and individuation *and* a desire to identify and belong: a focus on both individual and community, psyche and society.

Perhaps this confusion of change is a reaction to the previous polarities and extremes of individualism and community-ism. Hillman and Ventura (1992), in an explicitly-titled book *We've had a hundred years of psychotherapy and the world's getting worse*, question the received wisdom from psychoanalysis that the psyche is inside the skin: 'psychotherapy is only working on that "inside" soul. By removing the soul from the world and not recognizing that the soul is also *in* the world, psychotherapy can't do its job anymore . . . the sickness is out *there*' (pp. 3–4, original emphases). Psychology itself as has been discussed (Chapters 4 and 5) needs to become more social. At the same time Ahmed (1992) discusses religious and political fundamentalism as 'the attempt to resolve how to live in a world of radical doubt. It is a dialogue with the times, a response to it . . . ethno-religious revivalism is both cause and effect of postmodernism' (p. 13). Hofstede's (1980) dimensions, in particular those of individualism–collectivism and uncertainty–avoidance, provide the basis for some dialogue (and location) between these extremes. However, just as mental illness and mental health may be viewed as two separate continua (as described in Chapter 1) so individualism and collectivism may also be usefully seen as two parallel continua. Postmodern approaches to mental health in the context of social change then essentially emphasise it as multiple, relational and dynamic.

Mental health and mental illness

Having argued that mental health and mental illness are two separate realities, it is time to represent their interrelation. Having suggested a relation between mental health, mental ill-health and mental illness (Chapter 1), having examined the relationship between MHP and mental illness prevention (Chapter 3), having acknowledged (in Chapter 7) that some measures of psychological mental health are closely and usefully associated with physiological ill-health and dis-ease, the two continua may now be joined (see Figure 10.4) in the figure of the caduceus, the wand carried by Mercury, messenger of the Gods, usually and here represented with two serpents (symbols of wisdom and healing) entwined around it: a symbol for the eternal science of transformation, of healing into wholeness. 'The continuity with the past . . . remains a strong feature of postmodernism' (Ahmed, 1992, p. 16).

Figure 10.4 The caduceus

We shall not cease from exploration
And the end of all our exploring
Will be to arrive where we started
And know the place for the first time

(Eliot, 1942, p. 222)

Mental health and the city

'Because large parts of the population live in urban areas and a larger part still are influenced by ideas originating from these areas, the metropolis becomes central to postmodernism' (Ahmed, 1992, p. 18). Whilst this may be true, it is also the case that the concept and integrity of the metropolis is being challenged by forces such as economics and by health initiatives. The creation of office space which remains unoccupied, the decline of many city centres in terms of habitation, and the removal to the periphery of huge shopping centres and complexes: all bear witness to the lost heart and soul of many conurbations. Health initiatives such as the World Health Organisation's Healthy Cities project (see Kickbush, 1989) challenge the unhealthy environment and stress caused by the pollution and pace of urban life. Whilst there are necessary mental illness projects in cities, many consider the countryside in itself a source of mental health and well-being. With its emphasis on deconstruction and reflexivity, postmodernism offers a critique of Ahmed's somewhat urban-centric view. Furthermore, postmodern mental health needs to encourage dialogue between the urban and rural: both as a social intervention in external reality as well as in understanding these as metaphors of an intra-psychic conflict between realities.

Mental health and class

The concept and practice of mental health and well-being is open to the criticism that it is only for the chattering classes: those who can afford to pay for their 'chat'. Whilst the middle class may have provided an intellectual lead in the field of mental health (and mental illness), from a reflexive and critical perspective it is the masses who define these terms. The dimensions of mental health and the eight elements of mental health and their promotion are accessible to all at least conceptually, although the impact of different and differential social and economic conditions on people also affects their ability, for example, to cope with psychosocial stressors as well as their impetus for self-development and change.

Mental health promotion: integration and eclecticism?

Postmodernism dismisses eclecticism as 'the degree zero of contemporary general culture' (Lyotard, 1984, p. 76) and at the same time promotes a radical eclectism of taste and outlook – obvious in contemporary dress fashion.

Mental health, then, is about integration and eclecticism. It involves maximising our (cap)abilities across a range of knowledge, skills and interests through, for instance, the eight elements of mental health. It is also and essentially about developing an ability to reflect on oneself, one's thoughts, actions, etc., *critically*, in the sense of growth and development (critical self-reflection rather than critical self-criticism), including questioning those same eight elements and deconstructing such structures. It follows that mental health is also about putting that reflexivity into practice, in relation to and with others. So, mental health and its promotion may be thought of on three familiar levels: of content (the eight elements, particular skills, etc.); of meta-theory (critical self-reflection of the underlying assumptions of that and other content) and of process (interacting with others and our environments).

Postmodern mental health promotion is characterised by deconstruction through separation and *differance* – primarily of mental illness and the traditional medical and psychiatric (lack of) discourses; the juxtaposition of discourses – of mental health, mental ill-health and mental illness; the mixing of diverse and undecidable images of mental health – the literal and academic definitions and theories alongside the irrationality of the metaphorical and poetic. This is a mental health promotion in which underlying meta-theoretical assumptions of mental health and its promotion are examined and re-examined. Taking up Derrida's (1981) two movements, this postmodern process is one of 'overturning' hierarchies of mental health and how it is promoted, for instance, through the current local, national and international organisations concerned with mental health (and mental illness). This may initially be promoted through the serious integration and adoption of coherent conceptual frameworks (which is the current field of

MHP), after which we may deconstruct such integration with the serious play of 'exuberant eclecticism' (Ahmed, 1992, p. 25). Through this process mental health ultimately becomes a series of mutative metaphors which express its subjectivity, uncertainty and ambiguity and which may then be represented, reflected upon and 'written' about in every aspect of individual and community life.

Appendices

Appendix 1 Notes on community organising

This appendix is based on Bracht and Kingsbury (1990).

STAGE 1 COMMUNITY ANALYSIS

1.1 Define the community
1.2 Collect data/draw up a 'community profile'
1.3 Assess community capacity (including driving forces, e.g. as regards community mental health)
1.4 Assess community barriers (including restraining forces)
1.5 Assess readiness for change
1.6 Synthesise data and set priorities

STAGE 2 DESIGN AND INITIATION

2.1 Establish a core planning group and select a local organiser/co-ordinator
2.2 Choose an organisational structure
2.3 Identify, select and recruit organisation members (e.g. identify social roles such as innovators, experimenters, adapters, defenders, facilitators and bystanders)
2.4 Define the organisation's mission and goals
2.5 Clarify roles and responsibilities of board members, staff and volunteers
2.3 Provide training and recognition

STAGE 3 IMPLEMENTATION

3.1 Generate broad citizen participation
3.2 Develop a sequential work plan
3.3 Use comprehensive, integrative strategies
3.4 Integrate community values into the programmes, materials and messages

STAGE 4 PROGRAMME MAINTENANCE/CONSOLIDATION

4.1 Integrate intervention activities into community networks
4.2 Establish a positive organisational culture
4.3 Establish an ongoing recruitment plan
4.4 Disseminate results

STAGE 5 DISSEMINATION/REASSESSMENT

5.1 Update the community analysis
5.2 Assess effectiveness of interventions/programmes
5.3 Chart future directions and modifications
5.4 Summarise and disseminate results

Appendix 2 Mental health promotion targets

This appendix is based on the World Health Organisation's (1984/1991a) *Health for all targets*. It is a personal selection of those health for all targets specifically concerned with or with specific implications for mental health promotion – with the emphasis both on the *mental* and on *mental health*, as the logic of promoting an integrative view of mental health promotion (see Chapter 1) would suggest that all the health for all targets are concerned with mental health.

TARGET 2: HEALTH AND QUALITY OF LIFE

By the year 2000, all people should have the opportunity to develop and use their own health potential in order to lead socially, economically and mentally fulfilling lives.
   This target can be achieved if

- monitoring of health potential and quality of life is strengthened
- active participation in community life is encouraged
- access to the prerequisites for health, especially education, is improved
- healthy lifestyles based on effective coping skills become widely accepted
- health and environmental aspects of living and working are improved and social networks strengthened
- greater emphasis is placed on the quality of life in providing primary, secondary and tertiary care.

TARGET 3: BETTER OPPORTUNITIES FOR PEOPLE WITH DISABILITIES

By the year 2000, people with disabilities should be able to lead socially, economically and mentally fulfilling lives with the support of special arrangements that improve their relative physical, social and economic opportunities.
   This target aims at

- the provision of equal opportunities
- an improvement in the status of people with disabilities
- allowing people with disability to improve their quality of life and develop their health potential.

TARGET 6: HEALTHY AGEING

By the year 2000, life expectancy at birth in the Region should be at least 75 years and there should be a sustained and continuing improvement in the health of all people aged 65 years and over.

TARGET 7: HEALTH OF CHILDREN AND YOUNG PEOPLE

By the year 2000, the health of all children and young people should be improved, giving them the opportunity to grow and develop to their full physical, mental and social potential.

This target aims at achieving

- comprehensive support of children and their families, according to their health needs and socioeconomic circumstances.

The current (1994) activities of the mental health programme of the WHO's Regional Office for Europe include the development of a training programme for primary health care workers on the psychosocial development of 0-5 year olds, and strengthening psychosocial competence skills and coping skills in young people through work in schools (J.G. Sampaio Faria, personal communication, 16 March 1994).

TARGET 12: REDUCING MENTAL DISORDERS AND SUICIDE

By the year 2000, there should be a sustained and continuing reduction in the prevalence of mental disorders, an improvement in the quality of life of all people with such disorders, and a reversal of the rising trends in suicide and attempted suicide.

This target can be achieved through

- improvement in societal factors, such as unemployment and social isolation, that put a strain on the individual
- improved access to measures that support people and equip them to cope with distressing or stressful events and conditions
- improved access to measures that support carers, both formal and informal
- *development of comprehensive community-based mental health services with a greater involvement of primary health care* (my emphasis).

Many of the WHO's strategy targets (13-31) have an impact on the above targets; again, those specific to developing a mental health promotion strategy are noted.

TARGET 13: HEALTHY PUBLIC POLICY

By the year 2000, all member states should have developed, and be implementing, intersectoral policies for the promotion of healthy lifestyles, with systems ensuring public participation in policy-making and implementation.

TARGET 14: SETTINGS FOR HEALTH PROMOTION

By the year 2000, all settings of social life and activity, such as the school, workplace, neighbourhood and home, should provide greater opportunities for promoting health.

This can be achieved if in all member states action is taken in line with certain concepts and principles, such as those of the WHO Healthy Cities network, including steps to strengthen opportunities for health promotion in the various settings by

• concentrating health promotion on settings of daily living
• *facilitating community participation in decisions regarding health and the environment and health promotion* (my emphasis)
• fostering co-operation between sectors, to create better opportunities for healthy living
• *encouraging the involvement of various disciplines in health promotion* (my emphasis).

TARGET 15: HEALTH COMPETENCE

By the year 2000, accessible and effective education and training in health promotion should be available in all member states, in order to improve public and professional competence in promoting health and increasing health awareness in other sectors.

This can be achieved by

• making existing knowledge about health better known
• *emphasising a wider range of lifestyle issues, including self-esteem, personal skills and social support* (my emphasis)
• giving training and education in health promotion to all health professionals
• training other groups and disciplines to increase awareness of health promotion opportunities
• providing an effective infrastructure and adequate resources for implementing and co-ordinating health education programmes.

TARGET 16: HEALTHY LIVING

By the year 2000, there should be continuous efforts in all member states to actively promote and support healthy patterns of living through balanced nutrition, appropriate physical activity, healthy sexuality, good stress management and other aspects of positive health behaviour.

This target can be achieved by taking a holistic approach to promoting healthy patterns of living including

• increasing health and environmental awareness
• *developing and strengthening coping skills* (my emphasis)
• encouraging the giving and receiving of social support.

Appendix 3 A job description for community mental health promotion

This job description as outlined reflects – and represents a reflection – of the theory and practical implications of this inquiry. As such it indicates and encourages reflection on the content of the work of community mental health promotion (CMHP). Details, such as line management, supervision, salary and location, will be particular to the specific post and its context within a particular agency, organisation or relevant employing authority. At present there is no required qualification for, professional 'ownership' of, or particular career structure in this field; and, depending on how and where such a post is established, this will be more or less important and will influence the job and person specification. This job description is not intended as a fixed blue-print to be taken or implemented out of context; but, rather, as a point of reference for further discussion.

JOB DESCRIPTION: COMMUNITY MENTAL HEALTH PROMOTION

Summary

This post holds a key role in identifying initiatives with individuals, groups and organisations in the field of CMHP. It is recognised that this especially involves the fields of mental illness, mental health and health promotion. It carries special responsibilities for developing and maintaining working relationships within and between a number of relevant authorities, organisations, agencies and community groups as well as with individuals.

In addition to being a focus for local work in CMHP, as one of only a few in the country the post-holder will also have a broader developmental view of this innovative work.

Principal responsibilities

1   To work with individuals – professionals as well as identified 'clients' – and particularly with groups in the community:
    ● to promote the mental health of those with identified mental illnesses or who consider themselves as having a mental illness
    ● to promote the mental health of the population at large.
2   To promote positive mental health of individuals, groups and the community at large:

- through mental health education and promotion and developing materials for such work
- through developing a sense of the local community and its needs and by offering professional consultation to mental health workers
- through collaboration with and participation in local initiatives
- by identifying and working with people with mental health needs who are not served by existing groups or organisations.

3 To reflect on this work as it progresses with a view to
- developing interventions and initiatives in groups and organisations, including the employing agency, organisation and/or authority, which encourage reflection on and good practices in mental health
- presenting and promoting the work in terms of speaking, training/learning and writing
- evaluating the work.

4 To develop ideas and practice about which sources of knowledge and information are useful to such work.

Appendix 4 Mental health promotion course

AIMS OF THE COURSE

The course aims:

- To review and extend existing notions of mental health, health and health promotion, and community, by introducing participants to a sociopsychological conceptual framework.
- To help participants distinguish between mental health promotion and mental illness prevention and to draw out the implications of this for their practice.
- To introduce participants to a number of identified mental health skills.
- To introduce participants to practice skills relevant to mental health promotion such as reflexivity (self-critical reflection on practice); mental health consultation skills; and an appreciation of the elements of mental health policy (principles, strategies, targets, measures, etc.).
- To suggest different foci for promoting mental health: with individuals, groups and organisations and communities.
- To integrate anti-discriminatory theory and practice throughout the course.

The course takes place over twelve days.

Day 1 Welcome. Introductions. Learning styles and learning contracts. Social factors in mental health/mental illness. Listening skills.

Day 2 An introduction to mental health. Mental health and mental illness. Knowledge and society. A framework for thinking and practice. Reflection.

Day 3 Health and illness. Health education and health promotion. Paradigm analysis.

Day 4 Mental health promotion. Mental illness prevention. Eight elements of mental health. Mental health consultation. Reflection.

Day 5 Community. Community mental health. Community Mental Health Centres and Teams. Interdisciplinary working. Mental health consultation.

Day 6 Community care. *Caring for people. The Health of the nation.* Reflection.

Day 7 Community mental health promotion. Social action psychotherapy. User perspectives in mental health promotion. 'Paradigm shifts' and movement.

Day 8 Working with groups, organisations and communities. Mental health consultation. Reflection.

Day 9 Policy, objectives and principles. Developing mental health policy. Mental health assessment.

Day 10 Contracts, contracting and service agreements. Targets and measures. Reflection.

Day 11 Project presentations.
Day 12 Project presentations. Course evaluation. Endings.

Further details of this course are available from Keith Tudor at Temenos, 13A Penrhyn Road, Sheffield S11 8UL, England. Tel. (0114) 266 3931.

Notes

DEDICATION

1 This quotation is often (wrongly) attributed to Goethe. It is, in fact, from John Anster's (1835) highly extempore translation of Goethe's *Faust* and these lines do not appear in the original. I am grateful to Joan Tudor and friends for tracking this down.

INTRODUCTION

1 Future MHP information leaflets planned include *How to . . . deal with loneliness* and *How to . . . go to sleep*, available from MIND, address in bibliography.
2 However, a survey of health education policies in schools shows little practical response to mental/psychosocial health in primary schools and only a 12 per cent response to psychological aspects of health education in secondary schools studies (HEA, 1993a).

1 MENTAL HEALTH

1 Other work has examined the detrimental impact of gender roles on men's health including lifestyle, stress, risk-taking and preventive health practices (e.g. Verbrugge, 1985; Skelton, 1988) and in terms of psychological and psychiatric problems (Gomez, 1991).
2 'Black' is used here and throughout this work in the political sense to refer to black and Asian people.
3 Indeed, in the late 1930s, K. Davis (1938) identified the middle-class values of the mental hygiene movement in the United States and commented on those who then linked class, industrial conflict and mental health suggesting that industrial unrest connoted 'bad' mental hygiene and had to be corrected by 'good' mental hygiene with consequent good and increased productivity.
4 Laing never called himself an 'anti-psychiatrist' (Laing, 1985), the term being coined by his friend and colleague David Cooper (1967).
5 The World Health Organisation's definition of *health*, 'a state of complete physical, mental and social well-being and not merely the absence of infirmity' (WHO, 1946, p. 3), reflects one tautology yet (implicitly) recognises a health–infirmity continuum. Noack (1987) summarises the criticisms of the WHO's formulation as normative, fixed – as a state rather than a process – immeasurable, perfectionist and imperialist.

6 In this book I generally use the plural pronoun 'they' to refer to people generally; in quotations, I leave the integrity (and sexism) of the original.

7 Trent (1992a) (inaccurately) refers to this as the 'dual continuum' concept.

8 This argument has been applied in the physical health/illness field; e.g. Milz (1991).

9 Following Burrell and Morgan, in this book I use 'objectivist' and 'subjectivist' to refer to conceptual debates along this dimension and as distinct from the everyday use of subjective and objective.

10 In a paper discussing the contribution to MHP of cognitive neuropsychology, Parkins (1994) suggests 'the literature on mental health indicates that a positive model of mental health should be one in which the functioning of the mind is described in terms of the principles of homeostasis, and which is consistent with information concerning normal cognitive and neurophysiological development' (p. 288). This is interesting in that, in nature living organisms are dynamic rather than homeostatic; similarly, in the sociology of organisations, there are 'open' and 'closed' systems (Burrell and Morgan, 1979).

2 HEALTH PROMOTION

1 Illich (1975) offers a radical critique of the inadequacies of health care provision (see note 7 below).

2 Neumann et al. (1989a) argue, for instance that 'there are closer links between the mind and the immunosystem than hitherto assumed' (p. 10).

3 Controversial in that the lack of debate about the naturopathic and homeopathic alternatives to immunisation is due to the almost total domination of the field of medical research, epidemiology and health education by the Western medical model and powerful medical and financial interests (Chaitow, 1988).

J. Mitchell (1984) notes some of the protectionist measures and steps the medical profession has taken, historically, in order to defend its preserve:

• In the 1880s the medical profession consistently opposed the granting of a charter which would have given herbalists the status of registered practitioners.

• From 1911, with the passing of the *National Insurance Act*, it became virtually impossible for insured people to claim for attending the herbalist as they were able to do for seeing an allopathic doctor.

• In 1934 the Boothby Bill, which would have legitimised osteopathy, was thrown out by MPs under pressure from the British Medical Association.

• In 1979 the DoH funded an investigation of hakims, practitioners of the Unami system of medicine, utilised throughout the Islamic world. Its recommendations focused only on the dangers of using hakims and their 'abuse'.

4 Debates about health promotion indicators have been elaborated in a special issue of *Health Promotion* (Noack and McQueen, 1988).

5 The functionalist paradigm 'has developed as a branch of the natural sciences' (Burrell and Morgan, 1979). This paradigm has an extensive history and 'has provided the dominant framework for academic sociology in the twentieth century and accounts for by far the largest proportion of theory and research in the field of organisational studies' (Ibid., p. 48). Burrell and Morgan see Auguste Comte (1798–1857), the French philosopher, as the founding father of 'sociology'. Comte's third stage of the evolution of sociology is the Scientific or 'positive': the study of the laws of the universe and the cause of phenomena (the first two stages being the Theological and the Metaphysical). The theoretical

scheme of Comte's 'positive philosophy' was based on 'a definite view of the logic of scientific method and the character of scientific knowledge' (Giddens, 1974, p. 1). Comte envisaged a hierarchy of sciences, both historically and developmentally: sociology presupposes and is based on the laws of biology which are, in turn, predicated on the laws of chemistry, and so on, back to metaphysics and theology. The basic notion of positivism is that a science of society is directly comparable to the natural sciences. Three implications and assertions follow: that the methods of the natural sciences are applicable to the study of humans and human social action; that the outcome of social science research can be expressed as causal scientific laws; and that such results are value-free. Burrell and Morgan (1979) use the word 'positivist' 'to characterise epistemologies which seek to explain and predict what happens in the world by searching for regularities and causal relationships' (p. 5). The positivism–anti-positivism debate, therefore, can be viewed as a continum, the positivist end of which is representative of the functionalist paradigm.

In terms of the academic disciplines of health and health promotion, Doyal and Pennell (1979) suggest that social policy and social administration, two academic approaches to the study of medicine which emerged in the late nineteenth century and early twentieth century are the dominant disciplines and are limited by their problem orientation: 'the problems to which the practitioners of social administration address themselves are usually connected with the functioning or malfunctioning of the welfare state' (p. 13). Social administration has traditionally taken a functionalist approach, uncritically accepting, for instance, the medical profession's definitions of medicine. As far as the more recent sociology of medicine is concerned, the work of the sociologist Talcott Parsons who, although strictly a functionalist, has influenced theorists dealing with the social content and construction of the medical situation; social relationships; doctor–patient interactions; and the 'sick role'. Whilst maintaining a view about the function of medicine which is to do with social regulation and control, the tradition of the sociology of medicine has allowed of a more subjectivist element to its inquiry. Freidson (1970), for instance, reviews patterns of interaction between people involved in the process of medical treatment (e.g. doctor–patient) and argues that it is precisely such interaction between the medical profession and the 'layman' (*sic*) which has a positive influence in limiting the autonomy of professional practice. Similarly, Shapiro (1983) proposes that 'a values tradition, as a critic of scientific tradition, needs to be careful of its own potential biases' (p. 26).

6 The history of the intellectual tradition in which the interpretative paradigm has its roots can be traced back to the eighteenth-century German idealist philosopher Immanuel Kant (1724–1804), who argued that there are inherent organising principles by which all our mental perceptions of 'reality' are structured and understood. This *a priori* knowledge is independent of the external reality or particular object which evokes our sense of it. The development of idealism, and later interpretative sociology, confronted positivism both in the natural sciences, in that 'scientific method' was no longer seen as value free; and in the human sciences by acknowledging the spiritual nature of human beings. R. Holland (1990b) explains the development in the twentieth century of 'forms of knowledge which take account of the *meanings* human beings attach to objects, situations and events' (p. 3, original emphasis), citing the example of anthropologists having to learn the language of others before understanding and making sense of what might initially, and acontextually, be seen as bizarre. There are obvious parallels with mental illness, in particular, forms of thought

disorder in response to which mental health workers need to check their understanding of the client's meaning *in their context*.

7 Perhaps the most famous and influential radical humanist critic of contemporary medicine is Ivan Illich (1975). In his book *Medical nemesis* he defines and describes three categories of *iatrogensis*, that is, medically caused damage or medical pathology: *clinical iatrogensis* is the physical damage caused by doctors in 'curing' people, e.g. the use of electro-convulsive therapy (ECT) to treat depressed people; *social iatrogenesis* is the addiction of people to medical care as a solution to all their problems, e.g. 'I'm going to the GP because I'm depressed'; and, finally, *structural iatrogenesis* is the destruction of a person's autonomy in and responsibility for their own health and health care, e.g. no longer being able to think or feel that there are alternatives to going to the GP or having ECT. Ultimately Illich's view of medicine doing more harm than good leads him to a form of politics of abolition (Mathiesen, 1974). Illich argues that modern medicine as such needs to be destroyed and health care reappropriated by the people, and that the de-bureaucratisation and de-institutionalisation of society will accompany and contribute to this process. However, in his emphasis on personal autonomy and choice, as distinguished from organised, structural, radical change, Illich remains a radical humanist.

8 As Burrell and Morgan (1979) point out, Marx, in *The German ideology* (written in 1846), turned away from his earlier Hegelian idealism to a more materalist view and analysis of the social world, marking a movement away from philosophical concerns (idealist, subjectivist, radical humanist) to those of political economy and organisation (radical structuralist). Marx introduced two important methods in scientific inquiry: historical and dialectical materialism. Historical materialism is an approach to history which studies social life and 'social problems' in relation to the ways in which people produce their means of subsistence. Historical materialism also, importantly, explains the cause and nature of social change: 'at a certain stage of their development, the material productive forces of society come into conflict with the existing relations of production. . . . From forms of development of the productive forces these relations turn into their fetters. There begins an era of social revolution' (Marx, 1858/1971, p. 21). Thus, the motor of social change is in the dialectical and conflictual relationship between the forces and relationships of production – the specific nature of which can be determined only by empirical, objectivist analysis. Marxism is not simply a science of history but one which constantly analyses society's structure-in-process through the production and reproduction of material life.

> Dialectics makes it possible to think of a materialist process since it aims at the simultaneous recognition of 'things' as both objects and processes. In other words, dialectics aims at . . . grasping things immediately in their isolatedness, and immediately in their full relation to other things, and finally grasping the unity and disunity of both.
>
> (Coward and Ellis, 1977, p. 84)

Politzer (1976) identifies four important laws of dialectics. The first, that subjects/objects must be studied in motion and change, is familiar to those working in the field of mental health. The second, that everything is transitory in nature, is true of many psychiatric 'symptoms', conditions and crises. The third, that things change only because they contain contradictions within themselves, can be seen in the rare radical critiques of current policies to decant psychiatric hospitals, critiques which, from a psychological perspective, argue for subtlety in relation to institutionalisation (Banton et al., 1985) and, from an analysis of comparative social policy, argue for a reconsideration of de-institutionalisation (Tudor, 1990/91) (reviewed in Chapters 4 and 5). The fourth law of dialectics, that historical progress is made in a series of gradual changes which accumulate and then produce sudden and substantial change, is exemplified by the mental health illness reform movement and legislative reform in Italy.

9 If it is social policy and social administration which are dominant within the functionalist paradigm, and the sociology of medicine which has influenced the interpretative paradigm, and the sociology and psychology of *health* care (with its radical critique and complementary/alternative medical practice) which reflects the radical humanist paradigm, it is the kind of critical *social* policy of health, reflected in the work and writings of Doyal and Pennell (1979), J. Mitchell (1984), J. Robertson (1986) and Navarro (1986), which characterises the radical structuralist approaches to medicine, health care and policy. Doyal and Pennell (1979) move towards a 'critical understanding' of medicine which, in line with Burrell and Morgan's (1979) sociological analysis, 'must involve an understanding of the complex interrelationships between science and society' (p. 21). In pursuing this understanding they analyse the development and impact of capitalism; underdevelopment, colonialism and imperialism; social control and the politics of reproduction. Fanon (1970) writes about the links between medicine and colonialism: 'introduced into Algeria at the same time as racialism and humiliation, Western medical science, being part of the oppressive system, has always provoked . . . an ambivalent attitude' (p. 102). J. Mitchell (1984) argues that 'recognising that the struggle for better health happens primarily *outside* the health service is an absolute precondition of getting right what contribution health care cannot and can make' (p. 219, original emphasis) and advocates 'oppositional practice', e.g. developing more confidence and knowledge about our bodies and new forms of solidarity, a redistribution of knowledge and support for collective action. J. Robertson (1986) focuses on the economics of health: 'what is needed is an economics of well-being – including a real economics of health rather than a "health economics" oriented towards sickness – that will treat the creation of health as a form of wealth creation' (p. 83). Navarro (1978, 1986) writes a Marxist analysis of the evolution of the medical sector in Britain and offers an account of 'communist medicine'.

3 MENTAL HEALTH PROMOTION

1 Although this sequence is, in practice, most often seen in reverse: the concern of most doctors being to identify and diagnose 'disease', for which a particular treatment is prescribed. The emphasis in medical research is therefore to refine diagnostic criteria and categories and – and this is particularly true of research in psychiatry – to create ever more sophisticated drugs for medication. With the chemical industry often funding such research and the production of pharmaceutical drugs now a multi-million pound industry, it follows that industrialists as well as the medical profession are understandably nervous of any methods of treatment which challenge the traditional medical model, its implications and financing. Hence we see the general acceptance of the so-called 'side-effects' of drugs; and the lack of debate about immunisation, even within health education.

2 At a conference at which this framework was presented, in response to an intervention from a psychiatric patient about the closure of psychiatric hospitals, the conference was told not to criticise service provision and to think positively – and this within a context of 'Health For All' principles of reducing inequalities, community and intersectoral participation; anti-discrimination; and the promotion of mental health!

3 The notions of 'value' and 'values' are contentious ones, whether in philosophical terms, e.g. Ayer's (1936/1971) emotive theory of values, or in the
diverse psychological theories of values. Thus, values are defined as a belief
(Allport, 1963); a state or an object, a relationship between an emotional
feeling and cognitive categories (E.E. Jones and Gerard, 1967); and 'an
enduring belief that a specific mode of conduct or end-state of existence is
personally or socially preferable to [its] opposite' (Rokeach, 1973, p. 5) with
two functions: as standards and as motivational.

4 Freud (1894/1962) first introduced the term 'defensive process', later replacing
it with the word 'repression', later still reverting to 'defence' as a general
designation of which repression was one mechanism. By 1936 his daughter
Anna identified nine mechanisms of defence (A. Freud, 1936/1966), adding
three of her own. M. Klein (1932/1975) emphasised the defences of splitting
and projective-identification. Lazarus (1976) highlights another three, warning,
however, of the difficulty of categorisation and maintaining coherence between
terms.

5 Many of these creative adjustment coping mechanisms are, as the phrase
suggests, the positive aspect of the defence mechanism, primarily as and
when brought to consciousness. In developing these, I have drawn particularly
on gestalt psychology (Perls et al., 1951/1973; Clarkson, 1989).

6 Differing from Freud, Perls et al. (1951/1973) distinguish between introjection
and assimilation.

7 In the latest revision – DSMIV (APA, 1994) – this axis is now described as for
reporting 'psychosocial and environmental problems'.

8 H.B. Kaplan's (1983) components are personal attributes and behaviours; the
origin of values and self-evaluation; personal need-value system; specified
social influences; personal view of socially 'disvalued' attributes: all of which
have an influence in the resulting psychological distress.

9 Cross's (1971) model comprises the pre-encounter stage; the encounter stage;
immersion-emersion stage; internalisation stage; internalisation-commitment
stage.

10 Samples and Wohlford (1975), in their primer for self-actualisation, identify
four aspects of self-actualisation: personal openness, in terms of values and
prejudices; personal self-actualisation; the actualising environment in terms of
both insight and outsight (in relationships); and the actualising society.

11 Many Clinical Transactional Analysts and psychotherapists using Transactional
Analysis working with individuals and groups use and actively promote with
their clients Steiner's (1984) concept of emotional literacy; Tudor (1991), for
instance, describes using this material in working with groups of children.
Others have developed Steiner's work, although largely without acknowledgement, e.g. Rakusen's (1990) 'emotional education'.

12 Later, Erskine and Moursund (1988) developed and referred to this as the script
system. Although the debates are far from clear, I distinguish between the
racket system as describing a person's self-reinforcing, distorted system *in
relation to a particular issue* and the *script system* as a person's overall
script-bound system.

13 Although the influence of psychoanalysis, and in particular Winnicott, on a
developmental approach to mental health is widespread and has had an impact
on such documents as the Department of Education and Science's (1968)
publication on health education which refers to 'good health' and 'normal
development' (although it confuses mental ill-health with mental illness), its
influence has not spread wide in the field of MHP. Hill (1988) observes that this
has greater influence in the United States than in Britain (e.g. L. Kaplan, 1971).

A life-cycle approach to assessing health need has become more popular (e.g. Pickin and St Leger, 1993), an approach to assessing mental health need in MHP discussed in Chapter 7.

14 One WHO initiative which brings together these two concerns is that on Health Promoting Hospitals (WHO, 1991a).

4 COMMUNITY

1 This is developed from an original definition from a group exercise on the Trent Regional Health Authority Mental Health Promotion Course, October 1993–March 1994.

2 For M.S. Peck (1988) community building is more than therapeutic, having a quasi-religious purpose, for 'in and through community lies the salvation of the world' (p. 17).

3 Barić (undated) presents a summary of models in relation to the community approach, not dissimilar to the paradigm approach with his three models of locality development, social planning, and social action – selected and based on practice values.

4 However, in comparison with the £2 *billion* spent by the NHS on mental health, the MISG specific grant 'in itself is powerless to correct this major imbalance between hospital treatment and community-based services' (Sayce, 1990, p. 5). In 1993/94 the MISG was £34.4 million (MIND, 1993a).

5 The Italian psychiatric reform, its theoretical roots, its history, its implementation, the range and scope of its current services are all controversial and contested. Much of the literature available in English is written from the authors' implicit 'positions' on psychiatry, mental health and the process of institutional and individual change, and therefore their pre-theorised and pre-judiced views on the theory and practice of the reform. 'Conclusions' are presented thus: 'It doesn't work because it doesn't work throughout Italy' (K. Jones and Poletti, 1984), although at least they declared their scepticism before they 'cut a path through Italy' (p. 10), declining to visit Trieste 'where the movement has been well-documented and has clearly had some success' (Ibid., p. 10). Other 'conclusions' vary from 'It doesn't work because it's too radical' (Papeschi, 1985; K. Jones and Poletti, 1985) to 'It doesn't work because it's not radical enough' (Banton et al., 1985). A second shortcoming in the literature in English on 'the Italian experience' is a number of serious misconceptions about the background to and history of the reform, for example that Law 180/1978 came before or indeed initiated the reform movement – Heginbotham (1984), T. Becker (1985) and M. Davies (1990) among others – which it did not. More useful and accurate commentators on various aspects of the reform include Benigni et al. (1980), Onnis and Lo Rosso (1980), Piro and Oddati (1983) and Tudor (1990/91), whilst Maranesi and Piazza (1986) provide the first statistical survey, since the passing of Law 180/1978, of the effects of the reform and the (then) current state of psychiatric services and mental health resources and Ramon and Giannichedda (1988, 1990) provide the most accessible and comprehensive interleaving of 'the Italian experience' with British experiences of psychiatry in transition.

5 COMMUNITY MENTAL HEALTH PROMOTION

1 This particular reference is made ironic by the fact that on another occasion Thatcher talked about there being no such thing as society, thus rendering her

assumption of nation and her royal use of 'we' somewhat incongruous. The inaccuracy of the reference – in assuming Britain to be monocultural – also appeared lost on this great democrat and free marketeer.

2 Barham (1992) refers to the move from one institution to another (usually in the private or privatised sector) as 'transinstitutionalisation'.

3 Other statistics quoted in this section are from the same survey.

4 Øvretveit et al. (undated) offer a useful introduction to and summary of the issues involved in the organisation and management of CMHCs.

5 Equally, when CMHC services are withdrawn from the community environmental and social factors are ignored. C.J. Smith (1984), in a survey and analysis of service provision, notes the differential effect on women and Hispanic men of the closure, or 'recentralisation', of CMHC services: 'although longer distances, need to cross major routes, and unfamiliar public transport were relevant to this, they appeared less important than crossing of community boundaries, loss of cultural supports through the move, uncertainty of travelling in unknown areas, and identification of the new service with another community and racial group' (C.J. Smith, 1984, p. 141).

6 These are, commonly, identified as three: the psychoanalytic, the cognitive-behavioural, and what Maslow (1968) referred to as the 'third force', namely, the humanistic/existential tradition. There are current discussions as to whether transpersonal and integrative approaches to psychotherapy form separate traditions.

7 Corsini (1986) identifies 250 different schools or approaches to counselling and psychotherapy.

8 This was originally referred to as 'non-directive therapy', later as 'client-centred therapy' and, more recently, as 'person-centred therapy' or, in its wider applications, the 'person-centred approach'. Ivey et al. (1993) have identified these as representing three historical stages in Rogers' own process and development of theory.

9 Boadella (1985) presents some of the areas in which Reich faced problems: the interruption of pregnancy – contrary to conservative medical opinion of the time, Reich argued for a woman's right to choose in the matter of abortion; contraception – Reich promoted giving advice about contraception to young people; sex-affirmative education – Reich advocated counselling, focusing on the quality of adolescent love-life. 'At this time Reich still visualised himself as a Marxist psycho-analyst, and as such he still hoped to find some measure of support for the mental hygiene work he was engaged on, in both Marxist and psycho-analytic circles' (Boadella, 1985, p. 72). Reich was to be disappointed in both circles.

10 Social action psychotherapy has influenced not only WAMH but also the establishment of, amongst others, SHANTI and the Wimbledon Women's Group, reported by Collins (1993) who describes a movement from education to social change.

11 The Union of the Physically Impaired Against Segregation (1981) argues this point strongly against those who use the phrase 'people with disabilities', favouring 'physically impaired' as accurate, honest and descriptive of real, physical, social and economic differences between the able-bodied and disabled.

12 Conlan (1994), writing on behalf of the United Kingdom Advocacy Network (UKAN), identifies overlapping although slightly different forms and definitions of advocacy: legal advocacy, citizen advocacy, formal advocacy, peer advocacy and self-advocacy.

13 This incorporation – into the local state – is what most notably happened to

many Greater London Council (GLC) funded groups when the GLC was abolished - they went under. K. Thompson (1988) offers a powerful and useful critique of the problems of municipal anti-racism and the incorporation of dissent – equally applicable to the field of mental health.

14 Embleton Tudor and Tudor (1994) discuss issues of power, authority and influence in psychotherapy, identifying a number of different reactions to debates about power: defeatism, ignoring power, sharing power, doing away with or giving away power. Empowerment is seen essentially as about seizing power.

15 Developing Burrell and Morgan's (1979) subjective dimension and their four assumptions about the nature of social science, Embleton Tudor and Tudor (1994) identify four debates about power and human nature, ontology, episte-mology and methodology in relation to psychotherapy.

16 There is an ironic addendum to the points Beresford (1994) makes in that at the Third Annual Conference on the Promotion of Mental Health (European Conference), in Birmingham, at which his paper was presented, conference delegates received a message from the Birmingham Mental Health Pioneers drawing their attention to the fact that no user groups were consulted about the conference and that the cost of the conference was prohibitive to users.

17 Nevertheless 'culturally and professionally psychiatrists dominate the Italian scene in comparison to other welfare workers' (Ramon and Giannichedda, 1988, p. 15). This is evidenced by the chair left empty for the psychiatrist even in her absence in the local CSM that I visited in Trieste, Easter 1988 (see Tudor 1990/91). For a discussion of the changing professional roles in the Italian psychiatric/mental health reform movement see De Nicola et al. (1988).

18 In a moving description of one woman's psychiatric history over thirteen years, Gaglio and Sarli (1977) summarise the political analysis and practice of the early CSM in Trieste. The key elements of the early years in Trieste are synthesised: the social construction of 'Anita's' 'madness' in her unhappiness and conflict with the traditional female role; self-criticism of the psychiatrists' hesitancy to confront this contradiction; and an analysis of the wider social forces which impinged on her life, e.g. her husband's demand for her to be cured and returned to him 'better, like the other times'. There is a startling honesty about the effects Anita and her developing autonomy had on the inter-disciplinary team, with reference to an extra-marital relationship she had (described as 'the paradox of the crisis') during her contact with the CSM. The conclusion is equally quintessential: a rejection of psychiatric and medical norms in favour of an analysis of political, social, cultural and psychological contradictions in a class-divided society:

> what seems relevant to us is that now, and different from the past, Anita has been offered the opportunity to recognise and face the mechanisms which have impoverished and destroyed her; all this, without necessarily continuing to lose herself either in herself or in others in the closed circles which up to now she has known.
>
> (Gaglio and Sarli, 1977, p. 74)

6 MENTAL HEALTH POLICY

1 Continuity of care – between the hospital and the community – for those with a 'mental disorder' is implied in the *Mental Health Act 1983*, section 117 on after-care and clarified in the Act's *Code of practice* (DoH/Welsh Office, 1990, 1993) in which the strategy for implementation, i.e. through joint care planning, is also

laid out. The practice of a multi-disciplinary assessment, confirmed in an individual care plan and co-ordinated by a care manager, is given legislative weight in the *NHS and Community Care Act 1990*.

2 Psychiatrists offering counselling begs the question of their ability to offer such a service. Historically, and by virtue of their role, it has been assumed that psychiatrists offer counselling/psychotherapy, despite their lack of specific training in these distinct fields. In Britain, the British Association for Counselling (BAC) and the United Kingdom Council for Psychotherapy (UKCP) are the relevant national co-ordinating bodies in these respective fields and set appropriate standards for training, for supervision, and (in the case of the UKCP) for the necessity for registered psychotherapists to have undertaken their own personal therapy – a requirement not made of psychiatrists or psychologists.

3 The indicators which characterise and items which typify mental health are problematic, oriented as they are on the 'ideal' of the male personality or 'male' values or polarities (Broverman et al., 1981).

4 The service described by C. Murray et al. (1993) is the first district mental health team to be awarded the British Standards Institute BS5750 quality rating.

5 One of the more bizarre lapses between the two editions of the Key Area Documents is that the second edition (DoH, 1994b) drops the reference to 'regular consultation in general practice' in the section on the giving of opportunistic advice. This is particularly strange given *The health of the nation*'s almost exclusive focus on suicide prevention and the fact that the same edition quotes the statistic that 66 per cent of people who go on to commit suicide have consulted their GP in the previous month.

7 MENTAL HEALTH ASSESSMENT

1 For further details on definitions of assessment, the roles and responsibilities of the professionals involved, and the latest legal interpretations and references on this subject, see R.M. Jones (1994) and the Department of Health/Welsh Office (1993).

2 An example of the breakdown in community care due to inadequate funding and training occurred, ironically, during the writing of this chapter when a client of mine with a diagnosed 'mental illness' was refused a mental health (illness) assessment. One 'assessment' took the form of a counselling session (which was both inappropriate and had not been agreed), the other a five minute telephone conversation, the explicit purpose of both of which was to inform him (contradictorily) that he was not ill enough and therefore not eligible to receive services, and that there were sufficient local resources for his needs (which was untrue). Neither 'assessment' assessed his mental health or illness.

3 'Taking all things together, how would you say things are these days - would you say you were *very* happy, *pretty* happy or *not too* happy these days?'

4 This is based on the hypothesis that 'subjective well-being could be indicated by a person's position on two independent dimensions: positive and negative affect. Well-being is expressed as the balance between the two' (Bowling, 1991, p. 157).

5 Cognitive imagery also works on this dimension of mental health, see for instance (H. Graham, 1992, 1994).

6 These are reviewed in Abelin et al. (1987) and by Bowling (1991).

7 The suprapersonal or spiritual dimension is best represented by the works not so much of social scientists but of psychologists such as Jung (1978), Assagioli (1975) and Frankl (1939/1963) all of whom emphasised the importance of

meaning and spirituality in life. It is less conducive to even subjective or qualitative measurement.

8 These two questionnaires, together with the Community Placement Question-naire (Clifford, 1986), provide a set of schedules which may be used for individual care programme and service planning.

9 For instance in the situation of my client (see note 2 above), it would have been more honest for the authorities to have made a proper mental health (and illness) assessment and then told him that no appropriate facilities were available in his district and that they could not afford the facility out of the district which was available.

8 MENTAL HEALTH CONSULTATION

1 The lack of liability on the part of consultants for the outcome of their work and the lack of responsibility on the part of the commissioning organisation or authority to implement consultants' recommendations have become the subject of recent criticism. The British government's Management and Personnel Office's (1982) *Code of practice* offers useful guidelines on selection, terms of engagement and assessment of consultants which could equally be applied outside government departments.

2 In terms of drawing distinctions, there is arguably an additional distinction to be drawn between techniques and skills, with techniques, having echoes of a more mechanical metaphor, as something one can take on without them becoming an aspect of oneself. Skills are often viewed in the context of personal and professional development and as something 'I' have or am learning or devel-oping.

3 A. Brown (1984), however, does refer to four 'methods' of social work: case-work, community work, family work and group work, suggesting that differ-ences between these methods influence consultancy needs.

4 This does not mean, for Caplan, that the consultant ignores or does not pay attention to the consultee's feelings; it is rather that the consultation dos not focus on the consultee's feelings or problems. First, and fundamentally, this respects the consultee's privacy. Secondly, it means that if the consultee's ability to function in their work role and tasks is impaired due to personal problems or issues then the consultant addresses this 'in the form in which the consultee has displaced them onto the client's case and the work setting' (G. Caplan, 1970, p. 30). In a supervision context, using Hawkins and Shohet's (1989) double matrix model, this would involve focusing on the supervisee's counter transference and/or the here-and-now process in the supervision(/con-sultation) process, as a parallel of the there-and-then process between the supervisee and their client. Of course, the precise nature of the boundary between the personal and the professional as well as the interventions chosen by the consultant and supervisor will be influenced by their theoretical approach and training; thus, for instance, a person-centred consultant or supervisor might be more willing for the consultee or supervisee to talk more personally, at least initially, than one taking a more psychoanalytic/dynamic approach who would be more likely to make a facilitative interpretation à la Caplan (above).

5 A. Brown (1984) suggests further overlaps between evaluation, training, staff and professional development and consultancy.

6 This is an example of concordant reactive counter transference in Clarkson's (1992) view of transference and counter transference phenomena whereby 'the psychotherapist experiences the client's avoided experience or resonates empathically with the client's experience' (p. 155).

7 Menzies Lyth's analysis is pertinent and challenging to the number of professions involved in CMH, which spend little time in training considering personal psychology, motivation and mental health, and even less time when working dealing with the anxiety evoked by aspects of the work. Skynner and Schlapobersky (1989) point out that the focus of all professional training in mental health is on the understanding and solution of the patients'/clients' problems; litle attention is paid to the staff's own problems or what is evoked by the work. Institutions of training in social and health care/work support this by attributing and encouraging altruism, maturity, health and professionalism to the worker, thereby indirectly endorsing whatever strategies for dealing with anxiety were operational in the carer's family of origin.

8 Guggenbühl-Craig (1971/1978) draws an analogy of the primary task of social work to that of the Inquisition, both supposedly protecting and helping humanity in general and individuals in particular: 'for many of us, the medieval Inquisition represents the epitome of officially sanctioned sadistic lust for power. When, in modern social work, we sometimes force on an individual things which he himself rejects, our motives are surely better. Or perhaps not always?' (p. 8).

9 A useful developmental model of competency is described by Robinson (1974) and applied to training by Clarkson and Gilbert (1991).

10 Strangely, given increasing financial constraints on the public sector, the phrase 'as resources permit' does not appear in the revised edition of the *Code of practice*. (DoH/Welsh Office, 1993)

11 Menzies Lyth's analytic work has been highly influential on subsequent generations of organisational consultants. In a paper on social anxieties in public sector organisations, Obholzer (1994), for instance, follows her fundamental pessimism, based as it is on certain analytic bliefs such as 'in the unconscious, there is no such concept as "health"' (p. 171).

12 All four case examples are based on real situations, events and people. Some details have been altered so as to maintain confidentiality. In each case the consultant had the support of supervision or 'shadow consultancy' (Hawkins, 1993) in respect of their work.

13 Some attention has ben given to sexuality in organisations and of organisations, notably by Hearn et al. (1989).

14 In this case example the situation, the consultation and the reflection are developed throughout, marked in the text by the agreed and overt material (in normal type) distinguished from the analysis and reflection (in italic type).

15 The dynamic and interactive nature of this case example is reflected in its layout in columns, to be read across.

16 This case example was particularly pertinent to the process of mental health consultation in view of the statistic that 92.9 per cent of CMHCs claim themselves to offer consultation to mental health workers (Onyett et al., 1994).

9 MENTAL HEALTH EDUCATION AND TRAINING

1 Applying this to learning, Gardiner (1989) describes meta-learning as involving 'the ability to distinguish various orders of communication (meta-communication) and to ascribe accurate meaning to communications' (p. 135).

2 As far as integrative psychotherapy is concerned the therapeutic relationship is seen as a *method* (e.g. Khan, 1991) and as a conceptual framework for integration (e.g. Clarkson, 1990, 1994, 1995). Other components and considerations of integrative psychotherapy are described by Orlinsky and Howard (1987), Mahrer (1989) and Norcross and Goldfried (1992).

10 BEYOND MENTAL HEALTH PROMOTION

1 Morgan (1986) identifies eight images or metaphors for reading the structure of an organisation which R. Holland (1993) analyses as reflecting Morgan's own journey round the paradigm map.
2 MMPI: Minnesota Multiphasic Personality Inventory (Hathaway and McKinley, 1943/1970).

Bibliography

PUBLIC GENERAL STATUTES

12 Anne (2) c.23 (sometimes cited as 13 Anne c.26) *Vagrancy Act 1714*
17 Geo.II c.5 *Vagrancy Act 1744*
8 and 9 Vict. c.100 *Lunatics Act 1845*
49 and 50 Vict. c.41 *Idiots Act 1886*
53 Vict. c.5 *Lunacy (Consolidation) Act 1890*
3 and 4 Geo.V c.28 *Mental Deficiency Act 1913*
Mental Treatment Act 1930
Disabled Persons (Employment) Act 1944
7 and 8 Eliz.II c.72 *Mental Health Act 1959*
Local Authority Social Services Act 1970
Eliz.II c.20 *Mental Health Act 1983*. London: HMSO
Eliz.II c.33 *Disabled Persons (Services, Consultation and Representation) Act 1986*. London: HMSO
Eliz.II *NHS and Community Care Act 1990*. London: HMSO

Primary sources

Nurses, Midwives and Health Visitors' Rules Approval Order 1983. Statutory Instrument No. 873.
Nurses, Midwives and Health Visitors' (Registered Fever Nurses Amendment Rules and Training Amendment Rules) Approval Order 1989. Statutory Instrument No.1456.

REFERENCES

Abelin, T., Brzeziński, Z.J., and Carstairs, V.D.L. (1987). *Measurement in health promotion and health protection*. Copenhagen: WHO.
Adams, L., and Holroyd, G. (1989). 'Promoting mental health'. *Health for All News*, 8, Spring, 5–6.
Afzalnia, M.R. (1993). 'Television literacy and young children's mental health promotion'. In D.R. Trent and C. Reed (eds), *Promotion of mental health. Vol. 2* (pp. 89–104). Aldershot: Avebury.
Agel, J. (ed.) (1971). *The radical therapist*. New York: Ballantine.
Ahmed, A.S. (1992). *Postmodernism and Islam*. London: Routledge.
Albee, G.W. (1979). 'Primary prevention'. *Canada's Mental Health*, 27(2), 5–9.
Albee, G.W. (1982). 'Preventing psychopathology and promoting human potential'. *American Psychologist*, 37, 1043–1050.

Albee, G.W. (1986). 'Towards a just society: Lessons from observations on the primary prevention of psychopathology'. *American Psychologist*, *41*, 891–898.

Albee, G.W. (1988). 'Prevention is the answer'. *OpenMind*, *35* (October/November), 14–16.

Albee, G.W. (1990). 'Suffer the little children'. *Journal of Primary Prevention*, *11*, 69–82.

Albee, G.W. (1994). 'The fourth revolution'. In D.R. Trent and C. Reed (eds), *Promotion of mental health. Vol. 3* (pp. 1–16). Aldershot: Avebury.

Albrecht, K.G. (1980). *Brain power*. Englewood Cliffs, NJ: Prentice-Hall.

Alevras, J.S.A., and Wepman, B.J. (1994). 'Application of gestalt therapy principles to organizational consultation'. In B. Feder and R. Ronall (eds), *Beyond the hot seat: Gestalt approaches to group* (pp. 229–237). Highland, NY: Gestalt Journal Press. (Original work published 1980)

Alexander, C.N., Davies, J.L., Dixon, C.A., Dillbeck, M.C., Druker, S.M., Oetzel, R.M., Muehlman, J.M., and Orme-Johnson, D.W. (1990). 'Growth of higher stages of consciousness: Maharishi's vedic psychology of human development'. In C.N. Alexander and E.J. Langer (eds), *Higher stages of human development*. Oxford: Oxford University Press.

Allen, I. (1990). *Community care plannng and mental illness specific grant*. London: Policy Studies Institute.

Allport, G.W. (1961). *Pattern and growth in personality*. New York: Holt, Rinehart and Winston.

American Psychiatric Association (1987). *Diagnostic and statistical manual of mental disorders* (rev. 3rd edn). Washington, DC: APA.

American Psychiatric Association (1994). *Diagnostic and statistical manual of mental disorders* (4th edn). Washington, DC: APA.

Andrews, F.M., and Withey, S.B. (1976). *Social indicators of well-being*. New York: Plenum Press.

Anster, J. (1835). *Faustus I: A dramatic mystery*. London: Longmans.

Antonovsky, A. (1979). *Health, stress and coping: New perspectives on mental and physical well-being*. San Francisco, CA: Jossey-Bass.

Antonovsky, A. (1987). 'The salutogenic perspective: Toward a new view of health and illness'. *Advances*, *4*, 47.

Arnstein, S. (1969). 'A ladder of citizen participation'. *American Institute of Planners Journal*, *5*, 216–224.

Artemis Trust (undated). *Spreading personal growth in society*. Available from The Artemis Trust, 109 Park Hill, London W5 2JS.

Ashton, J., and Seymour, H. (1988). *The new public health*. Milton Keynes: Open University Press.

Assagioli, R. (1975). *Psychosynthesis*. Wellingborough: Turnstone Press.

Association of Metropolitan Authorities (1990). *Contracts for social care: The local authority view*. London: AMA.

Association of Metropolitan Authorities (1991). *Quality and contracts in the personal social services*. London: AMA.

Association of Metropolitan Authorities (1993). *Mental health services*. London: AMA.

Association of Metropolitan Authorities Social Services Committee (1991). *Report*. AMA SS 9153, October. London: AMA.

Audit Commission (1986). *Making a reality of community care*. London: HMSO.

Audit Commission (1993). *Putting quality on the map: Measuring and appraising quality in the public service*. London: HMSO.

Auerswald, E.H. (1987). 'Epistemological confusion in family therapy and research'. *Family Process*, *26*, 317–330.

Ayer, A.J. (1971). *Language, truth and logic*. Harmondsworth: Penguin. (Original work published 1936).

Bailey, R., and Brake, M. (1975). *Radical social work*. London: Edward Arnold.

Bailey, R., and Brake, M. (1980). *Radical social work practice*. London: Edward Arnold.

Baldwin, S., Godfrey, C., and Propper, C. (1990). *Quality of life: Perspectives and politics*. London: Routledge.

Banham, J. (1993). 'The cost of mental ill health to business'. In R. Jenkins and N. Coney (eds), *Prevention of mental ill health at work: A Conference*. London: HMSO.

Bannister, D., and Agnew, J. (1977). 'The child's construing of self'. In A.W. Landfield (ed.), *Nebraska symposium on motivation 1976* (pp. 99–125). Lincoln, NB: University of Nebraska.

Banton, R., Clifford, P., Frosh, S., Lousada, J., and Rosenthal, J. (1985). *The politics of mental health*. Basingstoke: Macmillan.

Barclay, P.M. (1982). *Social workers: Their role and tasks*. London: Bedford Square Press/National Council of Voluntary Organisations.

Barham, P. (1992). *Closing the asylum*. Harmondsworth: Penguin.

Barić, L. (undated). *Health promotion and health education: Module I – Problems and solutions*. Altrincham: Barns Publications.

Barnett, C. (1987). 'What will the neighbours say?' *Nursing Times*, 24 June, 31–32.

Barrera, M. (1981). 'Social support in the adjustment of pregnant adolescent assessment issues'. In B.H. Gottlieb (ed.), *Social networks and social support* (pp. 69–96). Beverly Hills, CA: Sage.

Barrera, M., and Ainley, S. (1983). 'The structure of social support: A conceptual and empirical analysis'. *Journal of Community Psychology, 11*, 133–143.

Barrett-Aranui, H. (1989). 'Nga matapihi o te waiora'. [Windows on Māori well-being]. In A. Munroe, B. Manthei and J. Small (eds), *Counselling: The skills of problem solving* (pp. 97–106). London: Routledge.

Basaglia, F. (1968). *L'istituzione negata*. [The institution denied]. Torino: Einaudi.

Basaglia, F. (1980). 'Problems of law and psychiatry: The Italian experience'. *International Journal of Law and Psychiatry, 3*, 17–37.

Basaglia, F. (1981). 'Breaking the circuit of control'. In D. Ingleby (ed.), *Critical psychiatry* (pp. 184–192). Harmondsworth: Penguin.

Bassett, T., Braisby, D., Edwards, S., and Newbigging, K. (undated). *Involving service users in community mental health services*. London: Good Practices in Mental Health.

Baudrillard, J. (1988). *Selected writings*. Oxford: Polity.

Bean, P., Bingley, W., Bynoe, I., Faulkner, A., Raffaby, E., and Rogers, A. (1991). *Out of harm's way: MIND's research into police and psychiatric action under section 136 of the Mental Health Act*. London: MIND.

Beardshaw, V., and Morgan, E. (1990). *Community care works*. London: MIND.

Beattie, A., Gott, M., Jones, L., and Sidell, M. (eds) (1993). *Health and well-being: A reader*. Basingstoke: Macmillan.

Becker, H.A. (1981). 'The four demons chasing the social scientist'. In H. Bonarius, R. Holland, and S. Rosenberg (eds), *Personal construct psychology* (pp. 1–11). London: Macmillan.

Becker, M.H. (ed.) (1984). *The health belief model and personal health behaviour*. Thorofare, NJ: Charles B. Slack.

Becker, T. (1985). 'Psychiatric reform in Italy: How does it work in Piedmont?' *British Journal of Psychiatry, 147*, 254–260.

Beeforth, M. (1991). 'A user only group'. In C. Thompson (ed.), *Changing the balance* (pp. 15–16). London: National Council for Voluntary Organisations.

Beers, C. (1908). *A mind that found itself*. New York: Longmans.

Benigni, B., Ciappi, F., Germano, G., and Martini, P. (1980). *Il nuovo servizio psichiatrico*. [The new psychiatric service]. Roma: La Nuova Italia Scientifica.

Beresford, P. (1994). 'Mental health and empowerment'. In D.R. Trent and C. Reed (eds), *Promotion of mental health. Vol. 3* (pp. 27–37). Aldershot: Avebury.

Berger, P., and Luckmann, T. (1967). *The social construction of reality*. Harmondsworth: Penguin.

Bergner, M., Bobbit, R.A., Carter, W.B., and Gilson, B.S. (1981). 'The Sickness Impact Profile: Development and final revision of a health status measurement'. *Medical Care, 14*, 57–67.

Berne, E. (1963). *The structure and dynamics of organisations and groups*. New York: Grove Press.

Berne, E. (1966). *Principles of group treatment*. New York: Grove Press.

Berne, E. (1968). *Games people play*. Harmondsworth: Penguin. (Original work published 1964)

Berne, E. (1973). *Sex in human loving*. Harmondsworth: Penguin. (Original work published 1970)

Berne, E. (1975). *What do you say after you say hello?* London: Corgi. (Original work published 1972)

Berne, E. (1981). *A layman's guide to psychiatry and psychoanalysis*. Harmondsworth: Penguin. (Original work published 1961)

Blaxter, M. (1990). *Health and lifestyles*. London: Tavistock/Routledge.

Boadella, D. (1985). *Wilhelm Reich*. London: Arkana. (Original work published 1973)

Bostock, J. (1991). 'Developing a radical approach: The contribution and dangers of community psychology'. *Clinical Psychology Forum*, June, 2–6.

Bostock, J. (1993). 'Experiences of collaborative community research and action in Nottingham'. In D.R. Trent and C. Reed (eds), *Promotion of mental health. Vol. 2* (pp. 143–152). Aldershot: Avebury.

Bowling, A. (1991). *Measuring health*. Milton Keynes: Open University Press.

Bozarth, J., and Temaner Brodley, B. (1986). 'The core values and theory of the person-centred approach'. Paper presented at the First Annual Meeting of the Association for the Development of the Person-Centred Approach, Chicago.

Bracht, N. (1991). 'Citizen participation in community health: Principles for effective partnership'. In B. Badura and I. Kickbusch (eds), *Health promotion research* (pp. 477–496). Copenhagen: WHO.

Bracht, N., and Kingsbury, L. (1990). 'Community organization principles in health promotion'. In N. Bracht (ed.), *Health promotion at the community level* (pp. 66–88). Newbury Park, CA: Sage.

Bradburn, N. (1969). *The structure of psychological well-being*. Chicago, IL: Aldine Publishing.

Bradshaw, J. (1972). 'The concept of social need'. *New Society, 21*, 30 March, 640–643.

Brearley, J.M. (1985). 'Anxiety in the organisational context: Experiences of consultancy'. *Journal of Social Work Practice, 1*(4), 33–47.

Bridges, W. (1980). *Making sense of life's changes*. Reading, MA: Addison-Wesley.

British Medical Association (1992). *Priorities for community care*. London: BMA.

Brogen, P.-O. (1985). *Promotion of mental health*. Gothenberg: Nordic School of Public Health.

Bronfenbrenner, U. (1977). 'Towards an experimental ecology of human development'. *American Psychologist, 32*, 523–531.

Bronfenbrenner, U. (1979). *The ecology of human development*. Cambridge, MA: Harvard University Press.

Broverman, I.K., Broverman, D.M., Clarkson, F.E., Rosenkrantz, P.S., and Vogel, S.R. (1981). 'Sex-role stereotypes and clinical judgements of mental health'. In E. Howell and M. Bayes (eds), *Women and mental health* (pp. 86–97). New York: Basic Books.

Brown, A. (1984). *Consultation: An aid to successful social work*. London: Heinemann Educational.

Brown, G.W., and Harris, T.O. (1978). *Social origins of depression*. London: Tavistock.

Brown, K. (1979). 'Towards a Marxist theory of personality'. Unpublished MA dissertation, University of Kent at Canterbury.

Brown, K., and Tudor, K. (1981). 'Social work education and practice: Reform and revolution – A theory for change'. *Contemporary Social Work Education, 4*, 101–112.

Browne, D., Francis, E., and Crowe, I. (1993). 'Black people: Mental health and the criminal justice system'. In W. Watson and A. Grounds (eds), *The mentally disordered offender in the era of community care* (pp. 102–117). Cambridge: Cambridge University Press.

Bulhan, H.A. (1980). 'Fritz Fanon: The revolutionary psychiatrist'. *Race and Class, 21*, 251–270.

Bulmer, M. (1987). *The social basis of community care*. London: Allen and Unwin.

Bunton, R., and Macdonald, G. (eds) (1992). *Health promotion: Disciplines and diversity*. London: Routledge.

Burden, C. (1994). *Promoting mental health through purchasing*. Conference report, March, South West Thames Regional Health Authority, Croydon.

Burnard, P. (1991). *Coping with stress in the health professions*. London: Chapman & Hall.

Burrell, G. (1988). 'Modernism, postmodernism and organisational analysis 2: The contribution of Michael Foucault'. *Organization Studies, 9*, 221–235.

Burrell, G., and Morgan, G. (1979). *Sociological paradigms and organisational analysis*. London: Heinemann.

Busfield, J. (1988). 'Mental illness as social product or social construct: A contradiction in feminists' arguments?' *Sociology of Health and Illness, 10*, 521-542.

Buss, A.R. (1979). *A dialectical psychology*. Irvington, NY: Halstead Press.

Camden Mental Health Consortium (1988). *Treated well? A code of practice for psychiatric hospitals based on the views of people who use them*. Available from Good Practices in Mental Health, 380-384 Harrow Road, London W9 2HU.

Campaign Against Psychiatric Oppression (undated). *Introduction, manifesto, demands*. Available from CAPO, c/o 18 Seymour Buildings, Seymour Place, London W1H 5TQ.

Campbell, P. (1989a). 'Speaking out on services'. *Social Work Today*, 9 November, 22.

Campbell, P. (1989b). 'The self-advocacy movement in the UK'. In A. Brackx and C. Grimshaw (eds), *Mental health care in crisis* (pp. 206-213). London: Pluto Press.

Cantril, H. (1965). *The pattern of human concerns*. New Brunswick, NJ: Rutgers University Press.

Caplan, G. (1961). *An approach to community mental health*. London: Tavistock.

Caplan, G. (1970). *The theory and practice of mental health consultation*. London: Tavistock.

Caplan, G. (1974). *Support systems and community mental health: Lectures on concept development*. New York: Behavioral Publications.

Caplan, G., and Killilea, M. (eds) (1976). *Support systems and mutual help: Multidisciplinary exploration.* New York: Grune & Stratton.

Caplan, R. (1986). 'The implications of socio-theoretical constructs for the evaluation of health education theory'. Unpublished MSc dissertation, King's College, University of London.

Caplan, R. (1989). 'Proposal for the establishment of a fellowship to investigate conceptual issues and implementation of community mental health promotion'. Paper available from the Health Education Authority, Hamilton House, Mabledon Place, London WC1H 9TX.

Caplan, R., and Holland, R. (1990). 'Rethinking health education theory'. *Health Education Journal, 49*, 10-12.

Castel, R., Castel, F., and Lovell, A. (1982). *The psychiatric society.* New York: Columbia University Press.

Cervi, B. (1990). 'Election pandering'. *Community Care*, 26 July, 9.

Chaitow, L. (1988). *Vaccination and immunization: Danger, delusions and alternatives.* Saffron Walden: C.W. Daniel.

Chambers, L.W., Sackett, D.L., and Goldsmith, C.H. (1976). 'Developments and application of an index of social function'. *Health Services Research, 11*, 430-441.

Chesler, P. (1972). *Women and madness.* New York: Avon.

Childs, K. (1992). ' "Look after your mental health": A mental health roadshow'. In D.R. Trent (ed.), *Promotion of mental health. Vol. 1* (pp. 247-256). Aldershot: Avebury.

Chiu, H. (1992). 'Mental health and daoism'. In D.R. Trent (ed.), *Promotion of mental health. Vol. 1* (pp. 31-40). Aldershot: Avebury.

Christmas, P., and Ewles, L. (1992). *Approaches to monitoring health promotion in contracts.* Available from Directorate of Public Health, Southampton and South West Hampshire Health Authority, Western Hospital (A Block), Oakley Road, Southampton SO9 4WQ.

Chwedorowicz, A. (1992). 'Psychic hygiene in mental health promotion'. In D.R. Trent (ed.), *Promotion of mental health. Vol. 1* (pp. 241–246). Aldershot: Avebury.

Clare, A. (1976). *Psychiatry in dissent.* London: Tavistock.

Clarkson, P. (1989). *Gestalt counselling in action.* London: Sage.

Clarkson, P. (1990). 'A multiplicity of psychotherapeutic relationships'. *British Journal of Psychotherapy, 7*, 148–163.

Clarkson, P. (1992). *Transactional analysis psychotherapy.* London: Routledge.

Clarkson, P. (1993). 'Bystander games'. *Transactional Analysis Journal, 23*, 158–172.

Clarkson, P. (1994). 'The psychotheraputic relationship'. In P. Clarkson and M. Pokorney (eds), *The handbook of psychotherapy* (pp. 28–48). London: Routledge.

Clarkson, P. (1995). The therapeutic relationship. London: Whurr.

Clarkson, P., and Gilbert, M. (1990). 'Transactional analysis'. In W. Dryden (ed.), *Individual therapy in Britain.* Milton Keynes: Open University Press.

Clarkson, P., and Gilbert, M. (1991). 'The training of counsellor trainers and supervisors'. In W. Dryden and B. Thorne (eds), *Training and supervision for counselling in action* (pp. 143–169). London: Sage.

Clifford, P. (1986). *Community placement questionnaire.* London: Research and Development in Psychiatry.

Clifford, P. (1987). *Problems questionnaire.* London: Research and Development in Psychiatry.

Clifford, P. (1991). *Why haven't I joined the normies? Some doubts about normal-*

isation. London: Research and Development in Psychiatry. (Original work published in 1986)

Clifford, P., and Morris, I. (undated). *Social functioning questionnaire*. London: Research and Development in Psychiatry.

Clifford, P., Leiper, R., Lavender, A., and Pilling, S. (1991). *Assuring quality in mental health services*. London: Research and Development in Psychiatry/Free Associations.

Clifford, P., Leiper, R., Lavender, A., and Pilling, S. (1991). *Assuring quality in mental health services*. London: Research and Development in Psychiatry/Free Associations.

Cochran, M. (1988). 'Addressing youth and family vulnerability: Empowerment in an ecological context'. *Canadian Journal of Public Health*, *79* (suppl. 2), S10–S16.

Coleman, E. (1985). 'Developmental stages of the coming out process'. In J.C. Gonsoriek (ed.), *A guide to psychotherapy to gay and lesbian clients* (pp. 31–43). New York: Harrington Park.

Collins, L. (1993). 'A community group for women who have or are at risk of having mental health problems'. In D.R. Trent and C. Reed (eds), *Promotion of mental health. Vol. 2* (pp. 177–187). Aldershot: Avebury.

Colman, A.D. (1992). 'Depth consultation'. In M. Stein and J. Hollwitz (eds), *Psyche at work* (pp. 92–117). Wilmette, IL: Chiron.

Conlan, E. (1944). 'Advocacy in mental health'. In NHS Executive Mental Health Task Force User Group (ed.), *Advocacy: A code of practice*. London: NHS Executive.

Cooper, D. (1967). *Psychiatry and anti-psychiatry*. London: Tavistock.

Coopersmith, S. (1967). *The antecedents of self-esteem*. San Francisco, CA: W.H. Freeman.

Corrigan, P., and Leonard, P. (1978). *Social work practice under capitalism: A marxist approach*. London: Macmillan.

Corsini, R. (ed.) (1986). *Current psychotherapies*. Itasca, IL: F.E. Peacock.

Costa, J. (1994). 'Occupational stress factors among European workers'. In D.R. Trent and C. Reed (eds), *Promotion of mental health. Vol. 3* (pp. 59-66). Aldershot: Avebury.

Council of Europe Committee of Ministers (1976). *On the organisation of preventive services in mental illness. Resolution (76)40*.

Coward, R., and Ellis, J. (1977). *Language and materialism*. London: Routledge & Kegan Paul.

Cox, D. (1979). 'Review of Burrell, G., and Morgan, G. (1979). *Sociological paradigms and organisational analysis*. London: Heinemann'. *Reviewing Sociology*, *1*, 1-3.

Cox, M., and Theilgaard, A. (1987). *Mutative metaphors on psychotherapy*. London: Tavistock.

Coyle, A., and Daniels, M. (1993). 'Psychological well-being and gay identity: Some suggestions for promoting mental health among gay men'. In D.R. Trent and C. Reed (eds), *Promotion of mental health. Vol. 2* (pp. 189-206). Aldershot: Avebury.

Craib, I. (1987). 'The psychodynamics of theory'. *Free Associations*, *10*, 32-56.

Cramer, D. (1994). 'Promoting mental health through acceptance'. In D.R. Trent and C. Reed (eds), *Promotion of mental health. Vol. 1* (pp. 67-76). Aldershot: Avebury.

Crepet, P., and De Plato, G. (1983). 'Psychiatry without asylums: Origins and prospects in Italy'. *International Journal of Health Services*, *13*, 119-129.

Critchley, B., and Casey, D. (1989). 'Organisations get stuck too'. *Leadership and Organisational Development Journal, 10*, 3-12.

Cross, W.E. (1971). 'The negro-to-black conversion experience: Towards a psychology of black liberation'. *Black World, 2.*

Dahrendorf, R. (1959). *Class and class conflict in industrial society.* London: Routledge & Kegan Paul.

Dalal, F. (1988). 'The racism of Jung'. *Race and Class, 29*(3), 1–22.

Dalgard, O.S., Sørensen, T., and Bjørk, S. (1991). 'Community psychiatry and health promotion research'. In B. Badura and I. Kickbush (eds), *Health promotion research* (pp. 421–439). Copenhagen: WHO.

Daly, M. (1978). *Gyn/Ecology.* Boston, MA: Beacon Press.

Daniels, M., and Coyle, A. (1993). 'Health dividends': The use of co-operative inquiry as a health promotion intervention with a group of unemployed women. In D.R. Trent and C. Reed (eds), *Promotion of mental health. Vol. 2* (pp. 207–220). Aldershot: Avebury.

Darwin, C. (1859). *The origin of species.* London: J. Murray.

Davidge, M., Elias, S., Jayes, B., Wood, K., and Yates, J. (1993). *Survey of English mental illness hospitals.* Health Services Management Centre, University of Birmingham.

Davidson, J. (1987). 'Health education in a psychiatric setting'. *British Journal of Occupational Therapy, 50*, 311–315.

Davies, J.K., and Kelly, M.P. (1993). *Healthy cities: Research and practice.* London: Routledge.

Davies, M. (1990). 'When in Rome . . . '. *The Health Service Journal,* 21 June, 915.

Davis, K. (1938). 'Mental hygiene and the class structure'. *Psychiatry, 1*, 55, 60.

Davis, N. (1976). *Sociological constructions of deviance: Perspectives and issues in the field.* Dubuque, IA: W.C. Brown.

Day, R., and Klein, P. (1984). 'Two sides of the same coin'. *Health and Social Service Journal,* 8 March, 285–286.

De Beauvoir, S. (1972). *The second sex.* Harmondsworth: Penguin.

Dekker, E. (1987). 'Health policy and mental health'. *Health Promotion, 2*, 139–147.

Del Giudice, G., Evaristo, P., and Reali, M. (undated). 'Can mental hospitals be phased out?' Unpublished paper, Trieste.

Dell'Acqua, G., and Mezzina, R. (undated). 'La storia, il soggetto, la capacita di intendere e di volere'. [A person's history, self and the full possession of their faculties]. Unpublished paper, Trieste.

Dell'Acqua, G., Mezzina, R., and Cogliati, M.G. (1986). 'Lesioni e minacce alla salute psichica nella "carrierra" del malato di mente'. [Injuries and threats to the mental health of the psychiatric patient]. Paper presented at an international conference, Trieste, June.

De Nicola, P., Giacobbi, E., and Rogialli, S. (1988). 'Changing professional roles in the Italian psychiatric system'. In S. Ramon and M.G. Giannichedda (eds), *Psychiatry in transition* (pp. 235–242). London: Pluto Press.

Department of Education (1993). *National curriculum: Guidance document 5.* London: HMSO.

Department of Education and Science (1968). *A handbook of health education.* London: HMSO.

Department of Health (1989a). *Caring for people.* London: HMSO.

Department of Health (1989b). *Working for patients.* London: HMSO.

Department of Health (1990a). *Community care in the next decade and beyond: Caring for people policy guidance.* London: HMSO.

Department of Health (1990b). *Specific grant for provision of social care for people with a mental illness*. Draft Health/Local Authority Circular, May.

Department of Health (1991). *The health of the nation*. London: HMSO.

Department of Health (1992). *The health of the nation*. London: HMSO.

Department of Health (1993a). 'Legislation planned to provide for supervised discharge of psychiatric patients'. Press release H93/908, 12 August. London: DoH.

Department of Health (1993b). *The health of the nation: Key area handbook mental illness*. London: HMSO.

Department of Health (1994a). *ABC of mental health in the workplace*. London: DoH.

Department of Health (1994b). *Draft guide to arrangements for inter-agency working for the care and protection of severely mentally ill people*. London: DoH.

Department of Health (1994c). *The health of the nation: Key area handbook mental illness* (2nd edn). London: HMSO.

Department of Health (1994d). *The report of the enquiry into the care and treatment of Christopher Clunis (Killing of Mr Zito)*. London: HMSO.

Department of Health (undated). *A guide to mental health in the workplace*. London: DoH.

Department of Health and Social Security (1976). *A review of the Mental Health Act 1959*. London: HMSO.

Department of Health and Social Security (1986). *Health and personal social services statistics for England 1986*. London: HMSO.

Department of Health/Home Office (1992). 'Services for people from black and ethnic minority groups: Issues of race and culture'. In *Review of health and social services for mentally disordered offenders and others requiring similar services. Vol. 1: A final summary report*. London: HMSO.

Department of Health/Welsh Office (1990). *Code of practice*. London: HMSO.

Department of Health/Welsh Office (1993). *Code of practice* (2nd edn). London: HMSO.

Derrida, J. (1978). *Writing and difference*. London: Routledge & Kegan Paul.

Derrida, J. (1981). *Positions*. Chicago: Chicago University Press.

Derrida, J. (1982). *Margins of philosophy*. London: Harvester.

Descartes, R. (1912). 'Meditations on the first philosophy'. In *A discourse on method* (J. Veitch, Trans.). London: Everyman. (Original work published 1641)

Dickson, A. (1982). *A woman in your own right: Assertiveness and you*. London: Quartet.

Doyal, L., and Pennell, I. (1979). *The political economy of health*. London: Pluto Press.

Doyle, R. (1989). 'A meeting of minds'. *The Health Services Journal*, 16 November, 1407.

Downey, R. (1990). 'Ready, steady – stop?' *Social Work Today*, 12 July, 9.

Downie, R.S., Fyfe, C., and Tannahill, A. (1990). *Health promotion: Models and values*. Oxford: Oxford University Press.

Doxiadis, S. (1987). 'Introduction'. In S. Doxiadis (ed.), *Ethical dilemmas in health promotion* (pp.xi–xiv). London: Wiley.

Durkin, L., and Douieb, B. (1975). 'The mental patient's union'. In D. Jones and M. Mayo (eds), *Community work: Two* (pp. 177–191). London: Routledge & Kegan Paul.

Dworkin, G. (1988). *The theory and practice of autonomy*. Cambridge: Cambridge University Press.

Eachus, P. (1991). 'Inequalities in health: Locus of control as a mediating factor'. *Journal of the Institute of Health Education*, *29*(2), 60–67.

Earp, J.A., and Ennett, S.T. (1991). 'Conceptual models for health education research and practice'. In D.V. McQueen (ed.), 'Theory [special issue]'. *Health Education Research*, *6*(2), 163–171.

Eaton, J.W. (1951). 'The assessment of mental health'. *American Journal of Psychiatry*, *108*, 81–90.

Echlin, R. (1988). *Community mental health teams*. Information pack available from Good Practices in Mental Health, 380–382 Harrow Road, London W9 2HU.

Edwards, G. (1989). 'Finding the Broad Street pump: Primary prevention in mental health'. *Changes*, *7*, 61–64.

Eisenberg, L. (1981). 'A research framework for evaluating the promotion of mental health and prevention of mental illness'. *Public Health Reports*, *96*, 3–19.

Eisenberg, L. (1987). 'Value conflicts in social policies for promoting health'. In S. Doxiadis (ed.), *Ethical dilemmas in health promotion* (pp. 99–116). London: Wiley.

Eliot, T.S. (1934). 'Choruses from "The Rock"'. In *Collected poems 1909–1962* (pp. 159–185). London: Faber & Faber.

Eliot, T.S. (1942). 'The Four Quartets. Little Gidding'. In *Collected poems 1909–1962* (pp. 187-223). London: Faber & Faber.

Embleton Tudor, L., and Tudor, K. (1994). 'The personal and the political: Power, authority and influence in psychotherapy'. In P. Clarkson and M. Pokorney (eds), *Handbook of psychotherapy* (pp. 384–402). London: Routledge.

Embleton Tudor, L., and Tudor, K. (1995). 'Acting up as acting out: Containing anxiety in social services'. *Changes*.

Epp, J. (1988). 'Promoting the mental health of children and youth: Foundation for the future'. *Canadian Journal of Public Health*, *79*(suppl. 2), S6-S9.

Erikson, E. (1968). *Identity, youth and crisis*. New York: W.W. Norton.

Erikson, E. (1977). *Childhood and society*. Harmondsworth: Penguin. (Original work published 1951)

Erskine, R.G. (1975). 'The ABCs of effective psychotherapy'. *Transactional Analysis Journal*, *5*, 163–165.

Erskine, R.G., and Moursund, J.P. (1988). *Integrative psychotherapy in action*. Newbury Park, CA: Sage.

Erskine, R.G., and Zalcman, M. (1979). 'The racket system: A model for racket analysis'. *Transactional Analysis Journal*, *9*, 51–59.

Esterson, A. (1972). *The leaves of Spring*. Harmondsworth: Penguin.

Evans, J. (1988). 'Healthy minds'. *Nursing Times*, 15 April, 55–56.

Falloon, I.R.H., Boyd, J.L., McGill, C.W., Williamson, M., Razani, J., Moss, H.B., Gilderman, A.M., and Simpson, G.M. (1985). 'Family management in the prevention of morbidity of schizophrenia'. *Archives of General Psychiatry*, *42*, 887–896.

Fallowfield, L. (1990). *The quality of life: The missing measurement in health care*. London: Souvenir Press.

Fanon, F. (1967a). *Black skins, white masks* (C.L. Markmann, Trans.). New York: Grove Press. (Original work published 1961)

Fanon, F. (1967b). *The wretched of the earth* (C. Farrington, Trans.). Harmondsworth: Penguin.

Fanon, F. (1970). *A dying colonialism* (H. Chevalier, Trans.). Harmondsworth: Penguin. (Original work published 1959)

Fanshal, A. (1972). 'A meaningful measure of health for epidemiology'. *International Journal of Epidemiology*, *1*, 318–319.

Farr, R. (1984). 'Social representations: Their role in the design and execution of laboratory experiments'. In R. M. Farr and S. Moscovici (eds), *Social representations* (pp. 125–147). Cambridge: Cambridge University Press.

Fernando, S. (1988). *Race and culture in psychiatry*. London: Croom Helm.

Fernando, S. (1990). 'Mental health promotion: The way forward'. In Health Education Authority, *National mental health promotion conference* (pp. 13–17). London: Health Education Authority.

Finch, J. (1986). 'Community care and the invisible welfare state'. *Radical Community Medicine*, *26*, 15–22.

Fitts, W.H. (1965). *Tennessee self-concept scale manual*. Nashville, TN: Counselor Recordings and Tests.

Flanagan, C.M. (1990). *People and change*. Hillsdale, NJ: Lawrence Erlbaum.

Fleming, P. (1985). 'The seven levels of listening in contribution training'. In *Pellin Diploma course notes* (pp. 8–10). Available from Pellin Training Courses, 15 Killyon Road, London SW8 2XS.

Foucault, M. (1971). *Madness and civilisation*. London: Tavistock.

Francis, E. (1991). 'Race in mind'. Presentation on *Approved Social Workers' Course*, Hillingdon, February.

Francis, E., David, J., Johnson, N., and Sashidharan, S. P. (1989). 'Black people and psychiatry in the UK: An alternative to institutional care'. *Psychiatric Bulletin*, *13*, 482-485.

Frankl, V. (1963). *Man's search for meaning* (I. Lasch, Trans.). New York: Pocket Books. (Original work published 1939)

Freidson, E. (1970). *Profession of medicine*. New York: Dodd, Mead.

Freire, P. (1972). *Pedagogy of the oppressed*. Harmondsworth: Penguin.

Freire, P. (1974). *Education: The practice of freedom*. London: Readers & Writers.

Freud, A. (1966). *The ego and mechanisms of defence* (C. Barnes, Trans.). London: Hogarth. (Original work published 1936)

Freud, S. (1962). 'The neuro-psychoses of defence'. In J. Strachey (Ed. and Trans.), *The standard edition of the complete works of Sigmund Freud. Vol. 3*. London: Hogarth. (Original work published 1894)

Freud, S. (1977). *On sexuality* (A. Richards, Trans.). Harmondsworth: Penguin. (Original work published 1905)

Freudenberg, R.K. (1979). 'Mental health education'. In I. Sutherland (ed.), *Health education: Perspectives and choice*. London: Allen & Unwin.

Fromm, E. (1956). *The sane society*. London: Routledge & Kegan Paul.

Fromm, E. (1971). *The crisis of psychoanalysis*. London: Cape.

Füredi, F. (1993). 'PC – The philosophy of low expectations'. *Living Marxism*, December, 17–19.

Gabriel, S. (1987). *The schizophrenic label and Afro-Caribbeans in Britain: Diagnosis or misdiagnosis?* Available from Bristol Inner City Mental Health Project, The Manse, Conduit Place, St Werburgh's, Bristol.

Gaglio, A., and Sarli, E. (1977). 'Bisogni e pratica psichiatrica'. [Needs and psychiatric practice]. *Aut-Aut*, *162*, 61–74.

Galdston, I. (ed.) (1955). *The epidemiology of health*. New York: Health Education Council.

Gardiner, D. (1989). *The anatomy of supervision*. Milton Keynes: Society for Research into Higher Education/Open University Press.

Gatherer, A. (1963). *The Northampton mental health project 1961: An experiment in mental health education*.

Gatherer, A., and Reid, J.J.A. (1967). *Public attitudes and mental health education:*

Northampton mental health project 1963. Available from Northamptonshire County Council, County Hall, PO Box 177, Guildhall Road, Northampton NN1 1AY.

Gergen, K.T. (1971) *The concept of self.* New York: Holt, Rinehart & Winston.

Gibran, K. (1926). *The prophet.* London: Heinemann.

Giddens, A. (1974). 'Introduction'. In A. Giddens (ed.), *Positivism and sociology* (pp. 1–22). London: Heinemann.

Giddens, A. (1984). *The constitution of society.* Oxford: Polity Press.

Glover, J. (1989). *I: The philosophy and psychology of personal identity.* Harmondsworth: Penguin.

Godfrey, C., Hardman, G., and Maynard, A. (1989). *Priorities for health promotion: An economic approach.* Discussion Paper 15. York: University of York, Centre for Health Economics.

Goffman, E. (1961). *Asylums.* Garden City, NY: Doubleday Anchor.

Goldberg, D.P. (1978). *Manual of the General Health Questionnaire.* Windsor: NFER/Nelson.

Goldberg, D.P., and Williams, P. (1988). *A user's guide to the general health questionnaire.* Windsor: NFER-Nelson.

Gomez, J. (1991). *Psychological and psychiatric problems in men.* London: Routledge.

Good Practices in Mental Health (1989). 'Centrally funded development projects'. *New Directions* Autumn, 1, 4–5.

Good Practices in Mental Health (1990). 'Centrally funded development projects'. *New Directions,* Spring, 6–9.

Good Practices in Mental Health (undated). *Survey of Department of Health funded projects for long-term needs.* Available from GPMH, 380–384 Harrow Road, London W9 2HU.

Goodbody, L. (1992). 'Community mental health centres: The natural setting for the prevention of mental health problems?' In D.R. Trent (ed.), *Promotion of mental health. Vol. 1* (pp. 185–196). Aldershot: Avebury.

Gordon, J.B. (1972). 'The meta-journey of R.D. Laing'. In R. Boyers and R. Orrill (eds), *Laing and anti-psychiatry* (pp. 48–76). Harmondsworth: Penguin.

Gordon, P. (1992). 'Early intervention for stress problems: Experience of 3 service delivery models'. In D.R. Trent (ed.), *Promotion of mental health. Vol. 1* (pp. 267–276). Aldershot: Avebury.

Gordon-Brown, I., and Somers, B. (1988). 'Transpersonal psychotherapy'. In J. Rowan and W. Dryden (eds), *Innovative therapy in Britain* (pp. 225–250). Milton Keynes: Open University Press.

Graham, H. (1992). 'Imaginative assessment of personal health needs'. In D.R. Trent (ed.), *Promotion of mental health. Vol. 1* (pp. 53–62). Aldershot: Avebury.

Graham, H. (1994). 'Imaginative stress management: Applying imagery in the assessment and management of stress'. In D.R. Trent and C. Reed (eds), *Promotion of mental health. Vol. 3* (pp. 103–116). Aldershot: Avebury.

Graham, P. (1986). 'Health education for mental health'. *Journal of the Royal Society of Medicine,* 79(suppl. 13), 28–29.

Green, L.W., and Lewis, F.M. (1986). *Measurement and evaluation in health education and health promotion.* Palo Alto, CA: Mayfield.

Griffiths, R. (1988). *Community care: An agenda for action.* London: HMSO.

Griffiths, S., Wylie, I., and Jenkins, R. (1992). *Creating a common profile for mental health.* London: HMSO.

Groder, M. (1977). 'Asklepieion: An integration of psychotherapies'. In G. Barnes (ed.), *TA after Eric Berne* (pp. 134–137). New York: Harper & Row.

Guernina, Z. (1994). 'Reforming mental health care and promoting mental health among ethnic minority families'. In D.R. Trent and C. Reed (eds), *Promotion of mental health. Vol. 3* (pp. 129–140). Aldershot: Avebury.

Guggenbühl-Craig, A. (1978). *Power in the helping professions* (M. Gubitz, Trans.). Irving, TX: Spring Publications. (Original work published 1971)

Guntrip, H. (1964). *Healing the sick mind*. London: Allen & Unwin.

Gurin, G., Veroff, J., and Feld, S. (1960). *Americans view their mental health*. New York: Basic Books.

Hagard, S. (1988). 'Is mental health promotion possible?' Lecture to the Annual General Meeting of the Cambridgeshire Mental Welfare Association, October.

Hall, P., Brockington, I.A., and Murphy, C. (1993). 'Presenters' perceptions of mental illness'. In D.R. Trent and C. Reed (eds), *Promotion of mental health. Vol. 2* (pp. 237–244). Aldershot: Avebury.

Halm, J. (1989). 'Mental health prevention'. In J. Neumann, H. Schroeder and P. Voss (eds), *Mental health within the health promotion concept* (pp. 83–91). Dresden: German Hygiene Museum/Copenhagen: WHO.

Hancock, B., and Hancock, D. (1993). 'Mastery of the environment'. *Elderly Care*, 5, No. 6 (November/December), 22–23.

Harpurhey Resettlement Team (1990). *Mental health project for schools*. Report available from Harpurhey Resettlement Team, Harpurhey Health Centre, 1 Church Lane, Harpurhey, Manchester M9 1BE.

Harré, R. (1983). *Personal being*. Oxford: Blackwell.

Harris, T. (1990). 'Time to change the record'. *Insight*, 10 January, 8.

Harrison, G., Owens, D., Holton, A., Neilson, D., and Boot, D. (1988). 'A prospective study of severe mental disorder in Afro-Caribbean patients'. *Psychological Medicine*, 18, 643–657.

Harrison, M. (1993). 'HOME-START: Support, friendship and practical help for young families under stress'. In D.R. Trent and C. Reed (eds), *Promotion of mental health. Vol. 2* (pp. 245–248). Aldershot: Avebury.

Harvey, L. (1982). 'The use and abuse of Kuhnian paradigms in the sociology of knowledge'. *Sociology*, 16, 85–101.

Hassard, J. (1993). 'Postmodernism and organizational analysis: An overview'. In J. Hassard and M. Parker (eds), *Postmodernism and organisation*. London: Sage.

Hassard, J., and Parker, M. (eds) (1993). *Postmodernism and organisation*. London: Sage.

Hastings Health Authority/East Sussex County Council Social Services Department (1989). *A strategy for action: The development of mental health services in the Hastings Health District*. Available from Hastings Health Authority, 729 The Ridge, St Leonard's-on-Sea TN37 7PT.

Hathaway, S.R., and McKinley, J.C. (1970). *Minnesota multiphasic personality inventory*. Minneapolis, MN: University of Minnesota. (Original work published 1943)

Hawkins, P. (1993). *Shadow consultancy*. Available from Bath Consultancy Group, 24 Gay Street, Bath BA1 2PD.

Hawkins, P., and Shohet, R. (1989). *Supervision in the helping professions*. Milton Keynes: Open University.

Health Education Authority (1989). *Strategic Plan 1990-1995*. London: HEA.

Health Education Authority (1990). *National mental health promotion conference*. London: HEA.

Health Education Authority (1993a). *A survey of health education policies in schools*. London: HEA.

Health Education Authority (1993b). *Health at work in the NHS*. London: HEA.

Health Education Authority (1993c). *Health Education Authority strategy 1993-98*. London: HEA.

Health Education Authority (1993d). *Health promotion in the workplace: A summary*. London: HEA.

Hearn, J., Sheppard, J.L., Tancred-Sheriff, P., and Burrell, G. (1989). *The sexuality of organization*. London: Sage.

Heginbotham, C. (1984). 'Lessons from the Italian school'. *Social Work Today*, 20 February, 18.

Heginbotham, C. (1990). 'A classic example'. *Insight*, 31 January, 25.

Henderson, S., Duncan Jones, P., Byrne, D.G., and Scott, R. (1980). 'Measuring social relationships: The Interview Schedule for Social Interaction'. *Psychological Medicine*, *10*, 723–734.

Hendon, J. (1992). 'The changing language of mental health'. In D.R. Trent (ed.), *Promotion of mental health. Vol. 1* (pp. 69–75). Aldershot: Avebury.

Hendon, J., and Lawson, M. (1990/1991). 'Mind your language'. *OpenMind, 48*, December/January, 10–11.

Higgins, P. (1984). 'Mental health education'. *Nursing Mirror, 159*, 28–29.

Hill, F. (1988). 'Mental health education: Where do we start?' *Westminster Studies in Education, 11*, 3–14.

Hillery, G.A. (1955). 'Definitions of community: Areas of agreement'. *Rural Sociology, 20*, 111–123.

Hillman, J. (1993). 'Loving the community and work'. In R. Bly, J. Hillman and M. Meade (eds), *The rag and bone shop of the heart* (pp. 229–232). New York: Harper & Perennial.

Hillman, J., and Ventura, M. (1992). *We've had a hundred years of psychotherapy and the world's getting worse*. San Francisco, CA: Harper.

Hitchings, P. (1994). 'Psychotherapy and sexual orientation'. In P. Clarkson and M. Pokorney (eds), *Handbook of psychotherapy* (pp. 119–132). London: Routledge.

Hofstede, G. (1980). *Culture's consequences: International differences in work related values*. Beverly Hills, CA: Sage.

Hoggett, P. (1990). 'Public hostility to the welfare state'. *Changes, 8*, 207–216.

Hoggett, P., and Lousada, J. (1985). 'Therapeutic interventions in working class communities'. *Free Associations, 1*, 125–152.

Holden, R. (1993). 'Laughter: The best medicine'. In D.R. Trent and C. Reed (eds), *Promotion of mental health. Vol .2* (pp. 259–264). Aldershot: Avebury.

Holland, R. (1977). *Self and social context*. London: Macmillan.

Holland, R. (1981). 'From perspectives to reflexivity'. In H. Bonarius, R. Holland and S. Rosenberg (eds), *Personal construct psychology: Recent advances in theory and practice* (pp. 23–29). London: Macmillan.

Holland, R. (1987). 'Experiments in perfectly reflexive teaching: The sociology of knowledge and of science'. Unpublished manuscript, Centre for Educational Studies, King's College, University of London.

Holland, R. (1988). *Sociopsychological studies: Course S3*. Available from the Management Centre, King's College, University of London, Campden Hill Road, London W8 7AH.

Holland, R. (1989). 'Visible and invisible curricula in professional education'. *Issues in Social Work Education, 8*, 83–111.

Holland, R. (1990a). 'Changing theories and changing families'. Unpublished manuscript. Available from the Management Centre, King's College, University of London, Campden Hill Road, London W8 7AH.

Holland, R. (1990b). 'Scientificity and psychoanalysis: insights from the controversial discussions'. *International Review of Psycho-Analysis, 2*, 133–158.

Holland, R. (1990c). 'The paradigm plague: prevention, cure and inoculation'. *Human Relations, 1*, 23–48.

Holland, R. (1991). 'Reflexivity'. Unpublished manuscript. Available from the Management Centre, King's College, University of London, Campden Hill Road, London W8 7AH.

Holland, R. (1992). 'Sanity, necessary complexities and mental health promotion'. *Changes*, *10*, 136–145.

Holland, R. (1993). 'A metatheoretical adventure'. In L. Harrison (ed.), *Substance misuse: Designing social work training* (pp. 24–70). London: Central Council for Education and Training in Social Work/University of Hull.

Holland, R., and Tudor, K. (1991). 'Psyche and society: Mental health promotion in theory and practice'. Paper presented at the annual meeting of the British Sociological Association, Manchester, March.

Holland, S. (1979). 'The development of an action and counselling service in a deprived urban area'. In M. Meacher (ed.), *New methods of mental health care* (pp. 95–106). London: Pergamon.

Holland, S. (1985). 'Loss, rage and oppression: Neighbourhood psychotherapy with working class, black and national minority women'. Paper presented at the Pam Smith Memorial Lecture, Polytechnic of North London, June.

Holland, S. (1988). 'Defining and experimenting with prevention'. In S. Ramon and M.G. Giannichedda (eds), *Psychiatry in transition* (pp. 125–137). London: Pluto Press.

Holland, S. (1990). 'Psychotherapy, oppression and social action: Gender, race and class in black women's depression'. In R. Perelberg and A. Miller (eds), *Gender and power in families* (pp. 256–269). London: Routledge.

Holland, S., and Hoggett, P. (1977). 'People's aid and action centre'. *Humpty Dumpty Radical Psychology Magazine*, *8*, 18–23.

Holland, S., and Holland, R. (1984). 'Depressed women: Outposts of empire and castles of skin'. In B. Richards (ed.), *Capitalism and infancy* (pp. 92–101). London: Free Association Books.

Hollander, D., Checkley, S., and Appleby, L. (1989). 'Mental health education for primary health care'. *Psychiatric Bulletin*, *13*, 73–76.

Hollingshead, A.B., and Redlich, F.C. (1958). *Social class and mental illness*. New York: Wiley.

Holmes, T.A., and Rahe, R.H. (1967). 'The social readjustment rating scale'. *Journal of Psychosomatic Research*, *11*, 213–218.

Holroyd, G. (1990) Promoting mental health by facilitating participation in planning. In J. Jones and J. Tilston (eds), *Roots and branches*. Papers from the Open University Winter School on Community Development and Health (pp.166–173). Milton Keynes: Open University Health Education Unit.

Holroyd, G. (1991). 'Promoting mental health – The Salford experience'. In *Community development and health*. Milton Keynes: Open University Press.

Hopkins, J. (1993). 'Staff care in the work community'. In D.R. Trent and C. Reed (eds), *Promotion of mental health. Vol. 2* (pp. 265–271). Aldershot: Avebury.

House of Commons Social Services Select Committee (1991). *Community care: Services for people with a mental handicap and people with mental illness*. London: HMSO.

Hunt, S.M., McEwan, J., and McKenna, S.P. (1986). *Measuring health status*. London: Croom Helm.

Icsoe, I., and Harris, L.C. (1984). 'Social and community interventions'. *Annual Review of Psychology*, *35*, 333–360.

Illich, I. (1973). *Deschooling society*. Harmondsworth: Penguin.

Illich, I. (1975). *Medical nemesis: The expropriation of health*. London: Calder & Boyars.

Ingleby, D. (ed.) (1981). *Critical psychiatry*. Harmondsworth: Penguin.

Insane Liberation Front (1971). 'Insane Liberation Front'. In J. Agel (ed.), *The radical therapist* (pp. 107–109). New York: Ballantine.

International Conference on Health Promotion (1987). 'Ottawa charter for health promotion'. *Health Promotion*, *1*(4), ii–v.

Ivey, A.E., Ivey, M.B., and Simek-Morgan, L. (1993). *Counseling and psychotherapy: A multicultural perspective* (3rd edn.). Boston, MA: Allyn & Bacon.

Jacoby, R. (1977). *Social amnesia*. Hassocks: Harvester.

Jahoda, M. (1958). *Current concepts of positive mental health*. New York: Basic Books.

James, M. (1981). *Breaking free*. Reading, MA: Addison-Wesley.

Jaques, E. (1953). 'On the dynamics of social structure'. *Human Relations*, *6*, 3–24.

Jaspers, K. (1964). *The nature of psychotherapy* (J. Hoenig and M.W. Hamilton, Trans.). Chicago: Phoenix Books/University of Chicago Press. (Original work published 1913)

Jenkins, R. (1993). 'Mental health promotion in the workplace'. In D.R. Trent and C. Reed (eds), *Promotion of mental health. Vol. 2* (pp. 311–320). Aldershot: Avebury.

Jenkins, R., and Griffiths, S. (eds) (1991). *How can we measure mental health?* London: HMSO.

Jervis, M. (1988). 'Support where it matters'. *Community Care*, 15 September, 22.

John, D.F. (1980). *Scientific proof of the existence of God will soon be announced by the White House!* Middletown, CA: Dawn Horse Press.

John, K., Gammon, G.D., and Weissman, M.M. (1987). 'Assessment of psychosocial status: Measures of subjective well-being, social adjustment and psychiatric symptoms'. In T. Abelin, Z.J. Brzeziński and V.D.L. Carstairs (eds), *Measurement in health promotion and health protection* (pp. 133–150). Copenhagen: WHO.

Jones, E.E., and Gerard, H.B. (1967). *Foundation of social psychology*. New York: Wiley.

Jones, K. (1972). *A history of the mental health services*. London: Routledge & Kegan Paul.

Jones, K., and Poletti, A. (1984). 'The mirage of a reform'. *New Society*, 4 October, 10–12.

Jones, K., and Poletti, A. (1985). 'Understanding the Italian experience'. *British Journal of Psychiatry*, *147*, 341–347.

Jones, R.M. (1993). *Encyclopedia of social services and community care law. Vol. 2*. London: Sweet & Maxwell.

Jones, R.M. (1994). *Mental Health Act manual* (4th edn.). London: Sweet & Maxwell.

Jung, C.G. (1978). *The collected works*. London: Routledge & Kegan Paul.

Kadushin, A. (1977). *Consultation in social work*. New York: Columbia University Press.

Kahn, M.D. (1991). *Between the therapist and the client: The new relationship*. New York: W.H. Freeman.

Kakar, S. (1984). *Shamans, mystics and doctors: A psychological enquiry into India and its healing traditions*. London: Unwin.

Kane, R. (1994). 'Performing arts, not as mere therapy but as a powerful public force'. In D.R. Trent and C. Reed (eds), *Promotion of mental health. Vol. 3* (pp. 181–192). Aldershot: Avebury.

Kaplan, H.B. (1983). 'Psychosocial distress in sociological context: Toward a general theory of psychosocial stress'. In H.B. Kaplan (ed.), *Psychosocial stress* (pp. 195–264). Orlando, FA: Academic Press Inc.

Kaplan, L. (1971). *Education and mental health*. New York: Harper & Row.

Kaplan, R.M. (1988). 'The value dimension in studies of health promotion'. In S. Spacapan and S. Oskamp (eds), *The social psychology of health* (pp. 207–236). Newbury Park, CA: Sage.

Kaplan, R.M., Bush, J.W., and Berry, C.C. (1976). 'Health status: Types of validity and the index of well-being'. *Health Services Research, 11,* 478–507.

Kaplun, A. (ed.) (1991). *Health promotion and chronic illness: Discovering a new quality of life.* Copenhagen: World Health Organisation.

Karpman, S. (1968). 'Fairy tales and script drama analysis'. *Transactional Analysis Bulletin, 7(26),* 39–43.

Keleman, S. (1989). *Patterns of distress.* Berkeley, CA: Centre Press.

Kennedy, A. (1988). *Positive mental health promotion: Fantasy or reality?* Glasgow: Greater Glasgow Health Board Health Education Department.

Kickbush, I. (1986). 'Introduction to the journal'. *Health Promotion, 1,* 3–4.

Kickbush, I. (1989). 'Healthy cities: A working project and a growing movement'. *Health Promotion, 4,* 77–89.

Killoran, A. (1992). *Putting health into contracts.* London: Health Education Authority.

Kittleson, M.J. (1989). 'Mental health vs. mental illness: A philosophical discussion'. *Health Education,* April/May, 40–42.

Klein, D.C. (1968). *Community dynamics and mental health.* New York: Wiley.

Klein, M. (1952). 'Some theoretical conclusions regarding the emotional life of the infant'. In M. Klein, P. Heimann, S. Isaacs and J. Riviere, *Developments in psycho-analysis* (pp. 198–236). London: Hogarth.

Klein, M. (1975). *The psychoanalysis of children* (A. Strachey, Trans.) (rev. edn.). London: Hogarth. (Original work published 1932)

Kohlberg, L. (1976). 'Moral stages and moralization: The cognitive-developmental approach'. In T. Lickona (ed.), *Moral development and behaviour: Theory, research and social issues* (pp. 31–53). New York: Holt, Rinehart and Winston.

Kohlberg, L. (1981). *Essays on moral development. Vol. 1.* New York: Harper & Row.

Kopp, S. (1974). *If you meet the Buddha on the road, kill him!* London: Sheldon.

Krantz, J., and Gilmore, T.N. (1990). 'The splitting of leadership and management as a social defense'. *Human Relations, 43,* 183–204.

Krejčiřova, D. (1989). 'Mental health of children in Czechoslovakia'. In J. Neumann, H. Schroeder and P. Voss (eds), *Mental health within the health promotion concept* (pp. 110–111). Dresden: German Hygiene Museum/Copenhagen: WHO.

Kuhn, T.S. (1970). *The structure of scientific revolutions* (2nd edn.). Chicago: University of Chicago Press.

Kuhn, T.S. (1976). *The essential tension.* Chicago: University of Chicago Press.

Labour Party (1991). *The better way to a healthy Britain.* London: Labour Party.

Laing, R.D. (1967). *The divided self.* Harmondsworth: Penguin. (Original work published 1960)

Laing, R D. (1985). *Wisdom, madness and folly.* London: Macmillan.

Laing, R.D., and Esterson, A. (1964). *Sanity, madness and the family: Families of schizophrenics.* London: Tavistock.

Lalonde, M. (1975). *A new perspective on the health of Canadians.* Ottawa: Information Canada.

Lamb, H.R., and Zusman, J. (1982). 'The seductiveness of primary prevention'. In F.D. Perlmutter (ed.), *Mental health promotion and primary prevention* (pp. 19–30). San Francisco, CA: Jossey-Bass.

Larre, C., Schatz, J., and Rochat de la Vallee, E. (1986). *Survey of traditional Chinese medicine* (S.E. Stang, Trans.). Paris: Institut Ricci.

Lawrence, D.H. (1964). 'Healing'. In V. de Sola Pinto and W. Roberts (eds), *The complete poems of D.H. Lawrence. Vol. 2*. London: Heinemann.

Lax, W. (1992). 'Postmodern thinking in a clinical practice'. In S. McNamee and K.J. Gergen (eds), *Therapy as social construction* (pp. 69–75). London: Sage.

Lazarus, R.S. (1975). 'A cognitively oriented psychologist looks at biofeedback'. *American Psychologist*.

Lazarus, R.S. (1976). *Patterns of adjustment*. Kogakusha, Tokyo: McGraw-Hill.

Leff, J., Kuipers, L., Berkowitz, R., Eberlein-Vries, R., and Sturgeon, D. (1982). 'A controlled trial of social interventions in the families of schizophrenic patients'. *British Journal of Psychiatry, 141*, 121–134.

Leonard, P. (1984). *Personality and ideology*. Basingstoke: Macmillan.

Lishman, G. (1989). 'Providing services: The perspective of age concern'. In *Should voluntary organisations provide more services? Contracts for care*. Conference Report no. 2 (pp. 4–7). London: National Council for Voluntary Organisations.

Littlewood, R., and Cross, S. (1980). 'Ethnic minorities and psychiatric services'. *Sociology of Health and Illness, 2*, 194–201.

Littlewood, R., and Lipsedge, M. (1982). *Aliens and alienists: Ethnic minorities and psychiatry*. Harmondsworth: Penguin.

Local Authorities' Conditions of Service Advisory Board/Association of Directors of Social Services (1989). *Survey of social services employment*. London: Author.

London Edinburgh Weekend Return Group (1980). *In and against the state*. London: Pluto Press.

Lotringer, S., and Marazzi, C. (1980). *Italy: Autonomia: Post-political politics*. New York: Semiotext(e).

Loumidis, K. (1992). *Can social problem-solving training help people with learning difficulties?* In D.R. Trent (ed.), *Promotion of mental health. Vol. 1* (pp. 77–87). Aldershot: Avebury.

Lousada, J. (1993). 'Self-defence is no offence'. *Journal of Social Work Practice, 7*, 103–113.

Lovell, A.M., and Scheper-Hughes, N. (1987). 'Introduction: The utopia of reality – Franco Basaglia and the practice of Democratic Psychiatry'. In N. Scheper-Hughes and A.M. Lovell (eds), *Psychiatry inside out: Selected writings of Franco Basaglia*. New York: Columbia University Press.

Lowe, B., and Tudor, K. (1995). *Class, consciousness and psychotherapy*. Manuscript submitted for publication.

Lukas, E. (1989). 'From self-actualization to global responsibility'. Paper presented at the Seventh World Congress of Logotherapy, Kansas City, June.

Lyotard, J.-F. (1984). *The post-modern condition: A report on knowledge*. Manchester: Manchester University Press.

Maccoby, N. (1988). 'The community as focus for health promotion'. In S. Spacapan and S. Oskamp (eds), *The social psychology of health* (pp. 175–206). Newbury Park, CA: Sage.

MacDonald, G. (1993). 'Defining the goals and raising the issues in mental health promotion'. In D.R. Trent and C. Reed (eds), *Promotion of mental health. Vol. 2* (pp. 371–394). Aldershot: Avebury.

MacDonald, G. (1994a). 'Promoting mental ? health'. Unpublished report available from Health Promotion Department, First Community Health, Arthur Sreet, Chadsmoor, Cannock WS11 2HD.

MacDonald, G. (1994b). 'Self-esteem and the promotion of mental health'. In D.R. Trent and C. Reed (eds), *Promotion of mental health. Vol. 3* (pp. 207–228). Aldershot: Avebury.

Macdonald, G., and Bunton, R. (1992). 'Health promotion. Discipline or disciplines?' In R. Bunton and G. Macdonald (eds), *Health promotion: Disciplines and diversity* (pp. 6–19). London: Routledge.

Macias, C. (1994). 'The role of case management within a community support system: Partnership with psychosocial rehabilitation'. *Community Mental Health Journal, 30,* 323–339.

Maciocia, G. (1989). *The foundations of Chinese medicine.* Edinburgh: Churchill Livingstone.

Mahler, M.S., Pine, F., and Bergman, A. (1975). *The psychological birth of the human infant.* London: Hutchinson.

Mahrer, A.R. (1989). *The integration of the psychotherapies: A guide for practicing therapists.* Ottawa: Human Sciences Press.

Management and Personnel Office (1982). *Code of practice for the use of management consultants by government departments* (4th edn.). London: HMSO.

Manktelow, R. (1993). 'A report on a study of views and attitudes of people in contact with former patients discharged from a Northern Ireland hospital'. In D.R. Trent and C. Reed (eds), *Promotion of mental health. Vol. 2* (pp. 395–412). Aldershot: Avebury.

Maranesi, T., and Piazza, A. (1986). 'Dossier: Dopo la 180 i dati della prima indagine sull'assistenza psichiatrica in Italia'. [Dossier: After Law 180 data from the first research on psychiatric welfare in Italy]. *Scienza Esperienza,* September, 17–21.

Marcuse, H. (1968). *One dimensional man.* London: Sphere.

Marcuse, H. (1969). *Eros and civilisation.* London: Sphere.

Martin, S. (1989). *Body and soul.* Harmondsworth: Arkana.

Martindale, D. (1961). *The nature and types of social theory.* London: Routledge & Kegan Paul.

Marx, K. (1971). *A contribution to the critique of political economy.* London: Lawrence & Wishart. (Original work published 1858)

Marx, K. (1975). 'Economic and philosophical manuscripts'. In R. Livingstone and G. Benton (Trans.), *Karl Marx early writings.* Harmondsworth: Penguin. (Original work published 1844)

Maslow, A.H. (1954). *Motivation and personality.* New York: Harper & Row.

Maslow, A.H. (1968). *Towards a psychology of being.* New York: Van Nostrand.

Mason, L.J. (1985). *Guide to stress reduction* (2nd edn.). Berkeley, CA: Celestial Arts.

Masson, J. (1989). *Against therapy.* London: Collins.

Mathiesen, T. (1974). *The politics of abolition.* London: Martin Robertson.

Mauri, D. (ed.) (1983). *La liberta é terapeutica?* [Is freedom therapeutic?]. Milan: Feltrinelli.

Mawhinney, B. (1993a). 'Making it happen: The mechanisms of purchasing and contracting'. In B. Mawhinney *Purchasing for Health: A framework for action* (pp. 21–36). London: NHS Management Executive.

Mawhinney, B. (1993b). 'Purchasing: the yardsticks for success'. In B. Mawhinney *Purchasing for Health: A framework for action* (pp. 37–52). London: NHS Management Executive.

Mawhinney, B. (1993c). 'The vision for purchasing'. In B. Mawhinney *Purchasing for Health: A framework for action* (pp. 9–20). London: NHS Management Executive.

Maximé, J.E. (1986). 'Some psychological models of black self-concept'. In S. Ahmed, J. Cheetham and J. Small (eds), *Social Work with Black Children and Their Families* (pp. 100–116). London: Batsford/British Agency for Adoption and Fostering.

McCormack, A. (1981). 'Promoting mental health'. *MindOut*, *42*, August, 17–18.

McDowall, R.J.S. (1943). *Sane psychology*. London: John Murray.

McDowell, I., and Newell, C. (1987). *Measuring health: A guide to rating scales and questionnaires*. Oxford: Oxford University Press.

McEwan, J., Hunt, S.M., and McKenna, S.P. (1987) 'A measure of perceived health: the Nottingham health profile'. In T. Abelin, Z.J. Brzeziński and V.D.L. Carstairs (eds), *Measurement in health promotion and health protection* (pp. 590–603). Copenhagen: WHO Regional Office for Europe.

McIlmoyl, M.L. (1994). 'Enhancing self-esteem in older women: A group facilitator approach'. In D.R. Trent and C. Reed (eds), *Promotion of mental health. Vol. 3* (pp. 245–258). Aldershot: Avebury.

McPheeters, H.L. (1976). 'Primary prevention and health promotion in mental health'. *Preventive Medicine*, *5*, 187–198.

Melville, J. (1980). *First aid in mental health*. London: MIND.

Mental Health Foundation (1990). *Mental illness: The fundamental facts*. London: MHF.

Mental Patients' Union (1973). *Declaration of intent*. Available from MPU, 37 Mayola Road, London E5.

Menzies Lyth, I.E.P. (1988). 'The functioning of social systems as a defence against anxiety: A report on a study of the nursing service of a general hospital'. In I. Menzies Lyth, *Containing anxiety in institutions* (pp. 43–85). London: Free Association Books. (Original work published 1959, 1961 and 1970)

Merry, U., and Brown, G.I. (1987). *The neurotic behaviour of organizations*. New York: Gestalt Institute of Cleveland Press.

Mid Staffordshire Mental Health Promotion Programme Development Group (1994). *Strategy for mental health promotion in Staffordshire*. Available from Health Promotion Department, South Staffordshire Health Authority, Arthur Street, Chatsmore, Cannock WS11 2HD.

Miller, E.J. and Gwynne, G.V. (1972). *A life apart*. London: Tavistock.

Miller, S.M., and Rein, M. (1975). 'Community participation: Past and future'. In D. Jones and M. Majo (eds), *Community work. Two* (pp. 3–24). London: Routledge & Kegan Paul.

Milton Keynes MIND (undated). 'Education project'. Leaflet available from Milton Keynes MIND, Cripps Lodge, Broadland, Netherfield, Milton Keynes MK6 4JJ.

Milz, H. (1991). 'Healthy ill persons – Social cynicism or new perspectives for living wth chronic illness'. In A. Kaplun (ed.), *Health promotion and chronic illness: Discovering a new quality of life*. Copenhagen: WHO.

MIND (1983). *Common concern*. London: MIND.

MIND (1990). *Advocacy: Different forms of empowerment*. Paper available from MIND, Granta House, 15-19 Broadway, London E15 4BQ.

MIND (1992). *The MIND guide to advocacy in mental health*. London: MIND.

MIND (1993a). *MIND policy on community care*. London: MIND.

MIND (1993b). 'Out of sight . . . Public attitudes about mental distress'. Factsheet available from MIND, Granta House, 15-19 Broadway, London E15 4BQ.

MIND (1993c). *Policy paper: The health of the nation – Comments by MIND*. London: MIND.

MIND (1994a). 'How to . . . assert yourself'. Leaflet available from MIND, Granta House, 15-19 Broadway, London E15 4BQ.

MIND (1994b). 'How to . . . look after yourself'. Leaflet available from MIND, Granta House, 15-19 Broadway, London E15 4BQ.

Minguzzi, G.F. (1974). 'Practice of madness'. *Minutes of the first meeting of Democratic Psychiatry*. Gorizia, Italy.

Minister of National Health and Welfare (1988). *Mental health for Canadians.* Ottawa: MNHW.

Ministry of Health (1963). *Health and welfare: The development of community care. Plans for the health and welfare services of the local authorities in England and Wales.* London: HMSO.

Ministry of Health [Province of British Columbia] (undated). *Healthy communities: The process.* Vancouver: Ministry of Health.

Minuchin, S. (1974). *Families and family therapy.* London: Tavistock.

Mishra, R. (1977). *Society and social policy: Theoretical perspectives on welfare.* London: Macmillan.

Mitchell, J. (1975). *Psychoanalysis and feminism.* Harmondsworth: Penguin.

Mitchell, J. (1984). *What is to be done about illness and health?* Harmondsworth: Penguin.

Mitchell, L. (1989). 'Whose health for all?' *Nursing Times,* 23 August, 48–50.

Money, M. (1993). 'The shamanistic path to health promotion'. In D.R. Trent and C. Reed (eds), *Promotion of mental health. Vol. 2* (pp. 453–462). Aldershot: Avebury.

Money, M. (1994). 'Following the shamanic path to mental health promotion'. In D.R. Trent and C. Reed (eds), *Promotion of mental health. Vol. 3* (pp. 259–268). Aldershot: Avebury.

Montessori, M. (1966). *The secret of childhood* (M.J. Costelloe, Trans.). New York: Ballantine. (Original work published 1936)

Moore, G., and McAdoo, P. (1992). 'Blyth Valley Walk-in Advice and Information Centre'. In D.R. Trent (ed), *Promotion of mental health. Vol. 1* (pp. 221–228). Aldershot: Avebury.

Moran, G. (1986). 'Radical health promotion: A role for local authorities?' In S. Rodmell and A. Watt (eds), *The politics of health education* (pp. 121–138). London: Routledge & Kegan Paul.

Morgan, G. (1986). *Images of organization.* London: Sage.

Morgan, G. (1993). *Imaginization: The art of creative management.* Newbury Park, CA: Sage.

Mosher, L.R., and Burti, L. (1989). *Community mental health.* New York: Norton.

Mubbashar, M.H. (1989). 'Promotion of mental health in schools'. *Positive Health,* 2(11), p. 4.

Murphy, E. (1991). *After the asylum.* London: Faber & Faber.

Murphy, H.B.M. (1986). 'The historical development of transcultural psychiatry'. In J.L. Cox (ed.), *Transcultural psychiatry* (pp. 7–22). London: Croom Helm.

Murray, C., Wills, S., and Hughes, J. (1993). 'Quality assurance within an innovative service providing community support to people with mental health problems'. In D.R. Trent and C. Reed (eds), *Promotion of mental health. Vol. 2* (pp. 469–481). Aldershot: Avebury.

Murray, M.C. (1989). 'Mental health promotion team'. Document available from Mid Staffordshire Mental Health Promotion Team, Mental Health Unit, St George's Hospital, Stafford ST16 3AG.

National Association for Mental Health (1971). *Mental Health.* Available from MIND, Granta House, 15–19 Broadway, London E15 4BQ.

National Health Service Executive (1994a). *Advocacy: A code of practice.* London: NHS Executive.

National Health Service Executive (1994b). *Building on experience.* London: NHS Executive.

National Health Service Executive (1994c). *Guidelines for a local charter for users of mental health services.* London: NHS Executive.

National Health Service Executive (1994d). *Health promoting hospitals.* London: DoH/NHS Executive.

National Health Service Management Executive (1994a). *Guidance on the discharge of mentally disordered people and their continuing care in the community.* (Health Service Guidelines (94)27). London: NHS Management Executive.

National Health Service Management Executive (1994b). *Introduction of supervision registers for mentally ill people from 1 April 1994.* (Health Service Guidelines (94)5). London: NHS Management Executive.

Navarro, V. (1978). *Class struggle, the state and medicine.* London: Martin Robertson.

Navarro, V. (1986). *Crisis, health and medicine: A social critique.* New York: Tavistock.

Neumann, J. (1989). 'Psychiatrists' responsibility for mental health'. In J. Neumann, H. Schroeder and P. Voss (eds), *Mental health within the health promotion concept* (pp. 52–56). Dresden: German Hygiene Museum/Copenhagen: WHO.

Neumann, J., Schroeder, H., and Voss, P. (1989a). 'Mental health and well-being in the context of the health promotion concept'. In J. Neumann, H. Schroeder and P. Voss (eds), *Mental health within the health promotion concept* (pp. 3–17). Dresden: German Hygiene Museum/Copenhagen: WHO.

Neumann, J., Schroeder, H., and Voss, P. (1989b). 'Mental health: Concepts and tasks from the psychological and psychiatric views'. In J. Neumann, H. Schroeder and P. Voss (eds), *Mental health within the health promotion concept* (pp. 26–37). Dresden: German Hygiene Museum/Copenhagen: WHO.

Newman, M.A. (1979). *Theory development in nursing.* Philadelphia, PA: Davis.

Newnes, C. (1988). 'Editorial: What is community psychology?' *Clinical Psychology Forum,* August, 2.

Newton, C. (1992). 'The emperor's new community care plans'. In C. Monkcom (ed.), *The first plans* (p. 17). London: National Council for Voluntary Organisations.

Newton, J. (1988). *Preventing mental illness.* London: Routledge.

Newton, J. (1992). *Preventing mental illness in practice.* London: Routledge.

Newton, K. (1975). 'Voluntary organizations in a British city: The political and organizational characteristics of 4264 voluntary organizations in Birmingham'. *Journal of Voluntary Action Research, 4,* 43–62.

Noack, H. (1987). 'Concepts of health and health promotion'. In T. Abelin, Z.J. Brzeziński and V.D.L. Carstairs (eds), *Measurement in health promotion and health protection* (pp. 5-28). Copenhagen: WHO/International Epidemiological Association.

Noack, H., and McQueen, D. (eds) (1988). 'Health promotion indicators [special issue]'. *Health Promotion, 3*(1).

Nobles, W.W. (1973). 'Psychological research and the black self-concept: A critical review'. *Journal of Social Issues, 29,* 11–31.

Nocon, A. (1990). 'No role for collaboration in the market place'. *Insight,* 11 April, 27.

Norcross, J.C., and Goldfried, M.R. (eds) (1992). *Handbook of psychotherapy integration.* New York: Basic Books.

North Derbyshire Mental Health Promotion Group (1991). *Mental health promotion strategy.* Available from Health Promotion, Scarsdale Hospital, Newbold Road, Chesterfield S41 7PF.

North Western Mental Health Promotion Group (1994). *Health of the nation targets for mental illness.* Available from East Lancashire Health Consortium, Lomeshaye Industrial Estate, Kenyon Road, Brierfield, Lancashire BB9 5SZ.

Northern Ireland Association for Mental Health (undated). *Mental health: What's it all about?* Education pack for schools available from Northern Ireland Association for Mental Health, 84 University Street, Belfast BT7 1HE.

Northern Ireland Centre for Learning Resources (1993). *Mental health matters.* Belfast: Author.

Northern Region Minds Matters Group (1993). *A policy framework for promoting mental health.* Available from 158 Durham Road, Gateshead NE8 4EL.

Obholzer, A. (1994). 'Managing social anxieties in public sector organizations'. In A. Obholzer and V.Z. Roberts (eds), *The unconscious at work* (pp. 169–178). London: Routledge.

O'Byrne, D. (1989). 'Introduction'. In J. Neumann, H. Schroeder and P. Voss (eds), *Mental health within the health promotion concept* (pp. 18–20). Dresden: German Hygiene Museum/Copenhagen: WHO.

Offer, D., and Sabshin, M. (1974). *Normality: Theoretical and clinical concepts of mental health.* New York: Basic Books.

Onions, C.T. (ed.) (1973). *The shorter Oxford English dictionary.* Oxford: Clarendon. (Original work published 1933)

Onnis, L., and Lo Rosso, G. (eds) (1980). *Dove va la psichiatria?* [Where is psychiatry going?]. Milano: Feltrinelli.

Onyett, S., Heppleston, T., and Bushnell, D. (1994). *The organisation and operation of community mental health teams in England.* London: Sainsbury Centre for Mental Health.

Orlinsky, D.E., and Howard, K.I. (1987). 'A generic model of psychotherapy'. *Journal of Integrative and Eclectic Psychotherapy, 6,* 6–27.

Orritt, E.J., Paul, S.C., and Behrman,J.A. (1985). 'The Perceived Support Network Inventory'. *American Journal of Community Psychology, 13,* 565–582.

Øvretveit, J., Temple, H., and Coleman, R. (undated). *The organisation and management of community mental health teams.* London: Good Practices in Mental Health.

Painter, C. (1994). *Sexual health, assertiveness and HIV.* Cambridge: Daniels.

Papeschi, R. (1985). 'The denial of the institution: a critical review of Franco Basaglia's writings'. *British Journal of Psychiatry, 146,* 247–254.

Parkins, E.J. (1994). 'Equilibrium and cognitive neuropsychology: Is mental health just a question of balance?' In D.R. Trent and C. Reed (eds), *Promotion of mental health. Vol. 3* (pp. 287–304). Aldershot: Avebury.

Parry, G. (1988). 'Mobilizing social support'. In F.N. Watts (ed.), *New directions in clinical psychology. Vol. 2* (pp. 83–104). Chichester: Wiley/British Psychological Society.

Patel, C. (1989). *The complete guide to stress management.* London: Optima.

Patmore, C., and Weaver, T. (1991). *Community mental health teams: Lessons for planners and managers.* London: Good Practices in Mental Health.

Peck, E., and Joyce, L. (1985). 'Community mental health centres: A view of the landscape'. In T. McAusland (ed.), *Planning and monitoring community mental centres* (pp. 56–60). London: Kings Fund.

Peck, E., and Smith, H. (undated). *Contracting in mental health services.* Bristol: National Health Service Training Authority.

Peck, M.S. (1988). *The different drum.* London: Century Hutchinson.

Pelikan, C. (1991). 'A marriage of convenience?', *Community Care* (19 September), pp. 17–19.

Perlmutter, F.D. (1982a). 'Editor's notes'. In F.D. Perlmutter (ed.), *Mental health promotion and primary prevention* (pp. 1–3). San Francisco, CA: Jossey-Bass.

Perlmutter, F.D. (1982b). 'New directions for mental health promotion'. In F.D.

Perlmutter (ed.), *Mental health promotion and primary prevention* (pp. 7–18). San Francisco, CA: Jossey-Bass.

Perls, F.S. (1971). *Gestalt therapy verbatim*. New York: Bantam.

Perls, F.S., Hefferline, R.F., and Goodman, P. (1973). *Gestalt therapy: Excitement and growth in the human personality*. New York: Bantam. (Original work published 1951)

Phillips, B., Crerar, A., and Davis, H. (1992). *Thoughts towards a mental well-being at work policy*. Available from Southern Birmingham Community Health Trust, West Heath Hospital, Rednal Road, West Heath, Birmingham B38 8HR.

Philpot, T. (1990). 'Comment. April fooled'. *Community Care*, 26 July, 13.

Piaget, J. (1964). *Six psychological studies*. New York: Random House.

Pickin, C., and St Leger, S. (1993). *Assessing health need using the life cycle framework*. Buckingham: Open University.

Piro, S., and Oddati, A. (1983). *La riforma psichiatrica del 1978 e il meridione d'Italia*. [The 1978 psychiatric reform and Southern Italy]. Roma: Il Pensiero Scientifico Editore.

Politics of Health Group (1980). *Cuts in the NHS*. Available from the Politics of Health Group, 9 Poland Street, London W1 3DG.

Politics of Health Group (1982). *Going private*. Available from Politics of Health Group, 9 Poland Street, London W1 3DG.

Politzer, G. (1976). *Elementary principles of philosophy*. London: Lawrence & Wishart.

Porter, P. (1987). *A social history of madness*. London: Weidenfeld and Nicolson.

Porter, P. (1990). *Mind-forg'd manacles*. Harmondsworth: Penguin.

Power, M. (1990). 'Modernism, postmodernism and organisation'. In J. Hassard and D. Pym (eds), *The theory and philosophy of organisations* (pp. 109–124). London: Routledge.

Powys Mental Health Promotion Working Group (undated). *A proposed mental health promotion strategy for Powys*. Available from Health Promotion Unit, Mansion House, Bronllys, Powys LD3 0LS.

Preston, G.H. (1943). *The substance of mental health*. New York: Farrar & Rinehart.

Price, J. (1992). 'Accentuate the positive, eliminate the negative: The role of boosting and putting-down signals in mental health'. In D.R. Trent (ed.), *Promotion of mental health. Vol. 1* (pp. 89–101). Aldershot: Avebury.

Procidano, M.E., and Heller, K. (1983). 'Measures of perceived social support from family and friends: Three validation studies'. *American Journal of Community Psychology*, *11*, 1–24.

Pro-Ed (1981). *Culture Free Self-Esteem Inventory*. USA: Pro-Ed.

Quirk, M., and Wapner, S. (1991). 'Notes on an organismic-developmental, systems perspective for health education'. *Health Education Research*, *6*, 203–210.

Rabkin, J.G., Muhlin, G., and Cohen, P.W. (1984). 'What the neighbours think: Community attitudes toward local psychiatric facilities'. *Community Mental Health Journal*, *20*, 304–312.

Raeburn, J.M., and Rootman, I. (1989). 'Towards an expanded health field concept: Conceptual and research issues in a new era of health promotion'. *Health Promotion*, *3*, 383–392.

Raimy, V.C. (1948). 'Self reference in counselling interviews'. *Journal of Consultating Psychology*, *12*, 92–110.

Rakos, R.F. (1991). *Assertive behaviour: Theory, research and training*. London: Routledge.

Rakusen, J. (1990). 'Emotional education'. *OpenMind*, *46*, August/September 10–11.

Ramon, S. (1983). 'Psichiatria Democratica: a case study of an Italian community mental health service'. *International Journal of Health Services*, *13*, 307–324.

Ramon, S., and Giannichedda, M.G. (eds) (1988). *Psychiatry in transition*. London: Pluto Press.

Ramon, S., and Giannichedda, M.G. (eds) (1990). *Psychiatry in transition* (2nd edn.). London: Pluto Press.

Randall, R., Southgate, J., and Tomlinson, F. (1980). *Co-operative and community group dynamics*. London: Barefoot Books.

Rappaport, J. (1977). *Community psychology, values, research and action*. New York: Holt, Rinehart & Winston.

Rawson, D. (1992). 'The growth of health promotion theory and its rational reconstruction'. In R. Bunton and G. Macdonald (eds), *Health promotion: Disciplines and diversity* (pp. 202–224). London: Routledge.

Rawson, D., and Grigg, C. (1988). *Purpose and practice in health education*. London: South Bank Polytechnic/HEA.

Read, J., and Wallcraft, J. (1994). *Guidelines on advocacy for mental health professionals*. London: MIND/UNISON.

Reason, D. (1977). 'The red queen's estate; or, grounds for interdisciplinarity'. *Studies in Higher Education*, *3*, 203–209.

Reed, J. (1985). 'Fighting mad . . . '. *Social Work Today*, 28 January, 14–15.

Reich, W. (1975). *The mass psychology of fascism* (V.R. Carfagno, Trans.) (3rd edn.). Harmondsworth: Penguin. (Original work published 1942)

Renshaw, J. (1987). 'The challenge of enabling the client to be a consumer'. *Social Work Today*, 27 July, 10–11.

Rigney, M. (1981). *A critique of Maslow's self-actualization theory: The 'highest good' for the aboriginal is relationship*. Videotape. Aboriginal Open College, Adelaide, Australia.

Roberts, E. (1984). 'Social work organizations: Constructive or destructive'. *Journal of Social Work Practice*, *1*(3), 43–53.

Robertson, G., and Tudor, K. (1993). 'Counselling in the context of community care'. *Counselling*, *4*, 188–190.

Robertson, J. (1986). 'Towards a new economics of health'. *Health Promotion*, *1*, 179–185.

Robinson, W.L. (1974). 'Conscious competency: The mark of a competent instructor'. *Personnel Journal*, *53*, 538–539.

Rodmell, S., and Watt, A. (1986) 'Radical health education'. In S. Rodmell and A. Watt (eds), *The politics of health education*. London: Routledge & Kegan Paul.

Rogers, A., and Faulkner, A. (1987). *A place of safety*. London: MIND.

Rogers, C.R. (1951). *Client-centred therapy*. London: Constable.

Rogers, C.R. (1961). *On becoming a person*. London: Constable.

Rogers, C.R. (1990). 'The politics of education'. In H. Kirschenbaum and V.L. Henderson (eds), *The Carl Rogers reader*. London: Constable. (Original work published 1977)

Rokeach, M. (1973). *The nature of human values*. New York: Free Press.

Romme, M., and Escher, S. (1993). *Accepting voices*. London: MIND.

Roosens, E. (1979). *Mental patients in town life: Geel – Europe's first therapeutic community*. Beverly Hills, CA: Sage.

Rose, H. and Hanmer, J. (1975). 'Community participation and social change'. In D. Jones and M. Majo (eds), *Community work. Two* (pp. 25–45). London: Routledge & Kegan Paul.

Rose, S.M., and Black, B.L. (1985). *Advocacy and empowerment*. Boston, MA: Routledge & Kegan Paul.

Rosenberg, M. (1965). *Society and the adolescent self image*. Princeton, NJ: Princeton University Press.

Rowan, D., and Eayrs, C.B. (1982). 'Coping with anxiety: An adult education evening class'. Paper presented to the Annual Conference of the British Association of Behavioural Psychotherapy, Sussex.

Royal Colleges of Physicians' Committee on Health Promotion/Society of Health Education and Health Promotion Specialists (1992). *Inclusion of health promotion within contracts*. Guidelines for Health Promotion no. 31. Document available from Royal Colleges of Physicians, 4 St Andrew's Place, London NW1 4LB.

Royal College of Psychiatrists' Council (1988). 'The Royal College of Psychiatrists' comments on the Griffiths Report: *Community care: agenda for action*'. *Bulletin of the Royal College of Psychiatrists*, *12*, 385–388.

Ryan, C.C. (1985). 'Gay health issues: Oppression is a health hazard'. In H. Hidalgo, T.L. Peterson and N.J. Woodman (eds), *Lesbian and gay issues: A resource manual for social workers*. Silver Spring, MA: National Association of Social Workers.

Saan, H. (1986). 'Health promotion and health education: Living with a dominant concept'. *Health Promotion*, *1*, 253–255.

Salford Health Authority Health Promotion Service (1987). 'Senior health promotion officer: Mental health'. Job description, Salford Health Authority Health Promotion Unit, Peel House, Eccles M30 0NJ.

Saljo, R. (1979). 'The educational construction of learning'. In J. Richardson, M. Eysenck and D. Warren Piper (eds), *Student learning*. Milton Keynes: Society for Research into Higher Education/Open University.

Samples, B., and Wohlford, B. (1975). *Opening: A primer for self-actualisation*. Menlo Park, CA: Addison-Wesley.

Samuels, A. (1993). *The political psyche*. London: Routledge.

Sandford, N. (1972). 'Is the concept of prevention necessary or useful?' In S. Golann and C. Eisdorfer (eds), *Handbook of community mental health*. New York: Appleton-Century-Crofts.

Sang, B. (1989). 'The independent voice of advocacy'. In A. Brackx and C. Grimshaw (eds), *Mental health care in crisis* (pp. 190–205). London: Pluto Press.

Sartorius, N. (1988). 'Health promotion strategies'. *Canadian Journal of Public Health*, *79*(suppl. 2), S3–S5.

Sartorius, N. (1992). 'The promotion of mental health: Meaning and tasks'. In D.R. Trent (ed.), *Promotion of mental health. Vol. 1* (pp. 17–23). Aldershot: Avebury.

Sayce, L. (1989). 'Community mental health centres – rhetoric and reality'. In A. Brackx and C. Grimshaw (eds), *Mental health care in crisis* (pp. 158–174). London: Pluto Press.

Sayce, L. (1990). 'Care reforms dislocated'. *OpenMind*, *46*, August/September, 5.

Sayce, L., and Charman, T. (1988). 'The obvious candidate for coordinator'. *Community Care*, 4 August, 16–18.

Sayce, L., Craig, T.K.J., and Boardman, A.P. (1991). 'The development of community mental health teams in the UK'. *Social Psychiatry and Psychiatric Epidemiology*, *26*, 14–20.

Scheff, T.J. (1966). *Being mentally ill*. Chicago: Aldine.

Schein, E.H. (1965). *Organizational psychology*. New York: Prentice-Hall.

Schein, E.H. (1969). *Process consultation*. Reading, MA: Addison-Wesley.

Schein, E.H. (1987). *Process consultation. Vol. 2: Lessons for managers and consultants*. Reading, MA: Addison-Wesley.

Scheuch, K. (1989). 'Stress and health'. In J. Neumann, H. Schroeder and P. Voss (eds), *Mental health within the health promotion concept* (pp. 72–78). Dresden: German Hygiene Museum/Copenhagen: WHO.

Schiff, J., Schiff, A.W., Mellor, K., Schiff, E., Schiff, S., Richman, D., Fishman, J., Wolz, L., Fishman, C., and Momb, D. (1975). *Cathexis reader: Transactional analysis treatment of psychosis*. New York: Harper & Row.

Schon, D.A. (1983). *The reflective practitioner*. New York: Basic Books.

Scott-Moncrieff, L. (1988). 'Comments on the Discussion Document of the Royal College of Psychiatrists regarding Community Treatment Orders'. *Bulletin of the Royal College of Psychiatrists, 12*, 220–223.

Scull, A.T. (1979). *Museums of madness*. London: Allen Lane.

Sedgwick, P. (1982). *PsychoPolitics*. London: Pluto.

Seeman, J. (1949). 'A study of the process of nondirective therapy'. *Journal of Consulting Psychology, 13*, 157-168.

Sennett, R. (1977). *The fall of public man*. Cambridge: Cambridge University Press.

Séve, L. (1975). *Marxism and the theory of human personality*. London: Lawrence & Wishart.

Séve, L. (1978). *Man in Marxist theory and the psychology of personality*. Hassocks: Harvester.

Seyle, H. (1956). *The stress of life*. New York: McGraw-Hill.

Shapiro, D.H. (1983). 'Science or sermon: Values, beliefs, and an expanded vision of psychological health'. In R. Walsh and D.H. Shapiro (eds), *Beyond health and normality: Explorations of exceptional psychological well-being*. New York: Van Nostrand.

Sheerer, E.T. (1949). 'An analysis of the relationship between acceptance of and respect for self and acceptance of and respect for others in ten counseling cases'. *Journal of Consultating Psychology, 13*, 169–175.

Siegler, M., and Osmond, H. (1966). 'Models of madness'. *British Journal of Psychiatry, 112*, 1193–1203.

Siegler, M., and Osmond, H. (1976). *Models of madness, models of medicine*. New York: Macmillan.

Simpkin, M. (1979). *Trapped within welfare*. London: Macmillan.

Skelton, R. (1988). 'Man's role in society and its effect on health'. *Nursing, 26*, February, 953–956.

Skynner, R., and Schlapobersky, J.R. (eds). (1989). *Institutes and how to survive them*. London: Methuen.

Sloboda, J., and Hopkins, J. (1992). 'Promoting mental health in the workplace: the staff care concept'. In D.R. Trent (ed.), *Promotion of mental health. Vol. 1* (pp. 297–304). Aldershot: Avebury.

Smith, C.J. (1976). 'Residential neighbourhoods as humane environments'. *Environment and Planning, 8*, 311–326.

Smith, C.J. (1984). 'Geographical approaches to mental health'. In H.L. Freeman (ed.), *Mental health and the environment* (pp. 121–168). New York: Churchill Livingstone.

Smith, C.J., and Hanham, R.Q. (1981). 'Any place but here! Mental health facilities as noxious neighbours'. *Professional Geographer, 33*, 326–334.

Smith, H. (1992). 'Quality in community care: Moving beyond mediocrity'. *Journal of Mental Health, 1*, 207–217.

Smith, H., and Brown, H. (1989). 'Whose community, whose care?' In A. Brechin and J. Walmsley (eds), *Making connections: Reflecting on the lives and experi-*

ences of people with learning difficulties (pp. 230–236). London: Hodder & Stoughton.

Social Services Inspectorate (1993). *Inspection of projects funded by the mental illness specific grant*. London: SSI.

Socialist Health Association (1987). *Goodbye to all that*. London: SHA.

South Thames Regional Health Authority (1994). 'Promoting mental health through purchasing: Checklist for developing a mental health promotion'. In C. Burden (ed), *Promoting mental health through purchasing*, Conference report, South West Thames Regional Health Authority, Croydon.

Spender, D. (1980). *Man made language*. London: Routledge & Kegan Paul.

Springfield Advice and Law Centre (1990). *Biennial report 1989-1990*. Available from Springfield Advice and Law Centre, Springfield Hospital, 61 Glenburnie Road, London SW17 7DJ.

Spy, T., and Watkins-Baker, K. (1980). 'Mental health education'. *Involve, 11*, Spring, 6.

Stark, W. (1986). 'The politics of primary prevention in mental health: The need for a theoretical basis'. *Health Promotion, 1*, 179–185.

Stein, M., and Hollwitz, J. (1992). *Psyche at work*. Wilmette, IL: Chiron.

Steiner, C. (1971). *Games alcoholics play*. New York: Ballantine.

Steiner, C. (1974). *Scripts people live*. New York: Grove Press.

Steiner, C. (1984). 'Emotional literacy'. *Transactional Analysis Journal, 14*, 162–173.

Stern, D. (1985). *The interpersonal world of the infant*. New York: Basic Books.

Stewart, A.L., Ware, J.E., Brook, R.H., and Davies-Avery, A. (1987). *Conceptualization and measurement of health for adults in the Health Insurance Study. Vol. II: Physical health in terms of functioning*. Santa Monica, CA: Rand Corporation. (Original work published 1978)

Stewart, A.L., Sherbourne, C.D., Wells, K.B., Burnam, M.A., Rogers, W.H., Hays, R.D., and Ware, J.E. (1993). 'Do depressed patients in different treatment settings have different levels of well-being and functioning?' *Journal of Consulting and Clinical Psychology, 61*, 849–857.

Stewart, I., and Joines, V. (1987). *TA today*. Nottingham: Lifespace.

Sullivan, K. (1993). 'A staff support service following major incidents at work'. In D.R. Trent and C. Reed (eds), *Promotion of Mental Health. Vol. 2* (pp. 551–560). Aldershot: Avebury.

Sunderland, M., and Clarkson, P. (1992). 'The role of affective education in society'. In D.R. Trent (ed.), *Promotion of mental health. Vol. 1* (pp. 103–116). Aldershot: Avebury.

Survivors Speak Out (1989). 'Addresses of groups'. List available from Survivors Speak Out, 33 Lichfield Road, London NW2 2RG.

Survivors Speak Out (1992). *Survivors' poetry: From dark to light*. London: Survivors' Press.

Survivors Speak Out (1994). *Self-advocacy pack* (rev. edn.). London: Survivors' Press.

Szasz, T. (1961). *The myth of mental illness*. London: Secker & Warburg.

Szasz, T. (1973). *Law, liberty and psychiatry*. New York: Macmillan.

Tannahill, A. (1985a). 'Reclassifying prevention'. *Public Health, 99*, 364–366.

Tannahill, A. (1985b). 'What is health promotion?' *Health Education Journal, 44*, 167–168.

Tarrier, N., Barrowclough, C., Porceddu, K., and Watts, S. (1988). 'The community management of schizophrenia: A controlled trial of a behavioural intervention with families to reduce relapse'. *British Journal of Psychiatry, 152*, 532–542.

Tart, C.T. (ed.) (1975). *Transpersonal psychology*. London: Routledge & Kegan Paul.

Taylor, I., and Robson, R.N. (1987, May). *Informing the public about mental health*. Unpublished paper. Available from Dyfed Health Authority, c/o St David's Hospital, Jobswell Road, Carmarthen, Dyfed SA31 3HB.

Taylor, J., and Taylor, D. (1989). *Mental health in the 1990s: From custody to care?* London: Office of Health Economics.

Temple, S., and Robson, P. (1991). 'The effect of assertiveness training on self-esteem'. *British Journal of Occupational Therapy*, *54*(9), 329–332.

Terborg, J.R. (1988). 'The organization as a context for health promotion'. In S. Spacapan and S. Oskamp (eds), *The social psychology of health* (pp. 129–174). Newbury Park, CA: Sage.

Thompson, C. (1989). 'Dilemmas for voluntary groups'. In National Council for Voluntary Organisations, *Contracts for care*. Conference Report No.2. (pp. 1–3). London: NCVO.

Thompson, D., and Pudney, M. (1990). *Mental illness: The fundamental facts*. London: Mental Health Foundation.

Thompson, K. (1988). *Under siege*. Harmondsworth: Penguin.

Thomson, M. (1985). 'Mental hygiene as an international movement'. In P. Wardling (ed.), *International health and welfare organisations between the First and Second World Wars*. Cambridge: Cambridge University Press.

Thorogood, N. (1992). 'What is the relevance of sociology to health promotion?' In R. Bunton and G. Macdonald (eds), *Health promotion: Disciplines and diversity* (pp. 42–65). London: Routledge.

Tissier, G. (1993). 'Not in our back yard'. *Community Care*, 26 August, 12–13.

Tones, K. (1987). 'Devising strategies for preventing drug misuse: The role of the health action model'. *Health Education Research*, *2*, 305–317.

Tones, K. (1990). 'Why theorise? Ideology in health education'. *Health Education Journal*, *49*, 2–6.

Townsend, J.L. (1987). 'Cigarette tax, economic welfare and social class patterns of smoking'. *Applied Economics*, *19*, 355–365.

Travis, A., and Brindle, D. (1990). 'Howe signals delay in care programme'. Guardian, 11 July, 20.

Trent, D.R. (1992a). 'Breaking the single continuum'. In D.R. Trent (ed.), *Promotion of mental health. Vol. 1* (pp. 117–126). Aldershot: Avebury.

Trent, D.R. (ed.) (1992b). *Promotion of mental health. Vol. 1*. Aldershot: Avebury.

Trent, D.R. (1993). 'The promotion of mental health: Fallacies of current thinking'. In D.R. Trent and C. Reed (eds), *Promotion of mental health. Vol.2*(pp. 561–568). Aldershot: Avebury.

Trent, D.R. (1994). 'Fighting the four horsemen'. In D.R. Trent and C. Reed (eds), *Promotion of mental health. Vol. 3* (pp. 377–384). Aldershot: Avebury.

Trent, D.R., and Reed, C. (eds) (1993). *Promotion of mental health. Vol. 2*. Aldershot: Avebury.

Trent, D.R., and Reed, C. (eds) (1994). *Promotion of mental health. Vol. 3*. Aldershot: Avebury.

Trent Regional Health Authority (1990). 'Strategic framework for health promotion'. Document available from Health Promotion, Trent Regional Health Authority, Fulwood House, Old Fulwood Road, Sheffield S10 3TH.

Trent Regional Health Authority (1992). 'A strategy for health in Trent'. Document available from Health Promotion, Trent Regional Health Authority, Fulwood House, Old Fulwood Road, Sheffield S10 3TH.

Trent Regional Health Authority/Centre for Mental Health Service Development (1994). *Focus on promoting mental health at work in the NHS*. Sheffield: Author.

Trent Regional Health Authority Psychology Advisory Committee (1990). 'The assessment of individual need and care planning'. Unpublished paper. Enquiries and correspondence to Psychology Department, Southern Derbyshire Mental Health Trust, Kingsway Hospital, Kingsway, Derby DE22 3LZ.

Trevillian, S. (1988/9). 'Griffiths and Wagner: which future for community care?' *Critical Social Policy*, 24, 65–73.

Trojan, A., Hildebrandt, H., Deneke, C., and Faltis, M. (1991). 'The role of community groups and voluntary organizations in health promotion'. In B. Badura and I. Kickbusch (eds), *Health promotion research* (pp. 441–466). Copenhagen: WHO.

Tudor, K. (1990). 'Conceptualising mental health promotion'. Paper presented at Health in Mind conference organised by South East Thames Regional Health Authority, June, Canterbury, Kent.

Tudor, K. (1990/91). 'One step back, two steps forward: Community care and mental health'. *Critical Social Policy*, 30(3), 5–22.

Tudor, K. (1991). 'Children's groups: Integrating TA and gestalt perspectives'. *Transactional Analysis Journal*, 21, 12–20.

Tudor, K. (1992a). 'Community mental health promotion: A paradigm approach'. In D.R. Trent (ed.), *Promotion of mental health. Vol. 1* (pp. 127–138). Aldershot: Avebury.

Tudor, K. (1992b). 'Promoting mental health'. Paper presented at the North Derbyshire Mental Health Promotion Seminar, Chesterfield, Derbyshire, September.

Tudor, K., and Worrall, M. (1994). 'Congruence reconsidered'. *British Journal of Guidance and Counselling*, 22, 197–206.

Turner, R.J. (1983). 'Direct, indirect and moderating effects of social support on psychological distress and associated conditions'. In H.B. Kaplan (ed.), *Psychosocial stress* (pp. 105–155). Orlando, FA: Academic Press Inc.

Tyson, A. (1987). 'User involvement: Going beyond the buzz-words to a new climate'. *Social Work Today*, 27 July, 12–13.

Union of the Physically Impaired Against Segregation (1981). *Disability Challenge*, 1, May.

Utting, W., Beardshaw, V., Crepaz-Key, D., Gask, L., Hally, H., Hewitt, C., Huka, G., Imbert, P., Major, J., Paykel, E., Prior, C., Runciman, R., Shepherd, G., Smallridge, P., Tylee, A., and Wistow, G. (1994). *Creating community care*. London: Mental Health Foundation.

Vallet, R. (1974). *Self-actualisation*. Niles, IL: Argus Communications.

Veit, C.T., and Ware Jnr, J.E. (1983). 'The structure of psychological distress and well-being in general populations'. *Journal of Consultating Psychology*, 51, 730–741.

Verbrugge. (1985). 'Gender and health: An update on hypotheses and evidence'. *Journal of Health and Social Behaviour*, 26, 156–182.

Verrall, J. (1990). 'Mental health promotion – A framework'. Presentation at Mental Health Promotion Day, North East Thames Regional Health Authority, London, June.

Viney, T. (1990). 'Community care – who's to benefit?' Unpublished paper available from Greenwich Welfare Rights Unit, Riverside House, Beresford Street, London SE18.

Ware, J.E. (1978). 'A study of psychological well-being'. *British Journal of Psychology*, 69, 111–121.

Ware, J.E., Johnston, S.A., Davies-Avery, A., and Brook, R.H. (1987). *Conceptualization and measurement of health for adults in the Health Insurance Study*.

Vol. III: Mental health. Santa Monica, CA: Rand Corporation. (Original work published 1979)

Ware, P. (1983). 'Personality adaptations: Doors to therapy'. *Transactional Analysis Journal, 13*, 11–19.

Warr, P. (1987). *Work, unemployment and health*. Oxford: Clarendon.

Watzlawick, P., Weakland, J.H., and Fisch, R. (1974). *Change*. New York: W.W. Norton.

Weare, K. (1992). 'The contribution of education to health promotion'. In R. Bunton and G. Macdonald (eds), *Health promotion: Disciplines and diversity* (pp. 66–85). London: Routledge.

Weiss, P. (1973). *The science of life: The living system – A system for living*. New York: Futura.

Wells, L.E., and Maxwell, G. (1976). *Self-esteem: Its conceptualization and measurement*. Beverly Hills, CA: Sage.

West Lambeth Health Authority Mental Health Unit Mental Health Education Group (1989). *Mental health problems*. Booklet available from Mental Health Unit, West Lambeth Health Authority, Tooting Bec Hospital, Church Lane, London SW17 8BL.

West Midlands Regional Working Party on the Promotion of Mental Health (undated). *The promotion of mental health*. Booklet available from Operational Research Unit, West Midlands Regional Health Authority, 326 High Street, Harborne, Birmingham B17 9PX.

Westheimer, I. (1977). *Practice of supervision in social work*. London: Ward Lock Educational.

Westwood, C. (1993). *Aromatherapy stress management*. Christchurch: Amberwood.

White, J. (1992). 'Use of the media and public lectures to publicise stress'. In D.R. Trent (ed.), *Promotion of mental health. Vol. 1* (pp. 331–343). Aldershot: Avebury.

Whitney, N.J. (1982). 'A critique of individual autonomy as the key to personhood'. *Transactional Analysis Journal, 12*, 210–212.

Whittington, C., and Holland, R. (1981). 'Social theory for social work'. *Issues in Social Work Education, 1*, 19–26.

Whittington, C., and Holland, R. (1985). 'A framework for theory in social work'. *Issues in Social Work Education, 5*, 25–50.

Wieland-Burston, J. (1992). *Chaos and order in the world of the psyche*. London: Routledge.

Williams, G. (1984). 'Health promotion: Caring concern or slick salesmanship?' *Journal of Medical Ethics, 10*, 191–195.

Williams, J., Watson, G., Smith, H., Copperman, J., and Wood, D. (1993). *Purchasing effective mental health services for women: A framework for action*. London: MIND.

Wing, J.K. (1989). *Health services planning and research: Contributions from psychiatric case registers*. London: Royal College of Psychiatrists.

Winnicott, D.W. (1975). 'Mind and its relation to the psyche-soma'. In D.W. Winnicott (ed.), *Through paediatrics to psycho-analysis* (pp. 243–254). London: Hogarth. (Original work published 1949)

Winnicott, D.W. (1988). *Human nature*. London: Free Association Books.

Wirth, L. (1938). 'Urbanism as a way of life'. *American Journal of Sociology, 44*, 3–24.

Wolfensberger, W. (1972). *The principles of normalisation in human services*. Toronto: National Institute on Mental Retardation.

Wolverhampton Health Authority (undated). *A strategy for mental health promo-*

tion. Available from Wolverhampton Health Care NHS Trust, Park Road West, Wolverhampton WV1 4PW.

Wood, C. (1986). *Mental health and mental illness: Educational materials for 5th and 6th year and further education students.* Available from Westminster MIND, 526 Harrow Road, London W9 3QF.

Wooton, B. (1959). *Social science and social pathology.* London: Allen & Unwin.

Worchel, S., and Goethals, G.R. (1985). *Adjustment: Pathways to personal growth.* New York: Prentice-Hall.

World Federation for Mental Health (1948). *Founding document.* Available from WFMH, 1021 Prince Street, Alexandria, VA 22314–2971, USA.

World Federation for Mental Health (1988). *Declaration 2000 on Mental Health.* Available from WFMH, 1021 Prince Street, Alexandria, VA 22314–2971, USA.

World Federation for Mental Health (1989). *Declaration of Human Rights and Mental Health.* Available from WFMH, 1021 Prince Street, Alexandria, VA 22314–2971, USA.

World Federation for Mental Health (1994). *Newsletter,* December. Available from WFMH, 1021 Prince Street, Alexandria, VA 22314-2971, USA.

World Federation for Mental Health European Regional Council (1991). *Manifesto.* Available from WFMHERC Secretariat, Franklin Street 110, 1040 Brussels, Belgium.

World Health Organisation (1946). *Constitution of the World Health Organisation.* New York: WHO.

World Health Organisation (1978). 'Primary health care'. *Report on the international conference on primary health care.* Geneva: WHO/UNICEF.

World Health Organisation (1981a). *Development of indicators for monitoring progress towards health for all by the year 2000.* Geneva: WHO.

World Health Organisation (1981b). *Social dimensions of mental health.* Geneva: WHO.

World Health Organisation (1985). *Targets for health for all.* Copenhagen: WHO.

World Health Organisation (1986). 'A discussion document on the concept and principles of health promotion'. *Health Promotion, 1,* 73–76.

World Health Organisation (1988). *A guide to assessing healthy cities.* WHO Healthy Cities Paper no.3. Copenhagen: FADL.

World Health Organisation (1991a). *Budapest declaration on health promoting hospitals.* Copenhagen: WHO Regional Office for Europe.

World Health Organisation (1991b). *Health for all targets.* Copenhagen: WHO. (Original work published 1984)

World Health Organisation (1991c). *Implications for the field of mental health of the European targets for attaining health for all.* Copenhagen: WHO.

World Health Organisation (1992). *The ICD-10. Classification of mental and behavioural disorders.* Geneva: WHO.

World Health Organisation (1993a). *Approaches to stress management in the community setting.* Copenhagen: WHO.

World Health Organisation (1993b). *Promoting the psychosocial development of children through primary health care services.* Report on a WHO meeting, Sofia. Copenhagen: WHO.

Ziglio, E. (1988). *Trends in Canadian health policy: Before and after the Lalonde report.* Edinburgh: Research Unit in Health and Behavioural Change.

Author index

Subject index